Praise for
STRATEGIC CLARITY

"*Strategic Clarity* offers executives a clear, research-grounded way to diagnose why strategy breaks down in behavior and how to fix it. A rare fusion of academic rigor and managerial clarity."

- VIJAY GOVINDARAJAN, THINKERS 50 HALL OF FAME, COXE DISTINGUISHED PROFESSOR OF MANAGEMENT, TUCK SCHOOL OF BUSINESS, DARTMOUTH COLLEGE

"*Strategic Clarity* is one of those rare strategy books that actually makes complex ideas feel usable. Kyle Harkema takes big academic concepts—entrepreneurial mindset, market orientation, opportunity spotting—and breaks them down into clear, practical guidance leaders can apply right away. If you want a smarter, more grounded way to make strategic decisions without the usual buzzwords, this book is the one you'll keep coming back to."

- DR. MARSHALL GOLDSMITH, THINKERS50 #1 EXECUTIVE COACH AND *NEW YORK TIMES* BESTSELLING AUTHOR OF *THE EARNED LIFE, TRIGGERS,* AND *WHAT GOT YOU HERE WON'T GET YOU THERE*

"Great companies are simultaneously more market-driven and more entrepreneurial than competitors. *Strategic Clarity* brings new insights into how these two orientations can coexist and reinforce one another and the ways in which they produce transformative approaches to creating, reaching, and serving markets."

- MICHAEL H. MORRIS, PHD, PROFESSOR, ENTREPRENEURSHIP AND SOCIAL INNOVATION, KEOUGH SCHOOL OF GLOBAL AFFAIRS, UNIVERSITY OF NOTRE DAME

"I've watched countless executives freeze, panic, or double down at exactly the wrong moment. Kyle's four-quadrant framework finally explains why—and more importantly, shows how to break these patterns. If you've ever wondered why your team's best thinking disperses during a crisis, read this book."

"World-class performance in entrepreneurial environments derives from adaptable models that harmonize with how firms think and act. Because successful firms must think and act in increasingly unique ways, the field of strategy needs new and dynamic firm-level approaches, like the one in this book, for use in both scholarly contexts and practical settings."

"As both an academic and a practitioner in Marketing, I have come to believe that the philosophy of Marketing held individually and collectively in the organization directly guides the practice of Marketing. The material provided by Dr. Harkema is very valuable because it helps the person and the organizational leader diagnose the orientation that is shaping the practice of Marketing. *Strategic Clarity* provides significant insights for business results. This is a resource that I want to use with my students and one that informs me as I work with organizations."

"The Strategic Orientation Index™ gave our executive team something we've been missing for years—a shared language for what we were feeling but couldn't measure. We've done strategic plans before, but SOI was the first tool that actually revealed how differently our teams were interpreting and enacting strategy.

"The results were eye-opening. Nine out of ten departments saw themselves in the Hybrid Zone, not because people were misaligned in intent, but because we were behaving out of sync. The SOI session didn't just diagnose the issue— it created clarity, energy, and momentum in the room. My team immediately recognized themselves in the findings, and more importantly, saw a path forward.

What stood out to me personally was how practical the framework felt. It wasn't academic theory—it explained what we were experiencing every day.

"The conversation it sparked across sales, product, operations, marketing, and engineering was one of the most productive strategic dialogues we've had as a leadership team.

"SOI helped us choose Insightful Optimizer™ as our strategic aspiration—a posture that fits our culture, our market, and the disciplined, relationship-driven way we want to grow. Dr. Harkema's work has already influenced our priorities, especially around Voice of Customer and cross-functional coordination.

"For any mid-market firm looking to grow with strategic discipline, SOI is one of the clearest and most actionable tools I've seen. It helped us see ourselves honestly and move forward with intention."

— MITCH KEHLER, CEO, KMC CONTROLS

"Harkema's *Strategic Clarity* extends the work of gurus at the intersection of strategy content and process, combining theory with operational precision. He provides an elegant system for turning strategic intent into ubiquitous organizational behavior in a focused manner. A must-read for founders and executives pursuing disciplined growth, especially in times of significant market and economic uncertainty and upheavals."

— JOE LIPUMA, CONSULTANT AND CLINICAL ASSOCIATE PROFESSOR,
QUESTROM SCHOOL OF BUSINESS, BOSTON UNIVERSITY

STRATEGIC
CLARITY

THE PRACTICAL METHOD FOR TRANSFORMING VISION INTO RESULTS

KYLE HARKEMA

CREATOR OF **THE STRATEGIC ORIENTATION INDEX™**

www.amplifypublishinggroup.com

Strategic Clarity: The Practical Method for Transforming Vision into Results

For more information, please contact:
Amplify Publishing, an imprint of Amplify Publishing Group
620 Herndon Parkway, Suite 220
Herndon, VA 20170
info@amplifypublishing.com

Library of Congress Control Number: 2026903836

CPSIA Code: PRV0226A

ISBN-13: 979-8-89138-904-5

Printed in the United States

CONTENTS

WHY I WROTE THIS BOOK

BRIDGING THE GAP BETWEEN STRATEGY AND BEHAVIOR

I didn't set out to build a diagnostic system. I set out to solve a problem that never seemed to go away.

For years, I watched organizations struggle with the same invisible disconnect: They had clear strategies on paper, but behavior across teams didn't align. Marketing listened. Product thought. Sales acted. But rarely did those disciplines move in sync. Growth efforts stalled. Customer signals were ignored. Bold ideas died in committee. Meanwhile, executives debated the plan without noticing the pattern underneath: Their strategy was misfiring because their teams didn't share the same behavioral orientation.

This insight became inescapable during my doctoral research, where I explored the intersection of **Entrepreneurial Orientation (EO)**, **Market Orientation (MO)**, and **Entrepreneurial Marketing (EM)**. Individually, these constructs were well studied. Collectively, they were underutilized—and rarely operationalized. I realized what was missing wasn't more theory. It was a usable framework—something firms could apply to **diagnose** where they were strong, where they were blind, and how to move forward.

That became the foundation of the Strategic Orientation Index™.

It was also the moment when I fully understood something my mentor, Dr. Harold Welsch, had challenged me to embrace from the beginning: The role of a **scholar-practitioner** is to build tools that bridge theory and practice. It's not enough to understand the literature. Our job is to make it usable—so it moves people and organizations forward.

The SOI™ is my answer to that challenge. It's a system that helps leaders:

- Map how their teams **think** (EO),
- Understand how they **listen** (MO), and
- Clarify how they **act** (EM) in the market.

It's a framework built for real-world behavior—not theoretical intention. And while it was born from academic rigor, it's designed for strategic clarity and action.

Whether you're a CEO, a strategy consultant, or a professor preparing the next generation of business leaders, I hope you'll find value in what follows—not just as a diagnostic, but as a new lens on how growth actually happens.

WHY THE STRATEGIC ORIENTATION INDEX™ MATTERS

Many firms stall—not because they lack ambition or talent—but because their strategic behaviors are misaligned.

They chase bold ideas (EO) but ignore market signals (MO). Or they listen closely to customers (MO) but fail to act with urgency or creativity (EO). Others make plans they never execute, because their real-world marketing behaviors (EM) don't match their strategic intent.

The Strategic Orientation Index™ (SOI™) exists to surface these blind spots.

It shows not just how a company thinks—but how it *behaves*.

It is the first diagnostic tool to integrate EO, MO, and EM into a unified framework—measuring your firm's posture, mapping it to one of five personas, and helping you recalibrate before growth stalls or misalignment hardens.

SOI™ is a mirror and a map.

Use it to understand where you are—and how to move forward with strategic clarity.

WHY DO SOME FIRMS SCALE WHILE OTHERS STALL?

The Strategic Orientation Index™ reveals the answer.

Built on two decades of executive leadership and four years of doctoral research, this breakthrough framework helps leaders align their entrepreneurial drive, market responsiveness, and real-world behavior to accelerate growth.

In this book, you'll learn to:

- Diagnose your firm's strategic posture across EO, MO, and EM
- Map your organization to one of five SOI™ personas
- Identify blind spots in execution—and close them
- Use strategic misalignment as a lens for leadership, not just a problem to fix

Whether you're a founder, executive, consultant, or educator, the SOI™ gives you a powerful new way to think about strategic clarity—and a practical roadmap to act on it.

THE STRATEGIC ORIENTATION INDEX™ (SOI™)— ROADMAP TO THIS BOOK

This book is built around one core idea: Strategy isn't just what you *plan*—it's how your company behaves. The Strategic Orientation Index™ (SOI™) helps you diagnose whether your firm's entrepreneurial mindset

(EO), market insight (MO), and real-world marketing behaviors (EM) are aligned—or dangerously out of sync.

The SOI™ model stands on the shoulders of empirically validated research across entrepreneurial, market, and behavioral strategy literature. While each dimension—EO, MO, and EM—has been independently tied to firm performance, SOI™ is the first framework to operationalize all three into a unified diagnostic. It does not claim to predict success—but it does reveal patterns that often determine it.

This roadmap shows how the SOI™ works, what it measures, and how to navigate this book to apply it.

WHAT DOES SOI™ MEASURE?

The SOI™ score is based on three foundational constructs:

ORIENTATION	WHAT IT MEASURES	KEY QUESTIONS
EO (**Entrepreneurial Orientation**)	Innovativeness, Proactiveness and Risk-Taking	Are we willing to lead, not follow? Are we bold enough?
MO (**Market Orientation**)	Customer Orientation, Competitor Orientation, and Interfunctional Coordination	Do we know what our customers and competitors are telling us?
EM (**Entrepreneurial Marketing**)	Six behavioral traits: Growth Orientation, Value Creation through Alliances, Opportunity Orientation, Informal Marketing Research, Two-Way Customer Contact, and Market Immersion	Are we actually behaving entrepreneurially in the market?

HOW ARE SCORES USED?

Your firm's EO, MO, and EM scores are combined into a strategic persona:

PERSONA	PROFILE	TYPICAL CHALLENGE
Visionary Vanguard	High EO + High MO	Focus and Scaling Systems
Fearless Inventor	High EO + Low MO	Customer Alignment
Insightful Optimizer	Low EO + High MO	Innovation Culture
Reluctant Responder	Low EO + Low MO	Total Reinvention
Hybrid Zone	Mid or mixed EO/MO	Alignment and Clarity

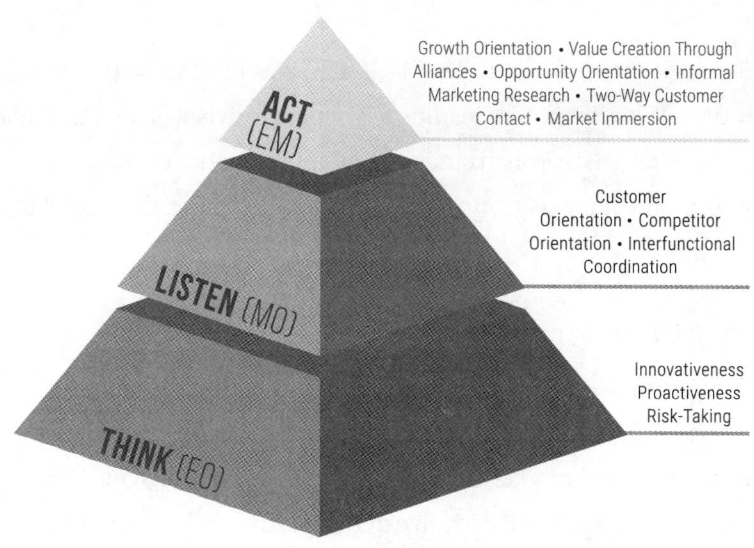

HOW TO NAVIGATE THIS BOOK

IF YOU WANT TO . . .	GO TO . . .
Understand EO, MO, and EM individually	Chapters 2–9
Diagnose your firm's SOI™ score	Chapter 10
Interpret your SOI™ persona	Chapter 10
Explore real-world firm patterns	Chapters 11–12
Create a strategic-growth plan	Chapters 13–14
Use SOI™ in consulting or teaching	Reach out at kylejharkema.com

HOW DIFFERENT AUDIENCES CAN USE THE SOI™ FRAMEWORK

The Strategic Orientation Index™ (SOI™) was built to be practical, not theoretical. Whether you're leading a company, advising clients, or teaching future strategists, this framework adapts to your context. Below are four common audience groups—and how each can put the SOI™ model into action.

EXECUTIVES AND LEADERSHIP TEAMS

Executives can use SOI™ to align their organization's strategic posture. Many firms stall because their entrepreneurial drive (EO), market responsiveness (MO), and marketing behavior (EM) are out of sync. The SOI™ diagnostic, when facilitated with an external partner, helps leadership teams:

- Diagnose current misalignment
- Identify blind spots across business units

- Clarify whether growth struggles are strategy-based or behavior-based
- Prioritize actions by firm persona (e.g., Fearless Inventor vs. Insightful Optimizer)

Best tools: kylejharkema.com consultation, persona grid, and persona action plans.

CONSULTANTS AND STRATEGY ADVISORS

Consultants can integrate the SOI™ framework into discovery sessions, team workshops, and strategic-planning engagements. Instead of only focusing on external analysis or metrics, SOI™ reveals internal behavioral patterns that affect alignment. Use it to:

- Guide executive teams through a facilitated scoring process
- Frame advisory services around persona-based interventions
- Add depth to innovation, marketing, or positioning engagements
- Offer repeatable IP and tools with licensing support

Best tools: Facilitated diagnostics, persona grid, quadrant workshop model.

EDUCATORS AND PROGRAM DIRECTORS

Educators in MBA or executive-education settings can use SOI™ to connect theory and practice. The model bridges entrepreneurship, marketing strategy, and organizational behavior in a way that's research-backed and intuitive. Instructors can:

- Use SOI™ personas for case-study analysis
- Assign student teams to map real companies onto the quadrant
- Structure classroom discussions around EO–MO–EM alignment
- Build capstone or simulation projects using the framework

Best tools: SOI™ persona grid and supplemental teaching guide.

CROSS-FUNCTIONAL TEAMS AND BUSINESS UNITS

Even within large organizations, different units exhibit different personas. The SOI™ framework helps cross-functional teams align around shared behaviors and market posture. Department leaders can use the model to:

- Compare strategic posture across departments
- Build shared language for risk, innovation, and customer responsiveness
- Diagnose execution challenges during planning cycles
- Surface hidden misalignment between stated vision and team behavior

Best tools: Team-level assessments, internal persona mapping, workshop facilitation.

WHAT THIS BOOK WILL DO FOR YOU

If you're a founder, executive, strategist, or educator seeking clarity on why some firms scale while others stall—this book gives you the answer.

The *Strategic Orientation Index™ (SOI™)* introduces a breakthrough framework that combines the entrepreneurial energy of start-ups with the customer-centric precision of market leaders. Built on two decades of executive experience and four years of doctoral research, this book helps you diagnose your firm's strategic posture—and then align it for sustainable growth.

Through rigorous evidence, practitioner insights, and real-world personas, you'll learn how to:

- Measure your firm's entrepreneurial orientation, market focus, and marketing agility
- Identify strategic misalignments before they become growth roadblocks
- Position your company in one of five SOI™ personas—from Visionary Vanguard to Reluctant Responder

- Navigate from where you are to where you want to be intentionally
- Equip your team, board, or client with a shared language for strategic focus

This is not theory for theory's sake. It's a practical tool kit for leaders serious about building companies that last.

SCALING STRATEGIC IMPACT THROUGH THE SOI™ FRAMEWORK

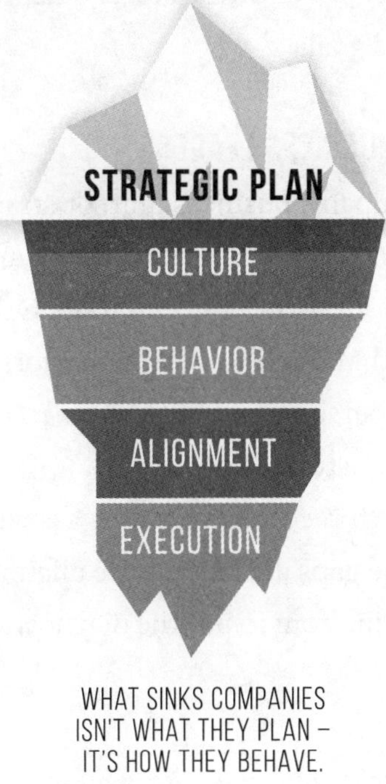

The Strategic Orientation Index™ (SOI™) was designed not only as a diagnostic lens, but as a scalable system for growth alignment across industries, team sizes, and leadership functions. As the framework continues to gain traction, we're committed to making it available through structured, value-added channels that preserve its strategic integrity and elevate its long-term impact.

HOW TO USE THIS BOOK

This book is designed to be more than just something you read—it's a tool you can use. Whether you're a business executive, consultant, educator, or student, *Strategic Clarity: The Practical Method for Transforming Vision into Results* provides a strategic framework, a diagnostic system, and a set of actionable personas to help any organization understand and improve its strategic posture.

But not every reader will use it the same way. Below is a simple guide to help you get the most out of the Strategic Orientation Index™ (SOI™) based on your role and goals.

FOR EXECUTIVES AND BUSINESS LEADERS

If you're leading a company, business unit, or strategic initiative

- Take note of the SOI™ framework, which maps your firm's Entrepreneurial Orientation (EO), Market Orientation (MO), and Entrepreneurial Marketing (EM) behaviors.
- Use the SOI™ persona grid in Chapter 10 to diagnose your company's current posture.
- Apply the growth recommendations associated with your firm's persona to close gaps and accelerate alignment.
- Visit kylejharkema.com to use the diagnostic with your leadership team.

Your goal: Strategic clarity, internal alignment, and execution that matches your ambition.

FOR CONSULTANTS AND ADVISORS

If you work with firms to improve strategy, growth, or organizational performance:

- Use this book to structure strategic diagnostics and client workshops.

- Chapters 4–9 provide deep behavioral insights across six EM dimensions—perfect for uncovering blind spots.
- Use the SOI™ to build a persona-driven advisory approach—show clients where they are, why it matters, and how to evolve.
- The quadrant map and persona transitions make excellent tools for team offsites, mid-year planning, and leadership development.

Your goal: Elevate your client conversations from symptoms to strategic root causes—and provide a roadmap for action.

FOR EDUCATORS AND STUDENTS

If you're teaching (or learning) strategy, marketing, or entrepreneurship:

- Integrate the SOI™ model into your curriculum to explore how EO, MO, and EM interact.
- Use Chapter 10's personas as case studies for student discussion, persona roleplay, or strategic-analysis exercises.
- Assign students to map real companies onto the SOI™ quadrant and recommend evolution paths.
- If you're an instructor or program lead, you can request university licensing at kylejaharkema.com to use the tool with your students.

Your goal: Connect academic theory to real-world firm behavior—and prepare future strategists to think like entrepreneurs.

No matter your role, the SOI™ framework gives you a language for strategic misalignment, and a pathway to correct it. It turns instinct into structure, confusion into clarity, and untapped potential into coordinated growth.

Let's get started.

AUTHOR'S NOTE

This book is the natural evolution of my doctoral research on entrepreneurial marketing and firm profitability. What began as a dissertation has grown into a practical guide for professionals—rooted in both academic rigor and real-world experience.

Every concept, case study, and strategic takeaway has been shaped by executive marketing leadership, years of graduate-level teaching, and countless refinements to ensure clarity, relevance, and impact.

This book is not just a product of writing—it's the outcome of lived expertise. I offer it to you as both a scholar and practitioner.

—Kyle J. Harkema, DBA, MBA

CHAPTER 1

UNDERSTANDING ENTREPRENEURIAL MARKETING

Entrepreneurial Marketing (EM) is a critical discipline that bridges the innovative spirit of entrepreneurship with the strategic principles of marketing. This approach is particularly vital for small and medium-sized enterprises (SMEs) and start-ups, which operate under conditions of uncertainty, limited resources, and intense competition. However, EM is not only relevant to smaller enterprises; it also provides significant advantages to large organizations that must navigate rapidly changing markets and complex competitive landscapes. EM emphasizes adaptability, proactiveness, and creativity, enabling businesses of all sizes to create unique value propositions and build strong, lasting customer relationships. This chapter explores the definition, historical context, key characteristics, and practical applications of Entrepreneurial Marketing, while also comparing it with traditional marketing approaches to highlight why EM is often the superior choice for modern businesses.

WHY THESE THREE FRAMEWORKS MATTER

In today's competitive environment, the firms that succeed aren't just the most well funded or the most established—they're the ones that can **sense change, respond quickly, and execute with agility.**

To do that consistently, they need three distinct strategic capabilities:

- **Entrepreneurial Orientation (EO)**—the capacity to pursue innovation, act proactively, and take calculated risks.
- **Market Orientation (MO)**—the ability to listen to customer needs, interpret market shifts, and collaborate cross-functionally to deliver value.
- **Entrepreneurial Marketing (EM)**—the behavior layer that ensures strategic intent shows up as action, especially when resources are constrained or markets are uncertain.

Each of these frameworks has strong academic foundations—but when used together, they form a practical, diagnostic system that can guide real organizational growth. This book introduces a new way to integrate them: the **Strategic Orientation Index™ (SOI™).**

SOI™ isn't just a way to describe your firm's posture. It's a way to identify blind spots, recalibrate execution, and move your team toward stronger strategic alignment.

THINK, LISTEN, ACT: SIMPLIFYING STRATEGIC ORIENTATION FOR BEHAVIORAL CLARITY

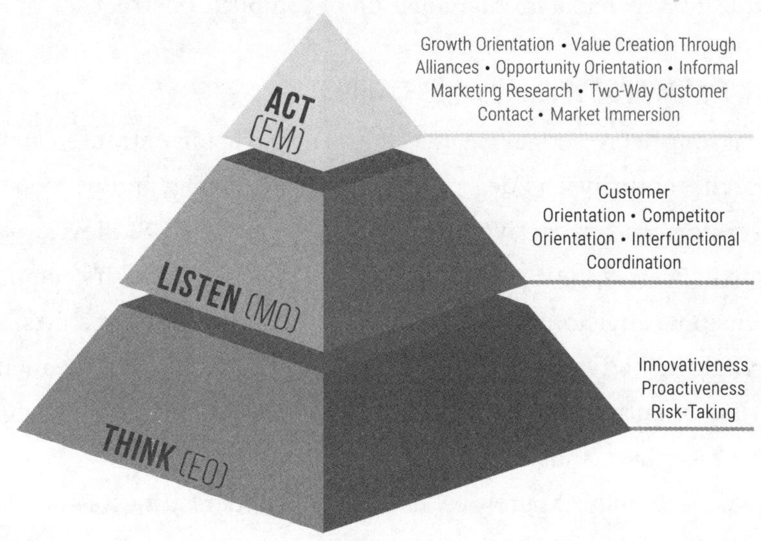

Strategic alignment often breaks down not because leaders lack vision, but because employees interpret and enact strategy differently across organizational levels. Scholars have long studied the behavioral underpinnings of strategic posture, particularly through the constructs of **Entrepreneurial Orientation (EO)**, **Market Orientation (MO)**, and **Entrepreneurial Marketing (EM)**. Together, these orientations describe how firms think, listen, and act in the marketplace. Yet, despite decades of empirical research, many executives and managers struggle to apply these constructs in practice.

The **Think–Listen–Act** simplification offers a more accessible framework. By translating EO as *Think*, MO as *Listen*, and EM as *Act*, it provides a language that resonates with practitioners and highlights the behavioral interplay among these constructs. However, the simplification must be nuanced: Each orientation implies not only a cognitive or perceptual mode but also a set of required actions. Thinking without moving forward, listening without responding, or acting without grounding can all undermine performance. Thus, the simplification works best when it is understood as a **sticky heuristic** that points toward deeper behavioral realities rather than a literal reduction of complex constructs.

THINK = ENTREPRENEURIAL ORIENTATION (EO)

EO has long been recognized as a central construct in entrepreneurship research, capturing the degree to which firms display innovativeness, risk-taking, and proactiveness (Miller, 1983; Covin & Slevin, 1989; Lumpkin & Dess, 1996). Framing EO as *Think* highlights its cognitive dimensions: envisioning possibilities, anticipating market shifts, and imagining new strategic options. In this sense, EO represents the **mental posture** of entrepreneurship—questioning assumptions, challenging existing routines, and pursuing new avenues of growth.

Yet, describing EO purely as thinking risks understating its inherently behavioral qualities. Proactiveness requires acting ahead of competitors, innovativeness requires bringing new products or processes to market, and risk-taking entails committing tangible resources under uncertainty (Covin & Miller, 2014). A firm cannot simply imagine opportunities; it must operationalize them through concrete initiatives. Thus, while "Think" captures EO's ideational spark, it must always be paired with mechanisms for implementation.

The simplification is nonetheless useful because it draws attention to **cognitive readiness**. Organizations with low EO often lack the imagination or boldness to conceive alternatives to the status quo. By framing EO as *Think*, leaders are reminded that strategic behavior begins with mindset. However, to prevent stagnation, firms must ensure that ideation is coupled with experimentation, resource allocation, and follow-through. The most effective entrepreneurial thinkers are those who recognize thinking as a precursor to action rather than an end in itself.

LISTEN = MARKET ORIENTATION (MO)

MO is one of the most extensively researched constructs in marketing and strategy, defined as the generation, dissemination, and responsiveness to market intelligence (Kohli & Jaworski, 1990; Narver & Slater, 1990). Translating MO into *Listen* underscores its perceptual dimension: attending to customers, monitoring competitors, and scanning environmental trends. Listening captures the act of attunement, which is essential for aligning organizational behavior with evolving market demands.

However, the framing risks implying passivity. True MO is never just about hearing; it requires **responding**. Firms that collect customer insights but fail to act on them exhibit what scholars have called "market myopia" (Day, 1994). The responsiveness element of MO is critical—customer feedback must lead to changes in product design, service delivery, or resource allocation. In fact, the responsiveness component is often the strongest predictor of performance outcomes in MO research (Kirca et al., 2005).

The Listen framing is powerful because it highlights the value of humility in organizational strategy. Firms that over-rely on EO may act aggressively without validating their assumptions, while firms that listen deeply are more likely to avoid misalignment with market needs. But listening is not sufficient if it does not culminate in decisive action. Leaders must remember that MO's ultimate purpose is to convert insights into improved performance. Listening is therefore best understood as a dynamic cycle of perception, interpretation, and behavioral response.

ACT = ENTREPRENEURIAL MARKETING (EM)

EM represents the executional side of strategy, where entrepreneurial thinking and market listening converge into tangible behaviors. Scholars have conceptualized EM as comprising six dimensions: Opportunity Orientation, Growth Orientation, Customer Intensity, Value Creation Through Alliances, Informal Market Research, and Resource Leveraging Through Immersion (Morris, Schindehutte, & LaForge, 2002). Framing

EM as *Act* highlights its inherently behavioral focus. Unlike EO and MO, which can be misconstrued as primarily cognitive or perceptual, EM is unavoidably about doing.

Yet, the simplification still requires nuance. Not all action is beneficial. Acting without clear thinking can lead to wasted resources, while acting without listening can alienate customers or miss competitive signals. EM is best understood as **aligned action**—the disciplined execution of strategies that emerge from entrepreneurial imagination and market intelligence. Its role is to ensure that firms not only move but move coherently in ways that strengthen market position.

The Act framing resonates with practitioners because it makes strategy tangible. Executives often ask, "What do we do next?" EM provides the behavioral answer to that question. However, the discipline of EM also demands prioritization, resourcefulness, and adaptability. Action for its own sake is not enough; the critical test of EM is whether those actions translate into sustainable performance advantages.

WHY THE FRAMING WORKS

The Think–Listen–Act model succeeds because it condenses decades of academic research into a simple, memorable heuristic. Human cognition favors triads, and leaders can easily recall and communicate these three verbs in ways they might not recall using "EO, MO, and EM" or their subdimensions. By attaching each construct to an everyday verb, the framework enhances both understanding and adoption.

Beyond memorability, the framing highlights **behavioral diagnosis**. Leaders can ask: Are we thinking boldly enough? Are we listening carefully enough? Are we acting decisively enough? This vocabulary makes abstract constructs actionable in team discussions. Moreover, the triad emphasizes **balance**. Overindexing on any one verb creates vulnerability: Thinking without listening leads to arrogance, listening without acting leads to paralysis, and acting without thinking leads to chaos. By making imbalance visible, the framework promotes strategic alignment.

Finally, the framing reinforces the **interdependence** of the constructs. Thinking without listening is misguided, listening without acting is wasted, and acting without thinking is reckless. The triad's simplicity reveals the systemic interplay among orientations in a way that resonates with both scholars and practitioners.

RISKS OF OVERSIMPLIFICATION

While simplification aids adoption, it can also obscure nuance. Scholars have cautioned that quadrant models and heuristics can appear normative, implying that certain postures are always superior (Lumpkin & Dess, 1996). Similarly, Think–Listen–Act may unintentionally suggest that EO is primarily about ideation, MO about perception, and EM about execution, when in fact each contains behavioral elements. EO requires resource commitment, MO requires responsive change, and EM requires disciplined prioritization.

A second risk is **false separation**. Firms may assume they can sequence orientations—first think, then listen, then act—rather than pursuing them concurrently. In reality, entrepreneurial firms often cycle rapidly among these orientations, listening while thinking, and acting in ways that generate new learning.

A third risk is **overshadowing depth**. The subdimensions of EO , MO, and EM offer rich diagnostic insight that the verbs alone cannot capture. Thus, while the simplification works as an entry point, leaders must be careful not to treat it as the entirety of the model.

STRATEGIC IMPLICATIONS FOR FIRMS

- **Think Without Acting = Strategic Paralysis.** Firms that invest heavily in ideation but fail to implement find themselves trapped in perpetual planning. They may be admired for creativity yet underperform in execution. This condition often arises in organizations with strong R&D but weak commercialization. Without action, even the boldest entrepreneurial ideas become irrelevant.

- **Listen Without Acting = Market Myopia.** Some firms excel at collecting customer feedback and monitoring competitors but hesitate to translate insights into change. They may fear alienating existing customers or disrupting internal processes. The result is stagnation. Listening must be paired with responsiveness, or else it becomes a hollow ritual that erodes credibility with stakeholders.

- **Act Without Thinking or Listening = Tactical Chaos.** Firms that rush to act without grounding often find themselves reacting impulsively to market noise. They may launch products without validation or pivot too frequently, confusing customers and draining resources. While action may create the appearance of agility, it often undermines long-term performance if not rooted in strategic clarity.

- **Integration = Alignment.** The highest-performing firms balance all three orientations, thinking creatively, listening deeply, and acting decisively. Research suggests that integration of EO and MO, when executed through EM behaviors, predicts stronger profitability and growth outcomes (Bhuian, Menguc, & Bell, 2005). Integration prevents overemphasis on any single mode and ensures that strategy is coherent, grounded, and actionable.

APPLICATION IN CONSULTING AND EDUCATION

In consulting practice, the Think–Listen–Act model functions as a rapid diagnostic tool. Executives can quickly self-assess where their organization is overdeveloped or underdeveloped. For example, if teams feel overburdened with data and are slow to implement change, the diagnosis may be "too much listening, not enough acting." This simple vocabulary enables leaders to articulate imbalances and chart corrective action.

In education, the model provides students with a gateway into complex research streams. Rather than beginning with technical definitions of EO, MO, and EM, instructors can introduce Think–Listen–Act as intuitive anchors. Once students grasp the behavioral implications, the subdimensions can be layered in. This sequencing improves retention and facilitates application.

The framework also strengthens cross-functional dialogue. Marketing managers, engineers, and executives may interpret strategy differently. By using verbs rather than academic jargon, Think–Listen–Act fosters shared language. This shared vocabulary enables organizations to align diverse teams around common behavioral expectations.

CONCLUSION

The Think–Listen–Act simplification offers a powerful way to make research on strategic orientations actionable for practitioners. By translating EO, MO, and EM into accessible verbs, it provides cognitive stickiness, diagnostic clarity, and strategic balance. Yet, it must be understood with nuance. Thinking requires action, listening requires responsiveness, and acting requires alignment. Oversimplification risks reducing the richness of decades of scholarship, but when treated as a heuristic rather than a reduction, the model offers executives a practical language for diagnosing and correcting behavioral misalignments.

Ultimately, the promise of Think–Listen–Act is not that it captures every detail, but that it makes strategy a lived behavior rather than an abstract concept. Firms that commit to thinking boldly, listening attentively, and acting decisively stand the best chance of sustaining competitive advantage in dynamic environments.

LIMITATIONS OF THE SOI™ MODEL

Like any strategic framework, the Strategic Orientation Index™ (SOI™) is a simplification of complex organizational dynamics. It is designed to help leaders and educators identify patterns of misalignment, but it does not claim to capture every variable that shapes firm performance. The SOI™ focuses specifically on three orientations—EO, MO, and EM—and does not explicitly address other important domains such as organizational culture, leadership style, or operational capability. In this way, it complements but does not replace other models such as McKinsey 7S or the Balanced Scorecard (Kaplan & Norton, 1996). The model's strength lies in diagnosing behavioral orientation, not in prescribing detailed execution tactics. Users should apply SOI™ alongside—but not in place of—existing planning and operational systems.

Second, the SOI™ is intentionally firm-level in focus, which means it may under-represent variations that exist within divisions, departments, or individual teams. A company may exhibit characteristics of more than one persona across functions—for example, a visionary product team inside a reluctant culture. While this model is useful for creating strategic alignment conversations at the enterprise level, it should not be used as a blunt instrument to label or judge subunits without deeper exploration. Practitioners should supplement the SOI™ diagnostic with department-level data and qualitative inputs when possible. Future versions of the tool may offer multitiered scoring to account for this complexity. For now, it is best used as a strategic mirror for executive-level pattern recognition and decision-making.

Third, the model is diagnostic, not predictive. Scoring high in EO, MO, or EM does not guarantee firm success—and scoring low does not automatically forecast failure. Strategic context, industry timing, team dynamics, and resource availability all play significant roles in firm performance. While the SOI™ offers useful strategic insights, it should be interpreted as a **conversation starter**, not a performance oracle. It identifies likely behavioral patterns and blind spots—but what happens next depends on leadership action. As such, users should treat their persona profile as a growth hypothesis, not a fixed identity.

Finally, while the SOI™ is grounded in peer-reviewed literature and doctoral research, it has not yet been statistically validated across a large sample of firms, industries, and geographies. Its empirical foundation draws heavily from the work of Morris et al. (2002), Miles and Darroch (2006), Kraus et al. (2010), and others—but the integrated model is still relatively new. As future researchers test and apply the SOI™ framework in classroom, consulting, or longitudinal settings, refinements may emerge. Readers are encouraged to treat this material as Version 1.0—a structured, research-backed platform ready for use, but open to evolution. Academic partners interested in formal validation are invited to collaborate. This intellectual humility ensures the SOI™ grows stronger over time—not more rigid.

WHY EO, MO, AND EM TOGETHER?

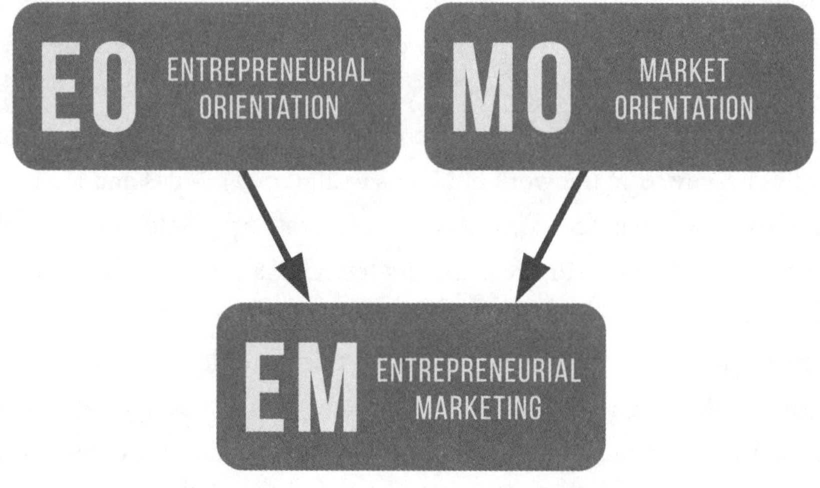

To understand a firm's strategic orientation clearly, it is not enough to study entrepreneurial intent (EO) or market intelligence (MO) in isolation. Many organizations exhibit a strong entrepreneurial posture but fail to translate that energy into market responsiveness, while others prioritize customer understanding but struggle with internal risk-taking or innovation. Prior studies suggest that both EO and MO are positively correlated with firm performance, but their combined impact is greater than either alone (Bhuian, Menguc, & Bell, 2005; Miles & Darroch, 2006). This is because alignment between these orientations creates a strategic posture that is both opportunity-seeking and customer-responsive. However, knowing how entrepreneurial and market-oriented a company is still doesn't fully explain executional behavior. That's where Entrepreneurial Marketing (EM) completes the picture—by translating intent into action.

EO, MO, and EM each address different but interdependent dimensions of strategic performance. EO captures the firm's internal willingness to innovate, take risks, and act proactively (Covin & Slevin, 1989; Lumpkin & Dess, 1996). MO reflects the firm's outward-facing discipline in gathering, disseminating, and responding to market intelligence (Narver & Slater, 1990). But EM operationalizes these two constructs—it's how firms behave in real market environments when deploying strategy (Morris, Schindehutte, & LaForge, 2002). EM includes behaviors such as Informal Marketing Research, Customer Immersion, and Value Creation Through Alliances—tactical actions that reveal whether EO and MO are actually being executed (Hills & Hultman, 2008). Without EM, strategy remains theoretical.

Table 2.1 below illustrates how the three constructs complement each other. Entrepreneurial Orientation supplies the strategic drive; Market Orientation provides the directional guidance; and Entrepreneurial Marketing reflects the behaviors that make both actionable. This relationship is not just theoretical. In practice, firms that align these three dimensions tend to outperform those that rely on only one or two (Miles & Darroch, 2006; Kraus, Harms, & Fink, 2010). More importantly, misalignment between them often creates performance breakdowns—for example, a company with high EO but low MO may innovate in ways the market doesn't value, while one with strong MO but low EO may fail to capitalize on trends. Entrepreneurial Marketing ensures these orientations are enacted at the customer level.

TABLE 2.1: DISTINCT ROLES OF EO, MO, AND EM IN STRATEGIC EXECUTION

CONSTRUCT	PRIMARY ROLE	CORE QUESTION ANSWERED	SAMPLE BEHAVIORS
EO	Strategic Intent	"Are we bold, fast, and innovative enough?"	Innovation, proactiveness, risk-taking
MO	Market Discipline	"Do we understand our customers and competitors?"	Customer-feedback loops, competitor tracking, cross-functional alignment
EM	Behavioral Execution	"Are we acting entrepreneurially in the market?"	Informal research, alliance-building, immersion, real-time responsiveness

The Strategic Orientation Index™ (SOI™) introduced in this chapter builds on this triangulated model. It measures each of these constructs—not in isolation, but in combination—to assess how strategically aligned a firm truly is. It then maps that alignment into a firm-level persona, offering practical insights into strategic gaps, growth pathways, and behavioral execution. The SOI™ is not just an assessment—it's a mirror that reflects how strategy, market understanding, and real-world behavior converge (or collide). By diagnosing where firms stand on EO, MO, and

EM, and how those dimensions interact, the SOI™ provides a roadmap for increasing both strategic clarity and market performance. The next chapter will walk you through that model in detail.

THEORETICAL GROUNDING: EO, MO, AND EM AS A STRATEGIC TRIAD

The Strategic Orientation Index™ (SOI™) framework is rooted in the triangulation of three foundational constructs: Entrepreneurial Orientation (EO), Market Orientation (MO), and Entrepreneurial Marketing (EM). While these constructs have been studied independently for decades, their convergence into a single diagnostic framework has been limited. Morris, Schindehutte, and LaForge (2002) provided the earliest and most influential articulation of this intersection, arguing that EM behaviors emerge when EO and MO are both present and interacting dynamically. In their view, EM is not a standalone philosophy but a behavioral manifestation of how opportunity-driven and market-aware firms operate. This conceptual model suggests that EM bridges the gap between strategy and execution, translating entrepreneurial posture and market insight into customer-facing behaviors. The SOI™ builds on this theoretical foundation and transforms it into an actionable diagnostic tool.

Miles and Darroch (2006) extended this argument by proposing that sustainable competitive advantage is most likely when firms simultaneously exhibit high levels of EO and MO. In their model, EM serves as a moderating force that enables larger firms to maintain entrepreneurial behavior while scaling. Similarly, Kraus, Harms, and Fink (2010) emphasized that EM is the behavioral engine that transforms strategic orientation into performance outcomes, particularly in small and medium-sized enterprises. Their findings reinforce the idea that EO and MO provide direction, but EM determines the effectiveness of execution. In this context, the three constructs are not redundant—they are interdependent. The SOI™ framework reflects this by measuring them in parallel and identifying where alignment or gaps exist.

In the chapters that follow, we'll unpack EO, MO, and EM in detail. But first, it's important to understand how these disciplines came to exist, why they matter more than ever, and how Entrepreneurial Marketing acts as the bridge between intention and execution.

DEFINITION AND HISTORICAL CONTEXT

Entrepreneurial Marketing emerged as a distinct discipline in the late twentieth century as scholars recognized the unique challenges faced by small businesses and start-ups. These challenges include operating in high-uncertainty environments, competing with larger firms with more resources, and the need for rapid adaptation to changing market conditions. Traditional marketing approaches, which rely on large budgets, extensive market research, and well-established processes, were found to be less effective in such contexts (Stokes, 2000; Carson, Cromie, McGowan, & Hill, 1995). In response, EM evolved as a flexible, opportunity-driven approach that blends marketing strategy with entrepreneurial agility, emphasizing innovation, risk-taking, and resourcefulness (Morris, Schindehutte, & LaForge, 2002).

The historical roots of EM lie in the broader evolution of marketing and entrepreneurship as academic disciplines. In the mid-twentieth century, marketing was primarily focused on mass markets, with a heavy emphasis on advertising, sales promotions, and distribution. As the business environment became more dynamic and competitive, particularly with the rise of technology and globalization, it became clear that traditional marketing methods were not always suitable for smaller, more agile businesses (Hills, Hultman, & Miles, 2008). This realization led to the development of EM as a distinct approach, tailored to the needs of entrepreneurs who must navigate uncertainty and make the most of limited resources (Kraus, Harms, & Fink, 2010).

THE SIX KEY FACTORS OF ENTREPRENEURIAL MARKETING

Entrepreneurial Marketing is distinguished by six key factors that together create a framework for a more dynamic, flexible, and customer-focused approach to marketing. These six factors are Growth Orientation, Opportunity Orientation, Two-Way Customer Contact, Value Creation Through Alliances, Informal Marketing Research, and Market Immersion. Each of these factors plays a critical role in driving the success of EM practices within an organization.

1. GROWTH ORIENTATION

Growth Orientation in Entrepreneurial Marketing refers to the strategic focus on expanding the business, whether through increasing market share, diversifying product lines, or entering new markets. Unlike traditional marketing, which may prioritize stability and incremental growth, EM embraces a more ambitious approach, setting bold goals for business expansion (Morris et al., 2002). This orientation drives companies to continuously seek new opportunities and push the boundaries of what is possible, fostering an environment of innovation and risk-taking.

For example, a company with a strong Growth Orientation might set a strategic goal to double its market presence within three years by expanding into international markets and introducing new product lines. This approach not only motivates the organization to pursue aggressive growth targets but also aligns the entire business toward achieving these goals.

2. OPPORTUNITY ORIENTATION

Opportunity Orientation is the ability to identify, evaluate, and capitalize on emerging opportunities in the market. This factor is central to EM, as it reflects the entrepreneurial mindset of being constantly on the lookout for new opportunities that can provide a competitive advantage (Morris et al., 2002). Unlike traditional marketing, which may focus on established markets and customer segments, EM encourages businesses to explore uncharted territories, including niche markets and emerging trends.

A practical example of Opportunity Orientation is seen in companies that pivot quickly in response to market shifts. For instance, a retail brand might adapt to the growing demand for eco-friendly products by introducing a new line of sustainable goods, capturing a significant share of this emerging market. This ability to recognize and act on opportunities as they arise is a defining characteristic of successful Entrepreneurial Marketing strategies.

3. TWO-WAY CUSTOMER CONTACT

Two-Way Customer Contact emphasizes the importance of open, ongoing communication between a business and its customers. This factor is crucial in building strong, lasting relationships, as it ensures that customers feel heard and valued (Fillis, 2010). Unlike traditional marketing, which often relies on one-way communication through advertising and promotions, EM fosters a dialogue with customers, using their feedback to inform product development, service improvements, and marketing strategies.

For example, an online service provider might regularly interact with customers through social media and live chat, using their feedback to refine services and enhance the user experience. This ongoing dialogue not only helps the business stay attuned to customer needs but also builds trust and loyalty, as customers appreciate being part of the decision-making process.

4. VALUE CREATION THROUGH ALLIANCES

Value Creation Through Alliances refers to the strategic partnerships that businesses form to leverage complementary strengths and resources. In EM, alliances are seen as a way to enhance competitive advantage by pooling resources, sharing knowledge, and accessing new markets (Morris et al., 2002). This approach contrasts with traditional marketing, where partnerships may be limited to supplier relationships or formal collaborations.

In practice, Value Creation Through Alliances can be seen in examples such as a software company partnering with a hardware manufacturer to co-develop a new integrated product. This partnership not only expands the market reach of both companies but also offers customers a more comprehensive solution, thereby increasing the value proposition.

5. INFORMAL MARKETING RESEARCH

Informal Marketing Research is a key factor in EM that involves gathering insights through non-traditional methods. Rather than relying solely on formal market research studies, entrepreneurial marketers often use direct customer interactions, observations, and informal conversations to gather data quickly and cost-effectively (Stokes, 2000). This approach allows businesses to be more responsive to changes in customer preferences and market conditions.

For example, a small business owner might regularly chat with customers in-store to gather feedback on product preferences, using this information to adjust inventory and introduce new offerings. This informal approach to market research enables businesses to stay agile and make informed decisions without the need for costly and time-consuming research projects.

6. MARKET IMMERSION

Market Immersion is the practice of deeply engaging with the market to understand customer behavior, industry trends, and competitive dynamics. This factor is crucial for staying ahead of the competition and ensuring that marketing strategies are relevant and effective (Fillis, 2010). Unlike traditional marketing, which may rely on periodic market analysis, EM encourages continuous immersion in the market, allowing businesses to stay attuned to changes and respond quickly.

For instance, a fashion retailer might frequently visit competitors' stores, attend industry events, and monitor social media trends to stay updated on the latest styles. This ongoing immersion in the market enables the retailer to adapt its product lines quickly, ensuring that it remains relevant and appealing to customers.

While Morris et al. (2002) originally introduced a seven-factor model of Entrepreneurial Marketing, this book adopts the six-factor model validated by Kilenthong (2011). Kilenthong conducted comparative empirical testing of five-, six-, and seven-factor configurations and found that the six-factor model demonstrated the strongest statistical fit across reliability, validity, and model parsimony. These six factors—Growth Orientation, Opportunity Orientation, Two-Way Customer Contact, Value Creation Through Alliances, Informal Marketing Research, and Market Immersion—form the behavioral foundation of the Strategic Orientation Index™ (SOI™).

This editorial decision reflects both empirical rigor and functional viability. By using the most robust version of the Entrepreneurial Marketing construct, the SOI™ remains grounded in peer-reviewed validation while enhancing usability for diagnostic, consulting, and instructional purposes. The goal is not to deviate from Morris et al.'s conceptual contribution, but to extend it—refining the model into a more practical, evidence-based structure that can drive real strategic behavior in firms of all sizes.

THE EVOLVING ROLE OF MARKETING IN ENTREPRENEURSHIP

FROM TRANSACTIONAL TO RELATIONAL MARKETING

Traditional marketing was initially developed in an era when the focus was primarily on transactional relationships. The primary goal was to drive sales through promotions, advertising, and distribution, with success measured by the volume of products sold. This approach was effective in mass markets, where businesses could rely on large-scale production and distribution networks to reach a wide audience (Stokes, 2000). However, as markets became more fragmented and competition intensified, the limitations of this transactional approach became apparent.

In contrast, Entrepreneurial Marketing emphasizes relational marketing, where the focus is on building and maintaining strong relationships with customers. This shift from transactions to relationships is crucial in the entrepreneurial context, where customer loyalty and long-term engagement are essential for sustained success (Gilmore, Carson, & Grant, 2001). Relational marketing involves understanding customer needs, preferences, and behaviors, and using this knowledge to create value and foster loyalty. In EM, the goal is not just to make a sale but to build a lasting relationship with the customer, one that is based on trust, mutual respect, and ongoing engagement (Bjerke & Hultman, 2002).

STRATEGIC MARKETING IN ENTREPRENEURIAL VENTURES

In entrepreneurial ventures, marketing takes on a broader strategic role than in traditional businesses. While traditional marketing often focuses on executing well-established processes and tactics, EM requires a more hands-on, flexible approach that aligns closely with the entrepreneurial mindset. Entrepreneurs must be willing to take risks, innovate continuously, and adapt quickly to changing market conditions (Hills et al., 2008). This strategic role of marketing is particularly important in entrepreneurship, where resources are often limited, and the ability to pivot quickly in response to new opportunities or challenges is critical (Collinson & Shaw, 2001).

COMPARING AND CONTRASTING ENTREPRENEURIAL MARKETING AND TRADITIONAL MARKETING

To fully appreciate the value of Entrepreneurial Marketing, it is essential to understand how it compares to traditional marketing across several key dimensions. These include strategic focus, resource utilization, customer engagement, innovation, and adaptability.

STRATEGIC FOCUS: FLEXIBILITY VS. RIGIDITY

One of the most significant differences between EM and traditional marketing is their strategic focus. Traditional marketing is often characterized by a rigid, process-driven approach. It typically involves long-term planning, with marketing strategies and campaigns developed months or even years in advance. This approach is suitable for large, established businesses with stable markets and predictable customer behavior (Carson et al., 1995). However, it can be a significant drawback for smaller businesses and start-ups, which operate in more volatile environments and need the flexibility to respond quickly to changes in the market (Stokes, 2000).

In contrast, Entrepreneurial Marketing is inherently flexible and adaptable. It is based on the understanding that markets are dynamic and that opportunities can arise unexpectedly. Entrepreneurs using EM are not bound by rigid plans; instead, they are always on the lookout for new opportunities and are willing to pivot their strategies as needed (Morris et al., 2002). This flexibility is a critical advantage in fast-paced industries, where the ability to adapt quickly can mean the difference between success and failure (Fillis, 2010).

For example, a start-up in the technology sector might use EM to continuously adapt its product and marketing strategy based on feedback from early adopters. This approach allows the company to stay ahead of competitors and quickly capitalize on emerging trends. In contrast, a traditional marketing approach would require a more extended planning period, which could result in missed opportunities and a slower response to market changes.

RESOURCE UTILIZATION: EFFICIENCY VS. ABUNDANCE

Another key difference between EM and traditional marketing is how they approach resource utilization. Traditional marketing often relies on large budgets, extensive market research, and significant investments in advertising and promotion. This approach is feasible for large corporations with deep pockets but is often out of reach for smaller businesses and start-ups (Carson et al., 1995). Moreover, traditional marketing can be inefficient, as it tends to focus on broad, mass-market campaigns that may not be well targeted or cost-effective (Kraus et al., 2010).

Entrepreneurial Marketing, on the other hand, is designed to make the most of limited resources. Entrepreneurs using EM are often working with tight budgets, so they must be creative and strategic in how they allocate their resources. This often involves leveraging low-cost marketing tactics, such as social media, content marketing, and guerrilla marketing, to reach their target audience without breaking the bank (Stokes, 2000). Additionally, EM emphasizes the importance of building strategic partnerships and alliances, which can help small businesses access resources and capabilities that they would not be able to afford on their own (Fillis, 2010).

For instance, a small business might use content marketing to build its brand and attract customers without the need for expensive advertising campaigns. By creating valuable, informative content that resonates with their target audience, the business can generate leads and build relationships at a fraction of the cost of traditional marketing methods. This approach is not only more cost-effective but also more sustainable in the long term, as it allows the business to build a loyal customer base without relying on expensive, short-term promotions.

CUSTOMER ENGAGEMENT: PERSONALIZATION VS. GENERALIZATION

Customer engagement is another area where EM and traditional marketing differ significantly. Traditional marketing often takes a broad, generalized approach to customer engagement, focusing on reaching as many people as possible through mass media channels such as television, radio, and print advertising. While this approach can be effective for building brand awareness, it is often impersonal and fails to create meaningful connections with individual customers (Stokes, 2000; Collinson & Shaw, 2001).

Entrepreneurial Marketing, on the other hand, emphasizes personalized, one-on-one engagement with customers. Entrepreneurs using EM understand that building strong relationships with customers is key to long-term success, so they prioritize direct, personalized communication and engagement. This often involves using digital marketing channels, such as social media, email, and mobile apps, to interact with customers in real time and tailor their marketing messages to individual preferences and behaviors (Gilmore et al., 2001).

For example, a start-up might use social media to engage directly with its customers, responding to their comments and feedback, and creating content that speaks directly to their interests and needs. This personalized approach helps build trust and loyalty, as customers feel valued and understood by the brand. In contrast, a traditional marketing approach would likely involve broadcasting a generic message to a broad audience, with little opportunity for direct interaction or feedback.

INNOVATION: EXPERIMENTATION VS. STANDARDIZATION

Innovation is at the heart of Entrepreneurial Marketing, and this is another area where it differs significantly from traditional marketing. Traditional marketing often relies on established, standardized practices that have been proven to work over time. While this approach can provide stability and predictability, it can also stifle creativity and limit the ability to innovate (Morris et al., 2002). Traditional marketers may be hesitant to try new ideas or take risks, preferring to stick with what has worked in the past.

In contrast, Entrepreneurial Marketing encourages experimentation and innovation. Entrepreneurs using EM are not afraid to take risks and try new approaches, even if they are untested or unconventional. This willingness to experiment is a critical advantage in fast-changing industries, where the ability to innovate can set a business apart from its competitors (Bjerke & Hultman, 2002; Fillis, 2010). EM also emphasizes the importance of staying agile and responsive to changes in the market, allowing businesses to quickly adapt their strategies and stay ahead of the curve.

For instance, an entrepreneur might experiment with a new product feature or marketing tactic, gathering feedback from customers and iterating on the idea until it resonates with the market. This approach allows the business to stay nimble and responsive, quickly adapting to changing customer needs and preferences. In contrast, a traditional marketing approach would likely involve a longer development cycle, with less room for experimentation and iteration.

ADAPTABILITY: AGILITY VS. INERTIA

Adaptability is another key difference between EM and traditional marketing. Traditional marketing often operates with a degree of inertia, relying on established processes and systems that can be slow to change. This approach can be effective in stable, predictable markets, but it can be a significant disadvantage in more volatile environments where rapid adaptation is essential (Hills et al., 2008; Gilmore et al., 2001).

Entrepreneurial Marketing, on the other hand, is inherently adaptable. Entrepreneurs using EM understand that markets are dynamic and that success requires the ability to pivot quickly in response to new opportunities or challenges. This adaptability is a critical advantage in industries where customer preferences, technology, and competition can change rapidly (Morris et al., 2002). EM also emphasizes the importance of staying attuned to the market, continuously gathering feedback and making adjustments to ensure that the business remains relevant and competitive.

For example, a start-up in the fashion industry might use EM to quickly adapt its product offerings based on the latest trends and customer feedback. This approach allows the business to stay ahead of competitors and ensure that its products resonate with the market. In contrast, a traditional marketing approach would likely involve a more extended planning period, with less flexibility to make changes in response to market shifts.

TABLE: TRADITIONAL MARKETING VS. ENTREPRENEURIAL MARKETING

DIMENSION	TRADITIONAL MARKETING	ENTREPRENEURIAL MARKETING
Strategic Orientation	Long-term planning, structured campaigns	Adaptive, opportunity-driven strategy
Market Research	Formal, data-heavy, time-intensive	Informal, real-time, and experiential (e.g., customer-feedback loops, gut instincts)
Customer Engagement	One-way communication; mass targeting	Two-way interaction; personalized, relationship-oriented
Risk Appetite	Risk-averse; focus on stability	Risk-tolerant; willing to experiment and pivot quickly
Innovation Approach	Incremental improvement of existing offerings	Proactive creation of new value and offerings
Budget & Resources	Large budgets; emphasis on economies of scale	Lean budgets; emphasis on creativity, resource leveraging, and partnerships
Decision Speed	Slow and hierarchical	Fast and decentralized
Goal Focus	Efficiency, brand consistency, and market share	Opportunity capture, strategic agility, and growth
Performance Metrics	Return on investment, awareness, market penetration	Customer traction, early revenue, proof of concept, and momentum
Culture & Mindset	Corporate, analytical, process-oriented	Entrepreneurial, intuitive, action-oriented

WHY ENTREPRENEURIAL MARKETING IS BETTER FOR SMES AND START-UPS

Given the differences outlined above, it is clear that Entrepreneurial Marketing offers several advantages over traditional marketing, particularly for SMEs and start-ups. These businesses often operate in environments that are highly dynamic and competitive, where the ability to adapt quickly and make the most of limited resources is critical for success. EM provides the flexibility, creativity, and customer focus that these businesses need to thrive in such environments.

FLEXIBILITY AND ADAPTABILITY

One of the most significant advantages of EM is its flexibility and adaptability. Unlike traditional marketing, which often relies on rigid processes and long-term planning, EM is designed to be responsive to change. This flexibility is particularly important for SMEs and start-ups, which may need to pivot quickly in response to new opportunities or challenges. By embracing EM, these businesses can stay agile and adapt their strategies as needed to stay competitive (Stokes, 2000; Kraus et al., 2010).

COST-EFFECTIVENESS

Another advantage of EM is its cost-effectiveness. Traditional marketing often requires significant investments in advertising, promotions, and market research, which can be out of reach for smaller businesses with limited budgets. In contrast, EM focuses on making the most of available resources, using creative solutions and low-cost tactics to achieve marketing goals. This cost-effectiveness is critical for SMEs and start-ups, which must be strategic in how they allocate their resources (Carson et al., 1995).

CUSTOMER-CENTRIC APPROACH

EM also offers a more customer-centric approach to marketing.

Traditional marketing often relies on broad, generalized messages that are designed to reach as many people as possible. While this approach can be effective for building brand awareness, it is often impersonal and fails to create meaningful connections with individual customers. EM, on the other hand, emphasizes personalized, one-on-one engagement, which helps build stronger relationships with customers and fosters loyalty over the long term (Gilmore et al., 2001).

INNOVATION AND EXPERIMENTATION

Finally, EM encourages innovation and experimentation, which are critical for success in today's fast-changing business environment. Traditional marketing often relies on established, standardized practices that can be slow to change. In contrast, EM encourages entrepreneurs to take risks and try new approaches, even if they are untested or unconventional. This willingness to experiment is a critical advantage in industries where the ability to innovate can set a business apart from its competitors (Morris et al., 2002).

WHY ENTREPRENEURIAL MARKETING IS BETTER FOR LARGE ORGANIZATIONS

While Entrepreneurial Marketing (EM) is often associated with small and medium-sized enterprises (SMEs) and start-ups, its principles and practices can also provide significant advantages for large organizations. In today's rapidly changing business landscape, where customer expectations, technological advancements, and competitive pressures are constantly evolving, large organizations can benefit from the flexibility, innovation, and customer-centric focus that EM offers.

NAVIGATING ORGANIZATIONAL INERTIA

Large organizations are often burdened by organizational inertia, a phenomenon where established processes, hierarchies, and bureaucracies slow down decision-making and innovation (Schilling, 2013). Traditional marketing approaches in large companies typically involve lengthy planning cycles, extensive market research, and rigid execution strategies. While these processes are designed to minimize risk, they can also stifle creativity and slow down the organization's ability to respond to market changes.

Entrepreneurial Marketing, on the other hand, emphasizes agility and flexibility, encouraging organizations to be more responsive to changes in the market. By adopting EM practices, large organizations can overcome the constraints of organizational inertia. EM fosters a more dynamic marketing environment where teams are empowered to experiment with new ideas, pivot quickly in response to feedback, and take calculated risks to capitalize on emerging opportunities (Kuratko, Hornsby, & Covin, 2014).

For example, a large corporation in the consumer goods industry might traditionally rely on extensive product testing and market research before launching a new product. While this approach reduces the risk of failure, it also slows down the innovation process. By incorporating EM principles, the company could adopt a more iterative approach, launching a minimum viable product (MVP) quickly, gathering customer feedback in real time, and refining the product based on actual market responses. This approach not only speeds up the innovation process but also ensures that the final product is more closely aligned with customer needs and preferences.

ENHANCING INNOVATION CAPABILITIES

Innovation is a critical component of long-term success for any organization, but it can be particularly challenging for large companies that have established ways of doing things. Traditional marketing in large organizations often focuses on maintaining the status quo, with an emphasis on incremental improvements rather than disruptive innovation (Teece, 2010). This approach can lead to missed opportunities, especially in industries where technological advancements and customer expectations are evolving rapidly.

Entrepreneurial Marketing encourages a culture of innovation by promoting experimentation, risk-taking, and a willingness to challenge conventional wisdom. By adopting EM practices, large organizations can enhance their innovation capabilities and become more proactive in identifying and pursuing new market opportunities. This is particularly important in industries like technology, health care, and retail, where the pace of change is accelerating, and the ability to innovate quickly can provide a significant competitive advantage (Hamel, 2006).

For instance, a large technology company might traditionally focus on improving existing products rather than exploring entirely new markets or technologies. However, by adopting EM practices, the company could create dedicated innovation teams that operate with the agility and entrepreneurial mindset of a start-up. These teams could explore new ideas, test them in the market, and iterate rapidly based on customer feedback. This approach not only drives innovation but also helps the company stay ahead of emerging trends and disruptors.

FOSTERING A CUSTOMER-CENTRIC CULTURE

Large organizations often struggle to maintain a close connection with their customers, particularly as they grow and expand into new markets. Traditional marketing approaches in large companies tend to focus on broad, mass-market strategies that may overlook the specific needs and preferences of individual customers. This can lead to a disconnect between the company and its customers, resulting in lower customer satisfaction and loyalty (Prahalad & Ramaswamy, 2004).

Entrepreneurial Marketing, with its emphasis on customer-centricity, can help large organizations foster a closer relationship with their customers. EM practices encourage organizations to engage directly with their customers, gather real-time feedback, and tailor their marketing strategies to meet the specific needs of different customer segments. This customer-centric approach not only enhances customer satisfaction and loyalty but also provides valuable insights that can inform product development, marketing campaigns, and overall business strategy (Baker & Sinkula, 2009).

For example, a large retail chain might traditionally rely on broad advertising campaigns to attract customers. While these campaigns can raise brand awareness, they may not effectively engage individual customers or address their specific needs. By adopting EM practices, the company could leverage digital marketing tools to engage with customers on a more personal level, using data analytics to tailor offers, recommendations, and communications based on individual customer preferences. This personalized approach can lead to higher customer engagement, increased loyalty, and ultimately, better business performance.

DRIVING COMPETITIVE ADVANTAGE

In today's hyper-competitive business environment, large organizations must continually seek ways to differentiate themselves from their competitors. Traditional marketing approaches, which often rely on well-established methods and practices, may not provide the level of differentiation needed to stand out in crowded markets. Moreover, the size and scale of large organizations can sometimes make them less nimble and slower to respond to competitive threats (Porter, 1996).

Entrepreneurial Marketing offers large organizations a way to drive competitive advantage by fostering a culture of agility, innovation, and customer focus. By adopting EM practices, large companies can become more responsive to market changes, more innovative in their product and service offerings, and more effective in engaging with their customers. This competitive edge is particularly important in industries where customer preferences are rapidly evolving, and new competitors are constantly emerging (Zahra, 1993).

For example, a large financial services company might traditionally focus on optimizing its existing products and services to maintain market share. However, by incorporating EM practices, the company could proactively explore new market opportunities, such as developing innovative financial products for underserved customer segments or leveraging technology to enhance the customer experience. This proactive approach not only helps the company stay ahead of competitors but also positions it as a leader in the industry.

ACCELERATING DIGITAL TRANSFORMATION

Digital transformation is a critical priority for large organizations across industries, as digital technologies continue to reshape customer expectations, business models, and competitive dynamics. However, traditional marketing approaches can sometimes hinder digital-transformation efforts, as they often rely on established channels, methods, and metrics that may not align with the rapidly changing digital landscape (Bharadwaj, El Sawy, Pavlou, & Venkatraman, 2013).

Entrepreneurial Marketing, with its emphasis on innovation, agility, and customer-centricity, can accelerate digital transformation in large organizations. EM encourages the use of digital tools and platforms to engage with customers, gather insights, and deliver personalized experiences at scale. It also promotes a more iterative, data-driven approach to marketing, where strategies can be quickly tested, refined, and optimized based on real-time feedback and performance metrics (Kotler, Kartajaya, & Setiawan, 2017).

For example, a large multinational corporation might traditionally rely on television and print advertising to reach its global audience. While these channels remain important, they may not be sufficient to engage digitally savvy customers who expect personalized, on-demand experiences. By adopting EM practices, the corporation could leverage digital-marketing platforms, such as social media, email marketing, and mobile apps, to deliver targeted, personalized content to customers in real time. This digital-first approach not only enhances customer engagement but also supports the organization's broader digital-transformation goals.

CULTIVATING AN ENTREPRENEURIAL MINDSET ACROSS THE ORGANIZATION

One of the key challenges for large organizations is maintaining an entrepreneurial mindset as they grow and mature. Over time, the processes, hierarchies, and risk-averse culture that often develop in large companies can stifle the creativity and innovation that are essential for long-term success (Kuratko et al., 2014). Entrepreneurial Marketing can help large organizations cultivate an entrepreneurial mindset across the organization, empowering employees at all levels to think creatively, take initiative, and embrace change.

By adopting EM practices, large companies can create a more dynamic and innovative work environment where employees are encouraged to experiment with new ideas, collaborate across departments, and take calculated risks. This entrepreneurial culture not only drives innovation but also enhances employee engagement and satisfaction, as employees feel more empowered to contribute to the organization's success (Ireland, Hitt, & Sirmon, 2003).

For example, a large manufacturing company might traditionally rely on top-down decision-making processes that limit the input and creativity of frontline employees. However, by adopting EM practices, the company could create cross-functional innovation teams that bring together employees from different departments to collaborate on new ideas and projects. This bottom-up approach not only fosters innovation but also helps the company tap into the diverse perspectives and expertise of its workforce, leading to more creative and effective solutions.

LEVERAGING SCALE FOR GREATER IMPACT

While Entrepreneurial Marketing is often associated with small, agile businesses, large organizations can leverage their scale to amplify the impact of EM practices. Large companies have access to vast resources, extensive networks, and significant market influence, all of which can enhance the effectiveness of EM strategies. By combining the agility and innovation of EM with the scale and reach of a large organization, companies can drive transformative change and achieve significant competitive advantages (Hitt, Ireland, Sirmon, & Trahms, 2011).

For instance, a large pharmaceutical company might use EM practices to rapidly develop and test new drug therapies in response to emerging health crises. By leveraging its extensive research and development capabilities, global distribution networks, and relationships with healthcare providers, the company can quickly bring innovative treatments to market, saving lives and establishing itself as a leader in the industry. This combination of entrepreneurial agility and organizational scale not only enhances the company's impact but also strengthens its market position and long-term competitiveness.

CONCLUSION

Entrepreneurial Marketing represents a significant departure from traditional marketing in several key areas, including strategic focus, resource utilization, customer engagement, innovation, and adaptability. These differences make EM a more effective approach for SMEs, start-ups, and even large organizations, which operate in dynamic and competitive environments where flexibility, creativity, and customer focus are critical for success. By embracing EM, businesses of all sizes can build strong relationships with their customers, make the most of limited resources, and stay ahead of the competition through continuous innovation and adaptability. As the business landscape continues to evolve, the principles of Entrepreneurial Marketing will become increasingly important for organizations of all sizes, offering a roadmap for success in an ever-changing world.

STRATEGIC INTEGRATION THROUGH THE STRATEGIC ORIENTATION INDEX™ (SOI™)

Entrepreneurial Orientation (EO), Market Orientation (MO), and Entrepreneurial Marketing (EM) each represent well-established lenses through which we can understand and evaluate firm behavior. EO captures a company's appetite for innovation, risk, and proactiveness. MO reflects the degree to which an organization listens to, learns from, and adapts to the needs of its customers and competitive environment. EM, while newer in the academic literature, serves as a behavioral expression of these two orientations in action.

To reflect this integrative reality—and to give practitioners a concrete, actionable way to evaluate and strengthen their firm's strategic posture—this book introduces a unifying framework: the Strategic Orientation Index™ (SOI™).

The Strategic Orientation Index™ is a three-dimensional diagnostic framework that unifies EO, MO, and EM into a cohesive strategic system. While EO captures a firm's ability to innovate and take strategic risks, and MO reflects its responsiveness to market signals, EM measures how these orientations show up behaviorally—how strategy is executed through resourceful, agile, market-facing activity. While EO reflects ambition and MO ensures responsiveness, Entrepreneurial Marketing (EM) is where orientation becomes behavior. EM reveals whether a firm can actually act on its strategic intent—through fast iteration, informal learning, customer co-creation, and market-based agility. That's why SOI™ gives EM its own six-point scoring model. Without EM, firms may know what to do—but fail to execute dynamically in the market. SOI™ enables leaders to score their firm's current posture, identify gaps, and prescribe growth-focused priorities.

The SOI™ was designed to solve a common issue: Many firms excel in one strategic dimension but underperform in others. Some companies are highly innovative (EO) but disconnected from customer insight (low MO). Others are market-responsive (MO) but lack the boldness to act on emerging opportunities (low EO). Still others develop high-level strategies but fail to execute them dynamically in the marketplace (low EM). The SOI™ framework helps identify these imbalances and provides a map for regaining alignment.

The model is built on academic foundations that span three decades. EO draws from the work of Covin and Slevin (1989) and Lumpkin and Dess (1996), highlighting the value of proactiveness, risk-taking, and innovation. MO builds on foundational contributions by Kohli and Jaworski (1990) and Narver and Slater (1990), who emphasized intelligence gathering, interfunctional collaboration, and market responsiveness. EM, as introduced by Morris, Schindehutte, and LaForge (2002), emerged as the behavioral bridge between entrepreneurship and marketing, emphasizing agility, creativity, and informality in execution.

Throughout the book, you'll encounter references to SOI™ as we unpack each of the three dimensions in more detail. But before we dive in, it's helpful to preview how the SOI™ actually works. At the heart of the model is a scoring system: Firms rate themselves across EO, MO, and EM, with EM being broken down into six subdimensions—Growth Orientation, Opportunity Orientation, Two-Way Customer Contact, Value Creation Through Alliances, Informal Marketing Research, and Market Immersion. These scores generate a strategic profile that maps the firm's current posture.

From there, the SOI™ diagnostic matches the firm to one of five strategic personas. Each persona reflects a unique configuration of EO, MO, and EM behaviors and is linked to specific growth challenges and opportunities. Once identified, the persona serves as a strategic mirror—guiding leaders to customized action plans and rank-ordered checklists designed to strengthen underdeveloped orientations and rebalance execution across all three dimensions.

Understanding your strategic posture isn't just an academic exercise—it's a practical starting point for transformation. Whether you're launching a start-up, scaling a midsize company, or modernizing a legacy enterprise, SOI™ helps reveal your blind spots, clarify your edge, and prioritize the next right steps. It's a diagnostic lens designed not just for reflection, but for momentum. These personas aren't arbitrary—they are based on observed patterns across firms, validated through consulting work, case-study research, and organizational diagnostics. Each persona includes a strategic summary, key vulnerabilities, and rank-ordered checklist recommendations tailored to that firm's profile.

SOI™ is not just descriptive—it is prescriptive. It translates orientation theory into a strategic-action system. And it's adaptable: equally valuable for start-ups, midsize firms, and large enterprises.

In that sense, SOI™ is both a mirror and a map. It reflects where your organization currently stands—and provides a roadmap for how to evolve your strategy across the three dimensions that matter most: entrepreneurship, market focus, and agile execution.

Chapter 10: Bringing It Together: EO, MO, and EM, features the full SOI™ scoring system, quadrant-placement visuals, and complete strategic-persona profiles. Each profile includes a radar chart, growth-trajectory summary, and actionable next steps tied to your firm's diagnostic results. For now, keep in mind that as you read each chapter on EO, MO, and EM, you're also building the foundation for a much larger system of integration. The SOI™ framework was built to bring these concepts together in a way that is both academically grounded and practically transformative. The scoring system itself—along with percentile benchmarks, interpretation guidance, and quadrant visuals—is detailed in the next section of the book.

That diagnostic doesn't just describe where a company is—it reveals who they are strategically. Based on SOI™ scores, firms fall into one of five strategic personas, each with a distinctive configuration of EO, MO, and EM behaviors. The Visionary Vanguard represents firms with high EO and MO: bold, customer-attuned, and capable of sustained strategic execution. The Fearless Inventor scores high on EO but low on MO— brimming with ideas but vulnerable to misalignment with market needs. The Insightful Optimizer reflects the opposite profile: highly responsive to market signals but often too cautious to seize emerging opportunities. The Reluctant Responder, with low EO and MO, tends to be reactive and resource-constrained, requiring transformational change. Finally, the Hybrid Zone captures those in strategic limbo—firms with uneven or moderate EO/MO that may be drifting or on the verge of alignment. These personas are unpacked in Chapter 10 through rich profiles, radar charts, and customized strategic checklists.

The SOI™ is not just a framework—it's a strategic operating system. It shows leaders where their firms currently stand and where to focus next. Whether you're running a start-up, guiding a midsize company, or leading transformation in a large enterprise, SOI™ equips you with the clarity and tools to close the gap between strategy and execution. As you explore the coming chapters, keep in mind: You're not just learning about EO, MO, and EM in isolation—you're building toward a powerful, integrated lens that can reshape how your organization grows.

STRATEGIC IMPLICATION

Firms that embrace Entrepreneurial Marketing act decisively in uncertainty. Leaders should assess how well their marketing behavior reflects flexibility, risk-taking, and innovation—not just planning.

CHAPTER 2

EMBRACING ENTREPRENEURIAL ORIENTATION

In the previous chapter, we established the theoretical foundations and empirical validation of the Strategic Orientation Index™ (SOI™), positioning it as a powerful diagnostic tool grounded in decades of research on Market Orientation (MO), Entrepreneurial Orientation (EO), and Entrepreneurial Marketing (EM). But theory alone doesn't move markets. To unlock real strategic traction, organizations must transition from orientation awareness to orientation activation. That's the focus of this chapter.

Let's move from diagnosing orientation to designing action.

Entrepreneurial Orientation (EO) is a strategic framework crucial for organizations aiming to thrive in competitive and dynamic markets. It encompasses a firm's proclivity toward innovation, proactiveness, and risk-taking, which collectively contribute to the firm's ability to achieve sustained competitive advantages (Covin & Slevin, 1989). This chapter delves into the definition and key dimensions of EO, explores its theoretical underpinnings, and provides actionable strategies for fostering an entrepreneurial culture within organizations. Through robust case studies and a critical examination of the literature, this chapter underscores EO's significance in driving long-term business success.

UNDERSTANDING ENTREPRENEURIAL ORIENTATION

DEFINITION AND CORE DIMENSIONS

Entrepreneurial Orientation (EO) refers to the strategic mindset and behavioral tendencies that shape how firms identify opportunities, pursue innovation, and respond to uncertainty. It captures the degree to which a firm is inclined to act entrepreneurially across key dimensions. While EO has been conceptualized with up to five dimensions, the most widely studied and consistently validated core components are **innovativeness, proactiveness, and risk-taking** (Covin & Slevin, 1989; Lumpkin & Dess, 1996). These three dimensions are central to how firms navigate dynamic markets and drive growth.

Innovativeness reflects a firm's commitment to creativity, experimentation, and the pursuit of novel ideas. It includes activities such as developing new products, embracing emerging technologies, and investing in R&D. Firms high in innovativeness are more likely to challenge the status quo and create breakthrough value (Miller, 1983; Covin & Slevin, 1991).

Proactiveness refers to a forward-looking posture in which firms actively seek out and exploit emerging opportunities. Proactive firms are often first movers, introducing new offerings or entering new markets ahead of competitors. This anticipatory behavior helps shape market trends rather than simply reacting to them (Lumpkin & Dess, 2001; Hughes & Morgan, 2007).

Risk-taking captures a firm's willingness to commit significant resources to uncertain ventures and make bold decisions in the face of ambiguity. Rather than avoiding uncertainty, risk-taking firms treat it as a necessary condition for innovation and growth (Miller & Friesen, 1982; Zahra & Garvis, 2000).

These dimensions interact dynamically, influencing a firm's overall entrepreneurial posture and its ability to sustain growth in a competitive environment. Together, these three dimensions represent the behavioral foundation of an entrepreneurial organization and serve as a critical lens for assessing firm-level strategic posture in the SOI™ framework.

The practical implications of EO are profound. Empirical studies have consistently shown that firms with high EO outperform their peers in terms of innovation, market responsiveness, and overall growth (Rauch et al., 2009; Covin & Miller, 2014). For example, companies like Amazon and Tesla have leveraged their strong EO to continuously innovate and dominate their respective industries (Sundararajan, 2016).

INNOVATIVENESS

IMPORTANCE OF FOSTERING CREATIVITY

Innovativeness, as a dimension of EO, is fundamental to a firm's ability to develop new products, services, and processes that distinguish it from competitors. Innovation is not merely about generating new ideas but also about creating value through the successful implementation of those ideas (Schumpeter, 1934; Drucker, 1985). A culture that fosters creativity is essential for sustaining innovation over time, particularly in industries characterized by rapid technological advancements (Hamel & Prahalad, 1994).

Research by Damanpour (1991) shows that organizations with a strong focus on innovation tend to have higher performance levels, especially in dynamic industries. Encouraging a culture of creativity involves creating an environment where employees are motivated to explore new ideas without the fear of failure, supported by the necessary resources and leadership commitment (Amabile, 1996; Tushman & O'Reilly, 1996).

STRATEGIES FOR ENCOURAGING INNOVATION

Establish an Innovation-Friendly Culture: Developing a culture that values and rewards innovation is crucial. This can be achieved by promoting open communication, encouraging cross-functional collaboration, and empowering employees to take ownership of their ideas. Leaders must model innovative behavior and provide a vision that inspires creative efforts (Dess & Picken, 2000; Kanter, 1983).

Provide Resources and Support: Sufficient investment in research and development (R&D) is critical for sustaining innovation. Firms should allocate resources not only to R&D but also to training programs that enhance employees' creative skills. For instance, 3M's commitment to allocating 15 percent of its employees' time to innovation has been a key driver of its success in developing breakthrough products (Govinda-rajan & Trimble, 2010).

Implement Innovation Processes: Structured processes such as design thinking, lean start-up methodologies, and innovation labs can facilitate the development of new ideas. These processes help firms systematically explore, prototype, and scale new products, thereby reducing the risks associated with innovation (Brown, 2008; Ries, 2011).

Recognize and Reward Innovation: Recognition programs that reward innovative efforts can significantly enhance motivation and encourage a culture of continuous innovation. Firms can implement both formal (e.g., innovation awards) and informal (e.g., public acknowledgment) recognition systems to sustain creative efforts (Glover, Friedman, & Jones, 2002).

CASE STUDIES OF INNOVATIVE COMPANIES

Tesla: Tesla's relentless focus on innovation has revolutionized the automotive industry. The company's advancements in electric vehicles, renewable energy, and autonomous-driving technology have set new industry standards. Tesla's innovation culture, championed by Elon Musk, emphasizes experimentation and calculated risk-taking, which has been critical to its success (Vance, 2015; Mangram, 2012).

Apple: Apple's approach to innovation is a key factor in its market dominance. The company's investment in design, user experience, and technological innovation has led to the creation of iconic products like the iPhone, iPad, and Apple Watch. Apple's innovation strategy is deeply embedded in its corporate culture, driven by a commitment to pushing the boundaries of what technology can achieve (Isaacson, 2011; O'Grady, 2009).

PROACTIVENESS

IMPORTANCE OF ANTICIPATING MARKET NEEDS

Proactiveness is essential for firms aiming to lead rather than follow in their industries. Proactive firms actively seek out and capitalize on new opportunities, often by introducing innovative products or services before competitors. This dimension of EO is particularly important in rapidly changing markets where the ability to anticipate and respond to emerging trends can be a significant competitive advantage (Lumpkin & Dess, 2001; Wiklund & Shepherd, 2005).

Proactive firms are characterized by their strategic foresight and ability to shape market dynamics. Research has shown that firms with a proactive orientation are more likely to achieve sustained growth and profitability, as they are better positioned to exploit first-mover advantages (Lieberman & Montgomery, 1988; Lumpkin & Dess, 1996).

TECHNIQUES FOR PROACTIVE BUSINESS STRATEGIES

Market Research and Trend Analysis: Comprehensive market research and trend analysis are vital for identifying future opportunities and threats. By staying informed about industry trends and consumer behavior, firms can develop proactive strategies that align with market needs (Narver & Slater, 1990; Day, 1994).

Customer Engagement: Regular engagement with customers allows firms to stay attuned to evolving needs and preferences. Firms that prioritize customer feedback and incorporate it into their product-development processes are more likely to anticipate and meet future demands (Jaworski & Kohli, 1993; Slater & Narver, 1998).

Scenario Planning: Scenario planning involves developing multiple strategic responses based on different potential futures. This approach helps firms prepare for various contingencies, enabling them to respond quickly to changes in the market environment (Schoemaker, 1995; Wack, 1985).

Early Adoption of Technologies: Proactive firms often gain a competitive edge by adopting new technologies early. This strategy allows them to leverage technological advancements to improve operations, enhance customer experiences, and develop innovative products (Porter, 1985; Christensen, 1997).

EXAMPLES OF PROACTIVE BUSINESSES

Netflix: Netflix's proactive approach to content delivery has disrupted the traditional entertainment industry. By transitioning from a DVD rental service to a streaming platform and investing in original content, Netflix was able to anticipate and capitalize on the shift toward on-demand entertainment. This proactive strategy has established Netflix as a global leader in streaming media (McDonald & Smith-Rowsey, 2016; Keating, 2012).

Amazon: Amazon's proactive strategies have been instrumental in its rise to dominance in e-commerce and cloud computing. The company's early adoption of technologies such as artificial intelligence and cloud infrastructure has allowed it to continually innovate and expand its market reach. Amazon's proactive approach to market opportunities has solidified its position as one of the most valuable companies in the world (Stone, 2013; Dumas, 2007).

RISK-TAKING

IMPORTANCE OF CALCULATED RISK-TAKING

Risk-taking is a critical dimension of EO, particularly in industries where innovation and market leadership are paramount. While risk-taking involves uncertainty, it is a necessary component of entrepreneurial success. Firms that excel in risk-taking are those that carefully balance bold actions with strategic foresight, ensuring that risks are calculated and aligned with the firm's long-term objectives (Covin & Slevin, 1991; Zahra, 1993).

Calculated risk-taking enables firms to pursue opportunities that have the potential for high returns while managing the associated uncertainties. Research by March and Shapira (1987) suggests that successful firms are those that strategically engage in risk-taking, leveraging it as a tool for competitive advantage.

STRATEGIES FOR MANAGING RISKS

Conduct Thorough Risk Assessments: Comprehensive risk assessments are essential for identifying potential challenges and developing mitigation strategies. This involves evaluating both the likelihood and impact of potential risks and ensuring that decisions are based on sound analysis (Miller & Friesen, 1982; Knight, 1921).

Diversify Investments: Diversification is a key strategy for managing risk. By spreading investments across multiple projects or ventures, firms can reduce the impact of any single failure and increase the overall resilience of their portfolio (Markowitz, 1952; Ansoff, 1957).

Build a Resilient Organization: Resilience is critical for navigating the uncertainties associated with risk-taking. Firms that foster a culture of resilience—where learning from failures is encouraged and rapid adaptation is possible—are better equipped to recover from setbacks and capitalize on new opportunities (Hamel & Valikangas, 2003; Vogus & Sutcliffe, 2007).

Set Clear Risk-Tolerance Levels: Establishing clear risk-tolerance levels helps firms make informed decisions about which opportunities to pursue. This involves defining acceptable levels of risk for different projects and ensuring that all decisions are aligned with the firm's strategic objectives (Kahneman & Tversky, 1979; Slovic, 1987).

REAL-LIFE EXAMPLES OF SUCCESSFUL RISK-TAKING

SpaceX: SpaceX, founded by Elon Musk, epitomizes successful risk-taking in the aerospace industry. The company's ambitious goal of making space travel more affordable and eventually enabling human colonization of Mars involved significant financial and technical risks. However, SpaceX's innovative approach, including the development of reusable rockets, has led to groundbreaking achievements and established the company as a leader in the aerospace sector (Vance, 2015; Belfiore, 2007).

Google's Alphabet: Google's parent company, Alphabet, has consistently engaged in high-risk, high-reward ventures. Projects such as Waymo (self-driving cars), Verily (life sciences), and Google Fiber (high-speed internet) illustrate Alphabet's willingness to take on significant risks in pursuit of transformative innovation. These ventures, while risky, have the potential to redefine industries and contribute to Alphabet's long-term growth (Schmidt & Rosenberg, 2014; O'Reilly & Tushman, 2016).

ADVANCED STRATEGIES FOR IMPLEMENTING EO

Entrepreneurial Orientation (EO) is a dynamic and multifaceted concept that requires advanced strategies for effective implementation within organizations. The strategic implementation of EO involves not only recognizing its key dimensions—innovativeness, proactiveness, and risk-taking—but also aligning these dimensions with the organization's overall strategy and operational practices.

1. ALIGNING EO WITH STRATEGIC GOALS

One of the critical advanced strategies for implementing EO is aligning it with the organization's broader strategic goals. This alignment ensures that entrepreneurial activities are not isolated or ad hoc but are instead integrated into the core strategic vision of the firm. According to Ireland, Hitt, and Sirmon (2003), strategic entrepreneurship, which blends strategic management and entrepreneurial activities, is crucial for achieving sustainable competitive advantage. Firms need to identify how EO can support long-term objectives such as market expansion, product innovation, and customer engagement.

For example, in multinational corporations like General Electric (GE),

EO is aligned with strategic goals through the company's "FastWorks" initiative, which applies lean start-up principles to drive innovation across the organization. This initiative encourages experimentation and rapid iteration, allowing GE to bring new products to market faster while aligning with its strategic goals of technological leadership and market penetration (Ries, 2011).

2. LEVERAGING DATA AND ANALYTICS FOR EO

In the digital age, leveraging data and analytics is an advanced strategy that can significantly enhance the effectiveness of EO. Data-driven decision-making allows firms to identify emerging-market trends, customer preferences, and potential risks with greater accuracy, thereby enabling more informed and proactive entrepreneurial activities (McAfee & Brynjolfsson, 2012). By utilizing big data and predictive analytics, companies can refine their EO strategies to target the most promising opportunities and mitigate risks.

For instance, Netflix's success in the entertainment industry is largely due to its data-driven approach to EO. The company uses advanced analytics to predict viewer preferences and guide content creation, leading to the production of popular shows like *House of Cards* and *Stranger Things*. This strategy not only ensures that Netflix remains a market leader but also aligns with its broader EO objectives of innovation and market responsiveness (Davenport & Harris, 2007).

3. FOSTERING STRATEGIC ALLIANCES AND PARTNERSHIPS

Forming strategic alliances and partnerships is another advanced strategy for implementing EO. Such collaborations can provide firms with access to new markets, technologies, and resources that are essential for entrepreneurial activities (Gulati, Nohria, & Zaheer, 2000). By partnering with other organizations, firms can leverage complementary strengths and capabilities, thereby enhancing their ability to innovate and respond proactively to market changes.

A notable example is the partnership between IBM and Apple, where both companies combined their expertise to develop enterprise mobility solutions. This alliance allowed IBM to enhance its mobile offerings, while Apple benefited from IBM's enterprise customer base. The collaboration exemplifies how strategic partnerships can enhance EO by pooling resources and capabilities to achieve innovation and market leadership (Ireland, Hitt, & Vaidyanath, 2002).

4. INTEGRATING EO INTO CORPORATE GOVERNANCE

Integrating EO into corporate governance structures is essential for ensuring that entrepreneurial activities are sustained and aligned with organizational goals. This involves embedding EO principles into the decision-making processes at the board and executive levels. According to Zahra and Pearce (1989), corporate governance plays a crucial role in shaping a firm's strategic direction, including its entrepreneurial posture. Effective governance ensures that the pursuit of innovation, proactiveness, and calculated risk-taking is balanced with oversight and accountability.

One way to integrate EO into governance is by establishing innovation committees within the board of directors. These committees can oversee entrepreneurial initiatives, allocate resources for innovation, and ensure that EO activities are aligned with the company's strategic objectives. For instance, Google's parent company, Alphabet, has a governance structure that supports its diverse portfolio of innovative ventures, including autonomous vehicles (Waymo) and life sciences (Verily). This structure ensures that entrepreneurial activities are monitored and guided by strategic oversight (Schmidt & Rosenberg, 2014).

5. ADOPTING AGILE METHODOLOGIES

Adopting agile methodologies is an advanced strategy that aligns closely with the principles of EO. Agile methodologies, which emphasize iterative development, flexibility, and customer feedback, are well suited to organizations aiming to enhance their EO. These methodologies enable firms to respond quickly to market changes, innovate continuously, and manage risks more effectively (Highsmith, 2004).

For example, Spotify's adoption of agile practices has been instrumental in its ability to innovate and scale rapidly in the competitive music-streaming industry. By organizing its teams into small, cross-functional squads that operate independently, Spotify has been able to maintain a high level of innovation and responsiveness, key components of its EO strategy (Kniberg & Ivarsson, 2012).

CREATING AN EO CULTURE

Creating a culture that supports EO is essential for embedding entrepreneurial practices throughout an organization. An EO culture encourages employees at all levels to think and act entrepreneurially, fostering an environment where innovation, proactiveness, and risk-taking are valued and rewarded.

1. LEADERSHIP COMMITMENT TO EO

Leadership plays a pivotal role in shaping and sustaining an EO culture. Leaders who are committed to entrepreneurial values can inspire similar behaviors across the organization. According to Schein (2010), organizational culture is largely a reflection of leadership. Leaders who demonstrate a willingness to take risks, support innovation, and encourage proactive behaviors set the tone for the entire organization.

For instance, under the leadership of Steve Jobs, Apple developed a culture of relentless innovation and design excellence. Jobs's vision and commitment to EO permeated every aspect of the company, from product development to customer service, fostering a culture where creativity and innovation were integral to the company's identity (Isaacson, 2011).

2. ENCOURAGING INTRAPRENEURSHIP

Intrapreneurship refers to the practice of fostering entrepreneurial behavior within an organization by encouraging employees to act like entrepreneurs. This involves providing employees with the autonomy to pursue new ideas and initiatives, even within the confines of a larger corporate structure (Pinchot, 1985). By empowering employees to innovate and take ownership of projects, organizations can cultivate a culture that supports EO.

Google's "20% time" policy is a prime example of encouraging intrapreneurship. This policy allows employees to spend 20 percent of their work time on projects that interest them, regardless of whether these projects align with their official job duties. This freedom has led to the development of successful products like Gmail and Google News, demonstrating the power of intrapreneurship in fostering an EO culture (Schmidt & Rosenberg, 2014).

3. BUILDING A LEARNING ORGANIZATION

Creating an EO culture also involves building a learning organization, where continuous learning and development are prioritized. A learning organization is one that constantly evolves by encouraging experimentation, learning from failures, and adapting to new information. According to Senge (1990), organizations that embrace a culture of learning are better equipped to innovate and sustain competitive advantages.

At Pixar Animation Studios, the concept of a learning organization is deeply embedded in the company's culture. Pixar fosters a culture of continuous learning through practices such as "post-mortems," where teams analyze both successes and failures after a project is completed. This approach not only improves future projects but also reinforces a culture of innovation and continuous improvement, key components of EO (Catmull & Wallace, 2014).

4. RECOGNITION AND REWARDS FOR ENTREPRENEURIAL BEHAVIOR

Recognizing and rewarding entrepreneurial behavior is crucial for sustaining an EO culture. When employees are rewarded for taking risks, innovating, and acting proactively, they are more likely to continue engaging in these behaviors. Recognition can take many forms, including financial incentives, promotions, public acknowledgment, and opportunities for professional growth (Gagné & Deci, 2005).

At 3M, the "Golden Step" award is given to employees who develop products that achieve significant commercial success. This recognition not only rewards innovation but also signals to the entire organization that entrepreneurial behavior is valued and essential to the company's success. Such practices help to embed EO into the organizational culture, encouraging a continuous flow of innovative ideas (Govindarajan & Trimble, 2010).

5. FOSTERING A COLLABORATIVE ENVIRONMENT

Collaboration is another critical element of an EO culture. When employees from different departments and backgrounds work together, they can combine their expertise to generate innovative solutions to complex problems. A collaborative environment also encourages the sharing of ideas and knowledge, which is essential for fostering innovation and proactiveness (Hansen & Birkinshaw, 2007).

IDEO, a global design company, exemplifies the importance of collaboration in fostering an EO culture. At IDEO, multidisciplinary teams work together in an open, collaborative environment to develop innovative solutions for clients. This approach not only leads to breakthrough innovations but also reinforces a culture where collaboration and creativity are integral to the company's success (Kelley & Littman, 2001).

TOOLS TO BUILD AN EO ORGANIZATION

Building an EO organization requires the use of various tools and methodologies that support innovation, proactiveness, and risk-taking. These tools can range from technological platforms to management frameworks, each contributing to the development of an entrepreneurial culture and operational excellence.

1. INNOVATION MANAGEMENT SOFTWARE

Innovation management software is a powerful tool for building an EO organization. These platforms enable organizations to capture, evaluate, and implement ideas from across the organization, ensuring that valuable insights are not lost and that innovation is systematically managed (Adams, Bessant, & Phelps, 2006). Innovation management software also facilitates collaboration and communication, allowing employees to contribute to the innovation process regardless of their location or department.

For example, companies like Siemens and General Electric use innovation management platforms such as IdeaScale and BrightIdea to manage their innovation processes. These platforms allow employees to submit ideas, collaborate on projects, and track the progress of innovations, thereby fostering a culture of continuous improvement and entrepreneurial thinking (Birkinshaw, Bouquet, & Barsoux, 2011).

2. AGILE PROJECT-MANAGEMENT TOOLS

Agile project-management tools, such as Jira and Trello, are essential for organizations seeking to enhance their EO. These tools support agile methodologies by enabling teams to manage projects in iterative cycles, respond quickly to changes, and continuously improve their processes. Agile tools also promote transparency and accountability, ensuring that everyone in the organization is aligned with the EO objectives (Highsmith, 2004).

Spotify's use of agile project-management tools has been instrumental in maintaining its innovative edge in the competitive music-streaming industry. By using tools like Jira, Spotify's teams can quickly adapt to market changes, experiment with new features, and deliver value to customers at a rapid pace. This agility is a key component of the company's EO strategy (Kniberg & Ivarsson, 2012).

3. KNOWLEDGE MANAGEMENT SYSTEMS

Knowledge-management systems (KMS) are critical tools for building an EO organization. KMS facilitate the collection, storage, and dissemination of knowledge within the organization, ensuring that valuable insights and expertise are accessible to all employees. By leveraging KMS, organizations can enhance their ability to innovate, respond proactively to market changes, and manage risks effectively (Davenport & Prusak, 1998).

For example, IBM's use of knowledge-management systems has been pivotal in supporting its EO initiatives. Through platforms like IBM Watson, the company is able to harness vast amounts of data and knowledge to drive innovation and improve decision-making. This systematic approach to knowledge management is essential for sustaining IBM's entrepreneurial culture and maintaining its competitive advantage (Zollo & Winter, 2002).

4. DESIGN-THINKING TOOLS

Design thinking is a user-centered approach to innovation that emphasizes empathy, experimentation, and iterative prototyping. Tools such as journey mapping, persona development, and rapid prototyping are central to the design-thinking process, enabling organizations to develop innovative solutions that meet customer needs (Brown, 2008). By incorporating design thinking into their EO strategies, organizations can enhance their ability to innovate and respond to market demands.

IDEO, a pioneer in design thinking, uses a variety of design-thinking tools to drive innovation. The company's approach to problem-solving, which involves close collaboration with clients and iterative prototyping, has led to the development of groundbreaking products and services. IDEO's use of design-thinking tools exemplifies how organizations can build EO by focusing on customer-centric innovation (Kelley & Littman, 2001).

5. SCENARIO-PLANNING TOOLS

Scenario planning is a strategic tool that helps organizations anticipate and prepare for potential future scenarios. By developing and analyzing different possible futures, organizations can make more informed decisions, manage risks more effectively, and capitalize on emerging opportunities (Schoemaker, 1995). Scenario-planning tools, such as the PEST analysis and scenario matrices, are essential for organizations aiming to enhance their EO.

Shell, a global energy company, is well known for its use of scenario planning. The company's scenario-planning process has enabled it to navigate complex and uncertain environments by anticipating future trends and challenges. Shell's use of scenario-planning tools has been instrumental in maintaining its competitive advantage and fostering a proactive, entrepreneurial culture (Wack, 1985).

TIPS ON HOW EVEN A SMALL BUSINESS CAN EMBRACE EO

For small businesses, adopting an Entrepreneurial Orientation (EO) is crucial for survival and growth in competitive markets. However, implementing EO in a small-business context requires a tailored approach that takes into account the unique challenges and opportunities faced by smaller firms.

1. START WITH A CLEAR VISION AND MISSION

A clear vision and mission are essential for guiding the entrepreneurial activities of a small business. The vision should articulate the long-term goals of the business, while the mission should outline how the business intends to achieve these goals through innovation, proactiveness, and risk-taking (Collins & Porras, 1996). A strong vision and mission provide a foundation for EO by aligning the efforts of all employees toward a common purpose.

For instance, Patagonia, a small outdoor-clothing company, has built its EO around a clear vision of environmental sustainability. The company's mission, "Build the best product, cause no unnecessary harm, use business to inspire and implement solutions to the environmental crisis," guides its entrepreneurial activities and has helped Patagonia differentiate itself in a competitive market (Chouinard, 2006).

2. LEVERAGE YOUR AGILITY

One of the key advantages of small businesses is their agility. Unlike larger firms, small businesses can pivot quickly in response to market changes, making them well suited to adopt an EO. To leverage this agility, small businesses should focus on rapid experimentation and iteration, allowing them to test new ideas, learn from failures, and refine their strategies (Blank, 2013).

For example, the success of Warby Parker, an online eyewear retailer, can be attributed to its agility. As a small start-up, Warby Parker was able to quickly adapt its business model and marketing strategies based on customer feedback, which helped it grow rapidly in a competitive industry. This agility is a key component of the company's EO and has been instrumental in its success (Zappos, 2012).

3. FOSTER A COLLABORATIVE TEAM ENVIRONMENT

Collaboration is critical for small businesses aiming to enhance their EO. By fostering a collaborative team environment, small businesses can encourage the sharing of ideas, knowledge, and expertise, which is essential for innovation and proactive decision-making (Edmondson, 1999). In a small business context, collaboration often involves close communication and teamwork, enabling employees to work together on entrepreneurial initiatives.

Basecamp, a small software company, emphasizes collaboration as a core component of its EO. The company's flat organizational structure and emphasis on teamwork allow it to innovate continuously and respond quickly to customer needs. Basecamp's collaborative approach has helped it maintain its competitive edge in the software industry (Fried & Hansson, 2010).

4. USE TECHNOLOGY TO ENHANCE EO

Technology is a powerful enabler of EO for small businesses. By leveraging digital tools and platforms, small businesses can enhance their ability to innovate, respond proactively to market changes, and manage risks effectively. Technology also enables small businesses to compete with larger firms by leveling the playing field in areas such as marketing, customer service, and operations (McAfee & Brynjolfsson, 2008).

For instance, Shopify, an e-commerce platform, has empowered thousands of small businesses to build and scale their online stores. By providing small businesses with access to powerful e-commerce tools, Shopify has enabled them to innovate and compete in the global marketplace. The use of technology has been a key factor in the success of many small businesses that leverage Shopify's platform (McKeown, 2012).

5. ENCOURAGE INTRAPRENEURSHIP

Even in small businesses, encouraging intrapreneurship can enhance EO by empowering employees to act entrepreneurially within the organization. Intrapreneurship involves giving employees the autonomy to pursue new ideas, develop innovative solutions, and take ownership of projects (Pinchot, 1985). This approach not only fosters innovation but also helps small businesses attract and retain talented employees.

Mailchimp, a small email marketing company, encourages intrapreneurship by allowing employees to work on side projects and experiment with new ideas. This culture of intrapreneurship has led to the development of new features and products that have contributed to Mailchimp's growth and success. Encouraging intrapreneurship is a powerful way for small businesses to enhance their EO and drive innovation (Smith, 2018).

6. EMBRACE RISK, BUT MANAGE IT WISELY

Risk-taking is an essential component of EO, but it must be managed wisely, especially in small businesses where resources are often limited. Small businesses should embrace calculated risks that have the potential to generate significant returns, while also developing strategies to mitigate potential downsides (Knight, 1921). Effective risk management involves thorough planning, contingency strategies, and continuous monitoring of the business environment.

For example, Threadless, a small online T-shirt company, embraced the risk of crowdsourcing designs from its community. While this approach involved uncertainty, it also allowed Threadless to tap into a large pool of creative talent and reduce the costs associated with traditional design processes. The calculated risk paid off, leading to the company's rapid growth and success. Managing risk effectively is crucial for small businesses aiming to enhance their EO (Burkus, 2013).

7. CONTINUOUSLY EVALUATE AND IMPROVE

Finally, small businesses must continuously evaluate and improve their EO strategies to ensure long-term success. This involves regularly assessing the effectiveness of entrepreneurial activities, gathering feedback from customers and employees, and making data-driven adjustments to strategies and processes (Kaplan & Norton, 1996). Continuous improvement ensures that small businesses remain agile, innovative, and responsive to changes in the market environment.

For example, Dropbox, a small start-up in the cloud-storage industry, has continuously refined its business model and product offerings based on customer feedback and market trends. This commitment to continuous improvement has helped Dropbox maintain its competitive edge and grow into a leading player in the industry. Continuous evaluation and improvement are essential for sustaining EO in small businesses (Gansky, 2010).

DEEP DIVE: ENTREPRENEURIAL INTENSITY

EI offers a powerful lens for understanding the vigor and cadence with which organizations pursue entrepreneurial activity. First conceptualized by Morris and Sexton (1996) as a two-dimensional construct, EI moves beyond the binary question of whether a firm is "entrepreneurial" to explore how much and how often. This perspective is critical for the Strategic Orientation Index™ (SOI™) because two organizations in the same quadrant may operate with radically different intensities, leading to divergent performance outcomes. EI reframes entrepreneurship as a spectrum, allowing leaders to calibrate activity rather than treat it as an all-or-nothing condition. In practice, it provides a bridge between theory and implementation, enabling organizations to match entrepreneurial effort to their context, resources, and strategic posture. By embedding EI in the SOI™ framework, executives gain an additional variable to align ambition with reality.

DIMENSIONS OF EI

EI is composed of two distinct yet interrelated dimensions: degree and frequency. Degree refers to the level of novelty, risk, and proactiveness embedded in entrepreneurial initiatives—ranging from incremental improvements to industry-defining innovations (Miller, 1983; Morris et al., 2002). Frequency refers to how often these initiatives are launched, whether sporadically in response to opportunities or continuously as part of a firm's strategic rhythm. High degree without high frequency can result in breakthrough innovation but long periods of stagnation; conversely, high frequency without degree may flood the organization with low-impact activities. Research shows that optimal configurations depend on context: Capital-intensive and regulated industries often succeed with fewer, higher-degree plays, while fast-moving markets reward high frequency coupled with moderate-to-high degree (Covin & Slevin, 1991). Understanding these dimensions allows leaders to diagnose and adjust their firm's entrepreneurial cadence.

STRATEGIC PROFILES AND ORGANIZATIONAL MANIFESTATIONS

Combining degree and frequency yields a matrix of strategic profiles, each with distinct behavioral markers. High Degree / High Frequency organizations are bold experimenters, rapidly launching disruptive products, entering new markets, and aggressively reallocating resources—behaviors often seen in hyper-growth technology firms. High Degree / Low Frequency organizations are more selective, focusing on occasional breakthrough bets, common in aerospace, pharmaceuticals, or specialized manufacturing. Low Degree / High Frequency organizations often excel in iterative innovation and rapid adaptation, as seen in consumer goods or retail formats where constant refreshes sustain market interest. Low Degree / Low Frequency organizations typically remain stable but risk obsolescence unless protected by structural advantages such as patents, regulation, or captive markets. For SOI™ application, mapping these profiles clarifies whether a firm's current EI is enabling or constraining its quadrant potential.

INTERACTION WITH EO, MO, AND EM

EI interacts dynamically with the three pillars of SOI™—Entrepreneurial Orientation (EO), Market Orientation (MO), and Entrepreneurial Marketing (EM). High EO combined with high EI can accelerate growth but also amplify risk exposure, particularly if market intelligence (MO) is underdeveloped. Conversely, high MO can focus EI on customer-validated opportunities, reducing wasted effort and increasing the probability of successful commercialization. EM behaviors—such as Two-Way Customer Contact, Value Creation Through Alliances, and Market Immersion—can serve as accelerants, ensuring that entrepreneurial initiatives resonate in the market. Misalignment occurs when EI outpaces the organization's ability to sense and respond (high EI, low MO) or when cultural resistance dampens initiative velocity (low EI, high EO intent).

Leaders who actively balance EI with EO, MO, and EM inputs create a more resilient and context-appropriate entrepreneurial engine.

QUADRANT MAPPING AND CONTEXT FIT

Each SOI™ quadrant exhibits natural EI tendencies, but these can be adjusted for context. Visionary Vanguards often thrive with sustained High Degree / High Frequency, but in capital-intensive B2B markets this may need tempering to avoid resource strain. Fearless Inventors benefit from maintaining high degree but may need to modulate frequency when operating in conservative or relationship-driven industries. Insightful Optimizers frequently excel with moderate-to-high degree innovations at lower frequency, ensuring that changes are market-driven and resource-efficient. Reluctant Responders may operate with low EI by design, but can still achieve strong results in protected niches if they commit to their chosen pace. Research supports that while context influences the "ideal" EI profile, commitment to a posture—rather than constant vacillation—is more predictive of performance (Zahra, 1991; Morris et al., 2002). In consulting, this insight becomes a central part of the quadrant-fit conversation.

IMPLICATIONS FOR LEADERS

For executives, EI is both a diagnostic tool and a lever for strategic change. Measuring EI provides clarity on whether entrepreneurial output matches strategic aspirations—a crucial step before reallocating resources or restructuring teams. Leaders can use EI to decide whether to push for more ambitious, high-degree moves or to focus on building a more consistent pipeline of smaller initiatives. A misfit between EI and quadrant posture often explains execution gaps: For example, a firm aspiring to Visionary Vanguard behavior but operating at low frequency may struggle to achieve market impact. Conversely, overdriving EI in an Insightful Optimizer context can create churn and erode the very advantages of disciplined, market-tuned execution. The key takeaway: EI alignment should be intentional, not accidental.

PRACTICAL APPLICATION IN CONSULTING

In practice, EI can be surfaced without adding another formal diagnostic. Consultants can integrate EI assessment into interviews, workshop activities, or SOI™ debriefs by asking targeted questions: How often do you launch new initiatives? How radical are they compared to industry norms? Facilitators can also use storytelling prompts—asking executives to recall their last three "big bets" and map them by degree and frequency—to create a shared view of current intensity. Visualizing EI alongside quadrant placement helps leaders see whether their behavioral cadence supports or undermines strategic alignment. In change programs, EI can be gradually adjusted through governance changes, innovation pipelines, or incentive structures. The advantage of embedding EI in SOI™ work is that it gives clients a tangible behavior to commit to, rather than an abstract strategic aspiration.

CONCLUSION

Entrepreneurial Intensity is not simply an academic construct; it is a practical, observable force shaping how organizations pursue opportunity. By dissecting degree and frequency, leaders gain a precise language for diagnosing entrepreneurial behavior and aligning it with their SOI™ quadrant. Research underscores that while context informs the optimal EI profile, consistent commitment to a chosen cadence is more important than chasing an ill-fitting ideal. Within the SOI framework, EI serves as both a mirror and a throttle—revealing current momentum and offering levers to accelerate or decelerate in service of strategic alignment. For practitioners, this means moving beyond the question of "Are we entrepreneurial?" to the more actionable "How entrepreneurial are we, and is it the right kind of entrepreneurial for where we want to go?" In doing so, they bridge vision with execution in a way that is both evidence-based and market-responsive.

CASE STUDY: ENTREPRENEURIAL INTENSITY AT PROCTER & GAMBLE

Procter & Gamble (P&G) offers a textbook example of a multinational corporation deliberately managing both the degree and frequency dimensions of Entrepreneurial Intensity (EI). As a consumer goods giant with more than 180 years of history, P&G operates in mature markets where incremental innovation is the norm—yet it has consistently produced breakthrough products from the launch of Tide in 1946 to Swiffer, Febreze, and the Crest Whitestrips platform in the late 1990s and early 2000s. Each of these high-degree initiatives reshaped entire product categories, demonstrating the company's capacity to pursue transformative opportunities even in highly competitive, brand-saturated environments (Morris & Sexton, 1996; Covin & Slevin, 1991).

P&G's innovation cadence reflects a dual-mode EI profile. At the high-degree end, the firm commits significant R&D resources—$1.9 billion in 2023 alone—to developing category-defining products that are launched roughly every five to seven years in key segments. Between these major leaps, P&G executes a high-frequency stream of moderate and low-degree innovations, such as scent extensions in Tide or packaging redesigns for Gillette, allowing the brand portfolio to remain fresh in consumer perception and responsive to emerging trends. This layering of intensity ensures that the company mitigates risk while maintaining a consistent perception of innovativeness in the market.

Crucially, P&G aligns EI decisions with Market Orientation and consumer insight systems. Its "Consumer is Boss" philosophy drives both the ideation and filtering process, ensuring that opportunities with high technical novelty also demonstrate clear market resonance before moving to scale. This approach balances entrepreneurial drive with disciplined execution—a factor that has allowed P&G to sustain brand leadership across dozens of product categories for decades (Narver & Slater, 1990; Morris et al., 2002).

From an SOI™ perspective, P&G operates largely as an Insightful Optimizer at the corporate level—deeply attuned to customer and competitor dynamics—while enabling Visionary Vanguard subcultures within its R&D and brand innovation teams. This structural hybrid allows for high EI where it matters most while preventing overextension in lower-potential areas. For firms studying EI, P&G illustrates how consciously managing the balance between degree and frequency can generate sustained advantage even in mature, slow-growth markets.

From a Strategic Orientation Index™ lens, P&G's EI profile reveals a deliberate positioning within the Insightful Optimizer quadrant at the corporate level. Its heavy investment in customer insight systems, rigorous competitive benchmarking, and disciplined innovation governance reflects the high Market Orientation (MO) posture characteristic of this quadrant. However, within innovation-focused units, P&G enables temporary shifts toward Visionary Vanguard behavior—allowing for higher Entrepreneurial Orientation (EO) and EI when category disruption is strategically justified. This dual-structure approach avoids the pitfalls of overnormative quadrant adherence by embedding flexibility without losing alignment. In practical terms, it means P&G's EI decisions are context-calibrated: Breakthrough initiatives emerge only when the opportunity profile meets both customer desirability and strategic fit, while routine innovations maintain frequency and market relevance. For organizations interpreting their own SOI™ results, the P&G case underscores that quadrant commitment does not require rigidity—it can, and often should, include deliberate intensity shifts in targeted areas to capture outsized returns.

STRATEGIC IMPLICATION

A firm's willingness to innovate and take calculated risks starts with leadership. Consider whether your team is fostering a culture of experimentation—or inadvertently stifling it through risk aversion.

CHAPTER 3

THE ROLE OF MARKET ORIENTATION

In today's dynamic business landscape, performance gaps are rarely caused by a lack of ambition or effort. Instead, they often stem from deeper, structural misalignments—between how a company thinks, how it listens to its market, and how it executes its marketing strategies. This chapter revisits the three foundational constructs that shape the Strategic Orientation Index™: Entrepreneurial Orientation (EO), Market Orientation (MO), and Entrepreneurial Marketing (EM). While each has been studied extensively on its own, their power emerges in how they interact—and often, how they conflict. Before diving into their individual definitions and subdimensions, we first explore why strategic coherence across these domains matters so profoundly.

STRATEGIC ALIGNMENT ACROSS EO, MO, AND EM

Strategic coherence across Entrepreneurial Orientation (EO), Market Orientation (MO), and Entrepreneurial Marketing (EM) is essential for sustained performance, yet is rarely achieved in practice. While these three constructs are deeply researched individually, most firms suffer from misalignment among them—bold innovation untempered by customer insight, or customer responsiveness crippled by a fear of risk (Morris et al., 2002; Narver & Slater, 1990; Kraus et al., 2010). The Strategic Orientation Index™ was designed to detect and diagnose these fractures early, offering a path to better fit between an organization's ambition, its market understanding, and its marketing actions. Rather than treat EO, MO, and EM as standalone traits, the SOI™ framework positions them as a dynamic system whose internal coherence determines a firm's strategic health. Companies with high alignment across these domains tend to outperform their peers in growth, adaptability, and competitive resilience (Kirca et al., 2005; Rauch et al., 2009; Hanaysha & Al-Shaikh, 2022). This systems lens provides the conceptual backbone for the rest of the chapter and ultimately for the SOI™ assessment that follows.

INTRODUCTION TO MARKET ORIENTATION

Market Orientation is a critical concept in contemporary business strategy, serving as a foundation for companies striving to achieve sustained profitability and competitive advantage. It represents an organizational commitment to understanding and responding to customer needs, closely monitoring competitors, and fostering collaboration across various functions within the company. This chapter will explore the definition, historical evolution, and key components of Market Orientation. Additionally, it will delve into customer orientation, competitor orientation, and interfunctional coordination, offering practical steps for implementing Market Orientation and examining its relevance, especially for small businesses and start-ups. Real-world examples and case studies will illustrate how market-oriented companies have achieved success and how empirical evidence links Market Orientation to increased profitability.

UNDERSTANDING MARKET ORIENTATION

Market Orientation involves an organization-wide focus on generating, disseminating, and responding to market intelligence regarding current and future customer needs (Kohli & Jaworski, 1990). This concept is foundational for businesses aiming to enhance adaptability, customer satisfaction, and competitive advantage in rapidly changing markets. Market Orientation is built on three essential components: customer orientation, competitor orientation, and interfunctional coordination.

Customer Orientation: This aspect of Market Orientation prioritizes understanding and meeting customer needs and preferences. Businesses that are customer-oriented actively engage with customers to gather insights into their preferences, behaviors, and feedback. These insights are then used to tailor products and services that align closely with customer expectations, leading to higher satisfaction and loyalty. Companies that excel in customer orientation often see long-term benefits in the form of repeat business and customer advocacy (Narver & Slater, 1990).

Competitor Orientation: Competitor orientation involves a vigilant focus on competitors' actions, strategies, and market positions. Businesses that adopt a competitor-oriented approach systematically analyze their competitors to anticipate market shifts and adjust their strategies accordingly. This proactive monitoring enables companies to stay ahead of market trends and competitive threats, ensuring they remain leaders in their industry. By understanding their competitors' strengths and weaknesses, companies can position themselves more effectively in the marketplace (Porter, 1980).

Interfunctional Coordination: Interfunctional coordination is the seamless collaboration across various departments within an organization to deliver superior customer value. This component ensures that marketing, sales, production, and customer-service teams work together toward common goals, fostering a unified approach to Market Orientation. Effective interfunctional coordination leads to better decision-making, improved operational efficiency, and enhanced customer satisfaction. Companies that successfully integrate their functions are better equipped to respond quickly to market changes and customer needs (Day, 1994).

HISTORICAL EVOLUTION AND RELEVANCE

The concept of Market Orientation has evolved significantly since the mid-twentieth century, where it branched out from the broader marketing concept. Initially, businesses focused primarily on production and sales orientations, emphasizing manufacturing efficiency and aggressive selling tactics. However, as markets became more competitive and customers more discerning, the need for a customer-centric approach became increasingly apparent. This shift led to the development of the marketing concept, which posits that the key to achieving organizational goals is identifying and satisfying customer needs better than the competition.

Market Orientation builds upon this concept by integrating customer focus with a thorough understanding of the competitive landscape and fostering cross-departmental collaboration. In today's dynamic business environment, Market Orientation has become more relevant than ever, with customer expectations constantly evolving and competitive pressures intensifying. Companies that embrace Market Orientation are better positioned to adapt to these changes and maintain a competitive edge, making it a critical component of long-term business strategy (Narver & Slater, 1990).

BUILDING A MARKET-ORIENTED CULTURE

Creating a market-oriented culture within an organization requires a multifaceted approach that includes leadership commitment, employee training, and the implementation of incentive programs that encourage market-oriented behaviors. These elements work together to embed Market Orientation into the organizational fabric, ensuring that all employees understand and contribute to the company's market-oriented goals.

Leadership Commitment: Leadership plays a crucial role in fostering a market-oriented culture by setting the tone and direction for the organization. Leaders must actively endorse and participate in market-oriented initiatives, demonstrating their commitment through actions such as engaging with customers and competitors. For instance, leaders can hold regular town hall meetings to share insights from customer interactions and market research, emphasizing the importance of Market Orientation to all employees. By modeling market-oriented behaviors, leaders can inspire their teams to prioritize customer needs and competitive awareness in their daily work (Homburg et al., 2011).

Employee Training and Development: Investing in employee training and development is essential for building a market-oriented culture. Training programs should focus on developing skills in customer service, market analysis, and competitive strategy, ensuring that employees are equipped to contribute to the organization's market-oriented goals. A comprehensive training curriculum might include workshops, online courses, and mentorship programs, all designed to enhance employees' understanding of market dynamics and customer needs. Ongoing development opportunities help keep employees engaged and informed, fostering a culture of continuous learning and adaptation (Kotter, 1996).

Incentive Programs: Implementing incentive programs that reward market-oriented behaviors is a powerful way to reinforce the importance of Market Orientation within the organization. These programs should be designed to recognize and reward employees who contribute to customer satisfaction, market-intelligence gathering, and cross-departmental collaboration. For example, a performance-based incentive system could include bonuses or recognition awards for employees who excel in integrating customer feedback into product development or successfully anticipating and responding to competitor moves. Such incentives not only motivate employees to align with the company's Market Orientation goals but also help create a culture that values and rewards market-driven success (Cameron & Quinn, 2006).

WHY MARKET ORIENTATION IS BENEFICIAL FOR LARGER BUSINESSES

Market Orientation (MO) offers numerous advantages for businesses of all sizes, but it holds particular significance for larger enterprises. As organizations grow, the complexity of their operations increases, and so does the need for a cohesive strategy that aligns with market demands. This section explores the specific benefits of MO for large businesses, highlighting how it contributes to sustained competitive advantage, enhances customer relationships, and drives innovation.

ENHANCED COMPETITIVE ADVANTAGE

One of the most significant benefits of MO for larger businesses is the ability to maintain and enhance competitive advantage. In large organizations, the stakes are high, and competition is fierce. A market-oriented approach enables these companies to stay ahead of their competitors by continually adapting to market changes and customer needs. According to Porter (1980), competitive advantage arises from a firm's ability to provide greater value to customers than its competitors. For large businesses, this often involves leveraging economies of scale, extensive resources, and established brand reputation.

Large enterprises with a strong MO are better equipped to anticipate market trends and respond proactively. This agility is crucial in industries characterized by rapid technological advancements and shifting consumer preferences. For example, in the tech industry, companies like Apple and Microsoft have maintained their market leadership by continuously monitoring customer needs and competitor strategies, allowing them to innovate and stay ahead of the curve (Cusumano, 2010). By fostering a market-oriented culture, these companies can make informed decisions that enhance their competitive positioning and ensure long-term success.

STRENGTHENED CUSTOMER RELATIONSHIPS

Another critical benefit of MO for larger businesses is the ability to build and maintain strong customer relationships. In large organizations, customer interactions are often more complex, involving multiple touchpoints across various channels. A market-oriented approach helps these companies integrate customer feedback into their strategies, ensuring that they consistently meet or exceed customer expectations. This focus on customer satisfaction leads to increased loyalty, higher retention rates, and ultimately, greater profitability (Narver & Slater, 1990).

Large businesses often have a diverse customer base, with varying needs and preferences. MO enables these companies to segment their markets effectively and tailor their offerings to different customer groups. For instance, multinational corporations like Procter & Gamble (P&G) use Market Orientation to understand regional differences in consumer behavior, allowing them to customize their products and marketing strategies accordingly. By aligning their operations with customer needs, P&G can deliver superior value across different markets, strengthening their relationships with customers and driving long-term growth (Aaker, 1998).

FACILITATED INNOVATION AND ADAPTATION

In large businesses, innovation is often a critical driver of growth and sustainability. Market Orientation plays a vital role in facilitating innovation by providing insights into customer needs and market trends. Companies that are attuned to the market are more likely to develop products and services that resonate with their target audience, leading to higher adoption rates and market success. According to Christensen (1997), understanding the "jobs" that customers need to be done enables firms to innovate more effectively, creating solutions that meet real needs.

For large organizations, the ability to innovate is closely tied to their capacity to adapt to changing market conditions. A market-oriented approach ensures that companies remain flexible and responsive, allowing them to pivot their strategies when necessary. This adaptability is particularly important in industries where disruption is common, such as the automotive or financial-services sectors. Companies like General Motors and Goldman Sachs have successfully navigated market challenges by maintaining a strong MO, enabling them to innovate in response to evolving customer demands and regulatory changes (Drucker, 1985).

IMPROVED ORGANIZATIONAL ALIGNMENT

Large businesses often face challenges related to organizational alignment, as different departments may have conflicting priorities or operate in silos. MO helps address this issue by fostering interdepartmental coordination and ensuring that all functions are aligned with the company's market-oriented goals. This alignment is crucial for achieving operational efficiency and delivering a consistent customer experience across all touchpoints (Day, 1994).

In market-oriented organizations, cross-functional teams are more likely to collaborate effectively, sharing information and insights that contribute to better decision-making. For example, in a large retail company like Walmart, marketing, sales, and supply-chain teams work closely together to ensure that their strategies are aligned with customer needs and market trends. This collaboration enables Walmart to respond quickly to market changes, optimize inventory management, and deliver value to customers at scale (Homburg et al., 2011).

LEVERAGING DATA AND TECHNOLOGY

Large businesses have access to vast amounts of data, which can be a significant asset when implementing a market-oriented strategy. By leveraging data analytics and technology, these companies can gain deeper insights into customer behavior, market trends, and competitive dynamics. This data-driven approach enhances their ability to make informed decisions that align with market demands, ultimately leading to better business outcomes (Davenport & Harris, 2007).

For instance, companies like Amazon use advanced analytics and machine-learning algorithms to personalize the customer experience, optimize pricing strategies, and predict market trends. This market-oriented approach enables Amazon to stay ahead of competitors and continuously improve its offerings based on real-time data. As a result, Amazon has maintained its position as a leader in the e-commerce industry, demonstrating the power of MO in driving business success (Brynjolfsson & McAfee, 2014).

GLOBAL MARKET REACH

For large businesses operating on a global scale, MO is particularly beneficial in navigating diverse markets and understanding regional differences in consumer behavior. A market-oriented approach allows these companies to adapt their strategies to local market conditions, ensuring that their products and services resonate with customers in different regions. This global perspective is essential for maintaining relevance and competitiveness in international markets (Yip, 2003).

Multinational corporations like Coca-Cola have successfully leveraged MO to expand their global reach and maintain brand consistency across diverse markets. By understanding the unique preferences and cultural nuances of their international customers, Coca-Cola can tailor its marketing strategies and product offerings to meet local demands while maintaining a strong global brand identity. This approach has enabled Coca-Cola to achieve sustained growth and profitability in markets worldwide (Allen, 1994).

CONCLUSION: THE STRATEGIC IMPORTANCE OF MO FOR LARGE BUSINESSES

In conclusion, MO offers significant benefits for larger businesses, enabling them to enhance their competitive advantage, strengthen customer relationships, facilitate innovation, improve organizational alignment, leverage data and technology, and expand their global market reach. By adopting a market-oriented approach, large organizations can better navigate the complexities of the modern business environment, ensuring that they remain agile, customer-focused, and poised for long-term success.

IMPLEMENTING MARKET ORIENTATION

Market Orientation is not just a theoretical concept; it is a practical approach that can be implemented across various types of organizations, including small businesses and start-ups. Implementing Market Orientation requires a commitment from leadership, a customer-centric culture, continuous learning and adaptation, and investment in technology and tools that support market intelligence and customer engagement.

Commitment from Leadership: The implementation of Market Orientation starts with leadership. Leaders must demonstrate their commitment to Market Orientation by setting clear goals, allocating resources, and leading by example. This involves actively participating in market research, engaging with customers, and staying informed about competitors. Leadership commitment is crucial for creating an organizational culture that values and prioritizes Market Orientation, ensuring that it becomes embedded in the company's strategic planning and decision-making processes (Homburg et al., 2011).

Customer-Centric Culture: Building a customer-centric culture is essential for successfully implementing Market Orientation. This involves fostering an environment where customer needs and preferences are consistently prioritized across all functions of the organization. Employees should be encouraged to think from the customer's perspective and to consider how their actions impact the customer experience. A customer-centric culture also requires empowering employees to make decisions that benefit the customer, even if it means deviating from standard procedures. For example, a company might implement a policy that allows customer-service representatives to offer refunds or discounts without managerial approval, enabling them to resolve issues quickly and to the customer's satisfaction (Cameron & Quinn, 2006).

Continuous Learning and Adaptation: Market Orientation is not a static approach; it requires continuous learning and adaptation based on market feedback and competitive insights. Companies must stay attuned to changing customer needs, emerging market trends, and competitive dynamics, adjusting their strategies accordingly. This can be achieved through regular market research, customer-feedback loops, and scenario planning. For instance, a company might conduct quarterly customer-satisfaction surveys and use the results to refine its product offerings, marketing campaigns, and customer-service processes (Kotter, 1996).

Investment in Technology and Tools: Implementing Market Orientation also requires investment in technology and tools that facilitate market intelligence gathering, customer engagement, and interdepartmental collaboration. This includes customer-relationship-management (CRM) systems, data-analytics platforms, and integrated communication tools. These technologies enable companies to collect, analyze, and act on market data more efficiently, ensuring that their strategies are informed by real-time insights. For example, a CRM system can help a company track customer interactions, monitor customer satisfaction, and personalize marketing efforts, all of which contribute to a more market-oriented approach (Chen & Popovich, 2003).

SYSTEMATIZING THE VOICE OF THE CUSTOMER

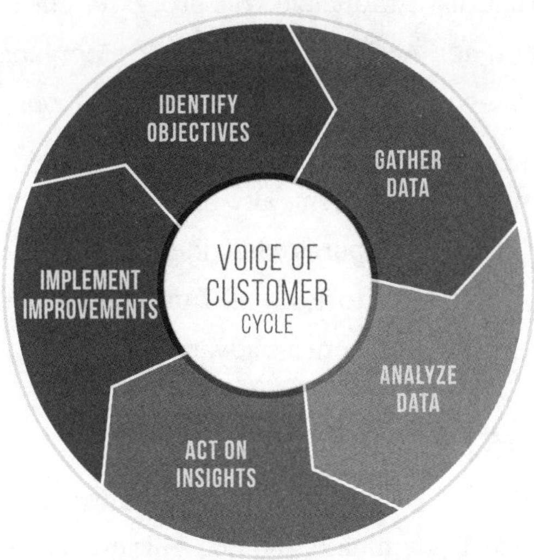

A truly market-oriented organization cannot rely solely on intuition or anecdotal customer feedback. Instead, it must adopt a systematic approach to capturing, analyzing, and disseminating the Voice of the Customer (VoC) across all levels and functions. VoC refers to the process of gathering comprehensive insights into customers' expectations, experiences, and preferences—then using those insights to guide decision-making across product development, marketing, operations, and customer service (Griffin & Hauser, 1993). By operationalizing VoC, organizations align their actions with actual customer needs rather than assumptions, creating a feedback-informed culture that drives innovation and enhances profitability.

THE STRATEGIC IMPORTANCE OF VOICE OF THE CUSTOMER

VoC goes beyond routine customer satisfaction surveys; it is a core capability of a high-functioning market-oriented firm. It fuels customer orientation by providing empirical data on wants and behaviors; it enables interfunctional coordination by equipping all departments with shared insight; and it influences competitor orientation by revealing customers' perceptions of alternative options in the market (Kohli & Jaworski, 1990).

Companies that institutionalize VoC processes consistently outperform those that do not. According to a study by Morgan, Anderson, and Mittal (2005), firms with strong customer-feedback loops see significantly higher customer satisfaction and loyalty, which correlates with superior financial performance. VoC systems also reduce the risk of product failure by ensuring that customer input is embedded into innovation and design cycles (Ulwick, 2005). In short, a well-functioning VoC system turns customer empathy into competitive advantage.

COMPONENTS OF AN EFFECTIVE VOC SYSTEM

An enterprise-level VoC system typically involves five core stages: Capture, Centralize, Analyze, Disseminate, and Act. This cyclical process creates a continuous feedback loop between the market and the organization.

1. CAPTURING THE VOICE

The first stage is collecting input from diverse channels across the customer journey. This includes both solicited feedback (e.g., surveys, reviews, interviews) and unsolicited feedback (e.g., social media comments, customer-support transcripts, in-app behavior). To ensure inclusivity, companies should gather feedback from existing customers, lost customers, and prospective buyers (Goodman, 2014).

Common VoC capture methods include:

- **Net-Promoter Score (NPS)** surveys to gauge customer loyalty
- **Customer-Satisfaction (CSAT)** surveys at transaction touchpoints
- **Customer interviews** and ethnographic studies
- **CRM integration** of customer-support interactions
- **Social listening** via tools like Brandwatch or Sprout Social

Leading firms create structured programs that schedule feedback collection at key journey moments—such as onboarding, product use, renewal, and churn (Lemon & Verhoef, 2016). This enables context-specific insights, not just generalized sentiment.

2. CENTRALIZING FEEDBACK IN A UNIFIED REPOSITORY

Many firms capture feedback but fail to centralize it, causing siloed insights and lost opportunities. A market-oriented organization treats customer data as a strategic asset, not a departmental tool. Centralized VoC repositories, often integrated within customer-relationship-management systems or dedicated VoC platforms (e.g., Qualtrics, Medallia), allow data to be searchable, categorized, and accessible across departments.

This centralized repository must include:

- Quantitative data from surveys
- Qualitative data from open comments

- Behavioral analytics
- Support tickets and transcripts

The use of dashboards and real-time analytics helps convert raw data into structured insights that can be easily distributed and acted upon (Bourne & Bourne, 2011).

3. ANALYZING FOR ACTIONABLE INSIGHT

Data without analysis is just noise. VoC systems should employ both quantitative techniques (e.g., segmentation, trend analysis, sentiment scoring) and qualitative coding (e.g., keyword tagging, customer-intent mapping). Text analytics and natural language processing (NLP) tools have become vital for parsing open-ended feedback at scale (He, Zha, & Li, 2013).

A critical component of the analysis phase is root-cause analysis. Instead of stopping at "customers are dissatisfied with pricing," for example, root-cause analysis seeks to answer "why"—perhaps revealing confusion due to poor product tiering or unclear value propositions.

Progressive firms conduct journey-based VoC analysis—mapping satisfaction and friction points across the life cycle instead of examining isolated events (Rawson, Duncan, & Jones, 2013). This holistic approach enables prioritization of systemic changes over cosmetic ones.

4. DISSEMINATING INSIGHTS ACROSS THE ORGANIZATION

One of the biggest pitfalls in VoC programs is failure to disseminate insights broadly. Market-oriented firms make VoC everyone's responsibility. Dissemination involves sharing insights through reports, dashboards, town halls, and team-specific summaries to ensure they inform action at all levels.

Best practices include:

- **Monthly VoC summaries** shared cross-functionally
- **Executive dashboards** with real-time VoC metrics

- **"Voice of the Customer" champions** in each department
- **Customer-insight briefings** at the start of new projects

According to Homburg, Workman, and Jensen (2000), firms with higher levels of cross-functional information sharing related to customer feedback are significantly more effective in implementing market strategies. Dissemination transforms feedback from isolated data points into shared organizational knowledge.

5. ACTING ON THE VOICE

Capturing and analyzing feedback is useless without follow-through. VoC programs must include closed-loop mechanisms that ensure responses to customers and internal teams. This could take the form of:

- Product or service improvements
- Policy changes
- Employee training based on customer pain points
- Customer communication about changes implemented due to feedback

Firms should also track VoC-to-Action conversion metrics—what percent of VoC inputs led to real changes—and communicate these outcomes internally and externally to reinforce trust and learning (Morgan et al., 2005). Some companies even involve customers directly in co-creation processes, turning feedback loops into collaboration cycles (Prahalad & Ramaswamy, 2004).

CASE EXAMPLE: HOW SLACK INSTITUTIONALIZES VOC

Slack, the popular workplace collaboration platform, is widely recognized for its commitment to customer-led development. The company uses a VoC framework that integrates structured survey data, in-app feedback, support-ticket reviews, and social media monitoring. More importantly, Slack routes all feedback into a centralized system that product, marketing, and customer-success teams can access in real time.

Each product-development sprint includes a dedicated "Customer Feedback Review" where engineers and designers analyze VoC inputs from the previous cycle. Slack also publishes a public changelog showing how user feedback has directly influenced updates. This not only drives loyalty but also accelerates innovation by ensuring that development is continuously aligned with customer needs (Croll & Yoskovitz, 2013).

EMBEDDING VOC INTO THE ORGANIZATIONAL CULTURE

Systematizing VoC is not just a process challenge—it is a cultural imperative. Organizations that truly embody Market Orientation infuse VoC into performance evaluations, team rituals, and strategic planning.

Leaders play a vital role here by:
- Referencing VoC data in decision-making forums
- Celebrating changes made due to customer feedback
- Making customer insight a key part of onboarding and training

In essence, a "customer-first" culture is sustained not by slogans but by **systems and incentives** that reward listening, learning, and iterating based on real-world customer voice (Denison & Mishra, 1995).

CONCLUSION: VOC AS THE ENGINE OF MARKET ORIENTATION

Voice of the Customer is not a standalone function—it is the engine that powers customer orientation, enhances cross-functional coordination, and sustains competitive advantage. Market-oriented organizations view VoC not just as a research initiative but as a **strategic infrastructure** that informs every major decision. By implementing a structured VoC system and cultivating a culture that values customer insight, firms of any size can achieve greater alignment, stronger customer loyalty, and ultimately, superior performance.

EMPIRICAL EVIDENCE OF MARKET ORIENTATION AND PROFITABILITY

Numerous empirical studies have demonstrated the positive impact of Market Orientation on business performance and profitability. These studies provide compelling evidence that companies that adopt market-oriented strategies tend to achieve superior financial outcomes compared to their less market-oriented counterparts.

Foundational Research: Kohli and Jaworski's foundational research on Market Orientation established a clear link between Market Orientation and improved business performance. Their study, which surveyed a wide range of industries, found that companies that actively gathered and responded to market intelligence reported higher levels of customer satisfaction, sales growth, and profitability. The research highlighted that Market Orientation enables businesses to better meet customer needs, adapt to market changes, and maintain a competitive edge, all of which contribute to increased profitability (Kohli & Jaworski, 1990).

The Influence of Market Orientation on Profitability: In their comprehensive study, Narver and Slater examined the impact of Market Orientation on profitability across multiple industries. They concluded that Market Orientation, characterized by customer orientation, competitor orientation, and interfunctional coordination, directly contributes to superior business performance. The study found that firms with higher levels of Market Orientation reported significantly better return on assets (ROA) and return on sales (ROS) compared to less market-oriented companies, underscoring the financial benefits of adopting a market-oriented approach (Narver & Slater, 1990).

Market Orientation in Global Contexts: Hult, Ketchen, and Nichols expanded the understanding of Market Orientation by exploring its effects in a global context. Their study, which involved data from multinational corporations operating in various countries, found that market-oriented firms consistently outperformed their competitors in terms of profitability, regardless of the market or region. The research emphasized the importance of adapting Market Orientation strategies to local market conditions to maximize profitability, demonstrating that Market Orientation is a valuable strategy for businesses operating in diverse environments (Hult, Ketchen, & Nichols, 2003).

Market Orientation and Innovation: Deshpandé, Farley, and Webster explored the relationship between Market Orientation and innovation, focusing on how these factors contribute to profitability. Their study found that market-oriented companies were more likely to successfully innovate, leading to the development of new products that met customer needs and captured market share. This innovation, driven by market insights, was identified as a key driver of increased profitability, illustrating the value of Market Orientation in fostering a culture of continuous improvement and competitive advantage (Deshpandé, Farley, & Webster, 1993).

Market Orientation in Small and Medium Enterprises (SMEs): Shoham, Rose, and Kropp conducted an empirical study focused on small and medium enterprises (SMEs), examining how Market Orientation affects profitability in this segment. Their research revealed that SMEs with a strong Market Orientation reported higher levels of profitability than their less market-oriented counterparts. The study highlighted that even with limited resources, SMEs could leverage Market Orientation to achieve significant financial gains, making it a critical strategy for smaller businesses seeking to compete in crowded markets (Shoham, Rose, & Kropp, 2005).

Meta-Analysis of Market Orientation and Performance: Kirca, Jayachandran, and Bearden conducted a meta-analysis of over 114 studies to assess the overall impact of Market Orientation on business performance. Their findings confirmed a robust positive relationship between Market Orientation and various financial performance metrics, including profitability. The meta-analysis highlighted that the benefits of Market Orientation were consistent across different industries and business environments, providing strong empirical support for the adoption of market-oriented strategies as a pathway to enhanced profitability (Kirca, Jayachandran, & Bearden, 2005).

CASE STUDIES OF SUCCESSFUL MARKET ORIENTATION

Market Orientation (MO) is a critical factor in the success of many leading companies across various industries. This section presents case studies of organizations that have effectively implemented MO by addressing its three key components: Customer Orientation, Competitor Orientation, and Interfunctional Coordination.

CASE STUDY 1: AMAZON'S MARKET ORIENTATION

Amazon is widely regarded as one of the most market-oriented companies globally, consistently demonstrating its commitment to customer orientation, competitor orientation, and interfunctional coordination.

Customer Orientation: Amazon places the customer at the core of its business strategy. The company utilizes extensive data analytics to understand customer behaviors, preferences, and purchasing patterns. For example, Amazon's recommendation engine, which suggests products based on past purchases and browsing history, exemplifies how the company tailors its offerings to meet individual customer needs. This focus on personalization enhances customer satisfaction and fosters long-term loyalty, which is critical to Amazon's success (Brynjolfsson, Hu, & Rahman, 2013).

Competitor Orientation: Amazon actively monitors its competitors, ensuring it remains competitive in the rapidly evolving e-commerce industry. The company keeps a close watch on competitors' pricing strategies, product offerings, and market trends. Amazon's dynamic pricing model, which adjusts prices based on real-time market data, is a direct result of its competitor orientation. This approach allows Amazon to remain competitive by offering better prices or more attractive deals than its rivals, maintaining its market leadership (Stone, 2013).

Interfunctional Coordination: Amazon's ability to coordinate across its various functions is one of its key strengths. The company integrates its marketing, logistics, customer service, and technology teams to deliver a seamless customer experience. For example, Amazon's Prime service, which offers fast delivery, is the result of coordinated efforts between logistics, customer service, and technology teams. This interdepartmental collaboration ensures that all aspects of the customer journey are optimized, contributing to Amazon's high customer satisfaction and loyalty (Reichheld, 2006).

CASE STUDY 2: PROCTER & GAMBLE'S GLOBAL MARKET ORIENTATION

Procter & Gamble (P&G) is a prime example of a company that has successfully implemented Market Orientation on a global scale by addressing customer orientation, competitor orientation, and interfunctional coordination.

Customer Orientation: P&G's customer orientation is evident in its deep commitment to understanding local markets and tailoring its products to meet the specific needs of consumers in different regions. For example, P&G conducts extensive market research to gather insights into consumer preferences and cultural nuances. This research informed the development of products like Tide Naturals, a detergent specifically formulated for the Indian market to meet local consumer preferences for affordability and effectiveness. By focusing on the specific needs of different markets, P&G ensures that its products resonate with local consumers, leading to stronger customer loyalty and higher market penetration (Aaker, 1998).

Competitor Orientation: P&G maintains a vigilant focus on its competitors, constantly monitoring their strategies and market positions. The company's ability to quickly adapt its marketing strategies in response to competitor actions is a testament to its strong competitor orientation. For instance, when a competitor launches a new product or adjusts its pricing, P&G swiftly responds by adjusting its own offerings or marketing campaigns to maintain its competitive edge. This agility allows P&G to protect its market share and continue to lead in the highly competitive consumer-goods industry (Deshpandé et al., 1993).

Interfunctional Coordination: P&G excels in interfunctional coordination, ensuring that its marketing, research and development (R&D), and supply-chain teams work closely together. This coordination is crucial for P&G's ability to innovate and bring new products to market efficiently. For example, the collaboration between R&D and marketing teams allows P&G to develop products that are not only scientifically advanced but also aligned with consumer needs and preferences, as identified by the marketing team's research. The synchronized efforts of these teams enable P&G to launch successful products that meet market demands and reinforce its leadership position (Kotler & Keller, 2006).

CASE STUDY 3: COCA-COLA'S MARKET ADAPTATION AND GLOBAL BRAND CONSISTENCY

Coca-Cola has maintained its market leadership through a strong market-oriented approach that addresses customer orientation, competitor orientation, and interfunctional coordination across its global operations.

Customer Orientation: Coca-Cola's customer orientation is reflected in its ability to adapt its product offerings to meet the diverse tastes and preferences of consumers around the world. The company's development of products like Coca-Cola Plus, a dietary fiber-fortified beverage for the Japanese market, illustrates its commitment to understanding and meeting local consumer needs. By conducting extensive market research and staying attuned to consumer trends, Coca-Cola ensures that its products are relevant and appealing to customers in different regions. This focus on customer needs has been key to Coca-Cola's ability to maintain its brand's relevance in various markets (Allen, 1994).

Competitor Orientation: Coca-Cola maintains a keen awareness of its competitors, adjusting its strategies to protect its market share. The company closely monitors competitors' product launches, marketing campaigns, and pricing strategies. For instance, when a competitor introduces a new beverage, Coca-Cola quickly assesses the potential impact and adjusts its own product offerings or marketing strategies to counteract the competitor's move. This proactive approach ensures that Coca-Cola remains competitive and continues to lead the global beverage market (Pendergrast, 2000).

Interfunctional Coordination: Coca-Cola's success is also driven by its strong interfunctional coordination. The company ensures that its marketing, production, and distribution teams are closely aligned to deliver consistent quality and brand messaging across all markets. This coordination is particularly important for maintaining Coca-Cola's global brand identity while allowing for localized adaptations in product offerings and marketing strategies. The seamless collaboration between these functions enables Coca-Cola to deliver a consistent brand experience worldwide, reinforcing its position as a global market leader (Pendergrast, 2000).

CASE STUDY 4: TOYOTA'S LEAN MANUFACTURING AND MARKET RESPONSIVENESS

Toyota's market-oriented approach is evident in its commitment to customer orientation, competitor orientation, and interfunctional coordination, particularly through its implementation of lean manufacturing and market responsiveness.

Customer Orientation: Toyota places a strong emphasis on understanding and responding to customer needs. The company's lean manufacturing system, known as the Toyota Production System (TPS), is designed to produce high-quality vehicles that meet customer expectations. For instance, Toyota's rapid response to the growing demand for fuel-efficient vehicles led to the development and mass production of hybrid models like the Prius, demonstrating the company's commitment to customer orientation and environmental sustainability. Toyota's focus on delivering products that align with consumer demands has been a critical factor in its success in the global automotive market (Liker, 2004).

Competitor Orientation: Toyota remains highly aware of its competitors, using this knowledge to refine its production processes and product offerings. The company continuously benchmarks its vehicles against those of its competitors, ensuring that its products offer superior value in terms of quality, reliability, and innovation. This competitor orientation helps Toyota maintain its competitive advantage in the global automotive market, particularly in the areas of fuel efficiency and environmental sustainability. By staying ahead of industry trends and competitors, Toyota has secured its position as a leader in automotive innovation (Liker & Hoseus, 2008).

Interfunctional Coordination: Interfunctional coordination is a cornerstone of Toyota's success. The company's production, R&D, and marketing teams work closely together to ensure that new vehicle models meet customer needs while maintaining high production efficiency. This coordination is exemplified in Toyota's Kaizen philosophy, which encourages continuous improvement and collaboration across all functions. By fostering a culture of teamwork and shared responsibility, Toyota is able to deliver vehicles that consistently meet high standards of quality and customer satisfaction. The integrated efforts of these teams have been crucial to Toyota's ability to innovate and lead in the automotive industry (Liker, 2004).

CASE STUDY 5: APPLE'S INNOVATION AND MARKET ORIENTATION

Apple's success is deeply rooted in its market-oriented approach, particularly its focus on customer orientation, competitor orientation, and interfunctional coordination.

Customer Orientation: Apple's customer orientation is reflected in its ability to anticipate and respond to consumer needs through innovative product design and functionality. The company invests heavily in market research to understand how customers interact with technology and what they expect from their devices. This understanding informed the development of groundbreaking products like the iPhone, which redefined the smartphone industry by offering a user-friendly interface combined with cutting-edge technology. Apple's focus on creating products that not only meet but exceed customer expectations has been key to its success (Isaacson, 2011).

Competitor Orientation: Apple maintains a strong focus on its competitors, using insights into their strategies to inform its own product development and marketing efforts. The company's ability to differentiate its products from those of its competitors, particularly in terms of design, user experience, and ecosystem integration, has allowed Apple to maintain a premium market position. For example, Apple's decision to integrate hardware, software, and services into a seamless ecosystem is a strategic response to competitor offerings, ensuring that its products offer a unique value proposition. This focus on maintaining a competitive edge through innovation and differentiation has been crucial to Apple's sustained success (Norman, 2002).

Interfunctional Coordination: Apple's success is also driven by its exceptional interfunctional coordination, particularly between its design, engineering, and marketing teams. This collaboration ensures that every aspect of a product, from its aesthetic design to its technical performance, aligns with the company's market-oriented goals. The integration of these functions is evident in products like the MacBook and iPad, where design excellence and technical innovation come together to create a cohesive user experience. This coordination is critical to Apple's ability to deliver products that are both innovative and highly desirable to consumers, maintaining its position as a leader in the technology industry (Isaacson, 2011).

CONCLUSION: THE IMPACT OF MARKET ORIENTATION ON BUSINESS SUCCESS

The case studies of Amazon, Procter & Gamble, Coca-Cola, Toyota, and Apple demonstrate how effectively addressing the three components of Market Orientation (MO)—Customer Orientation, Competitor

Orientation, and Interfunctional Coordination—can drive business success. These companies have shown that by deeply understanding customer needs, staying attuned to competitive dynamics, and ensuring seamless collaboration across all functions, they can achieve sustained profitability and maintain a competitive edge in their respective industries.

MO is not just a theoretical concept but a practical strategy that can be applied across various types of businesses, from e-commerce giants like Amazon to global consumer-goods leaders like P&G. The success of these companies underscores the importance of adopting a market-oriented approach as a key driver of long-term business performance in an increasingly competitive and dynamic market environment.

Strategic Implication: Customer focus is only strategic when it shapes decisions at every level. Evaluate whether your leadership team is responsive to market signals—or merely collecting data without adaptive follow-through.

CHAPTER 4

GROWTH ORIENTATION: AMBITION AND STRATEGY

Growth Orientation is not merely about expanding a business; it encompasses a strategic mindset that aligns ambition with foresight, continuous innovation, and adaptive resource management. In today's dynamic and competitive global market, firms that prioritize Growth Orientation are better equipped to respond to market fluctuations, seize emerging opportunities, and sustain competitive advantages over the long term (Ansoff, 1965). Growth-oriented businesses are characterized by their proactive pursuit of new opportunities, continuous innovation, and strategic resource allocation. These firms are committed to expanding their market presence, improving their competitive position, and achieving long-term success.

This chapter provides an in-depth exploration of Growth Orientation, discussing its theoretical foundations, practical applications, and the critical role it plays in Entrepreneurial Marketing. The chapter will also include robust case studies from various industries to demonstrate how Growth Orientation can drive business success, supported by relevant academic theories and practical examples.

UNDERSTANDING GROWTH ORIENTATION

Growth Orientation refers to a firm's commitment to achieving sustainable expansion by aligning its vision, resources, and actions toward long-term goals. This concept is rooted in strategic intent, which emphasizes the importance of an overarching vision that drives organizations toward ambitious objectives (Hamel & Prahalad, 1989). Growth-oriented firms are driven by a vision of long-term success and are willing to invest in new initiatives, enter new markets, and innovate continuously. This section explores the evolution of Growth Orientation, its key components, and its relevance in today's business environment.

KEY CONCEPTS OF GROWTH ORIENTATION:

Growth Orientation can be broken down into several key components that collectively contribute to a firm's ability to achieve sustainable growth:

Vision and Ambition: A strong vision provides a clear sense of direction and purpose, driving the organization toward ambitious growth goals. This vision must be communicated effectively across all levels of the organization to ensure alignment and commitment (Porter, 1980). A company's vision should be both inspirational and practical, guiding strategic decisions and resource allocation.

Strategic Planning: Effective strategic planning involves setting clear goals, developing detailed action plans, and continuously monitoring progress. Strategic planning must be flexible enough to adapt to changing market conditions while staying focused on long-term objectives (Mintzberg, 1994). This planning process should include scenario analysis, risk assessment, and resource allocation to ensure that the company is well prepared for future challenges and opportunities.

Continuous Innovation: Innovation is a key driver of growth, enabling firms to create new products, services, and processes that meet evolving customer needs. A culture of innovation encourages experimentation, risk-taking, and the continuous improvement of existing offerings (Schumpeter, 1934). Companies must invest in research and development (R&D) and foster an environment where new ideas can flourish. This innovation should be customer-centric, focusing on solving real problems and enhancing the customer experience.

Market Expansion: Expanding into new markets, whether geographic, demographic, or product-related, is essential for sustaining growth. This expansion often involves significant investments in market research, distribution networks, and marketing efforts (Ansoff, 1965). Companies must carefully analyze market conditions, customer behavior, and competitive dynamics before entering new markets to ensure that they can effectively compete and capture market share.

Resource Allocation: Strategic resource allocation ensures that the necessary financial, human, and technological resources are available to support growth initiatives. This includes investing in key areas such as R&D, talent management, and technology infrastructure (Barney, 1991). Effective resource allocation involves prioritizing high-impact projects, managing budgets efficiently, and ensuring that the right people and technologies are in place to drive growth.

Leadership and Organizational Culture: Leadership plays a critical role in fostering a growth-oriented culture. Leaders must inspire and motivate their teams, encourage innovation, and create an environment that supports continuous learning and development (Hamel & Prahalad, 1989). A strong organizational culture that aligns with the company's growth objectives is essential for sustaining momentum and driving long-term success. Leaders must also be adaptable, able to pivot strategies in response to changing market conditions and emerging opportunities.

Adaptability and Agility: In today's rapidly changing business environment, firms must be agile and adaptable. This requires a willingness to pivot strategies, embrace new technologies, and respond quickly to market changes (Teece, Pisano, & Shuen, 1997). Companies that can quickly adapt to new trends, customer demands, and competitive pressures are more likely to sustain growth and maintain their competitive edge.

SETTING GROWTH GOALS

Setting growth goals is a fundamental aspect of Growth Orientation. These goals provide a roadmap for the organization, guiding its actions and decision-making processes. However, setting effective growth goals requires more than just ambition; it requires careful consideration of the organization's capabilities, market conditions, and competitive landscape.

IMPORTANCE OF CLEAR AND ACHIEVABLE GOALS

Setting clear and achievable growth goals is essential for providing direction and focus to the organization. Goals act as a roadmap, guiding the company's efforts and ensuring that all stakeholders are aligned toward common objectives. Well-defined goals also serve as a basis for measuring progress and success (Drucker, 1954).

TECHNIQUES FOR SETTING EFFECTIVE GROWTH GOALS:

The SMART framework (defining objectives that are **s**pecific, **m**easurable, **a**ssignable, **r**ealistic, and **t**ime-bound) is a widely recognized tool for setting effective growth goals. However, in addition to SMART, organizations can employ several other techniques to enhance their goal-setting processes:

Scenario Planning: Scenario planning involves developing multiple potential scenarios based on different assumptions about the future. This technique helps organizations prepare for various outcomes and adjust their goals and strategies accordingly (Schoemaker, 1995). By considering different possibilities, companies can create more robust and flexible strategies that are better equipped to handle uncertainty.

Benchmarking: Benchmarking involves comparing the organization's performance against industry leaders or best practices. This technique helps identify gaps and opportunities for improvement, allowing the organization to set more realistic and achievable growth goals (Camp, 1989). Benchmarking also provides insights into what competitors are doing successfully, which can inform the company's own strategies.

Balanced Scorecard: The Balanced Scorecard is a strategic management tool that links growth goals to specific performance metrics across four key areas: financial performance, customer satisfaction, internal processes, and learning and growth (Kaplan & Norton, 1996). By using the Balanced Scorecard, organizations can ensure that their growth goals are aligned with their overall strategic objectives and that progress is measured across multiple dimensions.

EXAMPLES OF SUCCESSFUL GOAL SETTING

Amazon: Amazon's goal-setting approach is a prime example of how ambitious, well-defined goals can drive growth. Jeff Bezos, Amazon's founder, famously set the goal of making Amazon "the Earth's most customer-centric company" (Stone, 2013). This vision has guided Amazon's strategic decisions, leading to continuous expansion into new markets, the development of innovative products and services, and the establishment of a robust global infrastructure.

Airbnb: Airbnb's growth has been driven by its goal of creating a world where people can "belong anywhere." This vision has translated into specific goals around expanding the platform's reach, enhancing user experiences, and diversifying its service offerings. By setting clear, customer-focused goals, Airbnb has grown from a small start-up to a global hospitality leader (Gallagher, 2017).

Tesla: Tesla's goal of accelerating the world's transition to sustainable energy guides its strategic initiatives. By setting specific targets for production, market expansion, and innovation, Tesla has achieved significant growth in the electric vehicle and energy sectors (Musk, 2013). Tesla's ambitious goals have driven its investment in R&D, manufacturing, and global expansion, positioning it as a leader in the automotive and energy industries.

RESOURCE ALLOCATION FOR GROWTH

Strategic resource allocation is crucial for supporting growth initiatives. It involves distributing financial, human, and technological resources in a way that maximizes the impact on growth. Effective resource allocation ensures that critical projects receive the necessary support and that the organization can adapt to changing market conditions (Penrose, 1959; Barney, 1991). Resource allocation is particularly important in growth-oriented firms, where the focus is on maximizing the return on investment from resources deployed in various growth initiatives. This involves prioritizing projects that align with the company's strategic goals, developing detailed budgets, managing talent effectively, investing in technology, and forming strategic partnerships (Barney, 1991).

STRATEGIES FOR EFFECTIVE RESOURCE ALLOCATION

Portfolio Management: Portfolio management involves assessing and prioritizing the organization's projects and investments to ensure that resources are allocated to the most promising opportunities. This approach helps balance risk and reward, ensuring that the organization's resources are used efficiently (Markowitz, 1952). Portfolio management also allows companies to focus on high-impact projects that align with their strategic objectives.

Value-Chain Analysis: Value-chain analysis, introduced by Porter (1985), involves analyzing the organization's value-creating activities to identify areas where resources can be optimized for growth. By focusing on activities that add the most value, organizations can allocate resources more effectively and achieve higher returns on investment. Value-chain analysis helps companies identify areas for cost reduction, efficiency improvements, and competitive differentiation.

Resource-Based View (RBV): The Resource-Based View (RBV) of the firm posits that competitive advantage is derived from the unique resources and capabilities that an organization possesses (Barney, 1991).

By focusing on developing and leveraging these resources, organizations can achieve sustained growth and maintain a competitive edge. RBV emphasizes the importance of intangible assets such as brand equity, intellectual property, and organizational culture in driving growth.

CASE STUDIES IN RESOURCE ALLOCATION

Apple: Apple's strategic resource allocation has been instrumental in its success. The company allocates significant resources to R&D, enabling it to consistently introduce innovative products that set industry trends. Apple also invests heavily in its supply chain and marketing efforts, ensuring that its products are available globally and that its brand remains strong (Lashinsky, 2012). Apple's focus on design, user experience, and brand loyalty has allowed it to maintain a premium position in the market and drive sustained growth.

Google: Google's resource allocation is centered on its mission to "organize the world's information and make it universally accessible and useful." The company invests heavily in its core search-engine technology, as well as in adjacent areas such as cloud computing, artificial intelligence, and hardware. This strategic allocation of resources has enabled Google to maintain its dominance in the search market while expanding into new growth areas (Vise & Malseed, 2005). Google's investment in AI and machine learning has also positioned it as a leader in emerging technologies, driving future growth.

Amazon: Amazon's resource-allocation strategy involves continuous investment in technology and infrastructure. The company prioritizes projects that enhance customer experience and operational efficiency, such as its fulfillment centers and cloud computing services (AWS) (Stone, 2013). Amazon's strategic partnerships and acquisitions further support its growth objectives, enabling the company to diversify its offerings and maintain a competitive edge.

MONITORING AND ADJUSTING GROWTH STRATEGIES

Continuous monitoring of growth strategies is essential to ensure that they remain effective and aligned with the company's goals. Regular assessment allows businesses to identify potential issues, measure progress, and make data-driven adjustments. This ongoing process is critical for sustaining growth and ensuring that the organization can respond to changes in the market environment (Kaplan & Norton, 1996).

TECHNIQUES FOR EVALUATING AND ADJUSTING STRATEGIES:

Performance Metrics: Establish key performance indicators (KPIs) to measure the success of growth initiatives. Track metrics such as revenue growth, market share, customer acquisition, and product innovation (Kaplan & Norton, 1996). These metrics should be regularly reviewed to ensure that the company is on track to meet its growth objectives and that any deviations are promptly addressed.

Regular Reviews: Conduct regular reviews of growth strategies to assess progress and identify areas for improvement. Involve key stakeholders in the review process to gain diverse perspectives (Mintzberg, 1994). Regular reviews help ensure that the company remains agile and can quickly adapt to changing conditions.

Customer Feedback: Continuously gather and analyze customer feedback to understand their needs and preferences. Use this information to refine products, services, and marketing strategies (Drucker, 1954). Customer feedback is invaluable for identifying areas for improvement and ensuring that the company remains customer-centric.

Competitive Analysis: Monitor competitors' activities and market trends to stay informed about potential threats and opportunities. Adjust strategies based on competitive insights (Porter, 1980). Competitive analysis helps companies identify gaps in the market, anticipate competitor moves, and develop strategies to maintain a competitive edge.

Agile Approach: Adopt an agile approach to strategy execution, allowing for quick adjustments based on real-time data and feedback.

This involves iterative planning, rapid prototyping, and continuous improvement (Mintzberg, 1994). Agile methodologies enable companies to respond quickly to changes in the market and make data-driven decisions that drive growth.

EXAMPLES OF BUSINESSES THAT SUCCESSFULLY ADAPTED THEIR STRATEGIES

Netflix: Netflix's shift from a DVD rental service to a streaming platform is a prime example of strategic adaptation. By continuously monitoring market trends and customer preferences, Netflix identified the growing demand for on-demand content and pivoted its business model accordingly (Hastings & Meyer, 2020). This strategic adjustment has driven Netflix's growth and industry leadership, demonstrating the importance of agility in sustaining success.

Microsoft: Microsoft's transformation from a traditional software company to a cloud-computing leader demonstrates its ability to adapt to changing market conditions. The company's focus on cloud services (Azure) and subscription-based software (Office 365) has fueled its growth and positioned it as a key player in the tech industry (Nadella, 2017). Microsoft's ability to pivot its business model and invest in emerging technologies has allowed it to maintain relevance and drive long-term growth.

Salesforce: Salesforce is a prime example of a company that has leveraged Growth Orientation to become a dominant player in the software industry. From its early days as a pioneer in cloud-based customer relationship management (CRM), Salesforce has consistently expanded its product offerings, entered new markets, and acquired complementary companies to fuel its growth. Salesforce's growth-oriented approach has positioned it as the world's leading CRM platform, with a broad suite of solutions that serve businesses of all sizes (Benioff & Adler, 2009).

CHALLENGES IN SUSTAINING GROWTH

While Growth Orientation offers significant benefits, it also presents challenges. Sustaining growth over the long term requires organizations to navigate various obstacles, including market saturation, resource constraints, and the risks associated with rapid expansion.

MANAGING GROWING PAINS

Rapid growth can lead to operational challenges, such as increased complexity, resource constraints, and scalability issues. Organizations must anticipate these growing pains and implement strategies to manage them effectively. For example, as a company expands, it may need to invest in new infrastructure, hire additional staff, or restructure its operations to maintain efficiency and quality (Penrose, 1959). Companies must also develop robust processes and systems that can scale with growth, ensuring that quality and customer satisfaction are maintained as the business grows.

BALANCING SHORT-TERM AND LONG-TERM GOALS

One of the biggest challenges in sustaining growth is balancing short-term gains with long-term objectives. While it may be tempting to focus on immediate results, such as quarterly earnings or market share, organizations must also consider the long-term implications of their decisions. For example, prioritizing short-term profits at the expense of innovation or customer satisfaction can undermine long-term growth prospects (Kaplan & Norton, 1996). Companies must strike a balance between achieving short-term financial targets and investing in initiatives that will drive long-term growth.

SECURING AND MANAGING RESOURCES

Sustaining growth requires access to sufficient financial, human, and technological resources. However, as organizations grow, they may face challenges in securing these resources, particularly if they are competing with larger, more established firms. To overcome this challenge, organizations must build strong relationships with investors, suppliers, and other stakeholders, and demonstrate a clear path to profitability (Barney, 1991). Companies should also focus on developing a strong talent pipeline and investing in employee development to ensure that they have the skills and capabilities needed to support growth.

MAINTAINING ORGANIZATIONAL CULTURE

As organizations grow, maintaining the organizational culture that contributed to their early success can become challenging. Growth often brings increased bureaucracy, changes in leadership, and the need to integrate new employees and business units. To sustain growth, organizations must work to preserve their core values and culture while adapting to the demands of a larger, more complex organization (Hamel & Prahalad, 1989). A strong organizational culture that aligns with the company's growth objectives is essential for sustaining momentum and driving long-term success.

ADAPTING TO MARKET CHANGES

The market environment is constantly evolving, and organizations must be able to adapt to these changes to sustain growth. This requires staying informed about market trends, customer needs, and competitive dynamics, and being willing to pivot strategies when necessary. For example, companies in the technology sector must continually innovate and adapt to new technological advancements and shifting consumer preferences (Teece, Pisano, & Shuen, 1997). Companies that can quickly adapt to new trends, customer demands, and competitive pressures are more likely to sustain growth and maintain their competitive edge.

THE ROLE OF DIGITAL TRANSFORMATION IN GROWTH ORIENTATION

Digital transformation is playing an increasingly important role in Growth Orientation. Companies that embrace digital technologies, such as artificial intelligence, big data, and automation, are better positioned to scale their operations, enhance customer experiences, and drive growth. Digital transformation enables organizations to operate more efficiently, make data-driven decisions, and respond more quickly to market changes.

CASE STUDIES IN DIGITAL TRANSFORMATION

Netflix: As earlier noted, Netflix's digital transformation has been a key driver of its growth. By shifting from a DVD rental service to a streaming platform, Netflix was able to tap into the growing demand for on-demand content and expand its global reach. The company's use of big data and algorithms to personalize recommendations has also contributed to its success (Hastings & Meyer, 2020). Netflix's ability to leverage digital technology to enhance the customer experience has been a significant factor in its growth and success.

General Electric (GE): GE's digital transformation involved integrating digital technologies across its industrial operations, creating what it calls the "Industrial Internet." By leveraging data analytics and IoT technologies, GE has been able to improve operational efficiency, reduce costs, and drive growth in its core businesses (Immelt, 2016). GE's focus on digital transformation has allowed it to remain competitive in an increasingly digital world and continue to drive growth in its core industries.

Tesla: As noted above, Tesla's Growth Orientation is rooted in its commitment to sustainability and innovation. The company has embraced digital transformation in its production processes, product development, and customer-engagement strategies. By leveraging advanced manufacturing techniques, artificial intelligence, and data analytics, Tesla has been able to scale its operations rapidly while maintaining high levels of quality and innovation. Tesla's digital transformation efforts have also extended to its customer experience, with the company using data to personalize interactions and optimize the customer journey (Musk, 2013).

SUSTAINABILITY AND LONG-TERM GROWTH

Sustainability is becoming an increasingly important aspect of Growth Orientation. Companies that prioritize sustainable practices and products are better positioned to capitalize on the growing market for eco-friendly solutions. Sustainability-driven growth not only meets consumer demand but also aligns with broader environmental and social goals.

CASE STUDIES IN SUSTAINABLE GROWTH

Tesla: Tesla's growth strategy is deeply rooted in its mission to accelerate the world's transition to sustainable energy. By focusing on the development of electric vehicles and renewable energy solutions, Tesla has been able to differentiate itself in the automotive industry and drive significant growth (Musk, 2013). Tesla's commitment to sustainability has also attracted environmentally conscious consumers and investors, further supporting its growth objectives.

Unilever: Unilever's Sustainable Living Plan aims to decouple the company's growth from its environmental impact. By focusing on sustainability, Unilever has been able to reduce costs, enhance its brand reputation, and attract environmentally conscious consumers, driving long-term growth (Polman, 2014). Unilever's focus on sustainability has also helped it to build strong relationships with stakeholders, including customers, suppliers, and investors, further supporting its growth objectives.

Patagonia: Patagonia's commitment to environmental sustainability has been a key driver of its growth. The company has implemented a range of initiatives to reduce its environmental impact, from using recycled materials in its products to promoting sustainable business practices across its supply chain. Patagonia's focus on sustainability has not only driven customer loyalty but also positioned the company as a leader in the outdoor apparel industry, driving long-term growth (Chouinard, 2006).

FUTURE TRENDS IN GROWTH ORIENTATION

Looking forward, several trends are likely to shape the future of Growth Orientation:

Increased Focus on Digital and Data-Driven Strategies: As technology continues to evolve, businesses will increasingly rely on digital tools and data analytics to drive growth. The ability to harness big data for insights into customer behavior, market trends, and operational efficiencies will be a key differentiator.

Sustainability as a Competitive Advantage: Sustainability will move from being a niche consideration to a central component of growth strategies. Companies that can demonstrate a commitment to environmental and social responsibility will not only appeal to conscious consumers but also gain favor with investors and regulators.

Globalization and Market Expansion: The globalization of markets will continue, offering opportunities for businesses to expand their reach beyond local borders. However, this expansion will require a deep understanding of diverse cultures, regulations, and consumer preferences.

The Rise of AI and Automation: Artificial intelligence and automation technologies will play an increasingly important role in driving efficiency, reducing costs, and enabling scalability. Businesses that can effectively integrate these technologies into their operations will have a significant advantage.

Changing Consumer Expectations: As consumers become more sophisticated and demand more personalized experiences, businesses will need to adapt their growth strategies accordingly. This will require a deeper understanding of customer needs and the ability to deliver tailored solutions quickly and efficiently.

CONCLUSION

Growth Orientation is a vital strategy for entrepreneurial firms seeking to achieve long-term success and industry leadership. By prioritizing growth, companies can drive innovation, expand their market presence, and build a sustainable foundation for the future. The success of Growth Orientation depends on a company's ability to set ambitious goals, invest in innovation, and effectively manage the challenges that come with expansion. As the business landscape continues to evolve, companies that maintain a strong focus on growth will be better positioned to navigate challenges, capitalize on emerging trends, and achieve long-term success. This chapter has provided a comprehensive framework for understanding and implementing growth-oriented strategies, supported by real-world examples and case studies.

Strategic Implication: Growth is not a byproduct—it's a behavioral orientation. Firms must align their ambition with structured-growth levers and decide whether their current behaviors are producing scale or just movement.

CHAPTER 5

OPPORTUNITY ORIENTATION: PURSUING POTENTIAL

Opportunity Orientation is a critical aspect of Entrepreneurial Marketing, emphasizing a proactive approach to identifying, evaluating, and capitalizing on emerging opportunities in the market. In a business environment characterized by rapid change and intense competition, the ability to recognize and seize opportunities before competitors is a key determinant of success. This chapter delves into the concept of opportunity orientation, exploring its theoretical underpinnings, practical applications, and significance in driving business growth and innovation.

The modern business landscape is more dynamic and unpredictable than ever before, with technological advancements, globalization, and shifting consumer preferences continuously reshaping markets. Companies that can effectively navigate this environment by identifying new opportunities are better positioned to achieve sustained growth and competitive advantage (Drucker, 1985). Opportunity orientation is not just about being alert to changes; it involves a deliberate and systematic approach to exploiting these changes for strategic gain.

This chapter will guide businesses through the process of cultivating an opportunity-oriented mindset, utilizing tools and techniques for market research, evaluating opportunities, and overcoming common challenges. It will also feature detailed case studies of companies like Netflix, Airbnb, Tesla, and Spotify, which have successfully leveraged opportunity orientation to become industry leaders. By understanding and applying the principles discussed in this chapter, businesses can enhance their ability to innovate, grow, and maintain a competitive edge in today's fast-paced market environment.

UNDERSTANDING OPPORTUNITY ORIENTATION

DEFINITION AND KEY CONCEPTS

Opportunity orientation refers to a firm's proactive pursuit of new and emerging opportunities in the market, regardless of resource constraints. It is rooted in the belief that opportunities are the lifeblood of business growth and innovation, and that firms must be willing to seek out and exploit these opportunities to succeed (Fiet, 2002). This concept is closely associated with entrepreneurial thinking, where the focus is on recognizing market gaps, emerging trends, and unmet customer needs as avenues for creating value.

Key concepts within opportunity orientation include:

Proactivity: The ability to anticipate market changes and act ahead of competitors. Proactivity is crucial for firms aiming to stay ahead in fast-moving industries where timing can be the difference between success and failure (Lumpkin & Dess, 1996).

Market Sensing: This involves continuously monitoring the market for signals and trends that indicate potential opportunities. It requires a deep understanding of industry dynamics, consumer behavior, and competitor actions (Day, 1994).

Flexibility: Being adaptable and responsive to new information and changing circumstances is essential for capitalizing on opportunities. Firms that are too rigid in their strategies may miss out on emerging trends (Teece, Pisano, & Shuen, 1997).

Innovation: Developing new products, services, or processes that address emerging opportunities is at the heart of opportunity orientation. Innovation is often the vehicle through which opportunities are transformed into tangible business outcomes (Schumpeter, 1942). The concept of opportunity orientation has its roots in entrepreneurship theory, where the focus is on recognizing and exploiting opportunities as a means of creating value and achieving business growth. Joseph Schumpeter (1942) famously described entrepreneurs as innovators who disrupt existing markets by introducing new products or services that meet unfulfilled needs. This disruptive innovation is often driven by a strong opportunity orientation. Historically, businesses that have been successful in identifying and capitalizing on opportunities have demonstrated superior growth and a sustained competitive advantage. For instance, firms that identified the potential of the internet early on were able to establish dominant positions in e-commerce, digital advertising, and online services (Brynjolfsson & McAfee, 2014).

In today's fast-paced and dynamic business environment, opportunity orientation is more relevant than ever. With the rapid pace of technological change and globalization, firms must continuously adapt to new trends and changes. This requires not only the ability to recognize opportunities but also the agility to act on them quickly and effectively.

IMPORTANCE IN MODERN BUSINESS STRATEGY

Opportunity Orientation is essential for entrepreneurial firms that operate in dynamic and competitive markets. It enables companies to stay ahead of industry trends, adapt to changes, and continuously innovate to meet the evolving needs of their customers (Drucker, 1985). In a world where competitive advantages are increasingly temporary, the ability to identify and capitalize on new opportunities is crucial for long-term success (McGrath, 2013). For example, a beverage company that identifies a growing demand for health-conscious products and swiftly launches a line of organic, low-sugar drinks can capture a significant share of a rapidly expanding market segment. By entering the health-beverage market early, the company not only meets current consumer demand but also positions itself as a leader in a trend that is likely to grow in importance.

IDENTIFYING AND EVALUATING OPPORTUNITIES

TECHNIQUES FOR MARKET RESEARCH AND ANALYSIS

Identifying opportunities in the market requires a systematic approach to gathering and analyzing data. Market research and analysis are critical components of opportunity orientation, as they provide the insights needed to recognize emerging trends, understand customer needs, and identify gaps in the market. Several techniques can be employed to effectively identify opportunities:

Environmental Scanning: Environmental scanning involves regularly monitoring the external environment for trends, changes, and potential opportunities. This process includes analyzing market reports, industry publications, economic indicators, and technological advancements. By staying informed about changes in the macro-environment, firms can identify shifts that may signal new opportunities (Aguilar, 1967).

SWOT Analysis: Conducting a SWOT analysis (Strengths, Weaknesses, Opportunities, Threats) helps businesses evaluate their internal capabilities and external environment. This tool is particularly useful for identifying opportunities that align with the company's strengths while addressing external threats. A thorough SWOT analysis can reveal potential areas for expansion, product development, or market entry (Helms & Nixon, 2010).

Customer Feedback: Engaging with customers through surveys, focus groups, and social media allows firms to gather insights into their needs, preferences, and pain points. Customer feedback is invaluable for identifying unmet needs and areas where the company can innovate or improve its offerings. Firms that listen closely to their customers are often the first to recognize emerging opportunities (Griffin & Hauser, 1993).

Competitive Intelligence: Monitoring competitors' activities, products, and strategies is crucial for identifying gaps in the market that the company can exploit. Competitive intelligence involves tracking competitors' moves and understanding their strengths and weaknesses, which can provide insights into potential opportunities for differentiation (Porter, 1980).

TOOLS FOR EVALUATING OPPORTUNITIES

Once potential opportunities have been identified, they must be thoroughly evaluated to determine their feasibility and potential impact. Several tools can assist in this evaluation process:

Porter's Five Forces: Michael Porter's Five Forces framework is a powerful tool for evaluating the competitive intensity and attractiveness of an industry. This framework analyzes the bargaining power of suppliers and buyers, the threat of new entrants, the threat of substitute products, and the intensity of competitive rivalry. By understanding these forces, firms can assess whether an opportunity is likely to be profitable and sustainable (Porter, 1979).

PEST Analysis: A PEST analysis (Political, Economic, Social, Technological) helps firms assess the macro-environmental factors that could impact an opportunity. By analyzing these external factors, businesses can gain a better understanding of the broader context in which an opportunity exists and anticipate potential challenges (Yüksel, 2012).

Financial Modeling: Financial modeling involves creating projections to assess the potential profitability and return on investment of an opportunity. This includes forecasting revenue, expenses, and cash flow to determine whether the opportunity aligns with the company's financial goals. Financial models are essential for making informed investment decisions (Hitchner, 2011).

Risk Assessment: Identifying and evaluating the risks associated with an opportunity are critical to making sound strategic decisions. This involves assessing market, financial, operational, and strategic risks, and determining how they can be mitigated. A thorough risk assessment helps firms avoid potential pitfalls and increases the likelihood of success (Damodaran, 2015).

STRATEGIES FOR IDENTIFYING MARKET GAPS

Identifying market gaps—areas where customer needs are unmet or underserved—requires a keen understanding of the market and the ability to think creatively. Some strategies for identifying these gaps include:

Analyzing Customer Segments: By segmenting the market based on demographics, psychographics, and behavior, firms can identify specific groups of customers whose needs are not being fully met by existing products or services. For example, a company might discover that a particular demographic, such as eco-conscious millennials, is underserved in the market for sustainable products (Smith, 1956).

Exploring Adjacent Markets: Firms can identify opportunities by exploring markets adjacent to their current operations. Adjacent markets may share similarities with the firm's existing market, making it easier to leverage existing capabilities and resources. For example, a software company specializing in desktop applications might explore opportunities in mobile-app development, given the growing demand for mobile solutions (Zook & Allen, 2003).

Identifying Emerging Trends: Staying ahead of emerging trends is key to identifying market gaps before competitors. Firms that are attuned to changes in technology, consumer behavior, and societal values can spot opportunities early and capitalize on them. For instance, the rise of the sharing economy created opportunities for companies like Airbnb and Uber to disrupt traditional industries (Sundararajan, 2016).

Conducting Innovation Workshops: Innovation workshops, where employees are encouraged to brainstorm and develop new ideas, can lead to the identification of market gaps. These workshops foster creativity and collaboration, often resulting in innovative solutions that address unmet customer needs (Sawhney, Wolcott, & Arroniz, 2006).

STRATEGIES FOR ACTING ON OPPORTUNITIES

Once opportunities have been identified and evaluated, the next step is to seize them effectively. This involves developing strategies that enable the firm to act swiftly and decisively, leveraging its resources to capitalize on the opportunity. Key strategies include:

Agility and Flexibility: Firms must develop an organizational structure that allows for quick decision-making and rapid response to new opportunities. This includes empowering employees to take initiative and make decisions within a framework that supports agility. Agile organizations can pivot quickly when new opportunities arise, giving them a competitive edge (Doz & Kosonen, 2010).

Pilot Testing: Conducting pilot tests or small-scale experiments allows firms to validate an opportunity before committing significant resources. This approach minimizes risk by enabling the company to test and refine the concept based on real-world feedback. For example, a tech company might release a beta version of a new product to a select group of users to gather feedback and make improvements before a full launch (Thomke, 2003).

Strategic Partnerships: Forming strategic partnerships or alliances can help firms leverage external resources and capabilities to seize opportunities. Partnerships can provide access to new markets, technologies, and expertise, which can accelerate the company's ability to act on an opportunity. For example, a pharmaceutical company might partner with a biotech firm to co-develop a new drug, combining their respective strengths (Gulati, 1998).

Resource Allocation: Allocating resources strategically to support the opportunity is critical to its success. This includes financial investment, talent management, and technology deployment. Firms must ensure that the necessary resources are available and that they are deployed effectively to maximize the opportunity's potential (Bower, 1970).

CASE STUDIES OF SUCCESSFUL IMPLEMENTATION

UBER: DISRUPTING THE TAXI INDUSTRY

Uber identified an opportunity to disrupt the traditional taxi industry by leveraging technology to create a ride-sharing platform. The company recognized that consumers were dissatisfied with the existing taxi service, which was often inconvenient, unreliable, and expensive. By addressing these pain points with a user-friendly app that allowed consumers to book rides on demand, Uber quickly gained market share.

Uber's success can be attributed to its ability to act swiftly on the identified opportunity. The company rapidly expanded its operations, first in major cities in the United States and then internationally. Uber also continuously innovated, introducing new services like UberPOOL, which allows passengers to share rides and reduce costs. Despite regulatory challenges and competition, Uber's aggressive approach to seizing the opportunity has made it a global leader in the ride-sharing industry (Rogers, 2015).

SLACK: TRANSFORMING WORKPLACE COMMUNICATION

Slack recognized the need for improved workplace communication, particularly in organizations where teams were distributed across different locations. The company developed a messaging platform that was easy to use, integrated with other tools, and fostered collaboration. Slack's focus on addressing the specific needs of modern teams—such as reducing email clutter and improving communication efficiency—drove its rapid growth and widespread adoption.

To seize the opportunity, Slack employed a freemium model, allowing users to access basic features for free while offering premium features at a cost. This strategy enabled Slack to quickly build a large user base and convert many free users into paying customers. By continuously improving its platform based on user feedback and adding new features, Slack has maintained its position as a leader in workplace communication tools (Butterfield, 2020).

NETFLIX: REVOLUTIONIZING ENTERTAINMENT

Netflix is a prime example of a company that has successfully seized multiple opportunities to revolutionize the entertainment industry. Originally a DVD rental service, Netflix identified the emerging opportunity in online streaming and pivoted its business model to become a leading streaming platform. The company's decision to invest heavily in original content further solidified its position in the market.

Netflix's opportunity-oriented approach has allowed it to disrupt the traditional entertainment industry, become a global leader in streaming, and set the standard for content delivery. The company's ability to continuously identify and exploit new opportunities, such as expanding into international markets and leveraging data analytics to personalize content, has been key to its sustained success (McDonald & Smith-Rowsey, 2016).

ORGANIZATIONAL STRUCTURES THAT SUPPORT AGILITY

To effectively seize opportunities, organizations must be structured in a way that supports agility. This involves creating a culture that values flexibility, encourages innovation, and empowers employees to take initiative. Key elements of an agile organizational structure include:

Decentralized Decision-Making: Allowing decisions to be made closer to the action—by those with the most relevant information—enables the organization to respond more quickly to opportunities. Decentralized decision-making also empowers employees, fostering a sense of ownership and accountability (Mintzberg, 1979).

Cross-Functional Teams: Forming cross-functional teams that bring together employees from different departments allows for a diversity of perspectives and expertise. These teams are better equipped to identify and act on opportunities, as they can evaluate them from multiple angles and develop comprehensive strategies (Edmondson & Harvey, 2017).

Continuous Learning: An agile organization is one that continually learns and adapts. By fostering a culture of continuous learning, companies can stay ahead of market trends and be more responsive to changes. This involves encouraging employees to develop new skills, stay informed about industry developments, and share knowledge across the organization (Senge, 1990).

COMMON CHALLENGES IN OPPORTUNITY ORIENTATION

While opportunity orientation offers significant benefits, it also presents several challenges that businesses must overcome to be successful. Some of the most common challenges include:

Resource Constraints: Limited resources—whether financial, human, or technological—can hinder a firm's ability to pursue new opportunities. This is particularly challenging for small businesses and start-ups that may not have the same resources as larger competitors (Penrose, 1959).

Risk Aversion: Organizational culture and leadership may be risk-averse, which can prevent the company from pursuing bold opportunities. Fear of failure or reluctance to deviate from established practices can stifle innovation and prevent the company from capitalizing on new opportunities (Kahneman & Tversky, 1979).

Market Uncertainty: Uncertainty about market conditions and customer preferences can make it challenging to evaluate opportunities. In rapidly changing markets, it can be difficult to predict which trends will last and which will fade, leading to hesitation or indecision (Knight, 1921).

Execution Challenges: Successfully executing on opportunities requires alignment across the organization. This includes clear communication, coordination, and accountability. Without these elements, even the best opportunities can fail to materialize (Pfeffer & Sutton, 2000).

SOLUTIONS AND STRATEGIES FOR OVERCOMING CHALLENGES

Prioritizing Initiatives: To overcome resource constraints, firms should prioritize initiatives with the highest potential impact. This involves evaluating opportunities based on their alignment with the company's strategic goals and focusing on those that offer the greatest return on investment (Kaplan & Norton, 2004).

Fostering a Culture of Innovation: Encouraging a culture that values innovation and risk-taking is essential for overcoming risk aversion. This includes recognizing and rewarding employees who contribute to identifying and seizing opportunities, and creating an environment where experimentation is encouraged (Amabile, 1988).

Leveraging Data for Decision-Making: Using data-driven insights to navigate market uncertainty can help firms make more informed decisions. By analyzing market data, customer feedback, and competitive intelligence, companies can reduce uncertainty and increase their confidence in pursuing new opportunities (Davenport & Harris, 2007).

Building Strategic Flexibility: Maintaining flexibility in strategic planning and execution is key to overcoming execution challenges. Firms should be prepared to pivot and adapt based on real-time feedback and changing market conditions, ensuring that they remain agile and responsive (Teece, 2014).

CASE STUDIES OF OVERCOMING CHALLENGES

AIRBNB: NAVIGATING REGULATORY HURDLES

Airbnb's opportunity to revolutionize the travel and accommodation industry was met with significant regulatory challenges. In many cities, local laws were not conducive to the short-term rental model that Airbnb promoted, leading to legal battles and opposition from established hotel chains. To overcome these challenges, Airbnb engaged in proactive dialogue with regulators, advocating for changes to local laws that would allow its business model to operate legally. The company also implemented policies to address concerns about safety, taxation, and neighborhood impacts. By navigating these regulatory hurdles, Airbnb was able to expand its platform and achieve global success (Guttentag, 2015).

TESLA: SCALING PRODUCTION AMID RESOURCE CONSTRAINTS

Tesla faced significant resource constraints as it sought to scale production of its electric vehicles (EVs). The high costs of developing new technologies, building production facilities, and securing a supply chain for batteries were major hurdles. To address these challenges, Tesla secured substantial investment through public and private funding, formed strategic partnerships with suppliers, and vertically integrated its operations to reduce costs. The company also focused on continuous innovation, developing new manufacturing techniques to improve efficiency. Despite these challenges, Tesla successfully scaled its production and became a leader in the EV market (Ishibashi & Watanabe, 2004).

NETFLIX: ADAPTING TO CHANGING CONSUMER PREFERENCES

Netflix's shift from DVD rentals to online streaming was driven by changing consumer preferences and technological advancements. However, this transition posed significant challenges, including the need to secure streaming rights, invest in new technologies, and rebrand the company. Netflix overcame these challenges by making bold strategic decisions, such as investing heavily in original content and leveraging data analytics to personalize recommendations for users. The company's ability to adapt to changing market conditions and consumer preferences allowed it to dominate the streaming market (Keating, 2012).

OPPORTUNITY ORIENTATION IN ACTION: CASE STUDIES OF LEADING COMPANIES

To illustrate the power of opportunity orientation, this section presents detailed case studies of companies that have successfully leveraged this approach to achieve market leadership and sustained growth. Each case study highlights the company's strategic decisions, challenges faced, and the outcomes achieved, providing valuable insights into how opportunity orientation can be effectively implemented.

NETFLIX: TRANSFORMING ENTERTAINMENT THROUGH OPPORTUNITY ORIENTATION

Netflix is a quintessential example of a company that has continuously identified and capitalized on emerging opportunities, transforming itself from a DVD rental service into a global leader in online streaming. Netflix's journey is a testament to the importance of opportunity orientation in navigating disruptive changes and staying ahead of the competition.

INITIAL OPPORTUNITY IDENTIFICATION

Netflix was founded in 1997 as a DVD rental-by-mail service, a novel concept at the time when video rental stores like Blockbuster dominated the market. The founders, Reed Hastings and Marc Randolph, identified a gap in the market: the inconvenience of traditional video rental stores, where late fees and limited selection were common pain points for consumers (Keating, 2012). By offering a subscription-based model with no late fees and an extensive catalog, Netflix quickly gained a loyal customer base.

PIVOT TO STREAMING

As broadband internet became more widespread in the early 2000s, Netflix recognized a new opportunity in online streaming. The company's leadership foresaw the decline of physical media and the rise of digital content delivery, prompting them to invest heavily in developing a streaming platform. This decision was not without risks; the technology was still nascent, and the content industry was resistant to change. However, Netflix's opportunity-oriented mindset allowed it to move swiftly and decisively, launching its streaming service in 2007 (McDonald & Smith-Rowsey, 2016).

INVESTMENT IN ORIGINAL CONTENT

Recognizing that content would be the key differentiator in the increasingly crowded streaming market, Netflix made a bold move to invest in original programming. The company's first major success in this area came with the release of *House of Cards* in 2013, which was both a critical and commercial success. This strategy not only helped Netflix to attract and retain subscribers but also positioned it as a major player in content production, challenging traditional television networks and film studios (Lotz, 2017).

GLOBAL EXPANSION AND DATA-DRIVEN INNOVATION

Netflix's opportunity orientation extended beyond the US market. The company aggressively expanded its services internationally, recognizing the growing demand for streaming in global markets. By 2016, Netflix was available in over 190 countries, making it a truly global entertainment platform (McDonald & Smith-Rowsey, 2016). Additionally, Netflix leveraged data analytics to enhance user experience, using viewing data to personalize recommendations and inform content-creation decisions. This data-driven approach further solidified its market position and enabled it to continuously adapt to changing consumer preferences.

OUTCOME

Netflix's ability to identify and act on opportunities has made it a dominant force in the entertainment industry. The company's transition from DVD rentals to streaming, its investment in original content, and its global expansion have all been driven by a strong opportunity-oriented strategy. Today, Netflix is not only a leader in streaming but also a significant influencer in the production and distribution of digital content worldwide (Lotz, 2017).

AIRBNB: REVOLUTIONIZING TRAVEL WITH AN OPPORTUNITY-ORIENTED MINDSET

Airbnb's success story is a powerful example of how a company can disrupt a traditional industry by recognizing and capitalizing on a market gap. Founded in 2008, Airbnb transformed the hospitality industry by creating a platform that allows individuals to rent out their homes or spare rooms to travelers, offering an alternative to traditional hotels.

IDENTIFYING THE MARKET GAP

The idea for Airbnb was born out of the founders' personal experience of struggling to pay rent in San Francisco. They noticed that during a local conference, hotel rooms were fully booked, leaving attendees with limited accommodation options. The founders saw an opportunity to fill this gap by offering an online platform where people could list and rent out their extra space to visitors. This concept tapped into the growing trend of the sharing economy and addressed the needs of both home-owners seeking extra income and travelers looking for affordable, unique accommodations (Guttentag, 2015).

STRATEGIC SCALING AND EXPANSION

Airbnb's opportunity orientation was evident in its approach to scaling the business. The company initially focused on building trust within its community, recognizing that the success of a peer-to-peer platform would hinge on the safety and reliability of its service. Airbnb implemented features like user reviews, verified identities, and secure payment systems to build credibility. As the platform grew, Airbnb expanded its offerings to include entire homes, luxury properties, and even experiences hosted by locals, further differentiating itself from traditional hospitality services (Guttentag, 2015).

OVERCOMING REGULATORY CHALLENGES

As Airbnb expanded globally, it faced significant regulatory challenges, particularly in cities with strict housing and zoning laws. However, the company's leadership was proactive in addressing these issues, engaging with local governments to advocate for regulations that would allow home-sharing while addressing concerns about housing availability and neighborhood impacts. Airbnb's ability to navigate these regulatory hurdles was a key factor in its continued growth and success (Gurran & Phibbs, 2017).

OUTCOME

Airbnb's opportunity-oriented approach enabled it to disrupt the traditional hospitality industry and become a global leader in short-term rentals. The company's innovative platform not only provided a new way for people to travel but also created economic opportunities for millions of hosts around the world. Today, Airbnb is valued at billions of dollars and continues to expand its offerings, demonstrating the power of opportunity orientation in driving business success (Guttentag, 2015; Zervas et al., 2017).

TESLA: LEADING THE ELECTRIC VEHICLE MARKET THROUGH OPPORTUNITY ORIENTATION

Tesla's rise to prominence in the automotive industry is a testament to the power of opportunity orientation in driving innovation and market leadership. Founded in 2003, Tesla set out to revolutionize the automotive industry by producing electric vehicles (EVs) that were not only environmentally friendly but also high-performance and desirable to consumers.

IDENTIFYING THE OPPORTUNITY IN ELECTRIC VEHICLES

Tesla's founders, including Elon Musk, recognized the growing concern over climate change and the limitations of traditional internal combustion engines. They saw an opportunity to disrupt the automotive industry by developing electric vehicles that could compete with, and even surpass, traditional gasoline-powered cars in terms of performance and appeal. This vision was ambitious, given that the EV market was still in its infancy, and there were significant technological and infrastructure challenges to overcome (Ishibashi & Watanabe, 2004).

INNOVATION AND TECHNOLOGICAL ADVANCEMENTS

Tesla's opportunity orientation was evident in its approach to innovation. The company invested heavily in research and development to create battery technology that would extend the range and reduce the cost of its EVs. Tesla also focused on designing vehicles that were not only efficient but also stylish and high-performance, appealing to a broader market segment. The introduction of the Tesla Roadster in 2008, followed by the Model S in 2012, demonstrated the company's ability to deliver on its promise of making EVs desirable to consumers (Mangram, 2012).

VERTICAL INTEGRATION AND MARKET EXPANSION

To achieve its vision, Tesla adopted a strategy of vertical integration, producing many of its components in-house and developing its own charging infrastructure. This allowed Tesla to maintain control over the quality and cost of its products and ensured that it could scale production to meet growing demand. Tesla's Gigafactories, which produce batteries at scale, are a key part of this strategy, enabling the company to reduce costs and make EVs more accessible to consumers (Higgins, 2021; Stirngham et al., 2015).

OVERCOMING CHALLENGES AND DRIVING MARKET ADOPTION

Tesla faced numerous challenges in its journey, including skepticism from the automotive industry, financial constraints, and production bottlenecks. However, the company's strong opportunity orientation and commitment to its mission allowed it to overcome these obstacles. Tesla's ability to anticipate and respond to market needs, such as the demand for affordable EVs with the introduction of the Model 3, helped it gain a significant market share. Moreover, Tesla's focus on continuous innovation, such as the development of autonomous-driving technology, has kept it at the forefront of the industry (Mangram, 2012).

OUTCOME

Tesla's success in the EV market is a direct result of its opportunity-oriented approach. By recognizing the potential of electric vehicles early on and committing to continuous innovation, Tesla has established itself as a leader in the automotive industry. The company's ability to seize opportunities in a rapidly evolving market has not only driven its growth but also accelerated the global transition to sustainable energy (Higgins, 2021; Stringham et al., 2015).

SPOTIFY: CAPITALIZING ON THE SHIFT TO STREAMING MUSIC

Spotify's emergence as a global leader in music streaming is another compelling example of opportunity orientation in action. Founded in 2006, Spotify identified the opportunity to transform the way people consume music by offering a legal, user-friendly alternative to music piracy.

RECOGNIZING THE SHIFT TO DIGITAL MUSIC

In the mid-2000s, the music industry was grappling with the widespread issue of piracy, which was eroding revenues and undermining the traditional business model of selling physical albums. Spotify's founders, Daniel Ek and Martin Lorentzon, recognized that the future of music consumption was digital and that there was an opportunity to create a platform that would offer consumers easy access to music while compensating artists and rights holders (Morris & Powers, 2015).

BUILDING A USER-CENTRIC PLATFORM

Spotify's opportunity orientation was evident in its focus on creating a user-centric platform that would offer a superior experience compared to piracy and other legal alternatives. The company introduced features like personalized playlists, seamless streaming, and social sharing, which quickly attracted a large user base. Spotify's freemium model, which offered a free tier supported by ads and a premium tier with additional features, allowed the company to scale rapidly and convert free users into paying subscribers (Morris & Powers, 2015).

LEVERAGING DATA ANALYTICS FOR CONTINUOUS IMPROVEMENT

A key component of Spotify's success has been its use of data analytics to enhance the user experience. By analyzing user behavior, Spotify has been able to refine its algorithms for music recommendations, ensuring that users are consistently discovering new music that aligns with their tastes. This data-driven approach has not only improved user retention but also provided valuable insights to artists and record labels, further strengthening Spotify's position in the music industry (Prey, 2016).

EXPANDING GLOBALLY AND DIVERSIFYING OFFERINGS

Spotify's opportunity-oriented strategy also involved rapid global expansion. The company recognized that the demand for music streaming was not limited to specific regions and made its platform available in over 180 countries. Additionally, Spotify diversified its offerings by introducing podcasts and exclusive content, catering to the growing demand for audio entertainment beyond music (Morris & Powers, 2015).

OUTCOME

Spotify's ability to identify and act on opportunities has made it the world's leading music-streaming service. The company's focus on user experience, data-driven innovation, and global expansion has allowed it to dominate the market and redefine the music industry. Today, Spotify continues to explore new opportunities, such as entering the audiobook market, demonstrating its commitment to staying ahead in a competitive landscape (Morris & Powers, 2015).

THE FUTURE OF OPPORTUNITY ORIENTATION

As markets become more complex and competitive, the importance of opportunity orientation in Entrepreneurial Marketing will only increase.

Companies that develop and maintain a strong opportunity orientation will be better positioned to navigate challenges, seize new opportunities, and achieve long-term success. This section explores the emerging trends that will shape the future of opportunity orientation and offers recommendations for businesses looking to stay ahead.

EMBRACING EMERGING TECHNOLOGIES

The future of opportunity orientation will be closely tied to the adoption of emerging technologies. Companies that actively explore and integrate new technologies, such as artificial intelligence (AI), blockchain, and the Internet of Things, will be better equipped to identify and capitalize on opportunities in the digital age.

For example, AI can be used to analyze vast amounts of data, enabling companies to identify patterns and predict market trends with greater accuracy. This allows firms to anticipate changes in consumer behavior and adjust their strategies accordingly. Similarly, blockchain technology offers new opportunities for transparency and security in transactions, which can be particularly valuable in industries such as finance and supply-chain management (Brynjolfsson & McAfee, 2014).

ADAPTING TO GLOBALIZATION AND LOCALIZATION

Globalization and localization will continue to shape the landscape of opportunity orientation. Companies will need to balance global strategies with local market considerations, identifying opportunities to expand internationally while adapting to regional differences in culture, regulation, and consumer behavior. For instance, a consumer-goods company that expands into new international markets by partnering with local distributors and tailoring its products to meet local tastes and preferences will be better positioned to succeed. This approach allows the company to capitalize on global opportunities while remaining relevant in each market, demonstrating the importance of a nuanced understanding of both global and local dynamics (Yip, 2003).

FOSTERING SUSTAINABLE OPPORTUNITIES

Sustainability is becoming a critical factor in opportunity orientation. Companies that prioritize sustainable practices and products will be able to identify opportunities in the growing market for eco-friendly solutions. Sustainability-driven opportunity orientation not only meets consumer demand but also aligns with broader environmental and social goals. For example, a packaging company that develops biodegradable materials in response to the increasing demand for sustainable packaging positions itself as a leader in the eco-friendly market. By identifying and pursuing opportunities in sustainability, companies can enhance their brand reputation, meet regulatory requirements, and contribute to a more sustainable future (Porter & Kramer, 2006).

LEVERAGING DATA-DRIVEN DECISION-MAKING

The future of opportunity orientation will be increasingly data-driven. Companies that harness the power of big data and analytics to identify trends, understand customer behavior, and predict market shifts will be better equipped to seize new opportunities and make informed strategic decisions. For example, a retail chain that uses advanced analytics to track consumer purchasing patterns and identify emerging product trends can quickly adapt its product offerings and marketing strategies, staying ahead of competitors and capturing new market opportunities. Data-driven decision-making not only enhances a company's ability to identify opportunities but also improves its agility in responding to changes in the market (Davenport & Harris, 2007).

CONCLUSION

Opportunity orientation is a vital strategy for entrepreneurial firms seeking to thrive in today's fast-paced and competitive business environment. By actively identifying, evaluating, and exploiting new opportunities, companies can drive growth, foster innovation, and maintain a competitive edge.

The success of opportunity orientation depends on a company's ability to cultivate an opportunity-seeking culture, leverage market intelligence, and execute opportunities with agility. As the business landscape continues to evolve, companies that prioritize opportunity orientation will be better positioned to navigate challenges, capitalize on emerging trends, and achieve long-term success.

In conclusion, the examples of Netflix, Airbnb, Tesla, and Spotify demonstrate that opportunity orientation is not just a theoretical concept but a practical approach that can lead to transformative success. These companies have shown that by being proactive, flexible, and innovative, businesses can turn challenges into opportunities and maintain their relevance in a rapidly changing world.

Strategic Implication: Recognizing opportunity is not the same as pursuing it. Reassess whether your team has both the **discipline** and the **behavioral patterns** to convert insight into strategic action.

CHAPTER 6

TWO-WAY CUSTOMER CONTACT: BUILDING RELATIONSHIPS

Two-Way Customer Contact emphasizes the importance of engaging with customers in meaningful, reciprocal interactions. This behavior allows firms to build strong relationships, gain valuable insights, and enhance customer satisfaction. Two-Way Customer Contact is not just about communication; it is a strategic tool that can transform the way companies interact with their customers. By fostering open dialogue and active engagement, companies can build deeper relationships, gain valuable insights, and create a more customer-centric business model.

The importance of Two-Way Customer Contact cannot be overstated in today's business environment. With customers having more power and voice than ever before, businesses need to engage in meaningful dialogue to understand their customers' needs, preferences, and pain points. This form of communication is crucial for building trust and transparency, which are the foundations of long-term customer relationships (Grönroos, 1994). Historically, customer contact was primarily transactional, focusing on sales and customer-service inquiries. However, the rise of digital technologies, particularly social media, has revolutionized customer engagement. These platforms have enabled businesses to interact with customers in more personalized and immediate ways, shifting the focus from simple transactions to relationship-building.

For instance, the early days of retail primarily involved in-person sales, where the only customer feedback came from direct interactions with salespeople. With the advent of the internet and e-commerce, businesses began to receive customer feedback through online reviews and emails. Today, social media, mobile apps, and other digital platforms allow for real-time interaction, creating a more engaged and informed customer base (Chen & Popovich, 2003).

THE STRATEGIC IMPORTANCE OF TWO-WAY CUSTOMER CONTACT

Two-Way Customer Contact is not merely a communication strategy; it is a strategic tool that can transform a company's relationship with its customers. By fostering open dialogue and active engagement, businesses can gain valuable insights that drive innovation, improve customer experiences, and build a more customer-centric business model.

For instance, a company that actively listens to customer feedback can quickly identify issues with its products or services and make necessary adjustments. This proactive approach not only improves customer satisfaction but also reduces churn rates and enhances brand loyalty. Additionally, companies that engage in two-way communication are better positioned to develop products and services that truly meet their customers' needs, giving them a competitive edge in the market (Prahalad & Ramaswamy, 2004).

ENHANCING CUSTOMER SATISFACTION AND LOYALTY

Engaging in two-way communication allows companies to better understand their customers' needs, preferences, and pain points. This understanding enables companies to tailor their products, services, and customer experiences to meet those needs, leading to higher customer satisfaction and loyalty. For example, a software company that actively solicits user feedback through regular surveys and online forums uses this input to improve its product features and user interface. By addressing customer concerns and making continuous improvements, the company builds strong customer loyalty and reduces churn.

DRIVING CUSTOMER-CENTRIC INNOVATION

Two-Way Customer Contact provides direct access to customer insights, which can be a powerful driver of innovation. Companies can use this information to develop new products, enhance existing offerings, and create more personalized experiences that resonate with their target audience. For example, a consumer electronics brand that invites customers to participate in product development through beta testing programs receives feedback on new features and designs, which the company then incorporates into the final product, ensuring it meets customer expectations and stands out in the market.

BUILDING TRUST AND TRANSPARENCY

Open communication with customers fosters trust and transparency. When companies listen to their customers and respond to their feedback, they demonstrate that they value their customers' opinions and are committed to meeting their needs. This builds a strong foundation of trust, which is essential for long-term customer relationships. Trust and transparency are fundamental elements of a successful two-way customer communication strategy. Without trust, customers are unlikely to engage deeply with a brand, share valuable feedback, or remain loyal in the long term. Building trust involves more than just delivering quality products or services; it requires businesses to demonstrate integrity, honesty, and a genuine commitment to their customers' well-being.

For example, a financial-services company that uses social media to engage with customers can build trust by responding transparently to customer inquiries. This might involve clearly explaining the fees associated with certain services, openly discussing the risks involved in investment products, or providing regular updates about changes in policies. By doing so, the company not only addresses customer concerns but also positions itself as a trustworthy and customer-centric brand.

CASE STUDY: PATAGONIA—BUILDING TRUST THROUGH ENVIRONMENTAL RESPONSIBILITY

Patagonia, an outdoor clothing and gear company, is renowned for its commitment to environmental sustainability and social responsibility. This commitment is not just a marketing strategy; it is deeply embedded in the company's values and operations. Patagonia's transparency about its environmental impact, as well as its efforts to reduce that impact, has earned it the trust and loyalty of environmentally conscious consumers.

For instance, Patagonia's "Worn Wear" program encourages customers to buy used Patagonia gear or trade in their old items for store credit. This initiative not only promotes sustainable consumption but also builds trust by showing that Patagonia is willing to sacrifice short-term profits for the long-term health of the planet. The company's transparency about the environmental impact of its supply chain, as well as its advocacy for environmental causes, further reinforces its commitment to sustainability.

This case study highlights the importance of aligning company values with customer expectations and using transparency as a tool to build trust. Patagonia's success demonstrates that when companies are genuine in their commitment to ethical practices, they can foster deep, lasting relationships with their customers.

ENHANCING BRAND REPUTATION

Two-Way Customer Contact can significantly enhance a company's brand reputation. By engaging with customers in meaningful ways and demonstrating responsiveness, companies can build a positive image that resonates with both current and potential customers. For example, a retail brand that actively engages with customers on social media, responding to comments and questions in a timely and friendly manner, not only helps resolve customer issues quickly but also showcases the brand's commitment to customer service, enhancing its reputation.

TECHNIQUES FOR EFFECTIVE CUSTOMER ENGAGEMENT

COLLECTING AND ACTING ON CUSTOMER FEEDBACK

To effectively engage with customers, businesses must develop robust methods for collecting and acting on customer feedback. Surveys, social media listening, customer interviews, and feedback forms are some of the common techniques used to gather insights from customers. However, the real value lies in how businesses use this feedback to improve their offerings and enhance customer experience.

Surveys and questionnaires, for instance, provide a structured way to gather feedback on specific aspects of the business, such as product quality, service satisfaction, and overall customer experience. Companies can then analyze this data to identify trends and areas for improvement. Social media listening, on the other hand, offers a more dynamic approach, allowing businesses to monitor real-time conversations about their brand and respond to customer feedback promptly (Hennig-Thurau et al., 2010).

DEEPENING THE FEEDBACK LOOP

The feedback loop is a critical element in maintaining effective two-way customer communication. Businesses that excel in gathering, analyzing, and acting upon customer feedback can create a cycle of continuous improvement that not only satisfies customers but also drives innovation. However, to truly leverage this feedback loop, companies must go beyond simple collection methods and delve into the analysis that uncovers deeper customer insights.

One approach to deepening the feedback loop is through sentiment analysis, a method of processing and analyzing customer feedback to determine the emotional tone behind the words. By understanding how customers feel about their products and services, companies can prioritize which issues to address first and tailor their responses accordingly. This approach goes beyond traditional feedback methods, offering a more nuanced understanding of customer sentiments (Pang & Lee, 2008).

For example, a company that uses sentiment analysis on social media comments and customer reviews might discover that while customers appreciate the quality of their products, there is consistent frustration with the delivery times. Armed with this information, the company can then investigate its supply-chain operations and implement changes to reduce delivery times, thereby enhancing overall customer satisfaction .

Another advanced feedback method is predictive analytics, which can be used to anticipate customer needs and behaviors based on historical data. This approach allows companies to proactively address potential issues before they become widespread problems. For instance, if data indicates that customers who experience a specific issue with a product are likely to churn, the company can take preemptive action, such as offering a personalized solution or incentive, to retain those customers (Siegel, 2013).

THE ROLE OF FEEDBACK IN DRIVING CONTINUOUS IMPROVEMENT

Continuous improvement is a hallmark of companies that prioritize Two-Way Customer Contact. These businesses understand that customer needs and expectations are constantly evolving, and they must adapt to stay relevant. Feedback plays a crucial role in this process, serving as a roadmap for where improvements are needed and how they can be implemented (Evans & Lindsay, 2017).

In industries where innovation is key, such as technology or consumer electronics, customer feedback can be the difference between leading the market and falling behind. Companies that actively seek out customer input during the development phase of new products are more likely to create offerings that resonate with their target audience. This approach not only increases the chances of a successful product launch but also builds a stronger relationship with customers who feel their voices are heard and valued (Kumar & Pansari, 2016).

For example, a tech company developing a new software platform might engage with beta testers to gather feedback on user experience, functionality, and design. By incorporating this feedback into the final product, the company ensures that the software meets the needs of its users, which can lead to higher adoption rates and positive word-of-mouth marketing (Piller, Vossen, & Ihl, 2012).

CASE STUDY: MICROSOFT—EMBRACING CUSTOMER FEEDBACK FOR PRODUCT DEVELOPMENT

Microsoft provides an excellent example of how feedback can drive continuous improvement and innovation. The company has long been known for its customer-centric approach, particularly in the development of its flagship products like Windows and Office. Microsoft actively solicits feedback from a wide range of users, including enterprise customers, developers, and everyday consumers, through various channels such as user forums, surveys, and the Windows Insider Program.

The Windows Insider Program, in particular, has been a game-changer for Microsoft. This program allows users to test pre-release versions of Windows and provide feedback on new features and updates. Microsoft then uses this feedback to make adjustments before the official release, ensuring that the final product aligns with user needs and expectations. This iterative process not only helps Microsoft refine its products but also fosters a sense of community among its users, who feel invested in the development process (Microsoft, 2020).

The success of the Windows Insider Program is evident in the positive reception of recent Windows releases, which have been praised for their user-friendly features and stability. By embracing customer feedback and making it an integral part of the development process, Microsoft has been able to maintain its leadership position in the software industry while continually meeting the evolving needs of its users (Gawer & Cusumano, 2002).

TOOLS AND CHANNELS FOR TWO-WAY CUSTOMER CONTACT

CRM SYSTEMS

Customer-relationship-management (CRM) systems are integral tools for facilitating Two-Way Customer Contact. These systems allow businesses to manage and analyze customer interactions throughout the customer life cycle, with the goal of improving customer relationships, driving sales growth, and enhancing customer retention.

CRM systems centralize customer data, making it accessible to all relevant departments. This enables businesses to track customer interactions across various touchpoints, including phone calls, emails, social media, and in-person visits. By having a unified view of the customer, businesses can personalize their communications, respond more effectively to customer needs, and anticipate future demands.

For instance, a business might use CRM data to identify a customer's preferred communication channel, purchase history, and past feedback. This information allows the company to tailor its approach, offering products or services that align with the customer's interests, and addressing any past issues to improve the overall experience. Moreover, CRM systems often include features like automated follow-ups and reminders, ensuring that no customer interaction is overlooked (Buttle & Maklan, 2019).

EMAIL MARKETING

Email marketing remains one of the most effective channels for maintaining regular contact with customers. Unlike other forms of communication, email allows businesses to deliver personalized messages directly to the customer's inbox, where it can be accessed at their convenience. This makes email an ideal tool for nurturing relationships, delivering content, and promoting products or services.

To maximize the effectiveness of email marketing, businesses should focus on segmentation and personalization. By segmenting their email lists based on customer behaviors, preferences, and demographics, companies can send targeted messages that resonate with each group. Personalization further enhances engagement by addressing customers by name, recommending products based on past purchases, and offering exclusive deals tailored to their interests (Jenkins, 2016).

For example, an e-commerce retailer might use email marketing to send personalized product recommendations to customers based on their browsing history and past purchases. By doing so, the retailer not only increases the chances of a sale but also strengthens the customer's connection to the brand by demonstrating an understanding of their needs.

CHATBOTS AND LIVE CHAT

In today's fast-paced digital world, customers expect immediate responses to their inquiries. Chatbots and live chat tools provide businesses with the ability to meet this demand by offering real-time customer support on websites and mobile apps. These tools not only enhance the customer experience by providing instant assistance but also collect valuable data that can be used to improve products and services.

Chatbots, powered by artificial intelligence, can handle a wide range of customer queries, from answering frequently asked questions to guiding users through the purchasing process. More advanced chatbots can even provide personalized recommendations based on the customer's previous interactions with the brand. Live chat, on the other hand, offers a more human touch by allowing customers to interact directly with a support agent. This is particularly valuable for resolving complex issues that require a deeper understanding of the customer's needs (Adamopoulou & Moussiades, 2020).

SOCIAL MEDIA PLATFORMS

Social media platforms are arguably the most dynamic and versatile channels for Two-Way Customer Contact. These platforms allow businesses to engage with customers in real time, respond to feedback, and build a community around their brand. Social media also provides a public forum for customer feedback, where businesses can demonstrate their commitment to customer satisfaction by addressing issues promptly and transparently.

Different social media platforms offer unique opportunities for engagement. For example, Instagram and Pinterest are highly visual platforms, making them ideal for brands in industries like fashion, food, and lifestyle to showcase their products and engage with customers through visual content. Twitter, with its fast-paced and concise format, is often used for customer-service interactions and real-time communication. Facebook, with its extensive user base and diverse features, allows for a mix of content types and engagement strategies, from posts and stories to live videos and private messaging.

CASE STUDY: STARBUCKS—ENGAGING CUSTOMERS THROUGH "MY STARBUCKS IDEA"

Starbucks has been a leader in using Two-Way Customer Contact to enhance its product offerings and customer experience. One of the most notable examples of this is the "My Starbucks Idea" platform, which was launched in 2008 as a way to engage customers and involve them in the company's decision-making process.

The My Starbucks Idea platform allowed customers to submit ideas for new products, services, and store improvements. These ideas were then reviewed by Starbucks, and the most popular and feasible ones were implemented. This approach not only gave customers a voice in the company's operations but also helped Starbucks gather valuable insights that informed its business strategy.

For example, one of the ideas submitted through the platform was the introduction of a loyalty rewards program, which has since become a cornerstone of Starbucks's customer-engagement strategy. The program, which offers personalized rewards based on customers' purchasing habits, has been instrumental in driving customer retention and loyalty. Another idea that came to fruition was the expansion of non-dairy milk options, which addressed the growing demand for plant-based alternatives (Brenner, 2019).

The success of the My Starbucks Idea platform illustrates the power of Two-Way Customer Contact in driving innovation and strengthening customer relationships. By actively listening to and acting on customer feedback, Starbucks was able to create a more personalized and customer-centric experience, which has contributed to its continued growth and success.

MEASURING AND SUSTAINING CUSTOMER ENGAGEMENT

KEY METRICS FOR MEASURING ENGAGEMENT

Measuring customer engagement is crucial for understanding the effectiveness of Two-Way Customer Contact strategies. By tracking key metrics, businesses can gain insights into customer satisfaction, loyalty, and overall engagement, allowing them to make data-driven decisions that enhance the customer experience.

Customer Satisfaction (CSAT): This metric measures how satisfied customers are with a company's products, services, or interactions. It is typically assessed through post-interaction surveys or feedback forms. High CSAT scores indicate that customers are happy with their experience, while low scores highlight areas that need improvement (Oliver, 2014).

Net-Promoter Score (NPS): NPS is a popular metric used to gauge customer loyalty by asking customers how likely they are to recommend the brand to others on a scale of 0 to 10. Customers who score 9 or 10 are considered "Promoters," while those who score 0 to 6 are "Detractors." A higher NPS suggests a strong customer base that is likely to advocate for the brand (Reichheld, 2003).

Customer-Retention Rate: This metric tracks the percentage of customers who continue to do business with the company over a specific period. A high retention rate indicates strong customer relationships and effective engagement strategies. Retention is often linked to customer satisfaction and loyalty, making it a key indicator of long-term success (Heskett et al., 1994).

Customer Lifetime Value (CLTV): CLTV estimates the total revenue a customer is expected to generate over their lifetime with the company. This metric helps businesses prioritize high-value customers and tailor engagement strategies to maximize their value. By focusing on increasing CLTV, companies can improve profitability while building lasting relationships (Kumar & Shah, 2009).

Engagement Rate: Engagement rate measures customer interaction with content, such as email open rates, click-through rates, and social media interactions. High engagement rates indicate that the content is resonating with customers and encouraging them to take action. Monitoring engagement rates helps businesses refine their communication strategies to better align with customer preferences (Petersen et al., 2018).

CASE STUDY: AIRBNB—PERSONALIZED COMMUNICATION FOR ENHANCED CUSTOMER EXPERIENCE

Airbnb is a prime example of a company that has successfully leveraged Two-Way Customer Contact to build a personalized and responsive user experience. The company's platform allows both hosts and guests to interact directly with Airbnb, providing feedback and receiving support in real time.

Airbnb's approach to customer engagement includes personalized email communications, targeted notifications, and community engagement through its online forums. For instance, Airbnb uses machine-learning algorithms to analyze user behavior and send personalized recommendations for accommodations and experiences that match the customer's preferences. This personalized approach not only enhances the user experience but also drives higher engagement and booking rates (Guttentag, 2015).

In addition to personalized communication, Airbnb actively gathers feedback from its users to improve its platform. The company regularly surveys both hosts and guests to understand their needs and identify areas for improvement. This feedback is then used to refine the platform's features, such as the addition of new search filters, enhanced security measures, and improved customer support options.

The success of Airbnb's engagement strategies is reflected in its high customer satisfaction and retention rates. By focusing on personalized communication and actively incorporating customer feedback into its operations, Airbnb has created a platform that not only meets but exceeds user expectations, leading to sustained growth in a competitive market.

EXPANDING ON CUSTOMER-CENTRIC INNOVATION

THE INTERSECTION OF INNOVATION AND CUSTOMER INSIGHT

Innovation is often driven by a deep understanding of customer needs and preferences. Companies that excel in customer-centric innovation are those that not only listen to their customers but also anticipate their future needs. This proactive approach allows businesses to stay ahead of the competition by offering solutions that customers didn't even realize they needed (Christensen, Raynor, & McDonald, 2015).

To achieve this level of innovation, companies must invest in research and development (R&D) that is closely aligned with customer insights. This involves cross-functional collaboration between R&D teams, marketing, and customer service to ensure that new ideas are grounded in real-world customer experiences. Additionally, businesses should encourage a culture of experimentation, where employees are empowered to test new concepts and gather feedback early in the development process (Thomke, 2020).

For example, consider the automotive industry, where customer preferences are rapidly shifting toward electric and autonomous vehicles. Companies like Tesla have thrived by not only responding to these trends but also by pushing the boundaries of what is possible. Tesla's success can be attributed to its customer-centric approach, where feedback from early adopters is used to continuously refine its vehicles' performance, design, and features. This approach has positioned Tesla as a leader in the automotive industry, driving innovation in both electric vehicles and autonomous-driving technology (Stringham, Miller, & Clark, 2015).

CASE STUDY: TESLA—INNOVATING WITH THE CUSTOMER IN MIND

Tesla's approach to innovation exemplifies how a deep understanding of customer needs can drive technological advancements. From the outset, Tesla has positioned itself as a customer-centric company, focusing on building electric vehicles that not only meet but exceed customer expectations.

One of Tesla's key strategies is its over-the-air software updates, which allow the company to deliver new features and improvements to vehicles long after they have been purchased. This approach is unique in the automotive industry and has been a significant factor in Tesla's success. For example, when customers requested enhancements to the Autopilot feature, Tesla responded by releasing updates that improved the system's performance and safety. These updates were based on extensive feedback from Tesla drivers, demonstrating the company's commitment to listening to its customers and continuously improving its products (Boudette, 2017).

Tesla's direct sales model is another example of its customer-centric approach. By bypassing traditional dealerships, Tesla maintains a closer relationship with its customers, allowing for more personalized interactions and better control over the customer experience. This direct engagement has enabled Tesla to gather valuable insights that inform its product development and marketing strategies, further solidifying its position as a leader in automotive innovation (Matousek, 2019).

ENHANCING THE DISCUSSION ON THE FUTURE OF CUSTOMER CONTACT

THE RISE OF HYPER-PERSONALIZATION

As technology continues to evolve, the future of Two-Way Customer Contact will increasingly focus on hyper-personalization. This approach goes beyond traditional personalization by leveraging advanced data analytics and artificial intelligence to create highly individualized customer experiences (Lemon & Verhoef, 2016). Hyper-personalization allows companies to deliver the right message, at the right time, through the right channel, based on real-time customer data.

For example, a retail company might use hyper-personalization to send customized offers to customers based on their browsing history, purchase patterns, and even their social media activity. By predicting what a customer is likely to need or want next, the company can increase the effectiveness of its marketing efforts and enhance the overall customer experience (Arora, Dreze, Ghose, Hess, Iyengar, Jing, & Joshi, 2008).

Hyper-personalization also extends to customer service. With AI-powered chatbots and virtual assistants, companies can provide instant, personalized support that addresses customer inquiries based on their previous interactions with the brand. This level of service not only meets customer expectations for immediate responses but also builds stronger relationships by making customers feel understood and valued (Davenport, Guha, Grewal, & Bressgott, 2020).

THE INTEGRATION OF AI AND EMOTIONAL INTELLIGENCE

Another emerging trend in the future of customer contact is the integration of artificial intelligence (AI) with emotional intelligence (EI). While AI excels at processing data and automating tasks, EI involves the ability to recognize and respond to human emotions effectively. Combining these two elements allows companies to offer customer interactions that are not only efficient but also empathetic (Huang & Rust, 2021).

For instance, AI can be used to detect the emotional tone of a customer's voice or written communication and adjust the response accordingly. If a customer is frustrated, the AI system might prioritize the inquiry and route it to a human agent trained to handle sensitive situations. This blend of AI and EI helps companies maintain a human touch in their interactions, even as they scale their operations and automate more processes (Colson, 2019).

PREPARING FOR THE FUTURE: OMNICHANNEL STRATEGIES AND BEYOND

As customer expectations continue to rise, businesses must prepare for a future where omnichannel communication is not just a competitive advantage but a necessity. An effective omnichannel strategy ensures that customers receive a seamless experience across all touchpoints, whether they are interacting with the company online, via mobile, or in-store (Verhoef, Kannan, & Inman, 2015).

However, the future of customer contact will likely go beyond omnichannel to what some experts call "omni-experience." This concept involves creating a cohesive and consistent customer experience across all aspects of the brand, from marketing and sales to product use and customer support. Companies that succeed in delivering an omni-experience will be those that can integrate data, technology, and human touchpoints in a way that feels natural and effortless to the customer (Accenture, 2019).

CASE STUDY: SEPHORA—LEADING THE WAY WITH OMNICHANNEL AND OMNI-EXPERIENCE

Sephora, a global beauty retailer, is a pioneer in the use of omnichannel strategies to create a seamless and personalized customer experience. The company has successfully integrated its online and offline channels, allowing customers to move effortlessly between its website, mobile app, and physical stores.

One of Sephora's most notable innovations is its Virtual Artist feature, which uses augmented reality (AR) to let customers try on makeup virtually. This feature is available both on the Sephora app and in-store, where customers can use in-store tablets to experiment with different looks. The Virtual Artist feature not only enhances the shopping experience but also provides Sephora with valuable data on customer preferences, which can be used to personalize future interactions (Danziger, 2018).

Sephora's success in creating an omni-experience extends to its loyalty program, which is integrated across all channels. Customers can earn and redeem points whether they shop online or in-store, and they receive personalized offers based on their purchase history. This approach has helped Sephora build a loyal customer base that appreciates the convenience and personalization offered by the brand (Nagle, 2018).

Sephora's focus on omnichannel and omni-experience strategies demonstrates the importance of integrating technology, data, and human touchpoints to meet the evolving needs of today's customers. As the future of customer contact continues to unfold, businesses that follow Sephora's lead will be well positioned to thrive in an increasingly complex and competitive marketplace.

CONCLUSION

Two-Way Customer Contact is a powerful strategy for entrepreneurial firms looking to build strong, lasting relationships with their customers. By engaging in open, reciprocal communication, companies can gain valuable insights, drive customer-centric innovation, and enhance customer satisfaction and loyalty.

The success of Two-Way Customer Contact depends on the ability to create meaningful interactions, leverage the right channels, and sustain engagement over time. As the business landscape continues to evolve, companies that prioritize two-way communication will be better positioned to meet customer expectations, differentiate themselves in the market, and achieve long-term success.

The future of customer engagement will be shaped by new

technologies, such as AI, AR, and voice technology, and a deeper emphasis on personalization and real-time interaction. By staying ahead of these trends and continuously refining their customer engagement strategies, businesses can build strong, enduring relationships with their customers.

Strategic Implication: Dialogue—not just data—is the lifeblood of Market Orientation. Leadership should ask: Do we really listen to customers in ways that shape our behavior, or are we simply broadcasting louder?

CHAPTER 7

VALUE CREATION THROUGH ALLIANCES: COLLABORATING FOR SUCCESS

Value Creation Through Alliances involves forming strategic partnerships and collaborations to enhance a firm's capabilities, resources, and market reach. These alliances can provide access to new markets, technologies, and expertise, thereby driving growth and innovation. This chapter delves into the significance of alliances, the techniques for forming and maintaining partnerships, strategies for leveraging alliances for growth, and the challenges and solutions in managing these collaborations. Through robust case studies, we will illustrate how successful companies have used alliances to drive innovation and achieve substantial growth.

DEFINITION AND KEY CONCEPTS

Strategic alliances are partnerships that enhance an organization's capabilities, resources, and market reach. According to Das and Teng (2000), these alliances involve collaborating with other organizations to achieve mutual benefits, such as access to new markets, technologies, expertise, and resources, which are essential for driving growth and innovation.

KEY CONCEPTS IN VALUE CREATION THROUGH ALLIANCES INCLUDE:

Mutual Benefit: Ensuring that all parties involved in the alliance derive value from the collaboration.

Complementary Strengths: Leveraging the unique strengths and capabilities of each partner to achieve shared objectives.

Collaboration: Working together effectively to achieve common goals and overcome challenges.

Innovation: Co-creating new products, services, or solutions that enhance competitive advantage.

Techniques for Identifying and Establishing Partnerships: The success of alliances hinges on the ability to identify and establish partnerships that offer complementary strengths and resources. The process typically involves several key steps:

Identify Complementary Partners: Partners should offer resources or capabilities that complement each other. For instance, suppliers, distributors, technology providers, or businesses in related industries can form effective alliances.

Evaluate Strategic Fit: Assessing the strategic fit of potential partners by evaluating their goals, values, and capabilities ensures alignment with your organization's objectives and culture (Ireland, Hitt, & Vaidyanath, 2002).

Build Trust and Transparency: Establishing trust and transparency from the outset by clearly defining roles, responsibilities, and expectations is crucial. Open communication is key to a successful partnership (Gulati, 1998).

Negotiate Win-Win Agreements: Ensure that the terms of the alliance are mutually beneficial. Clearly outline the benefits, risks, and rewards for all parties involved (Parkhe, 1993).

STRATEGIES FOR EFFECTIVE COLLABORATION

Once an alliance is formed, maintaining the relationship requires ongoing effort and strategic management. Effective collaboration strategies include:

Regular Communication and Coordination: Maintaining open lines of communication and regular coordination helps build trust and ensures alignment on goals and strategies (Ring & Van de Ven, 1994).

Joint Planning and Execution: Collaborating on planning and executing joint initiatives, including setting shared goals and developing action plans, is essential for the success of the alliance (Doz & Hamel, 1998).

Conflict Resolution: Establishing mechanisms for resolving conflicts and addressing issues that arise during collaboration helps maintain a positive and productive relationship (Jehn, 1995).

Performance Measurement: Monitoring the performance of the alliance using key metrics allows for regular reviews of progress and necessary adjustments to achieve desired outcomes (Spekman, Forbes, Isabella, & MacAvoy, 1998).

The Role of Trust in Strategic Alliances: Trust is the cornerstone of any successful alliance. It serves as the foundation upon which collaboration, communication, and shared goals are built. Without trust, even the most strategically sound partnerships can falter. Building trust in strategic alliances requires time, consistent behavior, and transparency between partners.

TRUST IS BUILT THROUGH SEVERAL KEY PRACTICES:

Consistency in Actions: Partners need to demonstrate reliability by consistently meeting their commitments and delivering on promises. This includes adhering to deadlines, fulfilling agreed-upon roles, and being dependable in communication.

Transparency: Open and honest communication is crucial. Partners should share relevant information, including potential risks, challenges, and opportunities, to build mutual understanding and trust. This transparency fosters an environment where partners feel confident in the alliance's direction and decisions.

Mutual Respect: Respecting each partner's expertise, opinions, and contributions helps in creating a positive working relationship. It also encourages a collaborative atmosphere where both parties feel valued.

Once trust is established, maintaining it requires ongoing effort:

Regular Communication: Frequent and open communication helps in addressing issues as they arise and keeps both parties aligned on goals and expectations. Regular updates, meetings, and informal check-ins can reinforce trust and prevent misunderstandings.

Conflict Resolution: How conflicts are managed can either strengthen or weaken trust. Partners should have clear, agreed-upon processes for resolving disputes, and should approach conflicts with a mindset of collaboration rather than competition.

Accountability: Each partner must take responsibility for their actions within the alliance. Holding each other accountable for agreed-upon tasks and outcomes ensures that trust remains intact.

IMPACT OF TRUST ON ALLIANCE SUCCESS

Trust significantly impacts the success of an alliance. High levels of trust lead to better collaboration, more innovative outcomes, and a greater willingness to share resources and information. Conversely, a lack of trust can result in communication breakdowns, missed opportunities, and ultimately, the dissolution of the partnership. For example, the alliance between Toyota and its suppliers is often cited as a model of trust-based collaboration. Toyota's approach to supplier relationships, characterized by long-term commitments and mutual support, has led to a highly efficient and innovative supply chain (Dyer & Nobeoka, 2000).

TECHNIQUES FOR USING ALLIANCES TO DRIVE GROWTH

Alliances can be leveraged to drive growth through various strategies:

Access to New Markets: Alliances can facilitate entry into new markets and expansion of the customer base. Partners often provide valuable market insights, distribution channels, and local expertise (Contractor & Lorange, 2002).

Technology and Innovation: Collaborating with partners to co-create new products, services, or solutions can lead to breakthrough innovations by combining resources and expertise (Hagedoorn, 1993).

Resource Sharing: Partners can achieve economies of scale and reduce costs by sharing technology, facilities, and talent (Dyer & Singh, 1998).

Enhanced Capabilities: Alliances enhance an organization's capabilities by accessing the skills and knowledge of partners, such as technical expertise, market knowledge, and operational efficiencies (Lavie, 2006).

EXAMPLES OF SUCCESSFUL ALLIANCES

Spotify and Uber: Spotify partnered with Uber to enhance the ride-sharing experience by allowing passengers to control the music during their ride. This alliance provided added value to both Spotify and Uber customers, strengthening their market positions (Wagner, 2017).

Apple and Nike: Apple and Nike collaborated to integrate Apple's technology into Nike's fitness products, resulting in innovative products like the Apple Watch Nike+ and enhancing the customer experience for both brands (Nisen, 2013).

APPLE AND IBM: A STRATEGIC ALLIANCE FOR ENTERPRISE SOLUTIONS

The Apple-IBM alliance not only revolutionized enterprise mobility but also set a precedent for how consumer technology can be adapted for business environments. The partnership led to the development of mobile applications that combined IBM's big data and analytics capabilities with Apple's intuitive design and user experience. These applications were tailored to various industries, including health care, retail, and banking, offering solutions that improved operational efficiency and decision-making.

For instance, in health care, the alliance produced apps that allowed doctors and nurses to access patient data in real time, improving patient care and streamlining administrative processes. The success of this alliance is evident in the significant adoption of these applications by Fortune 500 companies, contributing to Apple's growing presence in the enterprise market and solidifying IBM's leadership in analytics and business intelligence.

This case exemplifies how strategic alliances can go beyond mere collaboration to create transformative impacts across entire industries. The Apple-IBM alliance leveraged both companies' strengths to address critical business challenges, setting a new standard for enterprise solutions.

RENAULT-NISSAN-MITSUBISHI ALLIANCE: DRIVING GLOBAL AUTOMOTIVE LEADERSHIP

The Renault-Nissan-Mitsubishi Alliance is one of the most significant examples of how long-term, multicompany alliances can drive industry leadership. The alliance allowed the companies to share research and development costs, standardize platforms, and achieve economies of scale, which were crucial for competing in the highly competitive automotive industry. This collaboration was particularly beneficial in the development of electric vehicles (EVs) and autonomous-driving technology.

By pooling their resources, the alliance partners were able to accelerate the development of EVs, making them more affordable and accessible to consumers. This strategic move positioned the alliance as a leader in the EV market, with models like the Nissan Leaf becoming one of the best-selling electric cars globally. The alliance's focus on innovation also enabled it to stay ahead of regulatory changes and consumer demand shifts toward more sustainable transportation options.

This case highlights the importance of strategic alliances in enabling companies to respond to industry trends and technological advancements more rapidly than they could individually. The Renault-Nissan-Mitsubishi Alliance demonstrates how collaborative innovation can lead to significant market advantages and long-term success.

STARBUCKS AND PEPSICO: EXPANDING THE READY-TO-DRINK COFFEE MARKET

The Starbucks-PepsiCo alliance is a classic example of how partnerships can help companies penetrate new markets and create new product categories. By combining Starbucks's expertise in coffee with PepsiCo's extensive distribution network, the two companies were able to create a new market segment for ready-to-drink coffee beverages. This partnership not only expanded Starbucks's product offerings but also allowed it to reach a broader consumer base beyond its traditional café customers.

The success of the Frappuccino product line is a testament to the power of strategic alliances in creating new revenue streams. The partnership also allowed Starbucks to diversify its product portfolio, reducing its reliance on in-store sales and increasing its presence in the retail sector. For PepsiCo, the alliance provided an opportunity to expand its beverage portfolio with a high-margin, premium product, enhancing its competitive position in the non-alcoholic beverage market.

This case illustrates how alliances can help companies leverage each other's strengths to create innovative products and enter new markets successfully. The Starbucks-PepsiCo partnership is a model for how companies can use alliances to drive growth and profitability.

COMMON CHALLENGES IN ALLIANCES

Managing alliances comes with its set of challenges, which include:

Cultural Differences: Organizational culture differences can lead to misunderstandings and conflicts. Establishing common ground and fostering a collaborative culture is essential (Lane & Lubatkin, 1998).

Resource Allocation: Ensuring that both parties allocate sufficient resources to the alliance can be challenging. Clear agreements and regular reviews can help manage resource commitments (Das & Teng, 1998).

Risk Management: Alliances involve risks, including dependence on partners and potential conflicts. Conducting thorough risk assessments and developing mitigation strategies are vital (Das & Teng, 2001).

Performance Measurement: Measuring the success of an alliance can be complex. Establishing clear metrics and regularly reviewing performance ensures alignment with goals (Ireland, Hitt, & Vaidyanath, 2002).

SOLUTIONS AND STRATEGIES FOR OVERCOMING CHALLENGES

To overcome these challenges, organizations can employ the following strategies:

Cultural Integration: Foster cultural integration by promoting mutual understanding and respect. Conduct joint training sessions and team-building activities to build trust and collaboration (Sirmon & Hitt, 2009).

Resource Planning: Develop detailed resource plans outlining each party's commitments. Regularly review resource allocation and adjust as needed to support the alliance (Lavie, 2006).

Risk Mitigation: Identify and evaluate potential risks and develop strategies to mitigate them, including contingency planning, regular risk assessments, and proactive communication (Dyer & Singh, 1998).

Regular Performance Reviews: Conduct regular performance reviews to assess the progress of the alliance. Use key metrics to measure success and identify areas for improvement (Ireland, Hitt, & Vaidyanath, 2002).

TECHNIQUES FOR FORMING AND MAINTAINING ALLIANCES

The techniques for forming and maintaining alliances include:

Identify Complementary Partners: Seek partners offering complementary strengths and resources. This can include suppliers, distributors, technology providers, or other businesses in related industries (Das & Teng, 2000).

Negotiating Win-Win Agreements: Ensure that alliances are mutually beneficial by clearly defining roles, responsibilities, and expectations to create a strong foundation for collaboration (Ireland, Hitt, & Vaidyanath, 2002).

Regular Communication and Coordination: Maintaining open lines of communication and regular coordination helps build trust and ensures alignment on goals and strategies (Ring & Van de Ven, 1994).

Joint Innovation Initiatives: Collaborate with partners on innovation projects. Combining resources and expertise can lead to the development of new products, services, or solutions (Hagedoorn, 1993).

EXPLORATION OF ADDITIONAL TYPES OF ALLIANCES

PUBLIC-PRIVATE PARTNERSHIPS (PPPS)

Public-private partnerships (PPPs) are a unique form of alliance where government entities collaborate with private companies to deliver public services or infrastructure projects. These partnerships are often used in sectors such as transportation, health care, and education, where significant investments are required, and the public sector seeks to leverage private-sector efficiency and expertise.

One of the most notable examples of a successful PPP is the London Underground's Public-Private Partnership, where private companies were brought in to help manage and improve the city's subway system. While the partnership faced challenges, it ultimately led to significant upgrades in infrastructure and service delivery, demonstrating the potential of PPPs to enhance public services.

PPPs offer several benefits, including risk-sharing, access to private capital, and the ability to leverage private sector innovation and management practices. However, they also require careful planning and clear agreements to ensure that public interests are protected, and the partnership delivers the intended benefits.

STRATEGIC CONSORTIA

Strategic consortia are alliances where multiple companies within an industry come together to pursue a common goal, such as setting industry standards, conducting joint research, or entering new markets collectively. These consortia allow companies to share the costs and risks associated with large-scale projects that would be too challenging to undertake alone.

An example of a strategic consortium is the GENIVI Alliance, a consortium of automotive manufacturers and suppliers that came together to develop an open-source software platform for in-vehicle infotainment systems. By collaborating, the consortium members were able to accelerate the development of the technology, reduce costs, and ensure compatibility across different vehicle brands, benefiting both the industry and consumers. Strategic consortia can be particularly effective in industries where technological advancements and standardization are critical for market success. They enable companies to pool their resources and expertise, driving innovation and creating new opportunities for growth.

THE ROLE OF DIGITAL TRANSFORMATION IN ALLIANCES

The rise of digital platforms has fundamentally changed how companies form and manage alliances. Platforms such as cloud computing, big-data analytics, and artificial intelligence are enabling more efficient collaboration by providing tools for real-time communication, data sharing, and joint decision-making. These technologies allow companies to work together more closely, even across geographical boundaries, enhancing the speed and effectiveness of their collaborations.

For example, digital-supply-chain platforms allow companies to share data with their partners in real time, improving coordination and reducing inefficiencies. Similarly, big-data analytics can provide insights into market trends and consumer behavior, helping alliance partners to make more informed decisions and tailor their strategies accordingly. Digital platforms also facilitate the creation of ecosystems, where multiple companies can collaborate within a shared digital environment. These ecosystems can drive innovation by bringing together diverse participants, including start-ups, established companies, and research institutions, to work on joint projects and share resources.

CYBERSECURITY AND TRUST IN DIGITAL ALLIANCES

As companies increasingly rely on digital platforms for collaboration, cybersecurity becomes a critical concern. The sharing of sensitive data between alliance partners can expose both parties to cyber threats, making it essential to implement robust security measures. Trust is a key factor in digital alliances, and companies must ensure that their digital platforms are secure and that data is protected. Establishing clear cybersecurity protocols and agreements between alliance partners is essential to mitigate risks and build trust. Companies should also invest in technologies such as blockchain, which can enhance transparency and security in digital transactions.

DIGITAL TRANSFORMATION AND COMPETITIVE ADVANTAGE

Digital transformation is not just about adopting new technologies; it's about using these technologies to create new business models and competitive advantages. In the context of alliances, digital transformation can enable companies to innovate faster, respond more quickly to market changes, and deliver more value to customers. For example, the strategic alliance between Microsoft and Adobe to integrate their cloud services is a case where digital transformation has been leveraged to enhance both companies' competitive positions. By combining Microsoft's cloud infrastructure with Adobe's creative and marketing software, the alliance has created a powerful platform for digital marketing and customer engagement, benefiting both companies and their customers.

CULTURAL INTELLIGENCE IN MANAGING GLOBAL ALLIANCES

Cultural intelligence (CQ) is the ability to understand and manage cultural differences effectively. In global alliances, where partners often come from different cultural backgrounds, CQ is critical for building strong, collaborative relationships. Cultural differences can impact communication, decision-making, and management practices, leading to misunderstandings and conflicts if not properly managed.

For example, in a cross-cultural alliance between a US-based company and a Japanese firm, differences in communication styles and business practices can lead to challenges. The US company may prefer direct communication and quick decision-making, while the Japanese firm may emphasize consensus-building and a more hierarchical approach. Understanding these differences and adapting communication and management practices accordingly is essential for the success of the alliance.

BUILDING CULTURAL COMPETENCE

Building cultural competence involves not only understanding cultural differences but also developing the skills to navigate them effectively. This can include training programs, cross-cultural workshops, and hiring or developing culturally aware leaders who can bridge cultural gaps. Incorporating cultural intelligence into alliance management can lead to better collaboration, stronger relationships, and more successful outcomes. Companies that invest in cultural competence are better equipped to manage global alliances and leverage the diversity of their partners to drive innovation and growth.

CULTURAL INTEGRATION STRATEGIES

Cultural integration is often a key challenge in mergers and acquisitions as well as in strategic alliances. Developing strategies for integrating different cultures involves creating a shared vision, establishing common values, and promoting mutual respect and understanding. One effective approach is to create cross-cultural teams that bring together members from different cultural backgrounds to work on joint projects. This not only facilitates knowledge sharing but also helps build trust and collaboration across cultural boundaries.

Another strategy is to establish a clear governance structure that reflects the cultural values of all partners. This can include setting up joint leadership teams, creating cultural advisory boards, and implementing cultural integration programs that align the alliance's goals with the cultural strengths of each partner.

THE ROLE OF LEADERSHIP IN MANAGING ALLIANCES

Leadership plays a critical role in the success of strategic alliances. Effective leaders can steer the alliance through challenges, inspire collaboration, and drive the partnership toward achieving its goals.

VISIONARY LEADERSHIP

Visionary leaders are essential in alliances, particularly in setting the long-term direction and ensuring that both partners are aligned with this vision. They can articulate a compelling future for the alliance that motivates all stakeholders. Leaders who can envision the future potential of the alliance are better equipped to guide it through periods of uncertainty and change.

For example, the leadership of Carlos Ghosn in the Renault-Nissan-Mitsubishi Alliance is often credited with the success of this partnership. Ghosn's ability to create a shared vision and foster collaboration across different cultures and organizations was instrumental in the alliance's growth and success (Rothaermel, 2013).

COLLABORATIVE LEADERSHIP

Collaborative leadership emphasizes teamwork, open communication, and joint problem-solving. Leaders who adopt this style encourage input from all partners, facilitate consensus-building, and promote a culture of mutual respect. Collaborative leaders are particularly effective in managing complex alliances where multiple stakeholders are involved.

CULTURAL INTELLIGENCE IN LEADERSHIP

In global alliances, cultural intelligence (CQ) is a critical leadership trait. Leaders with high CQ are adept at navigating cultural differences and can bridge the gaps that often arise in international partnerships. They are sensitive to cultural nuances and can adapt their leadership style to suit the cultural contexts of their partners.

REAL-WORLD CHALLENGES AND SOLUTIONS IN ALLIANCES

Alliances, while beneficial, are not without their challenges. Below are some common challenges faced in alliances, along with real-world examples of how these challenges have been successfully managed.

CHALLENGE: DIVERGING OBJECTIVES

One common challenge in alliances is the divergence of objectives over time. As markets evolve, partners may find that their strategic goals no longer align. This was the case in the alliance between Daimler and Chrysler. Initially formed to create a global automotive powerhouse, the partnership eventually faltered due to differences in corporate culture, management styles, and strategic priorities. The companies ultimately split, highlighting the importance of aligning long-term objectives (Vlasic & Stertz, 2000).

SOLUTION: REGULAR STRATEGIC ALIGNMENT MEETINGS

To address diverging objectives, successful alliances often implement regular strategic alignment meetings. These meetings provide a forum for partners to reassess their goals, make necessary adjustments, and ensure that the alliance continues to serve both parties' interests. The Renault-Nissan-Mitsubishi Alliance, for example, regularly reviews its strategic objectives to maintain alignment across its global operations.

CHALLENGE: CULTURAL DIFFERENCES

Cultural differences can create significant barriers to effective collaboration in alliances. These differences can manifest in communication styles, decision-making processes, and management practices.

SOLUTION: CROSS-CULTURAL TRAINING AND INTEGRATION PROGRAMS

One solution to this challenge is to implement cross-cultural training and integration programs. These programs help partners understand and respect each other's cultural norms and practices, fostering a more collaborative environment. The merger of Air France and KLM is a notable example where cultural integration was critical to the partnership's success. Despite significant cultural differences, the companies implemented a comprehensive integration program that included cross-cultural training and the establishment of joint leadership teams to manage cultural issues (Gittell, 2005).

CHALLENGE: INEFFECTIVE COMMUNICATION

Poor communication can derail an alliance, leading to misunderstandings, conflicts, and missed opportunities. Effective communication is crucial for ensuring that all partners are on the same page and that the alliance operates smoothly.

SOLUTION: ESTABLISHING CLEAR COMMUNICATION PROTOCOLS

To overcome communication challenges, alliances should establish clear communication protocols that define how, when, and through which channels partners will communicate. These protocols should include regular meetings, updates, and reporting structures to ensure that all parties are informed and aligned.

For instance, the alliance between Procter & Gamble (P&G) and its suppliers is known for its strong communication protocols. P&G has implemented a robust communication framework that includes regular meetings, real-time data sharing, and joint problem-solving sessions, which have contributed to the success of its supplier partnerships .

MANAGING AND SUSTAINING ALLIANCES: BEST PRACTICES

Once an alliance is formed, managing and sustaining it require ongoing effort and attention. Entrepreneurial marketers must focus on maintaining the health of the partnership, ensuring that it continues to deliver value over time (Gulati, 1998).

Regular Performance Reviews: Regular performance reviews are essential for ensuring that the alliance is meeting its objectives and delivering the expected value. These reviews provide an opportunity to assess progress, identify any issues, and make adjustments as needed (Spekman et al., 1998).

Adapting to Changing Conditions: Alliances must be flexible enough to adapt to changing market conditions, technological advancements, and evolving business needs. This adaptability is crucial for sustaining the value of the partnership over time (Lavie, 2006).

Fostering Collaboration and Innovation: Successful alliances are built on a culture of collaboration and innovation. Partners should encourage their teams to work together, share ideas, and explore new ways to create value (Hagedoorn, 1993).

Resolving Conflicts Effectively: Conflicts are inevitable in any alliance, but how they are managed can make or break the partnership. It is important to have mechanisms in place for resolving conflicts quickly and fairly, ensuring that they do not escalate and undermine the relationship (Jehn, 1995).

Celebrating Successes: Recognizing and celebrating the successes of the alliance can help strengthen the partnership and build morale among the teams involved. Celebrating milestones, achievements, and the value created through the alliance reinforces the commitment of both parties and motivates them to continue working together (Spekman et al., 1998).

CASE STUDIES: VALUE CREATION THROUGH ALLIANCES

To illustrate the power of Value Creation Through Alliances, let's review this chapter's previously discussed case studies of companies that have successfully leveraged partnerships to achieve significant growth and innovation.

APPLE AND IBM: A STRATEGIC ALLIANCE FOR ENTERPRISE SOLUTIONS

In 2014, Apple and IBM formed a strategic alliance to bring IBM's big data and analytics capabilities to Apple's mobile devices. The partnership aimed to create new business applications that would revolutionize the way enterprises operate. By combining Apple's user-friendly design with IBM's enterprise expertise, the alliance delivered powerful solutions that transformed industries like health care, finance, and retail (Apple Inc., 2014).

Outcome: The alliance enabled both companies to expand their market reach and create new revenue streams. Apple gained a stronger foothold in the enterprise market, while IBM enhanced its mobile capabilities, leading to the development of over one hundred industry-specific applications.

STARBUCKS AND PEPSICO: EXPANDING THE READY-TO-DRINK COFFEE MARKET

Starbucks and PepsiCo formed a strategic alliance in the 1990s to create and distribute ready-to-drink coffee beverages such as the popular Frappuccino. The partnership leveraged Starbucks's brand recognition and coffee expertise with PepsiCo's powerful distribution network and marketing capabilities. This alliance allowed Starbucks to rapidly enter and dominate the growing market for ready-to-drink coffee beverages (Starbucks Corporation, 1996).

Outcome: The alliance was highly successful, leading to the creation of a billion-dollar product line. The partnership allowed Starbucks to reach a broader consumer base, while PepsiCo benefited from adding a premium, high-demand product to its portfolio.

RENAULT-NISSAN-MITSUBISHI ALLIANCE: DRIVING GLOBAL AUTOMOTIVE LEADERSHIP

The Renault-Nissan-Mitsubishi Alliance is one of the most prominent examples of a successful automotive-industry partnership. Initially formed as an alliance between Renault and Nissan in 1999, the partnership later expanded to include Mitsubishi Motors. The alliance was created to share technology platforms and resources while maintaining the distinctiveness of each brand. This collaboration has allowed the partners to achieve significant cost savings, accelerate innovation, and expand their global market presence (Renault Group, 2019).

Outcome: The alliance has become one of the world's largest automotive groups, producing millions of vehicles annually across a wide range of markets. By pooling resources and technology, the alliance has been able to invest in electric vehicles, autonomous driving, and other advanced technologies.

SPOTIFY AND UBER: ENHANCING THE USER EXPERIENCE

In 2014, Spotify and Uber formed a strategic partnership that allowed Uber passengers to play their Spotify playlists during their rides. This alliance brought together two companies with complementary services to enhance the user experience, offering a unique and personalized service to customers of both brands (Wagner, 2017).

Outcome: The partnership helped differentiate Uber from other ride-hailing services by offering an added-value feature that appealed to music lovers. For Spotify, the alliance provided an opportunity to reach a wider audience and increase user engagement.

THE FUTURE OF VALUE CREATION THROUGH ALLIANCES

As the business landscape continues to evolve, the role of alliances in value creation is likely to become even more critical. The increasing complexity of markets, the rapid pace of technological change, and the growing importance of sustainability are all driving companies to seek partnerships that can help them navigate these challenges and seize new opportunities (Gulati, 1998).

EMBRACING CROSS-INDUSTRY ALLIANCES

The business world will likely see more cross-industry collaborations, where companies from different sectors come together to innovate and create new markets. These alliances can lead to the development of entirely new products and services that transcend traditional industry boundaries (Lavie, 2006).

LEVERAGING DIGITAL PLATFORMS FOR COLLABORATION

Digital platforms and ecosystems are enabling new forms of collaboration that were not possible before. These platforms allow companies to connect, share resources, and collaborate more efficiently, facilitating the creation of value through alliances on a global scale (Gawer & Cusumano, 2014).

FOCUSING ON SUSTAINABILITY THROUGH ALLIANCES

Sustainability is becoming a key focus for many companies, and alliances are playing a crucial role in advancing sustainable practices. By partnering with other organizations, companies can pool their resources and expertise to develop more sustainable products, processes, and business models (Hart & Dowell, 2011).

ADAPTING TO GLOBALIZATION AND LOCALIZATION

As globalization continues to expand, companies will need to balance global strategies with local market considerations. Alliances with local partners will be essential for navigating regional differences in culture, regulation, and consumer behavior, enabling companies to scale globally while remaining locally relevant (Johanson & Vahlne, 2009).

CONCLUSION

Value Creation Through Alliances is a powerful strategy for entrepreneurial firms looking to achieve sustained growth, innovation, and competitive advantage. By forming strategic partnerships, companies can amplify their capabilities, access new markets, accelerate innovation, and build stronger, more resilient businesses.

The success of these alliances depends on careful planning, clear communication, and a mutual commitment to creating value for all parties involved. As the business environment continues to evolve, the ability to form and manage effective alliances will remain a critical skill for entrepreneurial marketers.

The following chapters will explore how to integrate the principles of Value Creation Through Alliances with other Entrepreneurial Marketing strategies, providing practical tools, case studies, and insights to help firms implement these practices effectively and sustainably.

Strategic Implication: Firms that collaborate well compete better. Strategic alliances require not just partnerships, but behavioral readiness to co-create, share risk, and build value outside organizational boundaries.

CHAPTER 8

INFORMAL MARKETING RESEARCH: LISTENING TO YOUR GUT

In the dynamic and rapidly evolving landscape of modern business, traditional marketing research methods—while still valuable—are often too slow or rigid to respond effectively to changing consumer preferences and market conditions. This has led to an increased reliance on Informal Marketing Research, a method that leverages direct customer interactions, observations, and intuitive decision-making to gather insights quickly and adapt strategies accordingly (Carson, Cromie, McGowan, & Hill, 1995). Informal Marketing Research is particularly valuable for entrepreneurial firms and small businesses that may lack the resources for extensive formal studies but need to remain agile and responsive to stay competitive (Griffin & Hauser, 1993).

This chapter explores the importance of informal research techniques for collecting and analyzing data, strategies for integrating informal and formal research methods, and the benefits of using informal research to drive innovation. Through robust case studies, we will illustrate how successful companies use Informal Marketing Research to stay connected with their customers and make informed decisions, ultimately leading to greater market success.

DEFINITION AND KEY CONCEPTS

Informal Marketing Research involves gathering insights through less structured and more flexible methods such as direct customer interactions, observations, and intuition. This approach provides real-time, actionable insights that can complement more formalized research methods, such as surveys and focus groups (Carson et al., 1995). The key concepts of Informal Marketing Research include:

Direct Interaction: Engaging with customers through face-to-face conversations, phone calls, and online chats to gather immediate feedback (Leonard & Rayport, 1997).

Observation: Observing customer behavior in real-world settings to identify patterns and trends that may not be evident through formal research (Spiggle, 1994).

Intuition: Relying on gut instincts and accumulated experience to make informed decisions, particularly when formal data is either unavailable or inconclusive (Hayashi, 2001).

Flexibility: Adapting research methods based on the situation and the specific needs of the business, allowing for a more agile response to market changes (Griffin & Hauser, 1993). Historically, businesses relied heavily on formal market research methods such as surveys, focus groups, and quantitative analysis to guide decision-making. However, the rise of digital technologies and real-time communication has made informal research more accessible and valuable, particularly for small businesses and start-ups that need to respond quickly to market shifts (Pine & Gilmore, 1999). In today's fast-paced business environment, Informal Marketing Research is crucial for staying connected with customers and making agile, data-driven decisions (Spiggle, 1994).

THE IMPORTANCE OF INFORMAL RESEARCH FOR START-UPS AND SMALL BUSINESSES

For start-ups and small businesses, the stakes are high, and the resources are often limited. Formal market research, which can be expensive and time-consuming, may not always be a viable option. This is where Informal Marketing Research becomes indispensable. It offers a cost-effective and agile approach to gathering critical insights that can guide decision-making in these formative stages.

ADDRESSING RESOURCE CONSTRAINTS

Start-ups often operate with limited financial and human resources, making it challenging to conduct extensive formal research. Informal research methods, such as direct customer interactions, social media monitoring, and employee feedback, provide a more accessible means of gathering valuable data. According to Blank (2013), the lean start-up methodology emphasizes the importance of rapid iteration and customer feedback, which are core principles of informal research. By engaging directly with customers and observing their behavior, start-ups can make informed decisions without the need for costly research studies.

SPEED AND AGILITY

In the fast-paced world of start-ups, the ability to pivot quickly based on real-time insights is crucial. Informal research allows businesses to gather immediate feedback and adjust their strategies on the fly. Ries (2011) highlights that the "build-measure-learn" feedback loop is central to the lean start-up approach, enabling companies to test hypotheses quickly and refine their offerings based on customer input. This agility is often the difference between success and failure in the highly competitive start-up ecosystem.

BUILDING STRONG CUSTOMER RELATIONSHIPS

For small businesses, establishing strong, personal relationships with customers is often a key differentiator. Informal research, which relies heavily on direct interactions, helps businesses build these relationships by showing customers that their feedback is valued and acted upon. Hsieh (2010) notes that Zappos's success was built on a culture of listening to customers and exceeding their expectations, a strategy that was rooted in informal research practices.

TECHNIQUES FOR GATHERING INSIGHTS

Informal Marketing Research is inherently flexible, making it well suited for a variety of techniques that can be adapted to the specific needs of a business. Some of the most effective techniques include:

Customer Conversations: Engaging in regular conversations with customers to understand their needs, preferences, and pain points. This can be done through face-to-face interactions, phone calls, or online chats (Leonard & Rayport, 1997).

Observation: Observing customer behavior in real-world settings, such as retail stores, online platforms, or social media, helps identify patterns and trends that may not be captured through formal research (Spiggle, 1994).

Employee Insights: Leveraging insights from frontline employees who interact with customers daily. Their observations and experiences can provide valuable information about customer preferences and behaviors (Dabholkar, 1996).

Social Media Listening: Monitoring social media platforms for customer comments, reviews, and discussions about your brand. Engaging with customers by responding to their posts and addressing their concerns can provide a wealth of informal data (Pine & Gilmore, 1999).

CHALLENGES AND LIMITATIONS OF INFORMAL MARKETING RESEARCH

While Informal Marketing Research offers numerous benefits, it is not without its challenges. Relying too heavily on informal methods can introduce biases and lead to decisions based on incomplete or anecdotal evidence. It is important for businesses to recognize these limitations and take steps to mitigate them.

POTENTIAL FOR BIAS

One of the primary risks of informal research is the potential for bias. When decisions are based on observations or conversations with a limited group of customers, there is a risk that these insights may not be representative of the broader market. Carson et al. (1995) caution that while informal research can provide valuable insights, it is essential to validate these findings with more structured research methods to ensure they are not skewed by personal biases or outliers.

INCOMPLETE DATA

Informal research often relies on qualitative data, which, while rich in detail, may lack the comprehensiveness of quantitative data. This can lead to incomplete insights that may not fully capture the complexity of the market or customer behavior. Leonard and Rayport (1997) argue that while empathic design and informal research are powerful tools for innovation, they should be complemented by formal research to ensure a well-rounded understanding of customer needs.

DIFFICULTY IN SCALING

As businesses grow, the informal research methods that worked well in the early stages may become more challenging to scale. Larger organizations may struggle to maintain the same level of direct customer interaction or personalized feedback that smaller businesses can offer. To address this challenge, companies can leverage technology to scale their informal research efforts, as discussed in the next section.

THE ROLE OF TECHNOLOGY IN SCALING INFORMAL RESEARCH

Technology has revolutionized the way businesses conduct Informal Marketing Research, making it possible to scale these efforts while maintaining the agility and personal touch that characterize informal methods. Artificial intelligence (AI), machine learning, and big-data analytics are increasingly being used to enhance the efficiency and effectiveness of informal research.

AI AND MACHINE LEARNING

AI and machine-learning algorithms can process vast amounts of unstructured data, such as customer reviews, social media posts, and chat transcripts, to identify patterns and trends that might be missed by human analysts. This allows businesses to gather insights from a much larger pool of data, effectively scaling their informal research efforts without losing the depth of understanding. For example, HubSpot uses machine learning to analyze customer feedback and predict trends, helping them stay ahead of customer needs (Buttle, 2009).

SOCIAL MEDIA ANALYTICS

Social media platforms are a goldmine for informal research, providing real-time access to customer opinions and behaviors. Advanced social media analytics tools can track brand mentions, sentiment, and emerging trends across multiple platforms, giving businesses a comprehensive view of how their brand is perceived. Glossier, a beauty brand, uses social media analytics to gather informal insights from its highly engaged online community, allowing them to respond quickly to customer preferences (Weinstein, 2018).

CUSTOMER-RELATIONSHIP-MANAGEMENT (CRM) SYSTEMS

CRM systems integrate various data sources, including customer interactions, sales data, and social media feedback, to provide a holistic view of customer relationships. These systems can help businesses automate and scale their informal research efforts, ensuring that insights gathered from informal channels are effectively integrated into the overall strategy (Buttle, 2009).

DRIVING INNOVATION WITH INFORMAL RESEARCH

Informal research is not just a tool for understanding customer preferences—it is also a powerful driver of innovation. By staying closely connected to their customers and the broader market, businesses can identify emerging trends, uncover unmet needs, and develop innovative solutions that meet those needs before competitors do.

TECHNIQUES FOR USING INFORMAL INSIGHTS TO INNOVATE

Customer Co-Creation: Involving customers in the innovation process can lead to the development of products and services that better meet their needs. This can be done through crowdsourcing ideas, holding innovation contests, or running co-creation workshops where customers are invited to collaborate on product development (Prahalad & Ramaswamy, 2004). For example, LEGO has successfully used co-creation by inviting customers to submit their own designs for new LEGO sets. The best ideas are turned into actual products, which are then sold worldwide. This approach not only drives innovation but also deepens customer engagement with the brand.

Rapid Prototyping: Informal research enables businesses to quickly develop and test prototypes with real customers, gathering feedback that can be used to refine the product before it goes to market (Ries, 2011). This iterative process allows companies to make adjustments based on real-world data rather than assumptions. For instance, IDEO, a design firm known for its innovative approach, often employs rapid prototyping to test new product ideas with users, gathering insights that lead to further refinements.

Trend Spotting: By observing customer behavior and market dynamics, businesses can identify emerging trends that might not yet be visible through formal research methods (Gladwell, 2000). This ability to spot trends early can give companies a significant competitive advantage. Starbucks, for instance, has a history of identifying and capitalizing on emerging consumer preferences, such as the rise of artisanal coffee and the demand for plant-based milk alternatives, by using informal observations from their baristas and customer interactions.

Continuous Improvement: A culture of continuous improvement, driven by regular informal feedback from customers and employees, can help businesses stay ahead of the curve (Deming, 1986). Toyota's famous "Kaizen" approach is a prime example of how continuous improvement, fueled by informal feedback, can lead to significant innovations in product quality and manufacturing efficiency.

DROPBOX: PIONEERING CLOUD STORAGE WITH USER-CENTRIC DESIGN

Dropbox's success can be largely attributed to its user-centric approach to product development, which relied heavily on informal research methods. The company's early focus on gathering feedback from a small group of tech-savvy users allowed it to refine its product rapidly, ensuring that it met the needs of a broad user base. By continually iterating based on informal user feedback, Dropbox was able to create a simple, intuitive, and highly functional product that set the standard for cloud storage services (Blank, 2013).

INNOCENT DRINKS: INNOVATING WITH CUSTOMER FEEDBACK

Innocent Drinks has consistently used informal research to drive product innovation. By engaging directly with customers through social media and at events, the company has been able to identify emerging trends and customer preferences, which have informed the development of new products. For example, Innocent introduced its "Super Smoothies" line in response to growing consumer interest in health and wellness. This new product range, which features smoothies fortified with vitamins and nutrients, was directly influenced by customer feedback and market observations, demonstrating how informal research can lead to successful product innovation (Hatch & Schultz, 2008).

AIRBNB: REVOLUTIONIZING TRAVEL WITH INFORMAL RESEARCH

Airbnb, the online marketplace for lodging, exemplifies how informal research can drive innovation and disrupt traditional industries. In its early days, Airbnb's founders conducted informal research by staying with hosts and interviewing them to understand their experiences and pain points. This hands-on approach allowed them to identify key issues, such as the need for better guest verification processes and host support, which were critical to scaling the platform. The insights gathered from these informal interactions were instrumental in shaping Airbnb's customer experience and helped the company grow into a global leader in the travel industry (Gallagher, 2017).

UBER: USING INFORMAL RESEARCH TO ADAPT AND INNOVATE

Uber's success is also rooted in informal research. The ride-hailing giant started by engaging directly with drivers and passengers to understand their needs and concerns. These informal interactions helped Uber refine its app interface, improve the driver experience, and introduce new features, such as UberPOOL, which allows passengers to share rides and reduce costs. Uber's ability to quickly adapt to feedback and innovate based on informal research has been a key factor in its rapid expansion and dominance in the global market (Stone, 2017).

THE ROLE OF INFORMAL RESEARCH IN CUSTOMER RELATIONSHIP MANAGEMENT (CRM)

Customer Relationship Management (CRM) is a strategic approach to managing interactions with current and potential customers. While formal CRM systems are typically data-driven and rely on structured information, informal research plays a crucial role in enriching the customer experience by providing nuanced insights that structured data might overlook.

PERSONALIZED CUSTOMER EXPERIENCES

Informal research enables businesses to tailor their offerings to individual customer preferences, enhancing the overall customer experience. For example, Ritz-Carlton is known for its personalized service, which is largely informed by informal feedback gathered through direct interactions with guests. Employees at Ritz-Carlton hotels are trained to listen to guest preferences and observations, which are then used to personalize the guest experience, such as remembering a guest's preferred room type or favorite meal (Pine & Gilmore, 1999).

RESPONSIVE CUSTOMER SERVICE

By staying attuned to customer needs through informal research, businesses can provide more responsive and proactive customer service. Zappos, an online shoe and clothing retailer, excels in this area by encouraging its customer-service representatives to engage in informal conversations with customers, often going above and beyond to meet their needs. This approach has helped Zappos build a reputation for exceptional customer service and has fostered a loyal customer base (Hsieh, 2010).

BUILDING TRUST THROUGH TRANSPARENCY

Informal research can reveal what matters most to customers, allowing businesses to address these concerns openly and transparently. For example, Patagonia, the outdoor clothing brand, has used customer feedback gathered through informal channels to enhance its transparency about its supply-chain practices. By sharing detailed information about the environmental impact of its products, Patagonia has built strong trust and loyalty among its customers (Chouinard & Stanley, 2016).

FOSTERING CUSTOMER ADVOCACY

Engaging with customers through informal research can turn them into brand advocates, who promote the brand to others through word-of-mouth. Harley-Davidson, for instance, has cultivated a passionate community of brand advocates by regularly engaging with customers at events and through online forums. These informal interactions have helped the company foster a strong brand community and increase customer loyalty (Schouten & McAlexander, 1995).

INTEGRATING INFORMAL AND FORMAL RESEARCH

While informal research is valuable on its own, combining it with formal research methods, as resources allow, can provide a more comprehensive understanding of the market and customers. This integration allows businesses to benefit from the strengths of both approaches, leading to more informed decision-making.

BENEFITS OF COMBINING RESEARCH METHODS

Comprehensive Insights: Formal research methods provide quantitative data and statistical analysis, while informal research offers qualitative insights that add depth and context. For example, while a formal survey might indicate that a certain percentage of customers prefer a specific product feature, informal research can help uncover the reasons behind that preference (Griffin & Hauser, 1993).

Enhanced Decision-Making: Combining informal and formal research methods enhances decision-making by providing multiple perspectives. This approach allows businesses to validate assumptions made from informal research with hard data, reducing the risk of biased decisions (Leonard & Rayport, 1997).

Agility and Flexibility: Informal research enables businesses to quickly adjust their strategies based on real-time feedback, while formal research provides a solid foundation for long-term strategic planning.

This combination allows businesses to be both agile in the short term and strategic in the long term (Pine & Gilmore, 1999).

WARBY PARKER: INTEGRATING INFORMAL FEEDBACK WITH FORMAL SURVEYS

Warby Parker effectively combines informal research with formal methods to continually refine its product offerings. For instance, while the company uses informal customer feedback gathered in-store to make quick adjustments to its product line, it also conducts formal surveys to gather broader insights from a larger customer base. This combination of methods allows Warby Parker to stay agile while ensuring that its strategic decisions are based on comprehensive data (Leonard & Rayport, 1997).

TRADER JOE'S: MERGING EMPLOYEE OBSERVATIONS WITH MARKET RESEARCH

Trader Joe's integrates informal research gathered through employee interactions with customers with formal market-research data. This approach allows the company to validate trends observed in-store with broader market data, ensuring that its product decisions are both customer-driven and supported by formal research (Spiggle, 1994).

IMPLEMENTING INFORMAL MARKETING RESEARCH IN ENTREPRENEURIAL FIRMS

For entrepreneurial firms, the ability to adapt quickly to market changes is crucial for survival and growth. Informal Marketing Research provides the agility needed to stay competitive in dynamic markets. Implementing informal research within a company requires a commitment to continuous learning, customer engagement, and strategic adaptation. This section explores how entrepreneurial firms can effectively integrate Informal Marketing Research into their operations.

CULTIVATING A RESEARCH-ORIENTED CULTURE

To successfully implement Informal Marketing Research, it must become part of the company's culture. This involves encouraging employees at all levels to gather and share insights from their interactions with customers, competitors, and the market. A research-oriented culture empowers employees to be proactive in seeking out information and using it to inform decisions. For example, 3M, a company known for its innovation, encourages a culture of informal research by giving employees the freedom to explore new ideas and gather customer feedback without the constraints of formal processes. This approach has led to the development of numerous successful products, including the Post-it Note, which was born out of informal research and experimentation (Kelley & Littman, 2001).

TRAINING EMPLOYEES IN INFORMAL RESEARCH TECHNIQUES

Providing employees with training in informal research techniques can enhance the effectiveness of data collection. This might include teaching them how to engage customers in meaningful conversations, observe customer behavior, and use social media for market insights. Training ensures that all employees are equipped with the skills needed to gather and interpret informal data.

For instance, Ritz-Carlton provides its employees with training on how to listen for and act on customer preferences, a practice that has been key to the hotel chain's success in delivering personalized service. This training empowers employees to notice details that can enhance the guest experience, such as remembering a guest's favorite drink or preferred room temperature, which can then be used to surprise and delight customers (Pine & Gilmore, 1999).

INTEGRATING INFORMAL RESEARCH INTO STRATEGIC PLANNING

Informal research should be integrated into the strategic-planning process, ensuring that the insights gathered are used to inform business decisions and long-term strategies. This involves regular review and discussion of the data collected through informal channels. For example, at Procter & Gamble (P&G), informal research plays a crucial role in the company's strategy development. P&G often relies on informal insights gathered from consumer interactions and observations to identify unmet needs and emerging trends. These insights are then used to guide the development of new products and marketing strategies, helping P&G maintain its leadership position in the consumer-goods industry (Lafley & Martin, 2013).

LEVERAGING TECHNOLOGY TO ENHANCE INFORMAL RESEARCH

Technology can significantly enhance Informal Marketing Research by providing tools for data collection, analysis, and communication. This might include social media monitoring tools, customer-relationship-management (CRM) systems, and mobile apps for gathering customer feedback. For instance, Salesforce's CRM platform allows businesses to track and analyze customer interactions, including informal feedback gathered through support channels and social media. By leveraging this technology, businesses can gain a deeper understanding of customer preferences and behavior, which can be used to inform marketing strategies and improve customer satisfaction (Buttle, 2009).

INFORMAL MARKET ANALYSIS: UNDERSTANDING THE MARKET BEYOND THE NUMBERS

While formal market research provides valuable quantitative data, informal market analysis offers insights that are often more nuanced and actionable. Entrepreneurial marketers often rely on their intuition, observations, and direct interactions with customers and industry players to understand the market. This section explores various strategies for conducting informal market analysis.

DIRECT CUSTOMER INTERACTION

Direct interaction with customers, such as through informal conversations, social media engagement, or participation in community events, provides valuable insights that may not be captured through formal surveys or focus groups. These interactions allow businesses to gather real-time feedback and adjust their strategies accordingly. For example, Zappos, known for its exceptional customer service, actively engages with customers through social media and phone interactions. These informal conversations help Zappos identify customer pain points and preferences, which are then used to improve their service and product offerings (Hsieh, 2010).

OBSERVATIONAL RESEARCH

Observational research is another key component of informal market analysis. Entrepreneurial marketers observe customer behavior, competitor activities, and industry trends in real time, gaining insights that inform their strategies. For example, Starbucks often relies on observational research to identify emerging consumer trends. By observing customer orders and preferences in-store, Starbucks can quickly adapt its menu to include new offerings, such as the introduction of oat milk as a dairy alternative, which was a direct response to growing consumer demand observed through informal channels (Pine & Gilmore, 1999).

INDUSTRY NETWORKING AND INTELLIGENCE GATHERING

Industry events and networking functions provide opportunities to gather informal insights about competitors and market trends. These events often offer a behind-the-scenes look at what competitors are planning.

For instance, Tesla's CEO Elon Musk is known for attending industry conferences and engaging with peers in informal settings to gather insights about emerging technologies and competitor strategies. This informal research often informs Tesla's innovation roadmap, allowing the company to stay ahead of the competition in the rapidly evolving electric-vehicle market (Vance, 2015).

LEVERAGING SOCIAL MEDIA INSIGHTS

Social media is a valuable tool for informal market analysis. Entrepreneurial marketers monitor social media platforms to understand customer sentiment, track trending topics, and identify potential opportunities or threats in the market. For example, Glossier, a beauty brand, uses social media to gather informal insights from its highly engaged online community. By monitoring conversations and feedback on platforms like Instagram and Twitter, Glossier has been able to identify customer preferences and rapidly respond with new product launches that meet these demands (Gilliland, 2026).

CONCLUSION

Informal Marketing Research is a powerful tool for entrepreneurial firms, providing valuable insights that can drive innovation, enhance customer relationships, and strengthen competitive advantage. By embracing informal research methods, businesses can gather real-time data that is often more nuanced and actionable than formal studies. However, it is essential to recognize the limitations of informal research and to complement it with formal methods when necessary.

By integrating informal research into the strategic-planning process, cultivating a research-oriented culture, and leveraging technology to scale efforts, businesses can ensure that they are making informed decisions that are grounded in a deep understanding of their customers and the market. As the business landscape continues to evolve, those companies that prioritize informal research and adapt quickly to changing conditions will be better positioned to thrive in the long term.

The following chapters will build on the concepts discussed here, exploring specific strategies for integrating informal research with formal methods, leveraging technology for market analysis, and implementing best practices for data-driven decision-making in entrepreneurial firms.

INTUITION IN INFORMAL MARKET RESEARCH

In the context of Entrepreneurial Marketing and the Strategic Orientation Index™ (SOI™), intuition serves as a critical mechanism for making sense of incomplete, ambiguous, or rapidly changing information. While traditional marketing research relies on structured surveys, statistical models, and formal data collection methods, intuition reflects a different but complementary mode of knowledge creation. It represents the tacit, experience-based capacity to interpret weak signals, recognize patterns, and act decisively when formal information is lacking. Scholars across psychology, strategy, and entrepreneurship have long debated the role of intuition in decision-making, particularly in dynamic markets where uncertainty is high and formal data lags reality (Kahneman, 2011; Sadler-Smith, 2016).

Intuition in this sense is not mystical or irrational; rather, it is an emergent property of cognitive processing shaped by prior experience, domain knowledge, and repeated exposure to relevant stimuli (Dane & Pratt, 2007). In Entrepreneurial Marketing, intuition is often what allows managers to identify opportunities before competitors, to anticipate customer needs not yet visible in formal metrics, and to pivot in response to subtle shifts in cultural or industry dynamics. Within the SOI™ framework, intuition particularly undergirds **informal marketing research**, where entrepreneurs rely on direct customer contact, informal networks, and Market Immersion to guide strategy.

DEFINING INTUITION IN STRATEGIC AND ENTREPRENEURIAL CONTEXTS

The academic literature defines intuition in multiple ways, but a common thread is that it represents a **nonconscious process of recognizing patterns and reaching judgments without deliberate analytical reasoning** (Khatri & Ng, 2000). In organizational studies, intuition has been described as "affectively charged judgments that arise through rapid, nonconscious, and holistic associations" (Dane & Pratt, 2007, p. 40). For entrepreneurs, intuition often functions as a cognitive shortcut in uncertain contexts where time, information, or resources constrain formal analysis (Sadler-Smith, 2016).

This conceptualization aligns with dual-process theories of cognition. System 1 thinking, as Kahneman (2011) explains, is fast, automatic, and intuitive, while System 2 is slow, deliberate, and analytical. Both systems are essential, but in entrepreneurial settings where speed and adaptability matter, System 1 intuition is disproportionately valuable. Entrepreneurs often cannot wait for full datasets; instead, they must act on incomplete evidence, guided by intuitive pattern recognition informed by prior experience.

INTUITION AS TACIT KNOWLEDGE IN ACTION

One way to understand intuition is as the activation of **tacit knowledge** (Polanyi, 1966). Tacit knowledge consists of understandings that individuals cannot fully articulate but which shape perception and action—such as knowing how to ride a bicycle, recognizing a familiar face, or sensing when a market shift is underway. For entrepreneurs and marketers, tacit knowledge comes from accumulated exposure to customer interactions, industry norms, cultural shifts, and competitive behavior. Intuition mobilizes this tacit knowledge by enabling quick judgments without the need for conscious deliberation.

Empirical research supports this perspective. Mitchell et al. (2005) found that expert entrepreneurs rely heavily on cognitive scripts—deeply embedded mental models—that allow them to quickly interpret new situations and act effectively. These scripts are not innate but developed over time through repeated exposure, failure, and learning. Intuition, in this framing, is less about guessing and more about **recognizing familiar patterns in novel circumstances**. Informal Market Research provides fertile ground for these scripts to form, as entrepreneurs are constantly exposed to unstructured information from customers, suppliers, and competitors.

INTUITION AND INFORMAL MARKET RESEARCH

Informal Market Research emphasizes **close contact with customers, alliances, feedback loops, and immersive observation** (Morris, Schindehutte, & LaForge, 2002). These activities rarely generate neatly quantifiable data but instead provide raw impressions, anecdotes, and patterns that can guide strategy. Intuition becomes the processing mechanism by which entrepreneurs transform such fragments into meaningful insights.

For example, a series of casual conversations with customers may not constitute statistically significant evidence, but an experienced entrepreneur may intuitively recognize a recurring pain point that signals opportunity. Similarly, observing shifts in online communities or social media chatter may provide faint signals that, when filtered through intuitive judgment, forecast an emerging trend. This is precisely where formal market research would be too slow or insensitive to pick up changes, while intuition translates informal observations into strategic foresight.

STRENGTHS AND RISKS OF INTUITIVE JUDGMENTS

Intuition carries both advantages and risks. Its strengths lie in **speed, adaptability, and the ability to synthesize complex information holistically** (Dane & Pratt, 2007). For Entrepreneurial Marketing, these strengths are invaluable, as they allow firms to respond before competitors, identify latent needs, and experiment with emerging opportunities.

However, intuition is also vulnerable to **biases, overconfidence, and misinterpretation**. Cognitive biases such as availability heuristics, confirmation bias, and affective distortions can lead decision-makers to overweight certain signals and ignore contradictory evidence (Kahneman, 2011). Entrepreneurs who mistake personal hunches for grounded intuition risk pursuing opportunities that lack real market traction. Therefore, while intuition is indispensable in Informal Market Research, it must be complemented by mechanisms for validation—such as rapid experimentation, customer feedback, or triangulation with formal data when available.

KNOWLEDGE CORRIDORS AND THE FOUNDATIONS OF INTUITIVE JUDGMENT

One of the most influential explanations for entrepreneurial intuition lies in the concept of **knowledge corridors**. Shane (2000) argued that individuals are only able to perceive entrepreneurial opportunities through prior knowledge that channels their attention in specific directions. These corridors are built from prior experience, technical expertise, social networks, and cultural familiarity, which collectively shape the information an individual can process. Intuition emerges from within these corridors: It is not a random or mystical insight but a recognition of patterns that the decision-maker is uniquely equipped to see because of their background.

For example, an engineer steeped in battery technology may intuitively recognize the commercial potential of a new chemistry that others view as incremental. A marketing manager immersed in consumer behavior research may sense an unmet emotional need in a product category before surveys confirm it. Both are drawing on tacit knowledge embedded in their corridors to make intuitive leaps. Empirical studies confirm that entrepreneurs with deep industry experience identify and exploit opportunities more effectively, not because they have more data but because their prior knowledge gives them the cognitive schemas to "connect the dots" (Shane & Venkataraman, 2000).

In this sense, intuition is not detached from evidence—it is evidence filtered through lived expertise. Informal Market Research amplifies this effect by exposing individuals to unstructured signals, anecdotes, and observations, which their knowledge corridors help interpret. Managers and entrepreneurs with broader, richer corridors are more likely to perceive high-value opportunities from weak signals, while novices may miss or misinterpret the same cues. Thus, cultivating knowledge corridors through experience, education, and deliberate exposure is foundational to building reliable intuition in marketing and strategy.

MARKET IMMERSION AS A CATALYST FOR INTUITION

Closely related to knowledge corridors is the role of **Market Immersion**—the practice of embedding oneself deeply in the customer, cultural, and competitive environments. Immersion provides the raw material for intuition by creating repeated exposure to market cues, customer behaviors, and contextual subtleties that structured research often overlooks. In Entrepreneurial Marketing, immersion often takes the form of direct customer contact, ethnographic observation, or participation in industry communities (Brown, 2008).

The importance of immersion has been highlighted in design-thinking research, where empathic observation of users produces insights that are difficult to access through formal methods (Leonard & Rayport, 1997). Similarly, Entrepreneurial Marketing scholars emphasize that entrepreneurs often gather knowledge by "being in the market," engaging informally with lead customers, suppliers, and even competitors (Morris et al., 2002). These immersive experiences allow intuitive judgments to form because they provide the repeated, nuanced inputs that System 1 processes can encode and recognize (Kahneman, 2011).

For intuition to be effective, decision-makers must not only accumulate experience but remain close to the evolving realities of their markets. A marketing leader who spends significant time with frontline sales teams, customer-service logs, or user forums will build a far more refined intuitive sense than one who relies solely on quarterly reports. In this way, immersion extends and strengthens knowledge corridors, ensuring that intuitive insights are not based on outdated schemas but continuously updated through lived market interaction.

INTEGRATING KNOWLEDGE CORRIDORS AND MARKET IMMERSION

When considered together, knowledge corridors and Market Immersion provide a dual foundation for intuition in Informal Market Research. Knowledge corridors determine **what kinds of signals** an individual is predisposed to recognize, while immersion supplies **fresh streams of signals** that refine and recalibrate intuitive judgments. Without corridors, intuition risks being uninformed and idiosyncratic; without immersion, it risks becoming stale or disconnected from current market dynamics.

Scholarly work supports this integrative view. Corbett (2007) argued that opportunity recognition is not a onetime event but an iterative cycle where prior knowledge (corridors) and active learning (immersion) interact to create new insights. Entrepreneurs and marketing leaders who actively immerse themselves in markets are more likely to enrich their corridors with updated experience, thereby making their intuition both sharper and more adaptive. In the SOI™ framework, this interplay underscores why informal research behaviors such as customer contact, alliances, and Market Immersion are not "soft skills" but core drivers of strategic orientation.

CONCLUSION

Intuition is an indispensable element of Informal Market Research, particularly in entrepreneurial contexts where information is incomplete and time horizons are compressed. Far from being irrational, intuition reflects the rapid activation of tacit knowledge, the application of prior experience through knowledge corridors, and the absorption of signals through Market Immersion. Its value lies in enabling entrepreneurs and marketing leaders to recognize patterns, act decisively, and adapt strategies in real time.

Yet intuition must be balanced with humility and verification. While it provides speed and adaptability, it is vulnerable to bias and overconfidence. The most effective use of intuition, therefore, is not as a replacement for data but as a complement—guiding the direction of exploration, framing hypotheses, and informing rapid cycles of experimentation and feedback.

For organizations seeking to enhance their strategic orientation, cultivating intuition means investing in people's knowledge corridors, encouraging deep Market Immersion, and legitimizing informal research practices alongside formal analytics. In this way, intuition becomes not a fallback in the absence of data, but a structured competency embedded in the everyday behaviors of strategic leaders.

Strategic Implication: Insight doesn't always come from surveys. Entrepreneurial firms must legitimize informal market sensing—learning from intuition, sales feedback, and unstructured insight to move faster.

CHAPTER 9

MARKET IMMERSION: THINKING LIKE YOUR CUSTOMER

In today's highly competitive business landscape, Market Immersion is a critical strategy that enables companies to deeply understand their market environment, including customer behavior, industry trends, and competitive dynamics. This approach, which goes beyond traditional market research, enhances customer satisfaction, improves decision-making, and provides a sustainable competitive advantage (Narver & Slater, 1990). This chapter explores the importance of Market-Immersion techniques for staying connected to the market, strategies for fostering a customer-centric culture, and the benefits of thinking like your customer. Several case studies will illustrate how successful companies use Market Immersion to stay ahead in the industry and make informed decisions.

DEFINITION AND KEY CONCEPTS

Market Immersion is defined as the deep engagement and continuous learning within a market environment, focusing on customer behavior, industry trends, and competitive analysis (Kohli & Jaworski, 1990).

Unlike traditional market research that often relies on periodic surveys or focus groups, Market Immersion involves real-time, experiential learning through direct customer engagement and continuous monitoring of market dynamics. This concept transcends traditional market research by prioritizing direct engagement and experiential learning over passive data collection. Market Immersion is crucial for companies seeking to remain agile and responsive in a rapidly changing business environment. Historically, businesses relied heavily on market research and analysis to understand their customers and market dynamics. However, Market Immersion goes beyond these traditional methods by emphasizing direct engagement and experiential learning. This approach is particularly relevant in today's fast-paced business environment, where staying connected with customers and anticipating changes are crucial for making informed decisions (Kohli & Jaworski, 1990). The practice of Market Immersion has roots in the evolution of market research and competitive strategy. As markets became more dynamic and customer expectations more sophisticated, traditional methods proved insufficient. Market Immersion evolved as a response to this need, emphasizing the importance of real-time, qualitative insights gained through direct engagement with customers and the market.

TECHNIQUES FOR MARKET IMMERSION

Effective Market Immersion requires a combination of techniques that help businesses stay closely connected to their market environment. These techniques include:

Customer Empathy: Understanding customer needs involves developing empathy toward customers by delving into their lives, understanding their challenges, and identifying their pain points. This can be achieved through direct interactions, ethnographic research, and customer-journey mapping (Leonard & Rayport, 1997). The cornerstone of Market Immersion is customer empathy. This involves not just understanding what customers want but also why they want it. By empathizing with customers, businesses can design products and services that truly meet their needs. For example, Apple's success with the iPhone can be attributed to its deep understanding of how people use technology in their daily lives. Apple's designers and engineers immerse themselves in the customer experience, ensuring that every feature of the iPhone aligns with user needs and desires (Isaacson, 2011).

Industry Networking: Staying connected with industry trends requires active participation in industry events, conferences, and trade shows. Networking with peers and experts provides valuable insights and keeps businesses informed about the latest developments (Ibarra & Hunter, 2007). Industry networking is not just about attending events and conferences; it involves building meaningful relationships with industry peers, influencers, and thought leaders. Through these connections, businesses can gain insights into emerging trends and technological advancements. A notable example is Tesla's approach to networking within the automotive and tech industries. By fostering strong relationships with key suppliers and industry experts, Tesla has been able to stay ahead of the curve in electric-vehicle technology (Vance, 2015).

Competitive Analysis: Continuously monitoring competitors' activities is essential for identifying potential threats and opportunities. Techniques such as SWOT analysis, benchmarking, and market intelligence platforms help businesses maintain a competitive edge (Barney, 1991). Competitive analysis goes beyond tracking what competitors are doing; it involves understanding the strategic motivations behind their actions. For instance, Amazon's competitive analysis is so thorough that it often leads to proactive moves, such as launching Amazon Prime to preempt potential threats from other e-commerce platforms (Stone, 2013).

Market-Trend Analysis: Regularly analyzing market trends and emerging technologies helps businesses anticipate changes and adapt their strategies accordingly. This involves environmental scanning, trend spotting, scenario planning, and technology adoption (Christensen, 1997).

In today's fast-paced world, businesses must stay ahead of market trends to remain relevant. This requires a proactive approach to trend analysis, where businesses not only track current trends but also predict future shifts. Nike's ability to spot the rise of athleisure as a significant market trend allowed it to capitalize on this shift early, resulting in the successful launch of new product lines that cater to this growing market.

IMPORTANCE OF UNDERSTANDING CUSTOMER NEEDS

Customer empathy is the basis for Market Immersion, enabling businesses to create products, services, and experiences that genuinely resonate with their target audience. By understanding customers on a deeper level, businesses can tailor their offerings to meet specific needs, ultimately enhancing customer satisfaction and loyalty (Brown & Duguid, 2000).

THE PSYCHOLOGY BEHIND CUSTOMER EMPATHY

Understanding customer needs requires a psychological approach. It is not enough to know what customers want; businesses must also understand the underlying psychological factors that drive their behavior. This includes motivations, emotions, and cognitive biases that influence purchasing decisions. For example, understanding the concept of loss aversion—a principle in behavioral economics that suggests people prefer to avoid losses rather than acquire equivalent gains—can help businesses design more effective marketing strategies (Kahneman, 2011).

TECHNIQUES FOR BUILDING CUSTOMER EMPATHY

Ethnographic Research: Conducting ethnographic research allows businesses to observe and understand customers' behaviors, preferences, and pain points in their natural environment (Wasson, 2000). Ethnography, originally a tool of anthropologists, has become invaluable in market research. By observing customers in their natural environments, businesses can gain insights that are often missed in traditional research methods. For instance, Procter & Gamble's ethnographic studies in low-income households led to the development of products that are more affordable and better suited to the needs of these consumers (Aaker, 1991).

Customer-Journey Mapping: Creating customer-journey maps visualizes the steps customers take when interacting with a brand, helping identify pain points and areas for improvement (Richardson, 2010). A customer-journey map is more than a visual representation; it is a tool that helps businesses understand every interaction a customer has with their brand. This technique reveals pain points and moments of delight, enabling businesses to enhance the customer experience. For example, Disney uses customer-journey mapping to ensure that every aspect of a visitor's experience at their parks is optimized, from the moment they buy their ticket to the time they leave the park.

Customer Interviews: One-on-one interviews with customers provide deeper insights into their needs, motivations, and challenges. This qualitative data can inform product development and marketing strategies (Kvale, 1996).

Persona Development: Developing detailed customer personas based on insights gathered from customer research helps businesses tailor their marketing strategies to different segments of their customer base (Cooper, 1999). Developing customer personas helps businesses segment their audience and tailor their strategies accordingly. These personas are based on demographic data, psychographics, and behavioral patterns. For instance, HubSpot uses detailed personas to guide its content-marketing efforts, ensuring that each piece of content speaks directly to the needs of its target-audience segments (Halligan & Shah, 2009).

BENEFITS OF INDUSTRY NETWORKING

Industry networking is another crucial aspect of Market Immersion. It involves actively participating in industry events, conferences, and trade shows to stay informed about the latest trends and developments.

Networking provides valuable insights and opportunities for collaboration, helping businesses stay ahead of the competition (Cross & Parker, 2004).

THE ROLE OF SOCIAL CAPITAL IN INDUSTRY NETWORKING

Social capital, the networks of relationships among people who work in a particular field, plays a crucial role in industry networking. High social capital allows businesses to access valuable resources, such as information, advice, and support, which can lead to better decision-making and innovation. For example, Silicon Valley's success is partly due to the high social capital within its tech community, where ideas and knowledge are freely exchanged, leading to rapid innovation and growth (Saxenian, 1994).

STRATEGIES FOR EFFECTIVE NETWORKING

Attend Industry Events: Regularly attending industry events ensures that businesses stay informed about the latest trends and developments. Engaging with industry peers and experts provides valuable insights that can inform strategic decisions (Ibarra & Hunter, 2007).

Join Industry Associations: Joining industry associations and organizations helps businesses stay connected with industry trends. Participation in events, webinars, and discussions provides additional insights (Porter, 1980).

Build Relationships: Building relationships with industry peers, experts, and influencers is essential for fostering collaboration and mutual learning. These relationships often lead to valuable partnerships and business opportunities (Granovetter, 1973).

Stay Informed: Keeping up with industry news, trends, and developments by subscribing to industry publications, blogs, and newsletters ensures that businesses stay ahead of the curve (Cross & Parker, 2004).

Build Strategic Alliances: Strategic alliances are formal partnerships between companies that complement each other's strengths. These alliances can lead to co-innovation, joint marketing efforts, and shared resources. For example, the partnership between Starbucks and Spotify allows both companies to enhance their customer experience by integrating music with the coffeehouse environment, creating a unique value proposition for customers (Schultz, 2019).

Leverage Digital-Networking Platforms: In today's digital age, networking is not limited to in-person interactions. Platforms like LinkedIn, Twitter, and industry-specific forums provide valuable opportunities for businesses to connect with peers, share insights, and stay informed about industry developments. Companies like IBM have successfully leveraged digital networking to build communities around their products and services, driving engagement and loyalty (Gerstner, 2002).

IMPORTANCE OF COMPETITIVE ANALYSIS

Competitive analysis is a vital component of Market Immersion, as it involves continuously monitoring and analyzing competitors' activities, products, and strategies. This helps businesses identify potential threats and opportunities, allowing them to adapt and stay competitive (Porter, 1980).

UNDERSTANDING COMPETITOR BEHAVIOR

Understanding competitor behavior involves more than just observing their actions; it requires analyzing the strategic thinking behind those actions. By understanding the motivations and goals of competitors, businesses can anticipate their next moves and develop strategies to counter them. For example, when Apple noticed that Microsoft was focusing heavily on business software, it shifted its strategy to emphasize design and user experience, leading to the creation of iconic products like the iMac and iPhone (Isaacson, 2011).

TECHNIQUES FOR COMPETITIVE ANALYSIS

SWOT Analysis: Conducting a SWOT analysis (Strengths, Weaknesses, Opportunities, Threats) helps businesses evaluate their competitive position relative to others in the market (Barney, 1991).

Benchmarking: Comparing key performance metrics with those of leading competitors helps identify areas for improvement and allows businesses to maintain a competitive edge (Camp, 1989).

Market-Intelligence Platforms: Utilizing market-intelligence tools and platforms enables businesses to gather data on competitors' activities, pricing strategies, and customer reviews (Porter, 1980).

Mystery Shopping: Engaging in mystery shopping allows businesses to experience competitors' products and services firsthand, identifying areas for improvement (Finn & Kayande, 1999).

Game-Theory Applications: Game theory, a branch of mathematics that studies strategic interactions, can be used to model competitive scenarios and predict competitor behavior. Companies like Google use game theory to analyze how competitors might respond to their strategic moves, such as changes in pricing or new product launches (Varian, 2009).

War Gaming: War gaming involves simulating a competitive scenario where a company's team takes on the role of a competitor, attempting to anticipate and counter the company's strategies. This technique helps businesses prepare for various competitive scenarios and develop robust strategies. For instance, the US military has used war gaming extensively, and the concept has been adapted by businesses like Ford to anticipate competitive responses in the automotive industry (Collis & Montgomery, 1995).

IMPORTANCE OF ANALYZING MARKET TRENDS

Regularly analyzing market trends and emerging technologies is essential for businesses to anticipate changes and adapt strategies accordingly. Staying informed about market dynamics enables firms to identify opportunities and mitigate risks (Christensen, 1997).

THE ROLE OF BIG DATA IN TREND ANALYSIS

Big data has revolutionized the way businesses analyze market trends. By leveraging vast amounts of data from various sources—such as social media, customer transactions, and IoT devices—businesses can identify trends with greater accuracy and speed. For example, Netflix uses big-data analytics to track viewer preferences and predict which types of content will be popular, allowing it to invest in original programming that resonates with its audience.

TECHNIQUES FOR MARKET-TREND ANALYSIS

Environmental Scanning: Regularly scanning the external environment for trends, changes, and potential opportunities involves analyzing market reports, industry publications, and economic indicators (Aguilar, 1967).

Trend Spotting: Identifying emerging trends and opportunities by observing customer behavior and market dynamics helps businesses develop new products, services, or business models (Crawford & Di Benedetto, 2011).

Scenario Planning: Developing multiple scenarios based on different market conditions allows businesses to plan strategic responses for each scenario, helping them stay prepared for various possible futures (Schoemaker, 1995).

Technology Adoption: Staying informed about emerging technologies and evaluating their potential impact on the industry enable businesses to adopt new technologies early and gain a competitive edge (Rogers, 2003).

Predictive Analytics: Predictive analytics uses historical data to forecast future trends. This technique is particularly useful in industries where demand fluctuates based on various factors, such as fashion or consumer electronics. Zara, for example, uses predictive analytics to forecast fashion trends and adjust its production accordingly, ensuring that it remains at the forefront of fast fashion (Capell, 2008).

Crowdsourcing Insights: Crowdsourcing involves gathering insights from a large group of people, often through online platforms. This approach can reveal emerging trends and consumer preferences that might not be apparent through traditional research methods. Companies like LEGO have successfully used crowdsourcing to gather ideas for new products, engaging their community and ensuring that new offerings align with customer desires (Robertson & Breen, 2013).

BENEFITS OF THINKING LIKE YOUR CUSTOMER

Enhanced Customer Satisfaction: Developing customer empathy and staying immersed in the market helps businesses create products, services, and experiences that resonate with their customers. This leads to enhanced customer satisfaction and loyalty, as customers feel understood and valued (Brown & Duguid, 2000).

Improved Decision-Making: Market Immersion and customer empathy provide valuable insights that inform decision-making. By understanding customers' needs, preferences, and challenges, businesses can make data-driven decisions that drive growth and innovation (Kohli & Jaworski, 1990).

Increased Competitive Advantage: Staying immersed in the market and continuously analyzing competitors' activities help businesses identify opportunities and stay ahead of the competition. This leads to increased competitive advantage and market leadership (Porter, 1980).

Enhancing Customer Loyalty: Customer loyalty is built on a foundation of trust and satisfaction. By thinking like their customers, businesses can create experiences that meet or exceed expectations, fostering loyalty. For example, Amazon's relentless focus on customer satisfaction, exemplified by initiatives like one-click purchasing and same-day delivery, has made it a leader in customer loyalty (Stone, 2013).

Improved Brand Perception: When businesses demonstrate that they truly understand and care about their customers, it improves brand perception. This positive perception can lead to increased customer engagement, advocacy, and sales. For instance, Dove's "Real Beauty" campaign, which focused on authentic representations of women, significantly improved the brand's perception and led to increased market share (Bulik, 2006).

CASE STUDIES OF BUSINESSES USING MARKET IMMERSION

PROCTER & GAMBLE: THE "LIVING IT" PROGRAM

Procter & Gamble (P&G) is renowned for its Market-Immersion strategies, particularly through its "Living It" program. This initiative involves executives and employees living with consumers to experience their daily routines and challenges firsthand. By immersing themselves in the lives of their customers, P&G gains deep insights into consumer needs, which informs product development and marketing strategies. This approach has been instrumental in the success of products like Tide and Pampers, which are designed to meet the specific needs of their target consumers (Aaker, 1991).

NIKE: STAYING CONNECTED WITH ATHLETES

Nike's success can be attributed to its Market-Immersion strategy of maintaining close relationships with athletes and sports communities. The company's extensive network of sponsored athletes, coaches, and trainers provides valuable insights into performance needs and emerging trends. This ongoing engagement with its target audience drives innovation in product design and marketing, allowing Nike to stay ahead in the competitive sportswear market.

WARBY PARKER: DISRUPTING THE EYEWEAR INDUSTRY

Warby Parker's Market-Immersion strategy involved identifying a significant pain point in the eyewear market: the high cost of prescription glasses. By understanding that consumers were frustrated with the lack of affordable, stylish eyewear options, Warby Parker disrupted the industry by offering high-quality glasses at a fraction of the traditional price. The company's direct-to-consumer model and innovative home try-on program were directly informed by its deep understanding of customer needs and preferences, leading to rapid growth and strong brand loyalty (Marquis and Velez-Villa, 2013).

MARKET IMMERSION: A DEEP DIVE INTO CUSTOMER UNDERSTANDING

At the heart of Market Immersion lies an intense focus on understanding the customer. This goes beyond traditional customer surveys and focus groups, requiring a more holistic and nuanced approach to capturing the true needs, desires, and behaviors of customers.

CASE STUDY: MARKET IMMERSION AT NIKE

Market Immersion is a critical dimension of Entrepreneurial Marketing (EM) and the Strategic Orientation Index™ (SOI™), reflecting the degree to which firms embed themselves in the lives, behaviors, and cultures of their customers. Rather than relying solely on formal market research methods, firms practicing Market Immersion cultivate deep, lived familiarity with customer contexts. This process generates tacit knowledge, strengthens intuition, and allows firms to anticipate emerging needs and cultural shifts before they become visible in mainstream data (Brown, 2008; Leonard & Rayport, 1997).

Nike, Inc., a global leader in sportswear and athletic innovation, provides a compelling case study of Market Immersion. From its origins as Blue Ribbon Sports in 1964 to its status as a multibillion-dollar brand today, Nike has consistently grounded its strategic orientation in immersion within sports subcultures and athlete communities. This case demonstrates how immersion operates as both a **marketing practice** and a **strategic orientation**, illustrating how firms can institutionalize customer proximity to fuel innovation, loyalty, and long-term growth.

MARKET IMMERSION DEFINED

Market Immersion differs from traditional market research in both scope and method. While surveys and focus groups extract discrete data points, immersion emphasizes **long-term, experiential engagement** with customer worlds. In management scholarship, it is often linked to ethnography, participant observation, and design-thinking practices, which stress "walking in the customer's shoes" to uncover latent needs (Leonard & Rayport, 1997). For entrepreneurial firms, immersion provides raw insights that feed Informal Marketing Research and strengthen intuition (Morris, Schindehutte, & LaForge, 2002).

Theoretically, Market Immersion aligns with Polanyi's (1966) concept of tacit knowledge and Shane's (2000) notion of knowledge corridors. By spending sustained time within customer environments, firms develop nuanced, often unarticulated insights that can be translated into product design, messaging, and strategic posture. Nike exemplifies how this immersion becomes not an occasional research exercise, but a **cultural orientation** embedded into organizational identity.

NIKE'S IMMERSIVE ORIENTATION

From the start, Nike positioned itself not merely as a shoe company but as an advocate and partner within the athletic community. Co-founder Bill Bowerman was himself a track coach at the University of Oregon, and early product innovations—such as the iconic waffle sole—emerged directly from his immersion in athletes' training contexts (Knight, 2016). This pattern persisted as Nike grew: Product teams were staffed with former athletes, collaborations with sports teams were prioritized, and the brand consistently invested in grassroots immersion.

Nike's global expansion maintained this principle. Rather than treating markets as homogenous, Nike embedded local teams into cultural contexts to adapt products and messaging. For instance, in emerging basketball markets such as China, Nike immersed itself in playground basketball culture, supporting tournaments, sponsoring athletes, and engaging with communities before basketball became mainstream . This immersion created authenticity, allowing Nike to align its brand with aspirational cultural movements.

IMMERSION IN CUSTOMER CULTURE

Nike's immersion extends beyond functional performance into cultural identity. The firm does not only ask how athletes perform but also how they live, what they value, and how they construct identity through sport. This immersion manifests in campaigns like *Just Do It*, which resonate because they tap into the cultural ethos of persistence and empowerment rather than product specifications (Knight, 2016).

Nike also engages in immersive storytelling by embedding itself in the broader cultural movements of the day. The *Dream Crazy* campaign featuring Colin Kaepernick reflected Nike's immersion in conversations about race, identity, and activism in sports. While risky, this campaign demonstrated Nike's ability to intuitively align with cultural undercurrents—something that traditional surveys might have failed to capture. By immersing in athlete narratives and social movements, Nike positioned itself not only as a sportswear provider but as a cultural leader.

INSTITUTIONALIZING IMMERSION: NIKE SPORT RESEARCH LAB

A hallmark of Nike's strategy is the Nike Sport Research Lab (NSRL), established to bring immersion into a more systematic framework. The NSRL employs biomechanists, engineers, and kinesiologists who conduct extensive testing with athletes in real-world and lab contexts (Holt & Cameron, 2010). Unlike traditional R&D that begins with product concepts, Nike's research starts with immersion into the physical and psychological demands athletes face.

This practice aligns with design-thinking principles, where empathic observation and user immersion precede solution development (Brown, 2008). For example, the Flyknit shoe line emerged not from a survey asking consumers what they wanted, but from immersive observation of runners' needs for lightweight, sustainable, and performance-oriented footwear. By embedding researchers in athletes' training regimens, Nike could translate subtle pain points into breakthrough innovations.

INFORMAL MARKET RESEARCH THROUGH IMMERSION

Nike also leverages immersion as a form of **informal market research**. Beyond laboratory studies, Nike maintains direct, ongoing contact with athletes at all levels—from professionals to everyday runners. Programs like Nike Run Clubs, grassroots tournaments, and training apps create reciprocal feedback loops, where Nike gains constant informal insight into consumer needs while simultaneously deepening brand loyalty (Vincent, Hill, & Lee, 2010).

This aligns with Morris et al.'s (2002) argument that informal research is not anecdotal but systematic when institutionalized within a firm's behaviors. By embedding itself into the rhythms of athletic life, Nike converts informal signals—comments at a run club, data from a training app, or cultural cues from youth sports—into actionable strategy. Intuition plays a key role here: Product managers and designers must filter weak signals and recognize patterns before they crystallize in formal research.

KNOWLEDGE CORRIDORS AND MARKET IMMERSION AT NIKE

Nike's capacity to extract insight from immersion is enhanced by the **knowledge corridors** of its staff and leadership. Former athletes, coaches, and sports enthusiasts bring prior knowledge that allows them to interpret immersion experiences effectively. As Shane (2000) argued, individuals can only perceive opportunities within the bounds of their prior knowledge. Nike's organizational hiring strategy deliberately builds such corridors, ensuring that immersion yields meaningful insights rather than superficial impressions.

For example, a designer who has lived the life of a competitive runner can intuitively recognize when a small irritation—like sock slippage—could represent a widespread problem worth solving. By pairing immersion with deep expertise, Nike ensures that its intuitive insights are not arbitrary but grounded in corridors of experience. This integration explains why immersion at Nike consistently produces commercially viable innovations rather than disconnected observations.

MARKET IMMERSION AND INTUITION

Nike's immersion practices also illustrate how immersion strengthens intuition. Kahneman (2011) distinguishes between intuitive judgments that are skilled (rooted in repeated, relevant exposure) and those that are biased (based on limited or irrelevant exposure). Nike's immersion ensures that decision-makers accumulate the volume and variety of exposure needed to build skilled intuition. Over time, product teams become adept at recognizing patterns in athlete needs and anticipating future trends, even without formal data.

For example, Nike's early move into women's athletic apparel was informed not by survey data but by immersion in running clubs and communities where women athletes were underrepresented in brand narratives. This immersion enabled Nike to sense an opportunity that competitors ignored, fueling a multibillion-dollar category expansion (Vincent et al., 2010).

CHALLENGES AND RISKS OF IMMERSION

Despite its strengths, Market Immersion is not without risks. Firms can become overly identified with subcultures, leading to blind spots in broader market trends. Additionally, immersion generates vast amounts of informal, unstructured data, which can overwhelm decision-makers and amplify biases if not carefully filtered (Sadler-Smith, 2016). Nike itself has faced criticism for misjudging cultural currents, such as backlash to controversial campaigns or accusations of cultural appropriation. These missteps illustrate that immersion must be complemented with reflexivity and mechanisms for validation.

LESSONS LEARNED

Nike's case yields several broader lessons about Market Immersion:

Immersion must be institutionalized: Sporadic efforts yield limited insight; immersion must be embedded in culture, processes, and structures.

Knowledge corridors matter: Immersion is only as useful as the expertise interpreting it. Hiring and training must align with customer worlds.

Immersion builds skilled intuition: Repeated exposure creates reliable intuitive judgments that enable firms to anticipate shifts.

Balance immersion with validation: Immersion provides insights, but triangulation with data and reflexivity is necessary to avoid bias.

CONCLUSION

Market Immersion represents a strategic orientation as much as a research technique. Nike's sustained success demonstrates how immersion in customer culture, athlete experience, and broader social movements can drive innovation, strengthen brand identity, and create sustainable competitive advantage. By embedding itself in the worlds of its customers, Nike transforms informal signals into intuitive insights and strategic foresight.

The case highlights a central SOI™ thesis: Strategy lives in behavior. Nike's behavior of continual immersion ensures that its strategy is not an abstract plan but a lived engagement with its market. For entrepreneurial firms and legacy companies alike, Nike provides a model of how immersion can be both systematic and intuitive, informal yet strategic—a reminder that in dynamic markets, those closest to the customer are best positioned to lead.

Market Immersion involves a continuous dialogue with customers. Rather than relying solely on periodic feedback, entrepreneurial marketers engage with customers on an ongoing basis through various touchpoints, such as social media interactions, customer-service inquiries, and in-person meetings. For example, a SaaS company might maintain a dedicated customer-success team to regularly check in with users, gather feedback, and provide personalized support. This ongoing engagement would allow the company to quickly identify and address customer pain points, leading to higher satisfaction and retention rates.

INNOVATING THROUGH DEEP MARKET INSIGHTS

Market Immersion provides the deep insights needed to drive innovation. By understanding the market at a granular level, entrepreneurial marketers can develop new products, services, and business models that meet emerging needs and capitalize on new opportunities.

CUSTOMER-LED INNOVATION

Innovation driven by Market Immersion is often customer-led. Entrepreneurial marketers use their deep understanding of customer needs and pain points to guide the development of new solutions that address these challenges. For example, a tech company may develop a new mobile app feature based on customer feedback about usability issues. By directly addressing customer concerns, the company could enhance the user experience and differentiate itself from competitors.

CO-CREATION WITH CUSTOMERS

Co-creation is another approach to innovation that involves working directly with customers to develop new products and services. Entrepreneurial marketers who are immersed in the market often engage customers in the innovation process, leveraging their insights and feedback to create solutions that truly resonate. For example, a sportswear brand might invite athletes and fitness enthusiasts to participate in the design process for a new line of performance apparel. The brand could use customer input to refine the designs and ensure that the final products meet the specific needs of its target audience.

AGILE INNOVATION PROCESSES

Market Immersion supports agile innovation processes, where firms quickly develop, test, and iterate on new ideas. This approach allows entrepreneurial marketers to respond rapidly to market changes and capitalize on new opportunities, such as a start-up using a lean innovation process to develop and test new product ideas. By staying closely connected to the market, the start-up can quickly pivot its strategy based on customer feedback and market trends, reducing the risk of failure.

LEVERAGING EMERGING TECHNOLOGIES

Businesses that are immersed in the market are often the first to identify and leverage emerging technologies that can drive innovation. This might include new digital tools, artificial intelligence, blockchain, or other technologies that can enhance product offerings or improve operational efficiency. For example, a logistics company might adopt blockchain technology to improve transparency and traceability in its supply chain. By staying ahead of the curve, the company would be able to offer customers greater assurance about the provenance and quality of its products.

BUILDING STRONG CUSTOMER RELATIONSHIPS THROUGH IMMERSION

Market Immersion is essential for building strong, lasting relationships with customers. By continuously engaging with the market and understanding the evolving needs of their customers, entrepreneurial marketers can foster loyalty, trust, and advocacy.

CREATING A CUSTOMER-CENTRIC CULTURE

A customer-centric culture is one where the customer's voice is central to every decision the company makes. Market Immersion helps firms build this culture by ensuring that customer insights are integrated into all aspects of the business. For example, a retail company may train its employees to prioritize customer satisfaction in every interaction, from the sales floor to customer service. The company would then regularly gather feedback from frontline employees and customers to continually improve the shopping experience.

PERSONALIZED CUSTOMER ENGAGEMENT

Personalized engagement is a key component of strong customer relationships. Entrepreneurial marketers use Market Immersion to understand the unique needs and preferences of their customers, enabling them to offer personalized experiences that drive loyalty. For example, an online subscription service might use customer data to personalize recommendations, communication, and offers, creating a tailored experience that keeps customers engaged and subscribed for the long term.

BUILDING TRUST THROUGH TRANSPARENCY

Trust is built through transparency, and Market Immersion helps firms understand the issues that matter most to their customers. By addressing these concerns openly and honestly, firms can build stronger, more trusting relationships. For example, a food brand might provide detailed information about the sourcing, production, and nutritional content of its products. The brand's transparency could then build trust with health-conscious consumers who value knowing exactly what goes into the products they consume.

FOSTERING BRAND ADVOCACY

Strong customer relationships often lead to brand advocacy, where satisfied customers become ambassadors for the brand. Market Immersion enables firms to identify and nurture these advocates, turning them into powerful marketing assets. For example, a tech company could engage its most loyal customers through exclusive events, early product releases, and referral programs. These advocates would likely share their positive experiences with others, helping to spread the word about the brand and attract new customers.

GAINING COMPETITIVE ADVANTAGE THROUGH MARKET IMMERSION

Market Immersion is a powerful tool for gaining competitive advantage. Firms that are deeply immersed in the market are better equipped to anticipate and respond to competitive threats, differentiate themselves from rivals, and capture market share.

DIFFERENTIATION THROUGH CUSTOMER INSIGHT

Firms that are deeply immersed in the market have a unique understanding of their customers, which allows them to differentiate their offerings in meaningful ways. This differentiation is often based on a deep understanding of customer needs that competitors may overlook. For example, a luxury brand could use its deep understanding of customer preferences to offer highly personalized services, setting itself apart from competitors who offer more standardized experiences.

PROACTIVE COMPETITOR ANALYSIS

Market Immersion involves continuous analysis of competitor activities. By staying informed about competitor strategies, product launches, and market positioning, entrepreneurial marketers can anticipate competitive moves and develop proactive strategies to counter them. For example, a beverage company might monitor competitor pricing and promotional strategies, using this information to adjust its own pricing and marketing campaigns in real time, ensuring that it remains competitive in the market.

FIRST-MOVER ADVANTAGE

Market Immersion often leads to a first-mover advantage, where businesses that are closely attuned to market trends and customer needs are the first to introduce new products or services. This early entry into the market can establish a strong market position and create barriers for later entrants. For example, a tech start-up may identify an emerging need for secure, decentralized communication platforms and quickly develop and launch a solution before larger competitors can enter the space.

ADAPTABILITY AND RESILIENCE

Businesses that practice Market Immersion are inherently more adaptable and resilient. Their deep connection to the market allows them to pivot quickly in response to changes, ensuring that they remain competitive even in volatile or uncertain environments. For example, a global retailer could use Market Immersion to stay informed about shifting consumer behaviors during economic downturns. The retailer could then quickly adjust its product lines and marketing strategies to meet changing demands, maintaining its competitive position.

Strategic Implication: True Market Orientation goes beyond empathy—it requires immersion. Firms should ask whether their teams regularly inhabit their customers' world or merely assume they understand it.

CHAPTER 10

BRINGING IT TOGETHER: EO, MO, AND EM

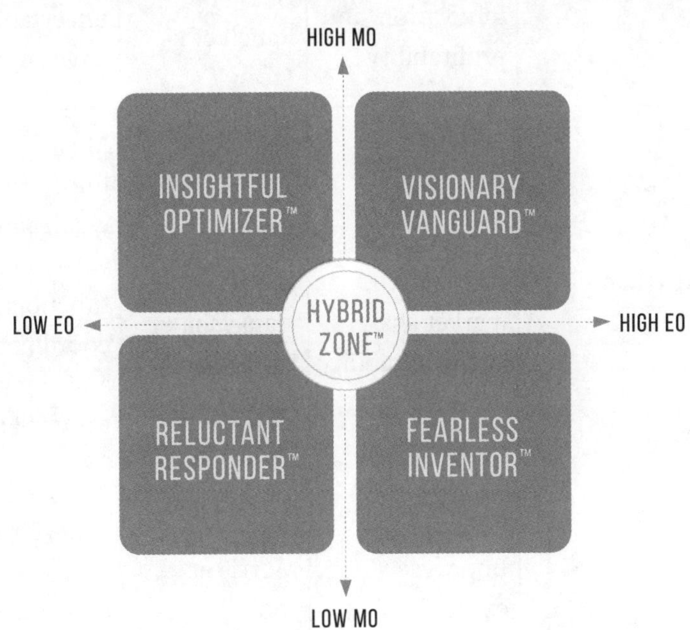

Over the past three decades, extensive empirical research has demonstrated that Entrepreneurial Orientation (EO), Market Orientation (MO), and Entrepreneurial Marketing (EM) each contribute meaningfully to firm performance. While individually valuable, the true strategic power of these constructs emerges when they are examined together. The Strategic Orientation Index™ (SOI™) is the first diagnostic framework to operationalize all three in a unified system.

The table below summarizes the empirical evidence supporting each dimension and highlights why integration is not just intuitive—it's evidence-based.

STRATEGIC CONSTRUCT	EMPIRICAL IMPACT ON PERFORMANCE	REPRESENTATIVE STUDIES	NOTES
Entrepreneurial Orientation (EO)	Positively associated with firm growth, innovation, and profitability	Covin & Slevin (1989); Lumpkin & Dess (1996); Rauch et al. (2009)	Especially effective in dynamic or uncertain environments
Market Orientation (MO)	Strong predictor of customer satisfaction, market share, and profitability	Narver & Slater (1990); Kirca et al. (2005); Hanaysha & Al-Shaikh (2022)	Most impactful when paired with inter-functional coordination and competitor vigilance
Entrepreneurial Marketing (EM)	Improves executional agility and market responsiveness	Morris et al. (2002); Miles & Darroch (2006); Kraus et al. (2010)	Acts as behavioral bridge between EO and MO; shows how strategy is enacted in practice

Combined EO + MO	Firms with high EO and MO alignment outperform peers in innovation and growth	Bhuian et al. (2005); Miles & Darroch (2006)	Alignment creates synergistic impact greater than either construct alone
EO–MO–EM Integration	Not yet meta-analyzed, but proposed as a behavioral triad for strategic execution	This book (Harkema, 2025)	SOI™ is the first model to diagnostically integrate all three dimensions at the firm level

WHY THIS MATTERS

A high EO gives a firm the courage to act. A high MO gives it the wisdom to listen. But without EM, intent and insight remain abstract. Entrepreneurial Marketing reveals whether those orientations are showing up in behavior—in real-time customer interaction, opportunity pursuit, and adaptive execution.

The SOI™ framework draws from these empirical foundations but extends them into an actionable diagnostic system. It provides leaders with a structured way to:

- Identify misalignment across strategic intent (EO), market understanding (MO), and behavior (EM)
- Map the firm's orientation into a strategic persona
- Prescribe tailored growth actions based on behavioral posture

As empirical validation of the SOI™ system continues across consulting, academic, and instructional use cases, this table serves as both grounding and invitation: to bring together the best of theory, research, and real-world application in pursuit of aligned, agile growth.

INTRODUCTION

In today's dynamic business environment, integrating Entrepreneurial Orientation (EO), Market Orientation (MO), and Entrepreneurial Marketing (EM) is critical for organizations seeking sustainable growth and competitive advantage. EO, which emphasizes innovation, proactiveness, and risk-taking, helps businesses navigate uncertainty and seize new opportunities. MO, on the other hand, focuses on understanding and responding to customer needs and competitor actions, ensuring that the company remains relevant and customer-centric. EM bridges these two orientations by providing the marketing strategies and tactics necessary to implement EO and MO effectively in the market. Together, these orientations create a robust framework that enables businesses to thrive in competitive markets (Kraus, Rigtering, Hughes, & Hosman, 2012; Covin & Miller, 2014).

BRIDGING THE GAP BETWEEN THEORY AND PRACTICE

One of the most significant challenges in integrating EO, MO, and EM lies in bridging the gap between theoretical concepts and practical application. While the principles of EO, MO, and EM provide a strong foundation for business strategy, their successful implementation requires a deep understanding of how these concepts translate into real-world practices. This section explores the importance of aligning theory with practice, the common pitfalls organizations face, and strategies for effectively bridging this gap.

Theoretical models such as EO, MO, and EM are essential for guiding strategic decision-making. They offer frameworks that help organizations understand the key drivers of innovation, market responsiveness, and customer engagement. However, the real value of these models lies in their application. Without practical implementation, these theories remain abstract concepts that fail to deliver tangible business results (Argyris & Schön, 1974). Bridging the gap between theory and practice is, therefore, a critical step in leveraging EO, MO, and EM to achieve competitive advantage.

One of the main challenges in applying these theories is the complexity of real-world business environments. Unlike the controlled settings of theoretical models, businesses operate in dynamic and often unpredictable markets where numerous variables can influence outcomes. For example, while EO encourages innovation and risk-taking, companies must also consider external factors such as market competition, regulatory changes, and economic conditions that can impact the success of their entrepreneurial initiatives (Lumpkin & Dess, 1996). Similarly, MO emphasizes the importance of being attuned to customer needs, but in practice, gathering and analyzing customer data can be resource-intensive and may require sophisticated tools and technologies (Narver & Slater, 1990).

Another common pitfall in bridging theory and practice is the misalignment between organizational culture and the principles of EO, MO, and EM. For instance, a company may adopt EO in its strategic planning but fail to foster a culture that supports innovation and risk-taking. Without a supportive culture, employees may be reluctant to embrace entrepreneurial behaviors, leading to a disconnect between the company's strategic goals and its operational practices (Covin & Slevin, 1991). Similarly, MO requires organizations to prioritize customer needs, but if customer orientation is not embedded in the company's culture, efforts to gather and respond to customer feedback may be superficial and ineffective (Jaworski & Kohli, 1993).

To effectively bridge the gap between theory and practice, organizations must take a holistic approach that integrates EO, MO, and EM into every aspect of their operations. This begins with leadership. Leaders play a crucial role in translating theoretical concepts into actionable strategies.

They must not only understand the principles of EO, MO, and EM but also be able to communicate these principles to their teams in a way that is relevant and practical. This involves setting clear expectations, providing the necessary resources and support, and creating an environment that encourages experimentation and learning (Schein, 2010).

Moreover, organizations need to invest in the right tools and technologies to support the practical application of EO, MO, and EM. For example, advanced data-analytics platforms can help companies gather and analyze customer data more efficiently, enabling them to respond to market trends in real time. Similarly, project-management tools can facilitate the implementation of entrepreneurial initiatives by providing teams with the structure and visibility needed to execute projects effectively (McAfee & Brynjolfsson, 2012).

Another important aspect of bridging the gap between theory and practice is continuous learning and adaptation. The business environment is constantly evolving, and companies must be willing to adapt their strategies and practices to stay competitive. This requires a commitment to ongoing education and development, both for leaders and employees. By staying informed about the latest trends and best practices in EO, MO, and EM, organizations can ensure that their strategies remain relevant and effective (Teece, Pisano, & Shuen, 1997).

For example, companies can conduct regular training sessions and workshops to educate employees on the principles of EO, MO, and EM and how they can be applied in their daily work. Additionally, creating cross-functional teams that bring together diverse perspectives can help to ensure that the organization's strategies are well rounded and grounded in practical experience. These teams can work collaboratively to identify potential challenges and develop innovative solutions that align with the company's strategic goals.

Lastly, companies should measure and evaluate the outcomes of their EO, MO, and EM initiatives to determine their effectiveness and identify areas for improvement. This involves setting clear metrics for success, such as customer-satisfaction scores, innovation outputs, and market-share growth, and regularly reviewing performance against these metrics. By monitoring progress and making data-driven adjustments, organizations can refine their strategies and ensure that they are effectively bridging the gap between theory and practice (Kaplan & Norton, 1996).

In conclusion, bridging the gap between theory and practice is a critical challenge for organizations seeking to integrate EO, MO, and EM into their operations. While theoretical models provide valuable guidance, their true value is realized through practical application. By aligning organizational culture, investing in the right tools and technologies, fostering continuous learning, and measuring outcomes, companies can effectively translate the principles of EO, MO, and EM into tangible business success. This approach not only enhances the effectiveness of these orientations but also ensures that organizations are well positioned to adapt to the complexities of the modern business environment.

The EM scoring framework used here is based on the six-factor structure validated by Kilenthong (2011), which streamlines the original seven-factor model proposed by Morris et al. (2002) for stronger empirical fit and practical usability.

THE SYNERGY BETWEEN EO, MO, AND EM

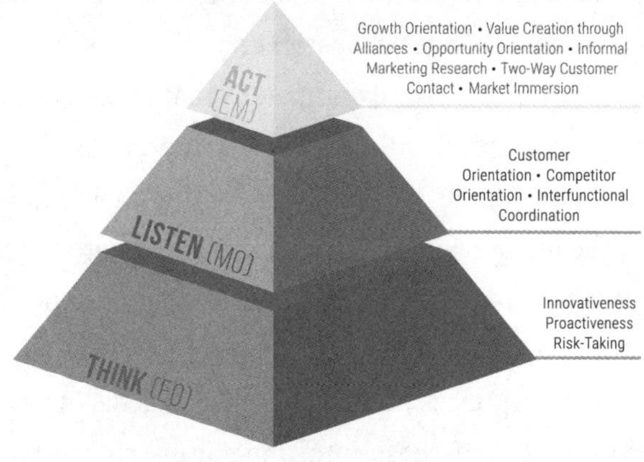

The integration of EO, MO, and EM represents a powerful synergy that enhances a company's ability to innovate, adapt, and deliver value to customers. EO's focus on innovation and risk-taking aligns with the core principles of MO, which emphasizes the importance of being attuned to customer needs and market dynamics. By integrating these orientations, companies can develop innovative products and services that are not only cutting-edge but also deeply aligned with market demands (Narver & Slater, 1990; Lumpkin & Dess, 1996).

EO drives the innovation process by encouraging a proactive approach to identifying and exploiting opportunities. This is particularly crucial in industries characterized by rapid technological changes and evolving customer preferences. When EO is combined with MO, the innovative efforts are guided by a deep understanding of customer needs, ensuring that new products and services are market-driven and customer-focused (Slater, Olson, & Hult, 2006). For instance, companies that excel in both EO and MO are more likely to launch successful products because they leverage customer insights throughout the innovation process.

EM plays a crucial role in operationalizing the strategies derived from EO and MO. While EO and MO set the strategic direction, EM provides the tools and tactics needed to implement these strategies effectively in the market. EM's emphasis on flexibility, customer engagement, and value creation ensures that the innovative ideas generated through EO are communicated effectively to the market and that the company remains responsive to ongoing changes in customer preferences (Hills & Hultman, 2013). This synergy is evident in companies that successfully adapt their marketing strategies to reflect both their entrepreneurial initiatives and their commitment to understanding and serving their customers.

Moreover, the integration of EO, MO, and EM creates a feedback loop that continuously enhances organizational learning and performance. As companies implement their marketing strategies, they gather valuable data on customer responses and market trends. This information feeds back into the innovation process, informing future entrepreneurial efforts and helping companies stay ahead of the competition (Baker & Sinkula, 2009). This continuous learning process is a key factor in sustaining competitive advantage in fast-paced industries.

PRACTICAL FRAMEWORK FOR INTEGRATING EO, MO, AND EM

To effectively integrate EO, MO, and EM, businesses can follow a practical framework that ensures these orientations are aligned with the company's strategic goals and operational practices. This framework includes several key components:

DEVELOP A STRONG ENTREPRENEURIAL CULTURE

Developing a strong entrepreneurial culture is the foundation for effectively integrating EO, MO, and EM. An entrepreneurial culture encourages employees at all levels to take initiative, embrace risk, and be proactive in seeking out new opportunities. This culture is not just about supporting innovation but also about fostering a mindset that sees challenges as opportunities for growth and improvement (Covin & Slevin, 1991). Leaders play a pivotal role in cultivating this culture by setting the tone, leading by example, and ensuring that entrepreneurial behaviors are recognized and rewarded. For example, Google's famous "20% time" policy, where employees are encouraged to spend 20 percent of their time on projects that interest them, is a testament to fostering an entrepreneurial culture that drives innovation.

Moreover, a strong entrepreneurial culture aligns with the principles of EO by creating an environment where employees are encouraged to think creatively and take calculated risks. This not only supports the development of innovative products and services but also drives the company toward new market opportunities. Companies can strengthen this culture by providing continuous training and development opportunities, which help employees develop the skills necessary for entrepreneurial thinking. Additionally, creating internal platforms for idea sharing, such as innovation labs or hackathons, can further embed entrepreneurship into the organization's DNA.

ENHANCE MARKET-SENSING CAPABILITIES

Market-sensing capabilities are crucial for aligning EO, MO, and EM effectively. Companies with strong market-sensing capabilities are better positioned to anticipate and respond to changes in customer preferences, competitor actions, and broader market trends (Jaworski & Kohli, 1993). These capabilities involve the continuous collection and analysis of data from various sources, including customer feedback, market research, social media, and industry reports. This data allows companies to make informed decisions that align with both EO's focus on innovation and MO's emphasis on customer orientation.

Enhancing market-sensing capabilities often requires investment in advanced technologies, such as artificial intelligence (AI) and machine learning, which can process vast amounts of data and identify patterns that might not be immediately apparent to human analysts. For example, AI can be used to predict emerging market trends by analyzing social media conversations or customer reviews in real time. These insights can then be used to guide the development of new products or marketing strategies that resonate with the target audience. Companies can also establish dedicated teams responsible for market sensing and ensure that their insights are communicated effectively across the organization.

Furthermore, effective market sensing goes beyond data collection; it involves interpreting and applying this data to strategic decisions. This requires cross-functional collaboration, where marketing teams work closely with product development, sales, and customer service to ensure that insights from market sensing are integrated into all aspects of the business. For instance, if market sensing indicates a growing customer demand for sustainable products, this insight should inform not only marketing campaigns but also product design and supply-chain management.

ALIGN MARKETING STRATEGIES WITH EO AND MO

Aligning marketing strategies with EO and MO is critical for translating entrepreneurial and market-oriented insights into actionable plans. This alignment ensures that the innovative ideas generated by EO are effectively communicated to the market in a way that resonates with customers and meets their needs. Agile marketing techniques, such as rapid prototyping, A/B testing, and iterative campaign development, allow companies to quickly adapt their marketing strategies in response to market feedback (Hills & Hultman, 2013). This approach is particularly valuable in dynamic markets, where customer preferences and competitive landscapes can change rapidly.

One way to align marketing strategies with EO and MO is through the development of customer personas and journey maps. These tools help companies understand their customers' needs, behaviors, and pain points, which in turn inform the development of targeted marketing messages and campaigns. For example, a company with a strong EO might develop a groundbreaking new product, but without a clear understanding of the target audience (MO), the marketing strategy might fail to connect with potential customers. By integrating customer insights into the marketing strategy, companies can ensure that their innovative offerings are positioned in a way that appeals to the right audience.

Additionally, aligning marketing strategies with EO and MO requires a commitment to ongoing measurement and optimization. Companies should regularly evaluate the performance of their marketing campaigns against key metrics, such as customer acquisition cost, lifetime value, and conversion rates. By analyzing these metrics, companies can identify areas for improvement and make data-driven adjustments to their strategies. For instance, if a particular marketing channel is underperforming, the company might reallocate resources to a more effective channel or adjust the messaging to better align with customer needs.

FOSTER CONTINUOUS LEARNING AND ADAPTATION

Continuous learning and adaptation are essential components of a successful integration of EO, MO, and EM. The business environment is constantly evolving, and companies must be willing to adapt their strategies and practices to remain competitive. This requires a commitment to ongoing education and development, both for leaders and employees (Baker & Sinkula, 2009). Companies can foster continuous learning by creating a culture that values curiosity, experimentation, and the sharing of knowledge. This can be achieved through initiatives such as regular training sessions, workshops, and seminars that focus on the latest trends and best practices in EO, MO, and EM.

Moreover, companies should encourage employees to learn from their experiences and apply those lessons to future projects. This can be facilitated by implementing feedback loops where employees regularly review and discuss the outcomes of their work. For example, after the launch of a new marketing campaign, teams could hold a debrief session to analyze what worked, what didn't, and how the insights gained can be applied to future initiatives. These feedback loops help ensure that the organization is constantly learning and improving, which is key to maintaining a competitive edge.

In addition to internal learning opportunities, companies should also encourage employees to engage with external sources of knowledge. This could include attending industry conferences, participating in online courses, or networking with peers in the field. By staying informed about the latest developments in EO, MO, and EM, employees can bring fresh ideas and perspectives back to the organization. This continuous influx of new knowledge helps the company stay ahead of industry trends and better anticipate market shifts.

MEASURE AND ADJUST

Finally, the importance of measurement and adjustment cannot be overstated when integrating EO, MO, and EM. Companies must establish clear metrics for success and regularly evaluate their performance against these metrics. Key performance indicators might include measures such as customer satisfaction, market-share growth, innovation success rates, and profitability (Kaplan & Norton, 1996). These metrics provide a quantitative basis for assessing the effectiveness of the company's strategies and making informed decisions about where to focus future efforts.

However, measurement alone is not enough; companies must also be willing to adjust their strategies based on the insights gained from these metrics. This might involve pivoting to new markets, reallocating resources, or even revisiting the company's overall strategic direction. For example, if market data reveals that a new product is not gaining traction, the company might decide to shift focus to a different product line or adjust the marketing strategy to better resonate with the target audience. This willingness to adapt is a hallmark of successful EO, MO, and EM integration and is critical for long-term success.

Moreover, companies should not view measurement and adjustment as a onetime activity but as an ongoing process. By continuously monitoring their performance and making incremental adjustments, companies can stay agile and responsive to changes in the market. This iterative approach ensures that the organization remains aligned with its strategic goals and can capitalize on new opportunities as they arise.

In conclusion, the practical framework for integrating EO, MO, and EM involves developing a strong entrepreneurial culture, enhancing market-sensing capabilities, aligning marketing strategies, fostering continuous learning, and implementing robust measurement and adjustment processes. By following this framework, companies can effectively leverage the synergies between EO, MO, and EM to achieve sustainable business success. This approach not only enhances the company's ability to innovate and respond to market demands but also ensures that it remains competitive in an increasingly dynamic business environment.

CHALLENGES AND PITFALLS

While integrating EO, MO, and EM offers significant benefits, it also presents challenges that companies must navigate carefully:

BALANCING INNOVATION AND MARKET DEMANDS

Companies may struggle to balance the need for innovation with the need to meet current market demands. Overemphasis on innovation can lead to neglect of customer needs, while a focus solely on the market can stifle creativity and limit long-term growth (Slater, Olson, & Hult, 2006). To address this challenge, companies should establish clear priorities and allocate resources strategically to support both innovation and market responsiveness. Regularly revisiting these priorities can help ensure that the company remains agile and responsive to changing market conditions. For example, setting aside dedicated resources for both R&D (reflecting EO) and customer engagement (reflecting MO) can help maintain this balance.

The balance between innovation and market demands is particularly challenging in industries where customer preferences evolve rapidly. For instance, in the technology sector, companies must innovate continuously to stay ahead of competitors while also ensuring that their innovations align with the current and future needs of their customers. Failure to balance these elements can result in products that are technologically advanced but fail to gain market traction due to a disconnect with customer expectations. Moreover, companies that focus too heavily on existing market demands may find themselves overtaken by more innovative competitors that introduce disruptive technologies or business models. Thus, maintaining a dynamic equilibrium between EO and MO is crucial for long-term success.

RESOURCE ALLOCATION

Effectively allocating resources between entrepreneurial activities, market research, and marketing initiatives can be challenging, particularly for smaller companies with limited resources (Covin & Slevin, 1991). Companies must carefully evaluate their resource-allocation strategies to ensure that they are investing in areas that will yield the highest returns. This may involve making difficult decisions about where to focus efforts and being willing to reallocate resources as needed to support the most critical initiatives. For example, during times of market volatility, a company may choose to invest more in market research (MO) to better understand shifting customer needs and less in short-term marketing campaigns.

The challenge of resource allocation is compounded by the fact that EO, MO, and EM each require significant investment in different areas. For instance, EO often demands substantial investment in R&D, talent acquisition, and infrastructure to support innovation. MO, on the other hand, requires continuous investment in market research, customer-relationship-management systems, and analytics tools. Meanwhile, EM necessitates resources for agile marketing campaigns, branding, and customer-engagement initiatives. Balancing these competing demands requires a strategic approach that aligns resource allocation with the company's overarching business goals. Companies must also remain flexible and willing to adjust their allocations as market conditions and business priorities evolve.

ORGANIZATIONAL ALIGNMENT

Ensuring that all departments are aligned with the integrated strategy can be difficult, especially in larger organizations with siloed functions (Narver & Slater, 1990). Organizational alignment requires clear communication, collaboration across departments, and a shared commitment to the company's strategic goals. Implementing cross-functional teams and encouraging open dialogue can help break down silos and ensure that all parts of the organization are working toward the same objectives. Additionally, aligning incentives and performance metrics with the integrated strategy can reinforce the importance of collaboration and shared goals.

For instance, tying employee bonuses to both innovation metrics (EO) and customer-satisfaction scores (MO) can help align efforts across the organization.

In practice, organizational alignment often requires cultural change, particularly in companies with entrenched silos or rigid departmental structures. Leaders must champion the integrated approach by demonstrating its benefits and encouraging collaboration across functions. This might involve restructuring teams, redefining roles and responsibilities, or introducing new communication channels that facilitate better information flow between departments. For example, companies can establish cross-functional innovation teams that include members from R&D, marketing, and sales, ensuring that new product development is informed by both market insights and customer feedback. Additionally, regular cross-departmental meetings and workshops can help build a shared understanding of the company's strategic goals and foster a culture of collaboration and mutual support.

Another aspect of organizational alignment is the integration of EO, MO, and EM into the company's performance management systems. This means that the success of these orientations should be reflected in the key performance indicators used to evaluate employee performance. For instance, incorporating metrics related to innovation outcomes, market responsiveness, and customer engagement into performance appraisals can help ensure that employees at all levels are aligned with the company's integrated strategy. Furthermore, providing training and development opportunities that focus on EO, MO, and EM can equip employees with the skills and knowledge needed to contribute effectively to the company's strategic objectives.

RELEVANCE OF EO, MO, AND EM IN THEORY AND PRACTICE

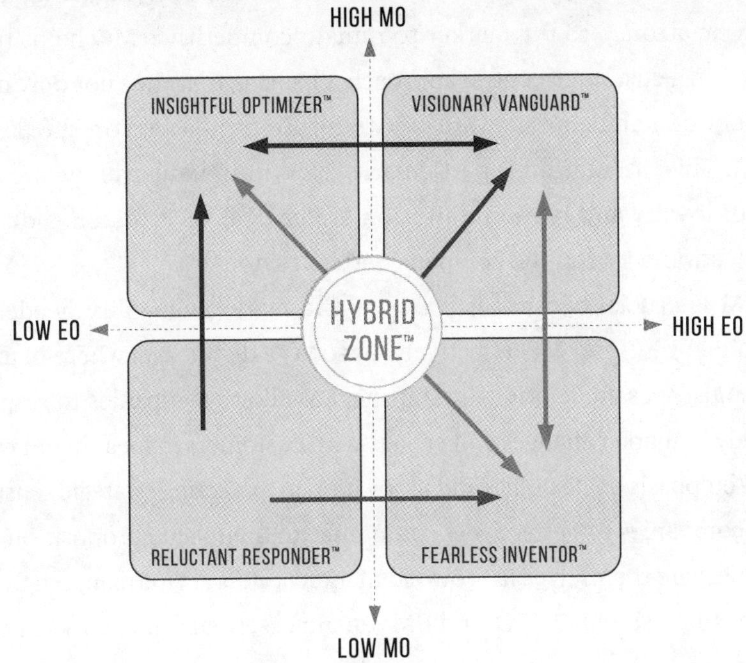

Entrepreneurial Orientation (EO), Market Orientation (MO), and Entrepreneurial Marketing (EM) continue to be highly relevant in both theory and practice, even as business environments evolve. These orientations provide a robust framework for navigating the complexities of modern markets, where innovation, customer focus, and agile marketing are critical to success.

EO remains relevant because it encourages companies to be proactive, innovative, and willing to take risks—qualities that are essential in today's fast-paced and competitive global markets. The ability to innovate and adapt quickly to changes is more important than ever, given the rapid technological advancements and shifting consumer preferences. Research shows that firms with a strong EO are more likely to achieve high performance, particularly in dynamic environments where the ability to innovate is a key differentiator (Covin & Miller, 2014).

MO continues to be vital because understanding and responding to customer needs is a cornerstone of sustainable business success. In an era where customer expectations are constantly evolving, companies must be attuned to the market to remain competitive. MO helps firms maintain a customer-centric approach, ensuring that they not only meet current demands but also anticipate future trends (Jaworski & Kohli, 1993). This orientation is particularly relevant in industries where customer loyalty and brand reputation are critical, as it fosters a deeper connection between the company and its customers.

EM is crucial because it provides the marketing agility needed to implement EO and MO effectively. In today's digital age, where marketing landscapes are continually shifting, EM allows companies to respond quickly to market changes and engage with customers in meaningful ways. EM's emphasis on flexibility and innovation in marketing strategies ensures that companies can effectively communicate their value proposition and differentiate themselves in crowded markets (Hills & Hultman, 2013).

In conclusion, EO, MO, and EM remain essential frameworks in both theory and practice. Their continued relevance is underscored by their ability to help companies navigate the complexities of modern business environments, drive innovation, stay attuned to market needs, and execute agile marketing strategies that resonate with customers.

INTRODUCING THE STRATEGIC ORIENTATION INDEX™ (SOI™)

As organizations increasingly navigate turbulent markets and shifting customer demands, the need for an integrated strategic compass has become urgent. While Entrepreneurial Orientation (EO), Market Orientation (MO), and Entrepreneurial Marketing (EM) are each well established, they are often discussed in parallel or isolation. Yet in practice, these constructs are deeply interdependent. This section introduces the Strategic Orientation Index™ (SOI™), a diagnostic framework designed to evaluate, unify, and apply EO, MO, and EM in a cohesive and actionable way. By providing a structured, evidence-based approach to scoring and classifying strategic posture, SOI™ empowers firms to better understand their current strategic alignment and identify high-leverage pathways for future growth.

PERSONA	EO	MO	PRIMARY TRAITS	KEY BLIND SPOT	POPULAR PHRASE (VOICE OF THE PERSONA)
Visionary Vanguard	High	High	Bold, innovative, customer-obsessed, aligned	Overextension or perfection paralysis	*"We move fast—but only when the customer moves with us."*
Fearless Inventor	High	Low	Aggressive, experimental, fast-moving	Lacks customer feedback and market validation	*"If we wait for feedback, we'll already be behind."*
Insightful Optimizer	Low	High	Disciplined, efficient, highly responsive to customers	Risk-averse, slow to innovate	*"Let's tweak what's working before we chase shiny objects."*
Reluctant Responder	Low	Low	Passive, reactive, often siloed and execution-starved	Strategic drift and cultural stagnation	*"We've always done it this way—let's not break what isn't broken."*
Hybrid Zone	Mid/ Uneven	Mid/ Uneven	Conflicted posture, internally inconsistent, often transitional	Misalignment and mixed strategic signals	*"Everyone's rowing hard—but in different directions."*

WHY A NEW FRAMEWORK IS NEEDED

In the current business environment, characterized by volatility, complexity, and accelerated innovation, strategy cannot be siloed. Entrepreneurial firms face immense pressure to innovate, disrupt, and move quickly—hallmarks of high EO. Simultaneously, customer expectations are rising, and the ability to generate and respond to market intelligence is more crucial than ever—a domain governed by MO. However, firms that focus heavily on one dimension without the other often falter. For example, a company that is highly entrepreneurial but lacks market insight may waste resources on innovations that don't resonate with buyers. Conversely, a company that is highly market-oriented but risk-averse may miss breakthrough opportunities. Meanwhile, EM offers an integrative behavioral lens, but its implementation across firms has been inconsistent and often anecdotal. There has been a theoretical gap—and a practical need—for a tool that integrates all three orientations into a single framework to guide strategic thinking and operational priorities.

WHAT IS THE STRATEGIC ORIENTATION INDEX™ (SOI™)?

The Strategic Orientation Index™ (SOI™) is a three-dimensional diagnostic framework that assesses a firm's posture along EO, MO, and EM dimensions. It is built on the premise that a firm's strategic performance is not just about how innovative or customer-centric it is, but how well it combines entrepreneurial drive with market responsiveness and marketing agility. SOI™ provides a structured scoring mechanism and visualization tool that generates a strategic persona for each firm based on its orientation profile. These personas—such as Visionary Vanguard, Fearless Inventor, Insightful Optimizer, Reluctant Responder, or Hybrid Zone—represent distinct combinations of the three core dimensions and are designed to be memorable, actionable, and strategically meaningful.

Beyond the label, each persona includes a description of current strengths, strategic risks, and recommendations for development. For example, firms in the Visionary Vanguard quadrant exhibit strong EO and MO, with EM behaviors flourishing as a result. In contrast, Fearless Inventors have high EO and EM but low MO—meaning they may push innovation but risk missing market fit. Insightful Optimizers, by contrast, execute well based on market insight but often lag in proactive, risk-taking innovation. The SOI™ framework not only names where the firm is—it points to where it should go next. The following hypothetical cases illustrate how a company in these persona categories applied the SOI™ framework in practice:

VISIONARY VANGUARD—SUMMARY PROFILE

Quadrant Location: High EO / High MO

Definition: The Visionary Vanguard is a firm that combines bold entrepreneurial drive with disciplined Market Orientation. It is both innovative and deeply in tune with customer needs—often setting the pace for its industry.

Common Behaviors:
- Launches disruptive offerings based on real customer pain points
- Embeds customer feedback throughout the innovation process
- Aligns internal teams around a clear strategic vision
- Cultivates partnerships and alliances to accelerate growth
- Uses data and intuition together to guide bold decision-making

Strategic Strengths:
- Rapid yet thoughtful innovation
- Strong brand differentiation grounded in real market needs
- High internal alignment between vision, culture, and execution
- Often viewed as a category leader or thought leader

Core Blind Spots:
- Can become over-reliant on "visionary" leaders
- May burn out teams with ambitious growth pacing
- Risk of chasing too many opportunities at once
- Vulnerable to internal complexity as scale increases

VOICE-OF-THE-PERSONA QUOTES:

"We don't just respond to the market—we shape it. And we do it with customer truth at the center."

"Every bold move we make starts with something our customers told us—directly or indirectly."

"We believe speed matters—but alignment matters more."

Growth Recommendation: To sustain momentum, Visionary Vanguard firms should invest in scalable systems, delegate strategic ownership beyond founding teams, and maintain clarity on core vs. peripheral innovation. Their next challenge is not creating value—but protecting focus and building infrastructure without losing edge.

CASE STUDY: VISIONARY VANGUARD IN ACTION

Company: BluePeak Robotics

Industry: Warehouse Automation

SOI™ Profile:

- High EO
- High MO
- EM: Balanced across all six subdimensions

Strategic Persona: Visionary Vanguard

BluePeak Robotics builds AI-powered automation systems for enterprise warehouses. The company is known for its strategic foresight, disruptive product launches, and deep client partnerships. A recent SOI™ assessment confirmed strong alignment across all three strategic dimensions: high EO, high MO, and a well-rounded EM profile with especially strong scores in Growth Orientation and Two-Way Customer Contact.

Despite strong performance, the leadership team noticed signs of complexity creep. With multiple product launches in development and customer pilots running across markets, internal focus began to waver. Leveraging the SOI™ framework, the team conducted a strategic-streamlining exercise, identified three core initiatives aligned with customer value, and paused lower-priority efforts. The result was a more focused execution pipeline and stronger internal alignment—helping them preserve their dominant position in the **Visionary Vanguard** quadrant without sacrificing agility.

ANECDOTAL CASE STUDY: VISIONARY VANGUARD

Westmont Instruments:

Building Bold, Listening Hard, Executing Fast

Westmont Instruments had every reason to play it safe. A sixty-year-old manufacturer of environmental control components, the firm had built its reputation on reliability, not risk. Yet in 2021, under new CEO Claire Tsao, Westmont launched an aggressive five-year transformation plan aimed at repositioning the company as a connected systems integrator for the smart-building economy.

The plan wasn't flashy. It wasn't even loud. But it was deeply aligned—and unmistakably bold.

Tsao had come from a venture-backed IoT firm. Her background was entrepreneurial, but her approach to culture change was surgical. Within six months, Westmont's executive team began operating differently. They implemented an internal innovation council composed of product, operations, and marketing leads. Monthly cross-functional "assumption testing" sessions were launched to challenge legacy thinking. And every strategic proposal had to include a customer-signal source, not just a market projection.

But the most telling indicator of Westmont's behavioral orientation was in how it handled failure.

One early pilot—a cloud-connected, airflow-monitoring module—missed its margin targets and fell short in commercial buildings. Rather than retreat, the team conducted structured voice-of-customer interviews with nine buyers who had passed. They didn't just listen; they changed the integration protocol, adjusted pricing models, and launched a second version within ninety days.

That second version became the foundation for a $5.6M multiyear partnership with a national HVAC distributor.

Internally, Westmont ran lean—but not silent. Innovation was a priority, but not at the expense of coherence. Strategic initiatives were mapped on a dashboard visible to all employees. That visibility created a culture of accountability: Teams were expected to act, but with shared intelligence.

Even suppliers noticed. "We get looped in earlier than ever," said a sourcing manager from one of Westmont's critical component partners. "They want to know how their design choices affect ours. That didn't happen before."

By 2024, Westmont had increased gross margin by 4 percent, grown OEM sales by 18 percent, and launched two new digital-service lines—all while maintaining its core product-delivery metrics.

What made it possible wasn't just a new vision—it was how the company thought, listened, and acted in unison.

Tsao would later describe it this way:

"Most companies execute on what they hope the market wants. We've trained ourselves to only execute on what the market proves."

In SOI™ terms, Westmont had achieved rare alignment:

EO (Entrepreneurial Orientation) was high—they acted with calculated boldness and a clear appetite for innovation.

MO (Market Orientation) was embedded—cross-functional coordination ensured that customer needs weren't just known but shared.

EM (Entrepreneurial Marketing) was visible—rapid iteration, strategic partnerships, and lean feedback loops defined their go-to-market behavior.

This wasn't luck. It was discipline.

The company still had internal debates, and not every launch was successful. But its behavioral consistency—the way its people *thought*, *listened*, and *acted*—formed a strategic posture that made adaptation inevitable.

Westmont didn't chase the market. It *co-evolved* with it.

FEARLESS INVENTOR—SUMMARY PROFILE

Quadrant Location: High EO / Low MO

Definition: The Fearless Inventor is bold, fast-moving, and innovation-driven—but often disconnected from customer needs and market signals. These firms thrive on experimentation and disruption but risk missing strategic fit and long-term traction.

Common Behaviors:

- Launches new products or services rapidly, often without deep customer validation
- Celebrates creativity, speed, and internal boldness
- Rarely pauses to collect structured feedback or formal research
- Prioritizes innovation and growth over market alignment
- Operates with a "build it and they will come" mindset

Strategic Strengths:

- High tolerance for risk and failure
- First-mover advantage in emerging categories
- Can pivot quickly and respond with agility
- Attracts entrepreneurial talent and early adopters

Core Blind Spots:

- Misjudges true customer demand or willingness to pay
- Lacks systematic voice-of-customer processes
- Often dismisses competitor signals or market norms
- Can outpace internal alignment or operational maturity

Voice-of-the-Persona Quotes:

- "We'd rather launch something imperfect today than wait for market research to tell us what we already know."
- "If we slow down for feedback, someone else will ship first."
- "The market catches up to us—not the other way around."

Growth Recommendation: Fearless Inventors must introduce disciplined market feedback loops without losing their creative edge.

Embedding informal research, structured customer contact, and light-weight testing can dramatically improve their product–market fit while retaining speed and innovation power.

HYPOTHETICAL CASE STUDY: FEARLESS INVENTOR IN ACTION

Company: NovaForge

Industry: Smart Home Technology

SOI™ Profile:

- High EO

- Low MO

- EM: Strong in Growth & Opportunity Orientation, weak in Market Immersion & Customer Contact

Strategic Persona: Fearless Inventor

NovaForge, a growth-stage smart-home start-up, built its brand on rapid innovation. The leadership team prided itself on launching new product features quarterly, often ahead of customer demand. Internally, the company's culture celebrated first-mover advantage and rewarded breakthrough ideas. Their Strategic Orientation Index™ results revealed a strong Entrepreneurial Orientation (EO), but their Market Orientation (MO) lagged—particularly in customer listening and cross-functional responsiveness.

This configuration placed NovaForge in the Fearless Inventor persona: high creativity and risk tolerance, but out of step with market needs. Their EM behaviors reflected the imbalance. They scored high in Growth and Opportunity Orientation but underperformed in Market Immersion and Two-Way Customer Contact. While the engineering team moved fast, customer feedback rarely influenced product direction. The disconnect became clear when one of their flagship products—a voice-controlled smart lock—faced backlash for usability issues and privacy concerns.

Guided by their SOI™ results and workshop recommendations, Nova-Forge took targeted action:

They formed a customer advisory panel and scheduled monthly feed-back loops.

They embedded customer-service representatives into product-design reviews.

They implemented an internal "market rotation" program, placing engineers in customer-facing roles one day per month.

Within two quarters, product returns dropped, customer-satisfaction scores improved, and the team's internal alignment strengthened. A follow-up SOI™ assessment showed marked gains in both MO and EM scores, nudging them closer to the Visionary Vanguard quadrant.

NovaForge's journey illustrates a key insight for Fearless Inventors: Innovation alone isn't enough. When bold thinking is grounded in customer understanding, it creates the conditions for scalable, sustainable growth.

ANECDOTAL CASE STUDY: FEARLESS INVENTOR

Cirqwave: Brilliant Tech, Missed Signals

Cirqwave Technologies launched with a vision to revolutionize industrial-safety systems through AI-powered anomaly detection. By their second year, they'd secured $12 million in Series A funding and hired a team of engineers from Tesla, Lockheed Martin, and Stanford. The firm operated like a war room—every conversation revolved around product breakthroughs, speed to IP, and how to stay ten steps ahead of the market.

On the surface, they were a textbook case of disruptive innovation. Internally, they identified as "category creators." What they weren't, however, was customer-centric.

Founder and CEO Erik Anders believed that true innovation required "insulating vision from noise." His approach to product development was unapologetically top-down. Sales teams were not consulted in roadmap decisions. Marketing was limited to technical brochures and trade-show demos. Beta users were hand-selected and treated more like test cases than learning partners.

When early feedback surfaced that Cirqwave's flagship sensor module was too complex to install and required too much end-user calibration, Anders dismissed it. "We're not here to make things easier," he said in a leadership meeting. "We're here to make things *possible*."

That attitude worked until scale became the goal.

By year three, Cirqwave had burned through more than half its funding. Sales were inconsistent. Enterprise prospects requested integration pilots and pricing flexibility—both of which Cirqwave considered distractions. Competitors with simpler, less advanced tech began winning the market with better onboarding, clearer value props, and channel-partner alignment.

Frustrated, Cirqwave doubled down. They expanded their engineering team, launched two more technical features, and delayed usability testing again. It wasn't until a major prospective customer—a \$2B energy utility—walked away after a sixty-day trial citing "engineering arrogance and lack of operational fit" that Cirqwave paused.

But by then, it was too late. The board installed a COO with commercialization experience and froze R&D spending. Several senior engineers left within six months.

In SOI™ terms, Cirqwave epitomized the **Fearless Inventor**:

EO (**Entrepreneurial Orientation**) was high—they were bold, risk-tolerant, and aggressively innovative.

MO (**Market Orientation**) was low—they deprioritized customer feedback, ignored sales signals, and lacked interfunctional coordination.

EM (**Entrepreneurial Marketing**) was strong in speed but weak in engagement—they iterated on tech, not on positioning.

Their downfall wasn't a bad product. It was a **behavioral imbalance**.

By refusing to *listen*, Cirqwave acted in a vacuum. And when the market didn't validate their assumptions, they had no playbook for adaptation.

As one former product lead said later, "We didn't just miss the signal. We were actively blocking it."

INSIGHTFUL OPTIMIZER—SUMMARY PROFILE

Quadrant Location: Low EO / High MO

Definition: The Insightful Optimizer is deeply customer-centric and operationally efficient but tends to be risk-averse and slow to innovate. These firms excel at refining what already works but rarely venture into bold new territory.

Common Behaviors:

- Gathers detailed customer feedback and acts methodically on it
- Prioritizes consistency, quality, and internal coordination
- Focuses on incremental improvements and optimizing current offerings
- Avoids high-risk ventures or markets with high uncertainty
- May invest heavily in CRM, surveys, and formal research processes

Strategic Strengths:

- High customer satisfaction and loyalty
- Efficient internal processes and strong cross-functional coordination
- Excellent at execution and continuous improvement
- Often dominates mature or niche markets with operational discipline

Core Blind Spots:

- Lacks appetite for disruptive innovation or major pivots
- May miss emerging opportunities or fail to act on early market shifts
- Over-relies on historical data rather than strategic foresight
- Struggles to attract entrepreneurial talent or challenge internal inertia

Voice-of-the-Persona Quotes:

- "If our customers aren't asking for it, we don't waste time building it."
- "We'd rather improve what's working than gamble on what might."
- "Innovation is fine—as long as it doesn't disrupt what our customers already love."

Growth Recommendation: Insightful Optimizers should cultivate entrepreneurial thinking internally starting with small pilot projects, external collaborations, or innovation sprints. Building tolerance for uncertainty and calculated risk can unlock new growth without sacrificing the customer responsiveness they're known for.

Hypothetical Case Study: Insightful Optimizer in Action

Company: CareWell Clinics

Industry: Health-Care Services

SOI™ Profile:

- Low EO

- High MO

- EM: Strong in Market Immersion and Informal Research; weak in Growth and Opportunity Orientation

Strategic Persona: Insightful Optimizer

CareWell Clinics is a regional health-care provider focused on community-based, personalized care. Their SOI™ assessment revealed strong Market Orientation (MO), especially in customer listening, service refinement, and internal alignment. However, their Entrepreneurial Orientation (EO) was low. EM scores showed a similar profile—strong in Market Immersion and Informal Research but underdeveloped in Growth and Opportunity Orientation.

Although patient satisfaction remained high, leadership recognized a pattern of missed innovation windows. Competitors were launching telehealth services and expanding regionally, while CareWell hesitated. Using the SOI™ results, they introduced two changes:

- A "low-risk innovation" budget to fund pilot initiatives across clinics

- An internal awards program for calculated risk-taking and new service ideas

Over the next year, CareWell launched a telehealth platform, improved patient access, and expanded into an adjacent market. A follow-up SOI™ assessment revealed growing EO scores and a more balanced EM profile—positioning the firm for future movement toward the Visionary Vanguard persona.

ANECDOTAL CASE STUDY: INSIGHTFUL OPTIMIZER

Breslow Supply: Masters of the Incremental

Breslow Supply had never been known for bold moves—and they were perfectly fine with that. A regional distributor of industrial fasteners and safety gear, the company had grown steadily over forty years through tight margins, reliable service, and strong vendor relationships. When competitors were chasing automation and digital platforms, Breslow doubled down on customer service, SKU accuracy, and relationship selling.

Internally, the company ran like a machine—one finely tuned for operational precision. Their executive team reviewed customer feedback quarterly and routinely interviewed key accounts to ensure expectations were being met. The marketing manager, who had once been a client-success lead, built email campaigns based on reorder patterns and line-level buyer behavior. Cross-departmental communication was strong, and no team operated in a silo.

What Breslow didn't do was bet big.

In 2022, a midsize competitor in a neighboring region began eating into Breslow's territory with a self-service digital portal and a fleet of last-mile delivery vans. The move surprised Breslow leadership, but rather than respond with speed or investment, they chose to optimize further. They revamped their inventory-forecasting model, tightened SLA language, and updated account manager scripts.

Over the next eighteen months, margins held steady, and customer churn remained low—but new business acquisition began to lag. Younger procurement officers increasingly selected vendors with integrated ERP tools or AI-driven quote engines—capabilities Breslow hadn't prioritized.

The product team proposed a pilot with a tech partner to digitize part of the order-entry process. Leadership declined, citing risk, distraction, and the belief that "our customers don't want fancy—they want dependable."

The pilot was never revisited.

In SOI™ terms, Breslow exemplified the **Insightful Optimizer**:

MO (**Market Orientation**) was high—they were attentive listeners, deeply in tune with customer needs, and operated with interfunctional coordination.

EO (**Entrepreneurial Orientation**) was low—they avoided risk, deprioritized innovation, and resisted future-focused experiments.

EM (**Entrepreneurial Marketing**) was present in tactical execution (emails, relationship loops) but absent in growth posture or opportunity orientation.

Their challenge wasn't in knowing the customer—it was in **translating knowledge into bold moves.**

Breslow succeeded in managing the present but failed to anticipate the future. Their organizational behavior favored optimization over reinvention, and while that preserved margins it limited growth.

A junior analyst put it bluntly during a leadership offsite:

"We're excellent at evolving within our current model—but I'm not sure we'd recognize a disruptive opportunity even if it punched us in the face."

RELUCTANT RESPONDER—SUMMARY PROFILE

Quadrant Location: Low EO / Low MO

Definition: The Reluctant Responder is passive, reactive, and often stagnant, lacking both entrepreneurial drive and market responsiveness. These firms operate in survival mode, typically anchored in legacy systems, internal silos, or outdated assumptions.

Common Behaviors:
- Rarely initiates change unless forced by external pressure
- Makes decisions based on internal politics or tradition rather than

market signals

- Avoids risk, experimentation, and investment in growth initiatives
- Has minimal or outdated customer insight infrastructure
- Focuses on short-term efficiency or protecting the status quo

Strategic Strengths:

- Institutional memory and deep legacy knowledge
- Stability in highly regulated or slow-moving industries
- Risk containment and operational control
- Familiar to longtime customers or partners

Core Blind Spots:

- Lack of vision, innovation, and proactive planning
- Misalignment with current customer expectations
- Low agility and slow response to competitors
- Inability to attract entrepreneurial or growth-minded talent

Voice-of-the-Persona Quote:

- "We've been doing it this way for twenty years—why change now?"
- "Our customers don't complain, so we must be doing something right."
- "Let's not reinvent the wheel—just stick to what we know."

Growth Recommendation: Reluctant Responders must first confront their strategic drift and commit to re-engaging with both their market and their internal potential. Starting with informal customer conversations, competitive analysis, and pilot innovations can reignite clarity and reorient the firm toward forward movement.

HYPOTHETICAL CASE STUDY: RELUCTANT RESPONDER IN ACTION

Company: MidState Manufacturing
Industry: Industrial Components
SOI™ Profile:

- Low EO

- Low MO
- EM: Weak across all six subdimensions, especially Opportunity Orientation and Value Creation Through Alliances

Strategic Persona: Reluctant Responder

MidState Manufacturing, a family-owned industrial parts supplier, maintained steady but stagnant operations. The company avoided risk, rarely sought new customers, and had no active marketing or product development functions. Their SOI™ assessment confirmed low EO, low MO, and weak performance across all six EM subdimensions.

Initially skeptical of the results, MidState's leadership began by focusing on two EM levers: Informal Marketing Research and Value Creation Through Alliances. They launched monthly client-listening calls and built a referral partnership with a regional distributor. The company also piloted a new reporting dashboard to identify growth opportunities in underserved segments.

Though progress was incremental, follow-up assessments showed improved EM behavior and early gains in MO scores. These shifts helped MidState evolve out of the Reluctant Responder quadrant and into the Hybrid Zone, laying the groundwork for more ambitious strategic shifts.

ANECDOTAL CASE STUDY: RELUCTANT RESPONDER

Harbridge Services: Playing Defense, Losing Ground

Harbridge Services specialized in back-office support for midsize credit unions—processing statements, managing call centers, and handling overflow transaction volume during seasonal peaks. With over three hundred employees and decades of industry presence, Harbridge had built a reputation for consistency, low error rates, and contractual dependability.

Internally, however, the mood was cautious—bordering on stagnant.

Every major initiative was passed through at least three committees. New technology purchases required yearlong evaluations. And while client-satisfaction scores remained respectable, Harbridge hadn't launched a new service line in over six years.

The company's executive team prided themselves on being "measured." But that posture often came at the cost of responsiveness. Frontline staff repeatedly escalated feedback about a growing number of credit unions asking for API integrations and real-time service dashboards. The IT director voiced concerns that Harbridge's legacy systems were becoming a liability. Sales leaders noticed longer deal cycles and more requests for features Harbridge didn't offer.

Still, leadership held back.

When the VP of marketing proposed a small-scale pilot to test a digital-onboarding experience with a single client cohort, the CEO tabled it. "If we test something and it fails, it could damage our reputation," he said. "Let's wait until we're sure."

Meanwhile, a newer entrant in the same space—backed by private equity—launched a self-serve client portal, implemented automation tools, and rapidly began winning deals that would have historically defaulted to Harbridge.

The turning point came when Harbridge lost its largest client to that competitor after a decade-long relationship. In the exit interview, the client praised Harbridge's team but noted, "We can't afford to wait for your systems to catch up. Our members expect more now."

In SOI™ terms, Harbridge was a textbook **Reluctant Responder**:

MO (Market Orientation) was present in principle—they gathered customer input and reviewed service metrics—but failed to act on key insights.

EO (Entrepreneurial Orientation) was low—they avoided risk, deferred strategic experimentation, and rarely initiated market change.

EM (Entrepreneurial Marketing) was nearly absent—there were no agile campaigns, partnership tests, or proactive market-shaping behavior.

Harbridge didn't suffer from arrogance or laziness. It suffered from **institutional inertia.**

Their processes were precise, their people capable, and their data abundant. But behaviorally, they defaulted to reactivity over reinvention. And in a market accelerating around them, that made the difference.

A departing sales director summed it up with quiet frustration:

"We were never wrong—but we were always too late."

HYBRID ZONE—SUMMARY PROFILE

Quadrant Location: Mid or Uneven EO / MO (mixed alignment or inconsistent execution)

Definition: The Hybrid Zone represents firms with a fragmented or fluctuating strategic posture—showing signs of both entrepreneurial intent and Market Orientation, but inconsistently or without internal alignment. These companies often experience internal conflict, directional ambiguity, or stalled momentum due to mixed signals.

Common Behaviors:

- Strong initiatives emerge in pockets, but lack organization-wide traction.
- Leadership says the right things strategically, but behavior is inconsistent.
- Efforts to innovate or serve customers are episodic or siloed.
- Team alignment depends on department or personality, not shared frameworks.
- The company shifts gears frequently without a clear long-term playbook.

Strategic Strengths:

- Latent potential across teams and functions
- Moments of brilliance in product, marketing, or customer experience
- Ability to connect with market trends when execution aligns
- Often in transition—early in turnaround, post-acquisition, or culture shift

Core Blind Spots:

- Misalignment between stated vision and actual behavior

- Confusion around decision-making and prioritization
- Energy spent reacting or recalibrating instead of executing
- Teams may feel demoralized by unclear expectations or shifting strategy

Voice-of-the-Persona Quote:

- "We're doing a lot of things—but I'm not sure we're pulling in the same direction."
- "Some teams are charging ahead, others are stuck—and nobody's sure which one is right."
- "We've got pieces of the puzzle—but no one's seeing the full picture."

Growth Recommendation: Hybrid Zone firms must clarify their strategic identity and align leadership, structure, and culture accordingly. Using the SOI™ diagnostic can help isolate gaps and prioritize which axis—EO, MO, or EM—requires focus first. Their power comes from potential—but only if they harmonize their conflicted strategic posture.

HYPOTHETICAL CASE STUDY: HYBRID ZONE IN ACTION

Company: Solara Learning

Industry: Educational Technology

SOI™ Profile:

- Mid-range EO
- High MO
- EM: Mixed—strong in Two-Way Customer Contact, weak in Growth Orientation and Value Creation Through Alliances

Strategic Persona: Hybrid Zone

Solara Learning offered a digital platform for school districts to manage classroom content, assessments, and teacher support. Their Market Orientation (MO) was strong—they listened well, adapted to user feedback, and had a deep understanding of customer pain points. But their EO score was moderate. They rarely initiated new product categories or pursued bold experimentation. EM behaviors were inconsistent: strong in Two-Way Customer Contact and Market Immersion, but weak in Growth Orientation and Value Creation Through Alliances.

This placed them squarely in the Hybrid Zone—a firm with partial alignment and unrealized potential. Leadership used the SOI™ assessment and workshop to identify low-risk innovation zones and tasked a cross-functional team with proposing one new feature every sixty days. They also pursued their first formal partnership with a state education agency, unlocking broader distribution.

Three quarters later, Solara had launched two new modules and expanded into two adjacent states. Their updated SOI™ scores showed rising EO and a more balanced EM profile, suggesting a potential future shift toward the Insightful Optimizer persona.

ANECDOTAL CASE STUDY: HYBRID ZONE

Pathcore Health: Between Ambition and Alignment
Pathcore Health was a growth-stage health-care software firm serving midsize clinics with scheduling, billing, and patient-communication tools. With $22 million in annual recurring revenue and 120 employees, the company was at a strategic crossroads—confident in its product-market fit, but unsure how to scale effectively.

Its founding team had strong entrepreneurial instincts. The CEO frequently spoke about disruption, market agility, and first-mover advantage. New feature concepts were brainstormed weekly, and the company often prioritized speed over structure. Their engineering team, led by a charismatic CTO, could launch prototypes in days.

At the same time, Pathcore had hired a head of customer success from a Fortune 500 background who implemented structured Net-Promoter Score (NPS) surveys, churn analytics, and playbooks for account expansion. The marketing team built buyer personas and ran segmented campaigns. Sales ops produced detailed win/loss reports and return-on-investment case studies.

In isolation, each function was high-performing.

But together, they were misaligned.

Product would launch new capabilities before enablement materials were ready. Marketing campaigns promoted features that sales hadn't been briefed on. Customer success collected valuable insights, but those insights rarely made it into roadmap planning. In executive meetings, leaders agreed on strategy in principle—but disagreed silently on which behaviors mattered most.

This lack of cohesion led to erratic performance. Quarterly revenue targets were missed despite strong lead volume. Clients expressed excitement about Pathcore's vision but struggled with inconsistent implementation experiences. Internally, departments worked hard but increasingly felt like they were running different races.

In an all-hands meeting, a senior engineer asked a pointed question:

"Are we a disruptor, a customer-service company, or a data platform? Because right now, I hear all three—and I'm building toward none."

Pathcore's executive team eventually brought in a third-party facilitator to assess behavioral alignment. What emerged wasn't a lack of talent or strategy. It was behavioral inconsistency.

In SOI™ terms, Pathcore sat squarely in the **Hybrid Zone**:

EO (**Entrepreneurial Orientation**) was present in leadership, but execution lacked cross-team adoption.

MO (**Market Orientation**) existed in data collection, but not in coordinated decision-making.

EM (**Entrepreneurial Marketing**) showed up in bursts but lacked consistency or feedback loops.

The company didn't need a new strategy—it needed a behavioral reset.

Pathcore began quarterly strategy-alignment sessions, created cross-functional "launch pods," and tied objectives and key results to quadrant-specific behaviors. Within six months, client-onboarding satisfaction rose 20 percent, internal product delays dropped, and their next pricing model was co-created with input from every team.

As the CEO later admitted:

"Our problem wasn't vision—it was translation. Once we started aligning how we thought, listened, and acted, the fog lifted."

TABLE: SUMMARY OF SOI™ STRATEGIC PERSONAS + EM BEHAVIORAL FOCUS

PERSONA	EO / MO PROFILE	KEY TRAITS	COMMON PITFALLS	EM BEHAVIOR PATTERNS	TOP PRIORITIES
Visionary Vanguard	High EO / High MO	Bold, aligned, visionary	Overextension, complexity creep	Strong across all EM subdimensions, especially Growth Orientation and Two-Way Customer Contact	Streamline focus, avoid overreach
Fearless Inventor	High EO / Low MO	Inventive, bold, experimental	Poor market fit, internal echo chamber	Strong in Growth and Opportunity Orientation; weak in Market Immersion and Customer Contact	Deepen market feedback loops, build MO & EM balance
Insightful Optimizer	Low EO / High MO	Insight-driven, steady, adaptive	Risk aversion, missed opportunities	Strong in Market Immersion and Informal Research; weak in Growth and Opportunity Orientation	Build EO confidence, experiment more boldly

PERSONA	EO / MO PROFILE	KEY TRAITS	COMMON PITFALLS	EM BEHAVIOR PATTERNS	TOP PRIORITIES
Reluctant Responder	Low EO / Low MO	Reactive, stable, internally focused	Stagnation, low innovation velocity	Weak across most EM factors, especially Opportunity Orientation and Value Creation Through Alliances	Strengthen both EO and MO fundamentals via EM levers
Hybrid Zone	Mixed or mid EO / MO	Versatile, transitional, fragmented	Drifting strategy, unclear direction	Variable EM profiles depending on the imbalance—some overindex on alliances, others on research	Clarify strategy, align EM to core priorities

STRATEGIC EVOLUTION PATHS ACROSS SOI™ PERSONAS

The Strategic Orientation Index™ (SOI™) personas are not fixed identities. They reflect your firm's current behavioral alignment across Entrepreneurial Orientation (EO), Market Orientation (MO), and Entrepreneurial Marketing (EM). Over time, firms evolve—by choice or by necessity. This evolution is driven by external pressures, internal leadership changes, market failures, or renewed growth ambition.

This section outlines the most common strategic transition paths between SOI™ personas. For each transition, it identifies the typical triggers, the primary strategic levers that drive transformation, and a realistic timeframe based on consulting observations and organizational pattern recognition.

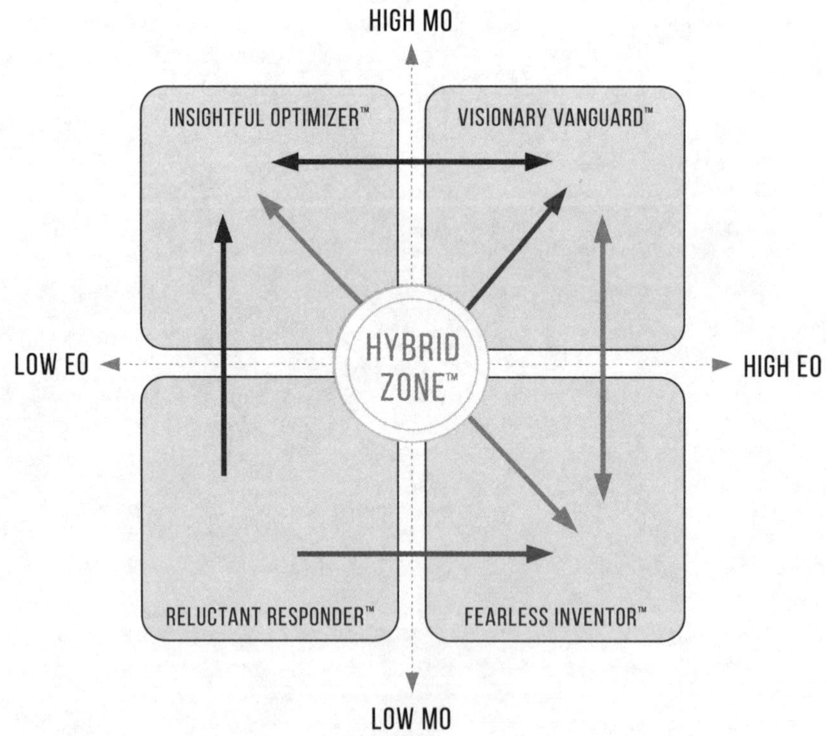

PERSONA TRANSITION MATRIX

CURRENT PERSONA	LIKELY EVOLUTION PATH	KEY TRIGGERS FOR MOVEMENT	PRIMARY STRATEGIC LEVERS	TYPICAL TIME-LINE
Reluctant Responder	Hybrid Zone or Insightful Optimizer	New leadership, Voice of Customer (VoC) investments, customer churn	Executive team reset, customer immersion, quick-win initiatives, team re-engagement	6–12 months
Insightful Optimizer	Visionary Vanguard	Cultural renewal, innovation pressure, market plateau	Innovation labs, growth-oriented leadership coaching, cross-functional risk-taking training	12–18 months
Fearless Inventor	Visionary Vanguard	Product failure, stalled growth, executive intervention	Customer segmentation, VoC integration, market-feedback loops, external benchmarking	12-18 months
Hybrid Zone	Any quadrant	Strategy offsite, executive turnover, strategic clarity	SOI™ diagnostics, persona workshop, alignment sprints by function	6–12 months
Visionary Vanguard	Sustain or slide to Hybrid	Leadership change, M&A disruption, complacency	Continuous VoC, innovation scaffolding, market revalidation, persona refresh	Ongoing vigilance

HOW TO USE THIS MATRIX

Diagnose your current persona using the SOI™ score.

Locate your current persona in the matrix.

Identify your desired strategic posture and whether evolution is proactive or reactive.

Implement the levers listed with executive buy-in, measurable milestones, and communication plans.

Strategic transitions rarely happen without intention. This table is your preview of the road ahead—so you can lead it, not react to it.

To customize this for your organization, use the full SOI™ assessment and workbook at kylejharkema.com.

HOW IT WORKS

Each of the three dimensions is scored on a standardized scale based on assessment inputs:

EO is assessed through metrics of innovativeness, proactiveness, and risk-taking (Lumpkin & Dess, 1996; Rauch et al., 2009).

MO is evaluated by customer orientation, competitor awareness, and interfunctional coordination (Narver & Slater, 1990; Kohli & Jaworski, 1990).

EM is operationalized through six granular subdimensions: Growth Orientation, Opportunity Orientation, Two-Way Customer Contact, Value Creation Through Alliances, Informal Marketing Research, and Market Immersion (Morris et al., 2002).

A scoring calculator or digital-assessment tool is used to generate raw scores and percentile classifications for each construct. These scores are then visualized in quadrant-based models and/or 3D scatterplots that enable strategic benchmarking against high-performing profiles. Unlike abstract models, the SOI™ is deliberately designed to bridge theory and practice, enabling decision-makers to immediately connect diagnostic insights with next steps.

VISUAL REPRESENTATION

The SOI™ framework can be depicted using multiple visual tools:

A **2x2 quadrant model** maps firms along EO (x-axis) and MO (y-axis). The four primary personas occupy each corner.

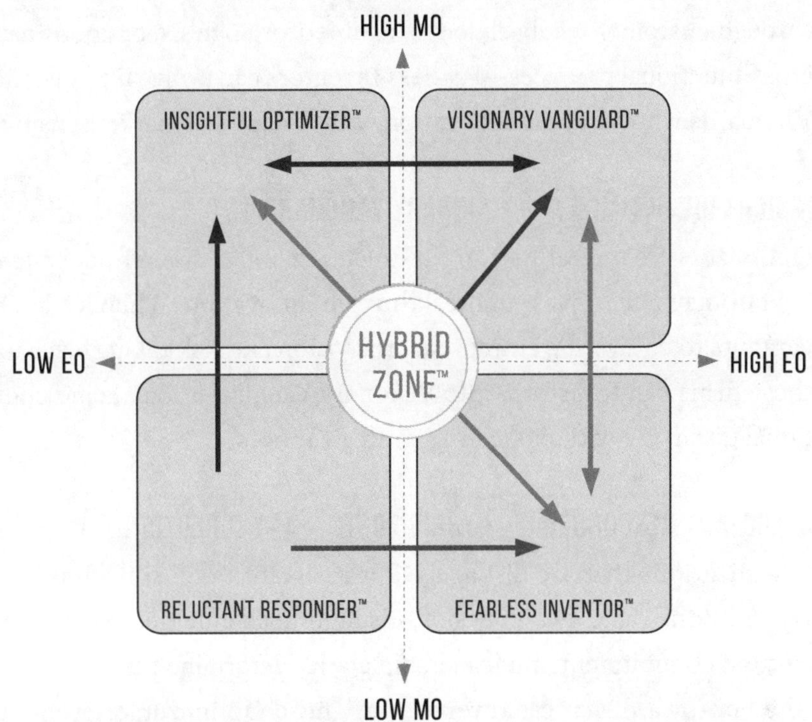

A **central Hybrid Zone** represents firms with mixed or moderate scores that defy clear classification.

These visuals are not just descriptive—they're prescriptive. They help teams quickly grasp where they stand and what types of strategy shifts would move them into higher-performance zones.

COMMON TRANSITIONS

FEARLESS INVENTOR → VISIONARY VANGUARD

Many firms begin with high entrepreneurial energy but lack structured listening mechanisms. By layering in systematic Market Orientation—through customer feedback loops, competitor analysis, or coordinated cross-functional practices—Fearless Inventors can evolve into Visionary Vanguards who pair bold innovation with disciplined market sensing.

INSIGHTFUL OPTIMIZER → VISIONARY VANGUARD

Optimizers are typically strong at execution and customer understanding but may underinvest in breakthrough innovation. When leadership commits to cultivating entrepreneurial vision and risk-taking behaviors, these firms can transform into Visionary Vanguards, balancing operational discipline with pioneering strategic moves.

RELUCTANT RESPONDER → HYBRID ZONE → ANY DIRECTION

Organizations that are disengaged or resistant often shift first into a Hybrid Zone once awareness of misalignment emerges. From there, cultural commitment and leadership clarity determine the trajectory—whether toward Fearless Inventor, Insightful Optimizer, or eventually Visionary Vanguard. This transition underscores the importance of momentum once inertia is broken.

VISIONARY VANGUARD → HYBRID ZONE

Even high-performing Vanguards can regress when leadership churn, rapid scaling, or loss of alignment erode their behavioral cohesion. The organization may retain ambition but lose cross-team synchronization, resulting in diluted strategy and confusion about priorities. Without intervention, this drift toward Hybrid is often the precursor to stalled growth.

VISIONARY VANGUARD → FEARLESS INVENTOR

When bold innovation begins to outpace structured market feedback, firms may drift away from balanced vision and toward unilateral experimentation. The result is a Fearless Inventor posture—still creative and pioneering, but increasingly vulnerable to customer blind spots and competitive surprises.

VISIONARY VANGUARD → INSIGHTFUL OPTIMIZER

Some Vanguards deliberately choose to scale back entrepreneurial risk once they achieve market leadership. By emphasizing executional excellence, compliance, and customer responsiveness, they can transition into Insightful Optimizers. This move often reflects a strategic decision to consolidate rather than expand risk horizons.

HYBRID ZONE → FEARLESS INVENTOR OR INSIGHTFUL OPTIMIZER

Most Hybrid firms resolve their misalignment by tilting one way or the other. If entrepreneurial drive reasserts itself before structure, the firm shifts toward Fearless Inventor. If market discipline and coordination are restored first, the organization stabilizes as an Insightful Optimizer. Either direction represents progress compared to the paralysis of Hybrid status.

PRACTICAL USE

The SOI™ framework is deployed through a diagnostic tool that executives, consultants, and educators can use to assess firms in real time. The tool provides:

- Firm-level scoring on EO, MO, and EM
- A quadrant classification (e.g., Visionary Vanguard)
- A radar view of EM subdimensions
- Checklist-driven recommendations prioritized by score
- Strategic action plans aligned with quadrant strengths and gaps

HOW THE SOI™ DIFFERS FROM OTHER STRATEGIC FRAMEWORKS

While the Strategic Orientation Index™ (SOI™) builds upon decades of strategic theory, it is not simply another addition to the toolbox—it fills a gap that many frameworks leave untouched. Traditional models like SWOT analysis and Porter's Five Forces help organizations evaluate external threats and opportunities, but they do not assess whether a firm's internal strategic behavior is aligned or executable. Tools like the Balanced Scorecard and the Business Model Canvas add operational clarity but tend to focus on metrics, not orientation (Kaplan & Norton, 1996; Osterwalder & Pigneur, 2010). SOI™ is different because it evaluates how firms behave, not just what they plan. It uncovers internal misalignment between entrepreneurial drive, market understanding, and marketing behavior—an area where other frameworks are often silent. This makes SOI™ a behavioral diagnostic tool as much as a strategic one.

Another key difference lies in how SOI™ moves beyond high-level strategy typologies to offer firm-level personas grounded in real-world execution. Frameworks like the BCG Matrix and Blue Ocean Strategy help firms make positioning choices but lack behavioral nuance (Kim & Mauborgne, 2005). SOI™, by contrast, connects strategic posture (EO), market-intelligence behavior (MO), and Entrepreneurial-Marketing execution (EM) into one integrated lens. Rather than simply deciding between cost leadership or differentiation, firms using SOI™ uncover why they aren't executing, even if the strategy is sound. It surfaces blind spots in behavior—like risk-aversion, siloed execution, or shallow customer contact—that can derail otherwise intelligent plans. That executional clarity is what gives the framework applied traction.

SOI™ also distinguishes itself by being the first operational model to triangulate EO, MO, and EM into a measurable diagnostic system. Morris, Schindehutte, and LaForge (2002) conceptually proposed that Entrepreneurial Marketing emerges at the intersection of entrepreneurial and Market Orientation. This model builds on that insight and extends it—offering firms not just theory, but a structured scoring system, visual quadrant, and actionable personas. Miles and Darroch (2006) emphasized that combining EO and MO leads to stronger competitive advantage, especially in larger firms. Kraus, Harms, and Fink (2010) added that EM is the missing link that turns orientation into performance. The SOI™ converts these academic principles into a usable strategic infrastructure for real firms of any size.

Additionally, the SOI™ is built for adaptability and strategic movement over time. It's not a snapshot—it's a dynamic map. While models like the McKinsey 7S focus on structure and systems, SOI™ focuses on behavioral alignment, allowing leaders to see how innovation, market focus, and execution interact—or conflict. It reveals not just where a firm is but why it's stuck, and how to move toward high-alignment personas like the Visionary Vanguard. It enables consultants, educators, and executives to design specific growth interventions based on persona archetypes, not generic best practices. The quadrant and transition model also make SOI™ useful in strategic-planning cycles, offsite workshops, and leadership coaching environments.

In short, SOI™ is a diagnostic system built for modern complexity. It does not replace other strategic tools—it enhances them by revealing behavioral gaps those models often miss. It offers a bridge between strategy and execution, between theory and behavior, between market truth and internal alignment. For any organization struggling with growth stagnation, strategic misfires, or cultural inertia, SOI™ offers a new way to see the problem—and a pathway forward. That's what makes it different. That's why it matters.

COMPARISON: SOI™ VS. OTHER STRATEGIC FRAMEWORKS

FRAMEWORK	PRIMARY FOCUS	UNIQUE VALUE	LIMITATION ADDRESSED BY SOI™
SOI™ (Strategic Orientation Index™)	Behavioral alignment across EO, MO, and EM	Maps strategic behavior and execution into firm personas	Integrates strategy, market understanding, and execution into a unified diagnostic
SWOT Analysis	Internal/external environmental scan	Identifies internal strengths/weaknesses and external threats/opportunities	Does not assess behavioral dynamics or execution readiness
Porter's Five Forces	Industry competitiveness and market positioning	Evaluates external forces shaping profitability	Ignores internal posture and strategic behavior
Balanced Scorecard	Performance metrics across strategic perspectives	Links strategy to KPIs in finance, operations, customers, and learning	Focuses on measurement but not behavioral alignment or strategic misfires
Business Model Canvas	Business model structure and component viability	Visualizes how value is created, delivered, and captured	Lacks diagnostic depth on internal misalignment or execution failure
Blue Ocean Strategy	Strategic differentiation and whitespace creation	Helps firms break out of crowded markets by creating new demand	Doesn't address internal capability to execute or sustain innovation

McKinsey 7S Framework	Organizational design and internal system alignment	Ensures cohesion across strategy, structure, systems, and culture	Assumes alignment but doesn't assess EO, MO, or market-driven behavior patterns
EOS (Entrepreneurial Operating System)	Traction, accountability, and operational execution	Provides simple tools for discipline, focus, and execution rhythm	Lacks market orientation and strategic-behavior profiling—SOI™ diagnoses how firms think, listen, and act in dynamic environments

SAMPLE SOI™ SCORECARD: "NOVATEK MANUFACTURING"

Industry: Industrial Automation

Size: 85 employees

Strategic Focus: Expanding into IoT and smart systems

Assessment Completed By: Executive team (5 responses averaged)

Strategic-Persona Classification:

Fearless Inventor

High EO + Low MO = Strong innovation drive, but disconnected from market needs.

STRATEGIC INSIGHTS:

Your executive team is entrepreneurial, confident, and innovation-driven.

However, weak Market Orientation indicates a lack of structured customer insight, competitor tracking, and cross-functional alignment.

You may be launching products faster than the market can absorb them—or without sufficient validation.

EM scores suggest opportunity sensing and growth mindset are strong, but customer contact and informal feedback are weak.

Introduce lightweight customer-discovery processes in new product development.

Assign one executive to lead informal research and frontline customer shadowing.

Build a Customer Advisory Board to increase early input and loyalty.

Consider strategic alliances with more market-aware partners or distributors.

LIMITATIONS AND FUTURE DEVELOPMENT OF THE SOI™ FRAMEWORK

Like any strategic model, the Strategic Orientation Index™ (SOI™) is a simplification. It offers a structured lens to understand firm-level alignment across Entrepreneurial Orientation (EO), Market Orientation (MO), and Entrepreneurial Marketing (EM), but it cannot capture every nuance of business behavior. Contextual variables—such as industry regulation, leadership changes, economic shocks, or organizational culture—may alter how EO, MO, or EM are expressed. The SOI™ does not replace detailed market analysis, operational auditing, or financial modeling. It is best viewed as a **behavioral diagnostic**—not a forecasting engine or standalone strategy-formulation tool.

Another limitation is the use of **self-reported data** as the foundation for scoring. This introduces the potential for cognitive bias, optimism distortion, or misperception among executive teams. When firms complete the SOI™ diagnostic, they are reporting how they perceive their behavior—not necessarily how customers, competitors, or frontline employees would rate it. That makes the SOI™ strongest when used as a **conversation catalyst**, not a fixed truth. To increase accuracy, firms are encouraged to gather cross-functional inputs, anonymize responses when possible, and follow up with qualitative discussions or customer feedback. The more perspectives included in the scoring process, the more diagnostic power the tool will have.

The SOI™ is also more effective at the **firm or unit level** than at an individual level. It is designed to evaluate strategic alignment across departments, teams, and leadership—not to score personal traits or performance. In firms with multiple business units, scores should be interpreted separately by division. Likewise, multinational firms should avoid applying a single persona across culturally or operationally distinct markets. While the SOI™ can highlight enterprise-wide trends, its best use is at the **operational zone** where strategy meets execution. In future editions, sub-score dashboards may be added to visualize internal variation more clearly.

Finally, while the SOI™ is built on well-documented constructs—**Entrepreneurial Orientation** (Lumpkin & Dess, 1996; Covin & Slevin, 1989), **Market Orientation** (Narver & Slater, 1990; Kohli & Jaworski, 1990), and **Entrepreneurial Marketing** (Morris et al., 2002; Miles & Darroch, 2006; Kraus et al., 2010)—it remains a relatively new framework. It has not yet been validated through large-scale longitudinal studies or cross-industry regression models. Future research could investigate how SOI™ scores correlate with financial outcomes, innovation rates, employee retention, or customer loyalty. Academic partners and research institutions are invited to engage in that process. This version of the model should be seen as a **Version 1.0 diagnostic framework**—useful, rigorous, and ready for use, but open to evolution. The goal isn't perfection—it's strategic clarity that sparks productive action.

STRATEGIC QUADRANT FIT CONDITIONS: ACCEPTABLE ORIENTATIONS AND ENVIRONMENTAL ALIGNMENT

The Strategic Orientation Index™ (SOI) framework identifies three dominant quadrants—Insightful Optimizer, Fearless Inventor, and Visionary Vanguard—that represent acceptable, and often optimal, combinations of how firms think (EO), listen (MO), and act (EM). Each of these quadrants is shaped not only by internal strategic behavior but by alignment with external environmental conditions, organizational structure, and cultural traits. Unlike traditional strategy models that imply a single path to optimality, SOI acknowledges the legitimacy of multiple pathways to performance, depending on industry context, market turbulence, and the organization's structural maturity (Zahra & Covin, 1995; Narver & Slater, 1990). Even the Reluctant Responder quadrant—typically associated with stagnation—is not inherently "wrong" in rare cases where market protection, monopoly power, or heavy regulation remove the need for adaptive behavior (Slater, Olson, & Hult, 2006). The quadrant model, therefore, functions as a strategic-fit framework rather than a simplistic hierarchy. Its value lies in matching behavioral posture with contextual demands, not prescribing uniformity.

Insightful Optimizer (**High MO, Low EO**) firms are particularly well suited for stable, trust-driven industries where the customer voice is central and innovation cycles are moderate. These organizations typically operate in legacy B2B sectors, family-owned manufacturing firms, regulated environments, and even higher education. They prioritize cross-functional listening systems and customer-satisfaction metrics over disruption or experimentation. Research has shown that firms high in Market Orientation tend to outperform their peers in customer satisfaction, adaptability, and long-term profitability (Narver & Slater, 1990; Kohli & Jaworski, 1990). However, these gains often require operational excellence and cultural alignment, including collaborative team structures and loyalty at the middle-management layer. Risk aversion is not a flaw in this context—it is a protective posture grounded in the organizational need to deliver reliability, build long-term relationships, and mitigate compliance exposure (Kellermanns et al., 2008). Insightful Optimizers are less likely to chase trends but more likely to succeed in navigating long sales cycles, procurement-driven buyer journeys, or political environments where disruption is punished rather than rewarded.

Externally, Insightful Optimizers thrive in markets with

low-to-moderate turbulence and with relatively stable customer segments. These environments reward consistency, relationship depth, and institutional trust over boldness or speed. Internal infrastructure must mirror these external conditions; firms in this quadrant typically display strong operational discipline, robust planning cycles, and low appetite for experimentation. In these contexts, EO-based strategies often backfire—pushing innovation for its own sake can alienate risk-averse buyers or destabilize carefully built alliances. High MO combined with strong EM execution creates an optimized posture for maximizing value within legacy constraints (Becherer, Haynes, & Fletcher, 2006). Rather than constantly reinventing themselves, Insightful Optimizers double down on operational listening, delivery, and long-term trust. This orientation may not appeal to venture capitalists or innovation evangelists, but it aligns powerfully with the incentives and constraints of legacy markets.

Fearless Inventor (High EO, Low MO) organizations represent a fundamentally different strategic fit. These are often found in early-stage start-ups, R&D-heavy verticals like biotech or aerospace, and founder-led innovation labs. Here, risk tolerance, visionary leadership, and first-mover advantage are key drivers of performance. These firms act before listening—not because they are negligent, but because speed, novelty, and bold experimentation are existential requirements. In highly uncertain markets, customer needs may not yet be knowable, and structured listening systems may slow down essential innovation cycles. This orientation fits disruptive technology firms where the market is still forming, and where being early—even at the risk of being wrong—is preferable to being late (Zhou, Yim, & Tse, 2005). In these firms, strategic autonomy and lightly structured teams support rapid iteration, idea generation, and tolerance for failure as a growth mechanism.

While this quadrant is clearly incompatible with the measured stability of Insightful Optimizer firms, it is not inherently reckless. The EO posture has been shown in many empirical studies to correlate with opportunity recognition, speed of decision-making, and successful navigation of ambiguity (Lumpkin & Dess, 1996; Covin & Slevin, 1991). The low MO score in this quadrant is not a deficiency—it is an intentional deprioritization. Listening too early in a product or category life cycle can actually increase risk, as customers themselves may not be able to articulate what they want or need. Instead, internal conviction, technical vision, and agile sprints become the guiding principles. Importantly, this quadrant is often a temporary posture. As the market matures and feedback loops become more available, successful Fearless Inventors may evolve into Visionary Vanguards or even Insightful Optimizers, depending on the institutionalization of their structures and the strategic maturity of their leadership.

Visionary Vanguard (High EO, High MO) is perhaps the rarest and most celebrated quadrant. These are firms that combine bold, future-facing ideation with highly developed market sensing and customer engagement. They often emerge in hypergrowth SaaS sectors, fintech, consumer tech, or as new category creators. The strategic posture here is complex: Firms must integrate fast data loops with deep foresight while building cross-functional teams that can execute at speed. The risk of this quadrant is burnout, misalignment, or resource strain—Visionary Vanguards are often pulled in many directions at once. But when successful, they fundamentally reshape the competitive landscape. Scholars have found that firms with both high EO and MO achieve superior innovation outcomes, especially when they can resolve the tension between internal vision and external voice (Atuahene-Gima & Ko, 2001; Noble, Sinha, & Kumar, 2002).

Culturally, Visionary Vanguard firms exhibit both top-down clarity and bottom-up responsiveness. Their leaders often function as strategic integrators—able to connect big-picture narratives with ground-level behaviors. Internally, these firms require agile operations, comfort with iterative failure, and investment in branding and customer experience as core strategic levers. While these capabilities are difficult to maintain, especially at scale, they offer immense strategic upside. These organizations do not simply react to the market—they shape it. However, Visionary Vanguard is not always the "best" quadrant. In fact, deploying this posture in an environment that cannot sustain it—such as a compliance-driven B2B firm—can lead to organizational exhaustion, customer confusion, or failed transformation. The quadrant's value lies in its fit with high-velocity environments where adaptation speed and narrative ownership are critical to survival and growth.

It's also worth noting that in very rare and specific cases, even the **Reluctant Responder** quadrant (Low EO, Low MO) may be viable. This typically occurs in protected markets such as public utilities, monopolies, or heavily subsidized government contractors. In these situations, performance is often driven by compliance, regulatory alignment, or infrastructure dominance rather than market dynamics. While this quadrant is not aspirational for most firms, it can offer a rational, even profitable, strategic posture when incentives do not reward innovation or customer-centricity (Slater et al., 2006). However, the SOI framework intentionally discourages firms from defaulting into this quadrant without rigorous justification. In nearly all cases, remaining in this posture leads to organizational decline over time—especially as deregulation, competitive encroachment, or technological disruption erode the original protection.

While the Strategic Orientation Index™ (SOI) emphasizes the relative strength and strategic coherence of the three major quadrants—Insightful Optimizer, Fearless Inventor, and Visionary Vanguard—it is critical to acknowledge the prevalence and complexity of the Hybrid Zone. Unlike the other quadrants, the Hybrid Zone is not a destination but a signal of misalignment. It represents a behavioral pattern where organizational actions, listening mechanisms, and thinking models are either at odds or unclear across leadership layers. These firms often exhibit inconsistent strategic behaviors, such as high innovation rhetoric with low risk-taking in practice, or customer-centric language that is not reflected in market-sensing routines. Empirical research on strategic misalignment confirms that mixed signals across strategic dimensions lead to diminished execution quality, reduced internal trust, and cultural fragmentation (Slater, Olson, & Hult, 2006). The SOI™ framework further breaks this zone into three diagnostic subtypes—**Conflicted**, **Diluted**, and **Aspirational** hybrids—each with distinct behavioral signatures and risks. For instance, Conflicted Hybrids tend to experience interdepartmental tension due to clashing narratives and divergent priorities, while Diluted Hybrids stagnate due to lack of conviction or clarity. Aspirational Hybrids, on the other hand, may have a visionary executive team whose strategic posture fails to penetrate the middle tiers of the organization, creating a gap between rhetoric and reality. These subtypes provide a practical mechanism for strategic consultants and executives to diagnose the source of organizational drag, and they underscore that being in the Hybrid Zone is often not a strategic choice but a symptom of narrative overreach or siloed decision-making. While no quadrant is inherently superior, the Hybrid Zone is best treated as a transitional posture—one that requires clarity, coherence, and often, a realignment of internal behaviors with external aspirations.

What matters most across all quadrants is alignment. Misalignment—between internal behavior, team beliefs, customer realities, and environmental conditions—is what drives performance erosion. This is where the SOI™ diagnostic offers unique value. It identifies not just where a firm sits, but how coherently that posture is understood across the organization. For example, one team may believe they are a Visionary Vanguard while another behaves like a Conflicted Hybrid. These gaps can be more damaging than the quadrant itself. Quadrant aspiration must be co-diagnosed based on both internal truths and external demands. As Morris, Schindehutte, and LaForge (2002) emphasized in their work on Entrepreneurial Marketing, true strategic strength comes from aligning entrepreneurial behavior with market responsiveness and firm-level action. SOI™ aims to operationalize that alignment.

In practice, the SOI™ quadrant framework provides a behavioral roadmap rather than a static categorization. Each quadrant comes with trade-offs, risks, and performance levers. It is not enough to label a firm; what matters is how the firm moves, listens, and thinks. The quadrant visual is merely a starting point for richer conversation about fit, readiness, and future direction. As environments shift and leadership transitions occur, quadrant fit must be re-evaluated. Ultimately, the SOI™ framework reflects a behavioral theory of strategy—one that integrates classic constructs (EO, MO, EM) with real-world complexity and implementation nuance. For educators, consultants, and executives alike, it offers a language system to bridge theory and action in a way that is both rigorous and actionable.

CONCLUSION

The Strategic Orientation Index™ (SOI™) is more than a model—it is a strategic mirror and map. By integrating EO, MO, and EM into a single, interpretable framework, it enables firms to diagnose their current positioning, recognize blind spots, and prioritize high-impact changes. It translates the richness of academic literature into a framework that is both analytically rigorous and user-friendly. For firms navigating today's complex strategic terrain, SOI™ offers clarity, alignment, and direction.

Detailed case studies aligned to each SOI™ persona—including Airbnb, Tesla, Slack, and others—are available in the course-exclusive workbook. These robust cases extend the strategic insights found here and provide real-world examples of quadrant movement, behavior mapping, and growth execution.

CASE STUDY EXAMPLES

CASE STUDY 1: AIRBNB

APPLYING THE SOI™ FRAMEWORK IN THE REAL WORLD

While the Strategic Orientation Index™ provides a behavioral map for assessing firms, its true power emerges in application. The following case studies illustrate how EO, MO, and EM dimensions manifest in practice—shaping culture, decision-making, and growth. These examples span both regional and global firms, highlighting strategic inflection points where behavior, not just strategy, determined trajectory. Each case invites the reader to analyze how orientation—and misalignment—drives performance outcomes.

The Airbnb case was constructed using behavioral evidence from executive decisions, product innovations, regulatory strategies, and cultural practices—as reported in peer-reviewed research and public documentation. The SOI™ model, as a behavioral diagnostic framework, can be credibly applied in this way, much like academic assessments of Entrepreneurial Orientation or Market Orientation in published firm profiles.

DIMENSION	SOI™ RATING	OBSERVATIONS
Entrepreneurial Orientation	**High**	Airbnb redefined the lodging category by transforming spare rooms and homes into a global hospitality platform. Its innovativeness is reflected in its creation of trust mechanisms (reviews, verification, insurance) that enabled widespread adoption of the sharing economy. Proactiveness is evident in entering new markets before regulators had frameworks in place, scaling globally at speed, and later diversifying into "Airbnb Experiences." Risk-taking was high, as the company challenged hotel incumbents, faced repeated regulatory battles, and leaned into a model reliant on customer trust and decentralized assets.
Market Orientation	**High**	Airbnb continuously gathers and applies customer insights, using data from millions of hosts and guests to optimize platform design, pricing, and policies. Its responsiveness is seen in rolling out safety and cleaning protocols during the COVID-19 pandemic and adapting product categories to meet shifting travel behaviors (e.g., longer stays, rural escapes). Competitor orientation has been demonstrated in monitoring both hotel industry responses and copycat platforms, often outpacing them through branding and community engagement. Interfunctional coordination occurs across technology, trust and safety, marketing, and operations to align around seamless user experience and regulatory navigation.

Entrepre-neurial Marketing	**High**	All six EM dimensions are visible: (1) **Growth orientation** through rapid scaling from a niche travel idea to a multibillion-dollar global platform; (2) **Opportunity orientation** by recognizing the latent demand for affordable, authentic travel and unlocking underutilized housing supply; (3) **Two-way customer contact** via reviews, host–guest messaging, and direct community engagement; (4) **Value creation through alliances** with city governments, tourism boards, and industry stakeholders to gain legitimacy; (5) **Informal marketing research** through continual observation of user interactions, feedback loops, and host/guest behaviors; (6) **Market immersion** by positioning itself as not just a booking platform but a cultural brand that integrates travel, lifestyle, and community identity.

STRATEGIC-PERSONA FIT: VISIONARY VANGUARD

Airbnb exemplifies the Visionary Vanguard quadrant—driven by bold innovation, informed by constant market sensing, and behaviorally aligned across all internal teams. Its story reinforces the SOI™ thesis: that strategy lives in the behavior of a firm's decisions, feedback loops, and market posture. This case study is constructed from third-party observations of Airbnb's strategic behavior. Like many HBR and Blue Ocean profiles, this analysis uses publicly available evidence to infer strategic orientation, not direct company participation.

OVERVIEW

Airbnb, founded in 2008, is a groundbreaking platform that has transformed the hospitality industry by allowing individuals to rent out their homes or rooms to travelers. This business model not only disrupted the traditional hotel industry but also introduced a new segment of the sharing economy. Airbnb quickly expanded its operations globally, offering millions of listings in more than 220 countries and regions. The company's ability to adapt to various markets and its innovative approach to business have made it a leader in the hospitality sector. By leveraging technology and focusing on user experience, Airbnb has created a unique value proposition that appeals to both hosts and guests. The company's success can be attributed to its strategic application of the six key elements of Entrepreneurial Marketing (EM).

ENTREPRENEURIAL ORIENTATION (EO)

Innovativeness

Airbnb redefined the hospitality industry by transforming underutilized private spaces into monetizable accommodations through a scalable digital marketplace. This product innovation was paired with continuous platform enhancements, such as Experiences, which expanded the brand beyond lodging into lifestyle and local culture (Guttentag, 2015). Airbnb has also pioneered trust-building mechanisms—like host reviews and secure payment systems—that helped it scale in a previously unregulated peer-to-peer model. These innovations reflect a strong commitment to user-centered design and novel service offerings. As a result, the company has maintained a clear first-mover advantage in alternative lodging globally (Zervas, Proserpio, & Byers, 2017).

Proactiveness

Airbnb has demonstrated a proactive stance by entering and defining a new market segment before traditional competitors even acknowledged the threat. The company consistently identifies emerging trends—such as remote work or "digital nomadism"—and adapts product offerings like long-term stays accordingly. Airbnb also responds to regulatory pressures proactively, often partnering with cities to co-develop policies that balance innovation with compliance. This preemptive approach has helped maintain operational continuity in contested legal environments.

Such strategic foresight exemplifies a proactive, anticipatory posture in a rapidly evolving landscape.

Risk-Taking

From its earliest days, Airbnb took significant risks by challenging entrenched hotel norms and navigating complex legal gray areas regarding short-term rentals. The founders famously maxed out credit cards to keep the business afloat during the 2008 financial crisis (Gallagher, 2017). More recently, Airbnb's decision to go public in the midst of the COVID-19 pandemic—when global travel had nearly halted—underscored its continued willingness to take calculated strategic risks. These bold moves paid off, positioning the company to rebound quickly post-crisis. Airbnb's risk posture remains a defining element of its entrepreneurial identity.

MARKET ORIENTATION (MO)

Customer Orientation

Airbnb has maintained a deep and consistent focus on understanding and serving both its core customer segments: hosts and guests. The company invests heavily in UX testing, feedback loops, and trust-enhancing features that create a seamless user experience across touchpoints (Zervas et al., 2017). Innovations like "Superhost" status and guest guarantees were developed directly in response to observed pain points. Airbnb also segments users by travel intent—leisure, business, or extended stay—and optimizes offerings accordingly. This strong customer orientation has been a driver of loyalty and platform stickiness (Guttentag, 2015).

Competitor Orientation

While Airbnb created a new market category, it has remained highly attentive to both traditional hotel chains and emerging platform-based competitors. The company tracks competitor pricing, amenity trends, and experience packaging to continuously refine its value proposition. For example, the rollout of Airbnb Luxe was a direct response to high-end travel offerings from hotel brands and start-ups alike (Gallagher, 2017). Airbnb's data-rich environment enables agile responses to competitive shifts, particularly in pricing and regional offerings. This vigilance underscores a robust competitor orientation.

Interfunctional Coordination

Airbnb's ability to align cross-functional teams—from engineering to community engagement—has been essential to its platform's scalability. Cross-departmental collaboration is evident in initiatives like localized regulatory compliance, which requires coordination between legal, public affairs, and operations. The product team works closely with customer service and data science to iterate platform changes based on user behavior and sentiment analysis. Airbnb's integrated internal structure allows for rapid testing, learning, and deployment of market-informed decisions. This coordination is central to Airbnb's market responsiveness and innovation velocity.

ENTREPRENEURIAL MARKETING (EM)

Growth Orientation

From the outset, Airbnb demonstrated a strong commitment to growth, aiming to establish itself as a global leader in the hospitality industry. The founders, Brian Chesky, Joe Gebbia, and Nathan Blecharczyk, envisioned a platform that could scale rapidly and reach a broad audience, which drove their decisions to continuously expand into new markets. This Growth Orientation is evident in Airbnb's relentless pursuit of new listings and its efforts to diversify its service offerings, including experiences and long-term stays. By consistently pushing the boundaries of its business model, Airbnb has maintained its competitive edge and achieved exponential growth. The company's ability to attract significant investment has also fueled its expansion, allowing it to develop new features and enter new markets swiftly. This focus on growth has enabled Airbnb to remain agile and responsive to market demands, ensuring its continued success in the ever-evolving hospitality industry.

Opportunity Orientation

Airbnb's success is deeply rooted in its ability to identify and capitalize on emerging market opportunities. The company recognized the growing demand for authentic and personalized travel experiences that traditional hotels could not offer. By tapping into the rising trend of the sharing economy, Airbnb was able to create a new market segment that catered to travelers seeking unique accommodations. This opportunity orientation allowed Airbnb to differentiate itself from competitors and establish a strong brand presence in the market. Additionally, Airbnb's expansion into experiences and long-term stays demonstrates its ability to continuously explore and exploit new opportunities. The company's proactive approach to identifying market gaps and addressing them with innovative solutions has been a key driver of its growth and success (Guttentag, 2015).

Two-Way Customer Contact

Airbnb has built its brand around strong, two-way communication with its users, which has been essential to its success. The platform facilitates direct interaction between hosts and guests, allowing them to communicate before, during, and after a stay. This open dialogue helps to establish clear expectations, build trust, and enhance the overall user experience. Airbnb also actively engages with its community through regular feedback mechanisms, customer support, and personalized communication channels. By maintaining continuous contact with both hosts and guests, Airbnb is able to address concerns, gather valuable insights, and make improvements to its platform. This commitment to two-way communication has not only strengthened Airbnb's relationship with its users but also fostered a loyal community that continues to support and promote the platform.

Value Creation Through Alliances

Airbnb has successfully leveraged strategic alliances to create additional value for its users and enhance its market position. The company has partnered with local businesses, tourism boards, and community organizations to offer curated experiences and unique travel opportunities for guests. These alliances have allowed Airbnb to diversify its offerings and provide a more comprehensive travel experience, which sets it apart from traditional accommodation providers. Furthermore, Airbnb has collaborated with governments and regulatory bodies to navigate the complex legal landscape surrounding short-term rentals. By forming these partnerships, Airbnb has been able to influence policy decisions and secure its place in various markets. These alliances have not only contributed to Airbnb's growth but have also played a crucial role in maintaining its competitive advantage.

Informal Marketing Research

Airbnb's approach to marketing research is characterized by its reliance on informal methods to gather insights and understand market trends. The company utilizes customer feedback, social media interactions, and data analytics to monitor user behavior and preferences. This informal approach allows Airbnb to remain agile and quickly respond to changing market conditions and consumer demands. For example, during the COVID-19 pandemic, Airbnb identified a shift in travel preferences toward longer stays and remote work-friendly accommodations. By swiftly adapting its platform to cater to these new needs, Airbnb was able to maintain its relevance and continue to attract users despite the global downturn in travel. The company's ability to gather and act on informal marketing insights has been a critical factor in its ongoing success.

Market Immersion

Airbnb's success is also due to its deep immersion in the markets it serves, which has allowed the company to stay ahead of trends and better understand its users. The company stays closely connected with its hosts and guests by engaging directly with them through various channels, including community events, forums, and social media. This constant interaction helps Airbnb gain a better understanding of the unique needs and preferences of its diverse user base. Additionally, Airbnb's employees often travel and stay in Airbnb accommodations, allowing them to experience the platform firsthand and identify areas for improvement. This level of Market Immersion enables Airbnb to continuously refine its offerings and maintain a competitive edge in the dynamic hospitality industry. By staying deeply involved in the markets it operates in, Airbnb has been able to anticipate and respond to shifts in consumer behavior, ensuring its continued growth and success (Guttentag, 2015).

CHALLENGES

Despite its success, Airbnb has faced significant challenges, particularly in navigating the regulatory environment in various cities around the world. Many cities have imposed restrictions on short-term rentals, leading to legal battles and the need for Airbnb to negotiate with local governments. These regulatory challenges have sometimes resulted in fines, restrictions on listings, and even bans in certain markets. Additionally, ensuring the safety and trust of both hosts and guests has been an ongoing concern for Airbnb. The company has had to implement robust verification processes, secure payment systems, and comprehensive review mechanisms to address these challenges. The complexity of managing a global platform with diverse legal and cultural environments continues to be a significant obstacle for Airbnb as it expands its operations (Guttentag, 2015).

LESSONS LEARNED

Airbnb's journey offers several key lessons for other businesses seeking to implement Entrepreneurial Marketing strategies. First, the importance of Growth Orientation and opportunity identification cannot be overstated; Airbnb's success has been largely driven by its ability to recognize and capitalize on emerging trends. Second, maintaining strong, two-way communication with customers is crucial for building trust and fostering loyalty, which are essential for long-term success. Third, strategic alliances can significantly enhance a company's value proposition and help navigate complex regulatory landscapes. Finally, the ability to gather and act on Informal Marketing Research and deeply immerse in the market is critical for staying ahead of the competition. Airbnb's experience underscores the importance of being adaptable, innovative, and customer-focused in today's fast-paced business environment.

CASE STUDY 2: TESLA

DIMENSION	SOI™ RATING	OBSERVATIONS
Entrepreneurial Orientation	**High**	Tesla demonstrates extreme innovativeness through EVs, battery chemistry, software updates, and AI; proactive in anticipating infrastructure and regulatory needs (e.g., Supercharger network); risk-taking evidenced by bold capital commitments, near-bankruptcy survival, and disruptive business models.
Market Orientation	**High**	Tesla maintains tight customer feedback loops via vehicle data, app integration, and social channels; shows competitor orientation by setting benchmarks for legacy automakers and monitoring subsidy/regulatory shifts; interfunctional coordination is enabled by vertical integration and cross-functional agility.
Entrepreneurial Marketing	**High**	All six EM dimensions are evident: (1) Growth Orientation through multisector expansion (EVs, energy, robotics); (2) Opportunity orientation in early EV and renewables markets; (3) Two-Way Customer Contact via direct engagement and Musk's active communication; (4) Value Creation Through Alliances with Panasonic and charging partners; (5) Informal research via social media and customer data; (6) Market Immersion through direct sales model, community engagement, and industry thought leadership.

PERSONA FIT: VISIONARY VANGUARD (TESLA)

Tesla exemplifies the Visionary Vanguard quadrant—pioneering disruptive innovation through electric vehicles, battery systems, and autonomous driving, all while shaping new markets before competitors respond. Its behavior reflects a company that combines bold technological bets with proactive market creation, reinforced by vertically integrated execution. The Tesla case underscores the SOI™ thesis: Strategy is not a plan on paper but the lived behavior of innovation pipelines, customer responsiveness, and risk acceptance. This case study is built from publicly available analyses of Tesla's actions and outcomes; like HBR-style company profiles, it infers strategic orientation from observed patterns rather than internal participation.

OVERVIEW

Tesla, founded in 2003 by Elon Musk, has become synonymous with innovation in the electric vehicle (EV) and sustainable energy sectors. The company's mission is to accelerate the world's transition to sustainable energy, which has driven its focus on developing cutting-edge electric vehicles, solar energy products, and energy storage solutions. Tesla's success has not only disrupted the traditional automotive industry but also set new standards for technological innovation and environmental responsibility. By leveraging its entrepreneurial approach to marketing, Tesla has rapidly expanded its global presence and built a loyal customer base that spans multiple continents. The company's ability to integrate its products into a cohesive vision for the future of energy and transportation has been central to its growth. Tesla's achievements are closely linked to its effective application of the six elements of Entrepreneurial Marketing (EM).

ENTREPRENEURIAL ORIENTATION (EO)

Innovativeness

Tesla exemplifies radical innovation by advancing electric vehicle (EV) technology, battery systems, and autonomous driving at a pace unmatched by traditional automakers. The company has pioneered proprietary battery chemistry, over-the-air software updates, and self-driving capabilities, disrupting multiple industries simultaneously (Stringham, Miller,

& Clark, 2015). Tesla's vertical integration—from battery production to software design—has enabled it to innovate at both the component and systems levels. Its continual expansion into solar energy, energy storage, and robotics reflects a multi-industry innovation portfolio. This relentless innovation strategy has elevated Tesla from a niche automaker to a global technology leader (Mangram, 2012).

Proactiveness

Tesla consistently moves ahead of market trends, launching products and infrastructure before mass demand fully materializes. Its early investment in the Supercharger network anticipated and removed key adoption barriers for EVs. The company also introduced the Cybertruck and AI-powered humanoid robot, betting on emerging markets with long-term strategic upside. Tesla's ability to anticipate regulatory shifts, such as zero-emission mandates, and adapt accordingly further underscores its proactive posture. These moves demonstrate forward-looking agility rather than reactive decision-making (Vance, 2015).

Risk-Taking

From its inception, Tesla has embraced risk, from entering capital-intensive industries to defying automotive norms. CEO Elon Musk bet his personal fortune on Tesla's survival during its early production crises, and the company faced multiple near-bankruptcies (Vance, 2015). Its bold entry into energy storage and autonomous driving required heavy R&D investment with uncertain short-term payoff. Tesla's direct-to-consumer sales model also challenged traditional dealership laws, exposing the company to political and legal risk. Yet these risks, taken deliberately, have often positioned Tesla as a first mover in transformational markets (Mangram, 2012).

MARKET ORIENTATION (MO)

Customer Orientation

Tesla maintains an intensely customer-centric approach, using real-time vehicle data and driver feedback to refine its products post-sale. Features like Autopilot, Sentry Mode, and customizable driving profiles reflect the company's responsiveness to user behavior and preferences . Tesla's mobile app and vehicle interface offer seamless, integrated control and service access, enhancing the customer experience. Additionally, the company crowdsources feedback through forums, Twitter, and software update polls to continuously enhance its offerings. This tight feedback loop exemplifies modern customer orientation (Vance, 2015).

Competitor Orientation

Although Tesla initially operated in a space with few direct rivals, it has remained intensely focused on benchmarking and outpacing both legacy automakers and new EV entrants. Tesla's pricing strategy, manufacturing scale (e.g., Gigafactories), and product differentiation respond directly to emerging competitive threats (Stringham et al., 2015). Its consistent acceleration of delivery timelines and vertical integration have become industry benchmarks, influencing competitor behavior. The company also closely monitors global regulatory and subsidy changes that affect its competitive position. Tesla's strategic responses show active monitoring and preemptive adjustments.

Interfunctional Coordination

Tesla's flat organizational structure and vertically integrated operations enable real-time coordination across R&D, manufacturing, software, and sales. Cross-functional collaboration allows Tesla to implement updates quickly, such as launching new software features globally overnight via over-the-air updates (Mangram, 2012). Teams collaborate to align design, engineering, and production timelines, reducing time-to-market for new models. Customer support, data analytics, and engineering also work in tandem to resolve issues and identify upgrade opportunities. This high degree of coordination supports both innovation and responsiveness to customer and market feedback (Vance, 2015).

ENTREPRENEURIAL MARKETING (EM)

Growth Orientation

Tesla's Growth Orientation is evident in its relentless pursuit of expansion across multiple sectors, including electric vehicles, energy storage, and solar energy. From the beginning, Elon Musk's vision for Tesla was not just to create a car company but to build an integrated energy company that could redefine the future of transportation and energy consumption. This ambitious growth strategy has led Tesla to continuously innovate and expand its product lineup, from the original Roadster to the Model S, Model 3, Model X, and Model Y, as well as energy products like the Powerwall and Solar Roof. Tesla's global growth has also been fueled by the construction of Gigafactories in key regions, allowing the company to scale production and meet the growing demand for its products. This focus on rapid and sustained growth has enabled Tesla to establish itself as a leader in both the automotive and energy industries, with a market capitalization that surpasses many traditional automakers (Stringham et al., 2015; Mangram, 2012).

Opportunity Orientation

Tesla's success is deeply rooted in its ability to identify and seize opportunities in emerging markets. The company recognized the potential of electric vehicles at a time when the automotive industry was heavily reliant on internal combustion engines. By focusing on the growing demand for environmentally friendly transportation solutions, Tesla was able to position itself as a pioneer in the EV market (Stringham et al. 2015). Tesla's entry into the energy storage and solar energy markets further exemplifies its opportunity orientation, as the company has capitalized on the increasing global emphasis on renewable energy. By continuously exploring and exploiting new opportunities, Tesla has been able to diversify its revenue streams and strengthen its market position, ensuring its long-term sustainability and growth (Brown & Duguid, 2000; Mangram, 2012).

Two-Way Customer Contact

Tesla places a strong emphasis on maintaining two-way communication with its customers, which is a cornerstone of its marketing strategy. The company engages directly with its customers through various channels, including social media, online forums, and its website, where users can interact with the brand, provide feedback, and share their experiences. Elon Musk's active presence on platforms like Twitter plays a significant role in this strategy, as it allows Tesla to respond quickly to customer inquiries and concerns while also keeping the public informed about new developments. This open line of communication has helped Tesla build a dedicated community of customers and brand advocates who are deeply invested in the company's mission. By fostering strong relationships with its customers, Tesla has been able to gather valuable insights that inform its product development and marketing efforts, ensuring that it meets the needs and expectations of its target audience (Stringham et al., 2015; Mangram, 2012).

Value Creation Through Alliances

Strategic alliances have played a crucial role in Tesla's ability to create value and drive innovation. One of the most significant partnerships has been with Panasonic, which supplies batteries for Tesla's electric vehicles and energy storage products. This collaboration has been instrumental in ensuring the quality and reliability of Tesla's battery technology, which is a critical component of its overall product offering. Tesla has also formed alliances with other companies and government entities to advance the development of EV infrastructure, such as charging stations, which are essential for the widespread adoption of electric vehicles. Additionally, Tesla's collaboration with SolarCity (before its acquisition) allowed the company to integrate solar energy solutions into its product portfolio, further enhancing its value proposition as a leader in sustainable energy (Brown & Duguid, 2000; Brown, 2008; Mangram, 2012). These alliances have not only strengthened Tesla's market position but have also enabled the company to accelerate its innovation efforts and bring new products to market more quickly.

INFORMAL MARKETING RESEARCH

Tesla's approach to marketing research is characterized by its reliance on informal methods to gather insights and stay ahead of industry trends. The company closely monitors social media platforms, customer feedback, and online communities to understand the preferences and behaviors of its target audience. This informal research approach allows Tesla to be agile and responsive to changes in the market, such as shifts in consumer demand or emerging technological advancements (Stringham et al. 2015). For example, Tesla's decision to introduce features like Autopilot and Full Self-Driving was influenced by the feedback and interests expressed by its customers and the broader tech community. By leveraging informal research, Tesla is able to continuously innovate and enhance its products in ways that resonate with its customer base, maintaining its competitive edge in the rapidly evolving automotive and energy sectors (Stringham et al., 2015; Mangram, 2012).

MARKET IMMERSION

Tesla's Market Immersion strategy involves deeply engaging with its customers and the broader industry to stay attuned to emerging trends and opportunities. The company maintains close relationships with its customers through direct sales channels, bypassing traditional dealerships and ensuring a consistent brand experience. This direct engagement allows Tesla to better understand the needs and preferences of its customers, which informs its product development and marketing strategies. Additionally, Tesla's employees, including Elon Musk, often participate in industry events, conferences, and online forums, where they can engage with thought leaders, experts, and enthusiasts. This immersion in the market helps Tesla stay ahead of technological advancements and regulatory changes, ensuring that the company remains at the forefront of innovation in the automotive and energy industries (Stringham et al. 2015). By staying deeply involved in its market, Tesla is able to anticipate and respond to shifts in consumer behavior and industry dynamics, which is crucial for maintaining its leadership position.

CHALLENGES

Despite its success, Tesla has faced numerous challenges, including production delays, supply chain disruptions, and regulatory hurdles. The company's ambitious production targets, particularly for the Model 3, have led to what Elon Musk described as "production hell," where bottlenecks and inefficiencies caused significant delays and cost overruns (Miller, 2020). Additionally, Tesla has had to navigate complex regulatory environments in various countries, where government policies on emissions, safety standards, and EV infrastructure can vary significantly. These regulatory challenges have sometimes resulted in delays in product launches or restrictions on Tesla's ability to sell its vehicles directly to consumers in certain markets (Brown & Duguid, 2000; Brown, 2008; Mangram, 2012). Furthermore, Tesla faces increasing competition from both established automakers and new entrants in the EV market, which puts pressure on the company to continuously innovate and differentiate its products.

LESSONS LEARNED

Tesla's journey offers several valuable lessons for businesses seeking to implement Entrepreneurial Marketing strategies. One key lesson is the importance of maintaining a strong Growth Orientation and continuously exploring new opportunities to drive expansion and innovation. Tesla's success also highlights the value of two-way communication with customers, which not only builds loyalty but also provides critical insights for product development and marketing. Additionally, strategic alliances can significantly enhance a company's ability to innovate and scale, as demonstrated by Tesla's partnerships with Panasonic and other key players in the industry. Tesla's reliance on Informal Marketing Research underscores the importance of staying agile and responsive to market trends and customer feedback. Finally, the company's deep Market Immersion has been crucial in anticipating and adapting to industry shifts, ensuring its continued leadership in the automotive and energy sectors. These lessons underscore the importance of being adaptable, innovative, and customer-focused in today's competitive business environment.

CASE STUDY 3: DOLLAR SHAVE CLUB

DIMENSION	SOI™ RATING	OBSERVATIONS
Entrepre-neurial Orientation	High	DSC entered a capital-intensive, brand-saturated market with boldness, challenging giants like Gillette through direct-to-consumer disruption. Its viral 2012 launch video exemplified risk-taking and category-defying innovativeness. Proactiveness was evident in anticipating subscription-based consumer demand years before incumbents pivoted.

Market Orientation	**Moderate**	Early strategy leaned more on bold market entry than systematic customer orientation. While DSC tapped into consumer frustration with razor pricing and complexity, structured customer feedback systems were limited in its early years. Competitor orientation was sharp—its entire positioning was built as a direct contrast to Gillette. Interfunctional coordination grew as the company scaled but was not a core strength in its start-up phase.
Entrepreneurial Marketing	**High**	Strong across multiple EM dimensions: (1) Growth Orientation via rapid expansion from razors into grooming and personal-care categories; (2) Opportunity orientation by seizing the emerging subscription economy model; (3) Two-Way Customer Contact fostered through online communities and humorous, relatable branding; (4) Value Creation Through Alliances with Unilever (acquisition) and logistics partners; (5) Informal Market Research by tracking consumer frustration and online culture; (6) Market Immersion through social media-driven brand identity.

PERSONA FIT: FEARLESS INVENTOR (DOLLAR SHAVE CLUB)

Dollar Shave Club represents the Fearless Inventor quadrant—defined by audacious market entry, humor-driven storytelling, and a readiness to challenge entrenched industry norms. Its viral launch and rapid expansion highlight a strategy built on entrepreneurial daring rather than structured planning, with MO elements emerging later as the company scaled. The case reinforces the SOI™ thesis: Strategy manifests in behavior—how a firm experiments, takes risks, and mobilizes opportunity into action. This analysis is constructed from external observations of DSC's market posture and growth trajectory, following the approach of widely published case profiles that interpret strategic orientation through publicly available evidence.

OVERVIEW

Dollar Shave Club (DSC), founded in 2011 by Michael Dubin, is a subscription-based razor and personal-care company that disrupted the traditional razor market by offering an affordable and convenient alternative to buying razors at retail stores. The company quickly gained traction through its viral marketing campaigns, particularly its humorous and engaging launch video, which resonated with consumers frustrated by the high cost and inconvenience of purchasing razors from traditional brands. Within a short period, DSC grew rapidly, attracting millions of subscribers and becoming a significant player in the grooming industry. The company's success can be attributed to its strategic application of Entrepreneurial Marketing (EM) principles, which allowed it to differentiate itself in a highly competitive market. By focusing on customer needs, leveraging digital platforms, and maintaining a strong brand identity, DSC was able to build a loyal customer base and challenge established industry giants like Gillette.

ENTREPRENEURIAL ORIENTATION (EO)

Innovativeness

Dollar Shave Club disrupted the men's grooming industry by introducing a direct-to-consumer subscription model that bypassed traditional retail channels. The innovation was not in the razor itself, but in the business model, pricing strategy, and brand experience that reimagined how men purchased personal-care products. Their viral launch video—humorous and irreverent—also demonstrated innovative marketing that resonated deeply with millennial consumers. Over time, Dollar Shave Club expanded its offerings into skincare, wipes, and hair care, continuously innovating within its niche. These moves reflect a strategic approach to innovation driven by customer insight rather than product complexity (Wessel & Christensen, 2016).

Proactiveness

From the outset, Dollar Shave Club moved quickly to capitalize on emerging trends in e-commerce and subscription services. Rather than waiting to scale organically, the company aggressively invested in brand-building and customer acquisition, aiming to disrupt Gillette's long-standing dominance. The company anticipated a shift toward digitally native consumer behavior and positioned itself early in the value chain. It also expanded product categories proactively based on customer feedback, rather than reacting to competitive threats. This speed and foresight contributed to its rapid growth and market penetration (Wessel & Christensen, 2016).

Risk-Taking

Launching with limited capital and taking on industry giants like Gillette represented significant risk. The company bet heavily on untested creative content and viral marketing, using humor to attract attention in a crowded market. Its decision to own inventory and manage fulfillment logistics internally early on also deviated from the standard lean start-up playbook. These operational risks, paired with a bold brand voice, could have backfired—but instead created viral momentum and investor interest. Dollar Shave Club's $1 billion acquisition by Unilever validated those early risks as high-return strategic bets (Wessel & Christensen, 2016).

MARKET ORIENTATION (MO)

Customer Orientation

Dollar Shave Club built its entire brand around solving customer pain points—high prices, locked cabinets, and complicated razor choices. The brand voice was intentionally casual, humorous, and transparent, reflecting how their target market actually spoke and thought about grooming (Bhasin, 2020). They frequently surveyed customers, refined product lines, and added features like customizable shipments and flexible subscriptions based on user feedback. This tight loop between brand, product, and customer preference fueled high retention and customer loyalty. Customer needs remained central to every major operational and marketing decision.

Competitor Orientation

While launching against an entrenched giant like Gillette, Dollar Shave Club maintained acute awareness of competitive pricing, branding, and positioning. Its entire origin story was a counterpoint to traditional brands—offering simplicity where others offered complexity and humor where others offered prestige (Bhasin, 2020). The company carefully observed competitive reactions, such as Gillette's subsequent entry into the subscription market, and adjusted messaging accordingly. This vigilance allowed them to hold ground even as legacy brands tried to imitate their model. Their focus remained not on matching features, but on differentiating experience.

Interfunctional Coordination

Cross-functional alignment between marketing, logistics, product development, and customer service was critical to Dollar Shave Club's success. The viral video that launched the brand was created by the founder himself, blurring lines between leadership, creative, and strategic roles . Operations and customer support worked closely to ensure fulfillment scaled with viral growth, avoiding service breakdowns. As the company scaled, interdepartmental coordination ensured the customer experience remained seamless—from subscription customization to unboxing. This cohesion allowed them to punch above their weight and maintain brand consistency at scale (Bhasin, 2020).

ENTREPRENEURIAL MARKETING (EM)

Growth Orientation

From its inception, Dollar Shave Club exhibited a strong Growth Orientation, with a clear focus on scaling its business rapidly. The company's subscription-based model provided a steady stream of recurring revenue, which allowed DSC to reinvest in marketing, product development, and customer acquisition. DSC's growth strategy was also supported by its decision to expand its product line beyond razors to include grooming products such as shaving cream, body wash, and skincare items. This diversification not only increased the average revenue per customer but also strengthened DSC's brand as a comprehensive personal-care solution. Additionally, the company's ability to secure significant venture capital funding enabled it to accelerate its growth and increase its market presence. By maintaining a relentless focus on growth, DSC was able to rapidly scale its operations, ultimately leading to its acquisition by Unilever for $1 billion in 2016 (Bhasin, 2020).

Opportunity Orientation

Dollar Shave Club's success was largely driven by its ability to identify and exploit a significant market opportunity. The company recognized that many consumers were dissatisfied with the high prices and inconvenience associated with buying razors from traditional retail channels. DSC capitalized on this frustration by offering a more affordable and convenient alternative through its subscription service, which delivered razors directly to customers' doors at a fraction of the cost (Teixeira, 2015). This opportunity orientation allowed DSC to differentiate itself from established competitors and quickly gain market share. Additionally, the company's focus on digital marketing and direct-to-consumer sales enabled it to bypass traditional distribution channels, further enhancing its competitive advantage. By continuously seeking out and capitalizing on new opportunities, DSC was able to disrupt the razor market and establish itself as a formidable challenger to industry leaders.

TWO-WAY CUSTOMER CONTACT

A key factor in Dollar Shave Club's success was its commitment to fostering two-way communication with its customers. DSC built a strong relationship with its customers by engaging them through multiple channels, including social media, email newsletters, and its website. The company's humorous and relatable brand voice resonated with customers, encouraging them to interact with the brand and share their experiences (Miller, 2018). DSC also actively sought customer feedback on its products and services, which it used to inform product development and improve customer satisfaction. This continuous dialogue helped DSC to build a loyal customer base that felt connected to the brand and valued by the company. By maintaining open lines of communication with its customers, DSC was able to create a sense of community and trust, which contributed to its rapid growth and success (Bhasin, 2020).

VALUE CREATION THROUGH ALLIANCES

Dollar Shave Club leveraged strategic alliances to enhance its value proposition and strengthen its market position. The company partnered with manufacturers to produce high-quality razors and grooming products at competitive prices, which allowed DSC to offer premium products at a lower cost than traditional brands. Additionally, DSC collaborated with content creators and influencers to amplify its marketing message and reach a broader audience. These partnerships were particularly effective in the early stages of the company's growth, as they helped to generate buzz and drive customer acquisition. By creating value through these alliances, DSC was able to differentiate itself from competitors and establish a strong brand presence in the market. Furthermore, the company's ability to form and maintain these partnerships was crucial in sustaining its growth and expanding its product offerings (Teixeira, 2015) (Kahn, 2017).

INFORMAL MARKETING RESEARCH

Dollar Shave Club's marketing strategies were heavily informed by informal research methods, including customer feedback, social media monitoring, and industry trends. The company closely tracked customer preferences and behavior through its digital platforms, which allowed it to stay attuned to emerging trends and adapt its offerings accordingly (Bhasin, 2020). For example, DSC's decision to expand its product line to include grooming and skin-care products was driven by customer demand and feedback gathered through informal channels. This approach enabled DSC to remain agile and responsive to changes in the market, ensuring that its products continued to meet the evolving needs of its customers. By leveraging Informal Marketing Research, DSC was able to maintain a competitive edge and sustain its growth in a rapidly changing industry.

MARKET IMMERSION

Dollar Shave Club's deep immersion in its market played a critical role in its ability to understand and meet the needs of its customers. The company maintained close relationships with its customers by actively engaging with them through social media, email, and other digital platforms. This constant interaction allowed DSC to gain valuable insights into customer preferences, pain points, and expectations, which informed its product development and marketing strategies. Additionally, DSC's strong online presence and digital-first approach enabled the company to stay connected with industry trends and consumer behavior, ensuring that it remained relevant in a competitive market. By staying deeply immersed in its market, DSC was able to anticipate and respond to shifts in consumer behavior, which was crucial for its continued growth and success (Teixeira, 2015; Kahn, 2017).

CHALLENGES

Despite its rapid growth and success, Dollar Shave Club faced several challenges as it scaled its operations. One of the primary challenges was intense competition from established razor brands, such as Gillette, which responded to DSC's disruption with aggressive pricing strategies and marketing campaigns. Additionally, DSC had to contend with other subscription-based services entering the market, which increased competition and made customer retention more challenging. The company also faced the challenge of maintaining product quality while keeping costs low, particularly as it expanded its product line beyond razors to include grooming and skin-care products (Teixeira, 2015; Kahn, 2017). Managing customer expectations and minimizing churn in a subscription-based model required ongoing engagement and innovation, which placed additional pressure on DSC's marketing and product-development teams. These challenges highlighted the complexities of sustaining growth in a competitive and rapidly evolving industry.

LESSONS LEARNED

Dollar Shave Club's journey offers several valuable lessons for businesses seeking to implement Entrepreneurial Marketing strategies. First, the importance of identifying and capitalizing on market opportunities is critical, as demonstrated by DSC's ability to disrupt the traditional razor market with its subscription-based model. Second, maintaining strong, two-way communication with customers is essential for building trust and fostering loyalty, which are key to long-term success. Third, creating value through strategic alliances can significantly enhance a company's competitive advantage and help it scale more effectively. Additionally, leveraging Informal Marketing Research allows companies to stay agile and responsive to market trends and customer feedback, which is crucial for sustaining growth in a dynamic industry. Finally, deep Market Immersion enables businesses to better understand and anticipate customer needs, ensuring that their products and services remain relevant and competitive to all (Bhasin, 2020; Gensler et al., 2012). These lessons underscore the importance of being adaptable, customer-focused, and innovative in today's business environment.

CASE STUDY 4: ZAPPOS

DIMENSION	SOI™ RATING	OBSERVATIONS
Entrepreneurial Orientation	**Moderate**	Zappos innovated primarily in customer experience rather than radical product breakthroughs. Risk-taking was selective, focused on cultural bets (e.g., holacracy, free returns) rather than industry-disruptive technology. Proactiveness was evident in pioneering online shoe retail before it was mainstream, but subsequent innovation leaned toward incremental service enhancements rather than bold new categories.
Market Orientation	**High**	Zappos is widely recognized for its customer-centricity, embedding service obsession into its culture. Its legendary customer-service model, free returns, and emphasis on "WOW" experiences illustrate deep commitment to understanding and meeting customer needs. Competitor orientation was less about head-to-head competition and more about differentiation through service culture. Inter-functional coordination was reinforced by values-driven alignment across all departments.

Entrepre-neurial Marketing	**High**	EM behaviors were embedded across the organization: (1) Growth Orientation sustained through scaling service culture, later reinforced by Amazon acquisition; (2) Opportunity orientation reflected in seizing the shift to e-commerce; (3) Two-Way Customer Contact through call centers, social media, and community building; (4) Value Creation Through Alliances (e.g., Amazon partnership, vendor relationships that supported risk-free returns); (5) Informal Marketing Research via frontline service interactions; (6) Market Immersion achieved by making every employee a steward of customer happiness.

PERSONA FIT: INSIGHTFUL OPTIMIZER (ZAPPOS)

Zappos exemplifies the Insightful Optimizer quadrant—anchored in deep customer orientation, sustained service culture, and disciplined growth built on consistency rather than radical disruption. Its posture demonstrates that competitive advantage can come from behavioral alignment and customer intimacy just as powerfully as from product innovation. The case reinforces the SOI™ thesis: Strategy is enacted in behavior—in this instance, how Zappos listens to customers, integrates service culture across functions, and aligns its organizational posture with its market environment. This case study is constructed from external analyses and company reports; like other HBR-style profiles, it interprets strategic orientation from observable evidence rather than direct participation.

OVERVIEW

Zappos, founded in 1999 by Nick Swinmurn and later led by CEO Tony Hsieh, started as an online shoe retailer and quickly grew into one of the most successful e-commerce companies in the world. Known for its customer service and unique company culture, Zappos has expanded its product offerings to include clothing, accessories, and more. The company's success can be largely attributed to its commitment to customer satisfaction, innovative use of technology, and strategic application of Entrepreneurial Marketing (EM) principles. By focusing on exceptional customer experiences, fostering strong relationships with suppliers, and maintaining a flexible and adaptive business model, Zappos has set new standards in the retail industry.

ENTREPRENEURIAL ORIENTATION (EO)

Innovativeness

Zappos revolutionized online retail by offering free shipping and returns, a move that eliminated major barriers to e-commerce adoption. Beyond logistical innovation, the company built a customer-service experience that was so engaging it became its primary brand differentiator (Hsieh, 2010). Zappos was also among the first to integrate real-time inventory systems with supplier networks, enabling rapid order fulfillment without holding excessive stock. The company experimented with management innovation as well, adopting a flat, holacratic structure to foster decentralized decision-making and agility. Innovation at Zappos is deeply cultural, extending far beyond product or technology (Denning, 2015).

Proactiveness

Zappos proactively pursued a customer-obsessed model well before "customer-centricity" became a mainstream strategic imperative. Founder Tony Hsieh designed the company to exceed expectations at every touchpoint, offering 24/7 call support and surprise shipping upgrades as standard practice (Hsieh, 2010). The company also moved early into lifestyle branding and content marketing through Zappos Insights, sharing its culture with entrepreneurs and HR professionals. Zappos anticipated the growing role of company values and culture as competitive assets and positioned itself accordingly. Its acquisition by Amazon was largely based on its brand equity and service model, not just revenue.

RISK-TAKING

From its inception, Zappos took strategic risks by prioritizing customer service over short-term profitability. Offering free returns on shoes—an item consumers traditionally wanted to try on—was considered a high-risk move at the time (Hsieh, 2010). The company also rejected conventional call center metrics, empowering reps to spend hours solving customer problems rather than rushing through scripts. Adopting holacracy, a self-management structure without traditional hierarchy, was another unconventional and controversial organizational risk (Denning, 2015). These bold moves often defied industry norms but helped Zappos create a cultlike following.

MARKET ORIENTATION (MO)

Customer Orientation

Zappos places the customer at the heart of every decision, measuring success not by transactions but by customer happiness. Its call center team has no scripts or time limits, allowing employees to build authentic, meaningful relationships with customers (Hsieh, 2010). The company empowers all employees to resolve issues on the spot, reducing friction and reinforcing customer loyalty. Customer feedback is actively used to improve website UX, product assortments, and service policies. This level of personalization and empathy defines Zappos's legendary service reputation.

Competitor Orientation

While Zappos closely tracks online retail trends, it chooses to differentiate rather than imitate. The company doesn't try to compete on speed alone—despite being owned by Amazon—but instead focuses on service depth, brand trust, and emotional connection. It monitors competitor behavior in terms of pricing and assortment but invests more in culture, team experience, and word-of-mouth marketing (Denning, 2015). Zappos's loyalty isn't price-driven; it's experience-driven. This competitor orientation is unique in that it uses emotional and experiential differentiation to avoid price wars.

Interfunctional Coordination

Zappos's legendary customer experience relies on seamless coordination between marketing, customer service, logistics, and IT. Teams collaborate to solve customer pain points holistically, not just within silos. The company's internal culture, driven by its ten core values, ensures alignment across functions and fosters shared ownership of the customer experience (Hsieh, 2010). Transparency and trust within teams enable fast, empowered decision-making across departments. This strong cultural glue allows for dynamic coordination, especially in high-touch service situations.

ENTREPRENEURIAL MARKETING (EM)

Growth Orientation

From its inception, Zappos demonstrated a strong Growth Orientation by focusing on expanding its product offerings and customer base. Initially starting as an online shoe store, Zappos quickly diversified into other product categories such as clothing, accessories, and home goods to attract a broader audience. The company's growth strategy was also supported by its commitment to customer satisfaction, which led to high levels of customer loyalty and repeat business. Zappos's innovative approach to customer service, including free shipping and returns, as well as a 365-day return policy, helped the company build a strong reputation and rapidly increase its market share (Hsieh, 2010). Additionally, Zappos embraced a customer-centric culture that empowered employees to go above and beyond for customers, further driving growth through word-of-mouth marketing and positive customer experiences. By maintaining a relentless focus on growth and customer satisfaction, Zappos was able to scale its operations and achieve significant success in the highly competitive e-commerce market.

Opportunity Orientation

Zappos's success is largely driven by its ability to identify and capitalize on emerging opportunities in the market. The company recognized early on that the future of retail was moving online, and it positioned itself to be a leader in e-commerce by offering a vast selection of products and an exceptional shopping experience (Hsieh, 2010; Frei & Morriss, 2012). Zappos also saw an opportunity to differentiate itself from competitors by focusing on customer service as a key competitive advantage. This focus on service excellence allowed Zappos to build a strong brand identity and attract a loyal customer base. Additionally, Zappos was quick to embrace new technologies and trends, such as social media and mobile commerce, to enhance the customer experience and stay ahead of the competition. By continuously seeking out and exploiting new opportunities, Zappos has been able to maintain its relevance and grow its business in the rapidly evolving retail landscape.

Two-Way Customer Contact

A central aspect of Zappos's success is its commitment to maintaining two-way communication with its customers. The company places a strong emphasis on listening to customers and using their feedback to improve its products and services. Zappos's customer-service team is trained to engage with customers on a personal level, taking the time to understand their needs and provide tailored solutions. This level of engagement not only enhances customer satisfaction but also builds trust and loyalty. Zappos actively encourages customers to share their experiences through reviews, social media, and direct-feedback channels, which the company uses to inform its decision-making and continuously improve the customer experience. By fostering strong two-way communication, Zappos has been able to create a sense of community and connection with its customers, which has been instrumental in driving customer loyalty and repeat business (Hsieh, 2010).

Value Creation Through Alliances

Zappos has created significant value through strategic alliances and partnerships, particularly with its suppliers. The company has built strong relationships with a wide range of brands and manufacturers, which has allowed it to offer a diverse selection of products to its customers . Zappos's commitment to maintaining open and transparent communication with its suppliers has been key to these successful partnerships, as it ensures that both parties are aligned in their goals and objectives. Additionally, Zappos has collaborated with various technology companies to enhance its e-commerce platform, making it more user-friendly and efficient. These partnerships have been crucial in helping Zappos stay ahead of technological advancements and provide a seamless shopping experience for its customers. By creating value through these alliances, Zappos has been able to differentiate itself from competitors and offer a superior shopping experience (Hsieh, 2010; Frei & Morriss, 2012).

Informal Marketing Research

Zappos's marketing strategies are heavily informed by informal research methods, including customer feedback, social media monitoring, and trend analysis. The company closely tracks customer interactions and reviews to gain insights into their preferences and pain points . This information is used to make data-driven decisions about product offerings, marketing campaigns, and customer-service improvements. For example, Zappos's decision to offer free returns was influenced by customer feedback indicating that the ability to return products easily was a key factor in their purchasing decisions (Hsieh, 2010). Zappos also leverages social media to engage with customers and monitor conversations about its brand, allowing the company to stay attuned to emerging trends and respond quickly to customer needs. By relying on Informal Marketing Research, Zappos has been able to remain agile and responsive to changes in the market, ensuring that its products and services continue to meet the evolving needs of its customers .

MARKET IMMERSION

Zappos's deep immersion in its market has been a critical factor in its ability to understand and meet the needs of its customers. The company's leadership and employees are deeply involved in the retail industry, regularly attending industry events, conferences, and trade shows to stay connected with trends and innovations (Hsieh, 2010; Frei & Morriss, 2012). Zappos also invests in training and development programs for its employees, ensuring that they are equipped with the knowledge and skills needed to provide exceptional customer service. This Market Immersion allows Zappos to stay ahead of industry trends and anticipate changes in customer preferences, which is crucial for maintaining its competitive edge. Additionally, Zappos's employees are encouraged to engage with customers directly, gathering feedback and insights that are used to inform the company's product development and marketing strategies .By staying deeply connected with its market, Zappos has been able to maintain its leadership position in the e-commerce industry and continue delivering a superior shopping experience.

CHALLENGES

Despite its success, Zappos has faced several challenges as it has grown and expanded its operations. One of the primary challenges has been scaling its customer-service model while maintaining the high standards of service that the company is known for. As Zappos has grown, it has had to invest heavily in technology and training to ensure that its customer-service team can handle increasing volumes of customer interactions without compromising on quality. Additionally, Zappos has faced challenges related to competition in the e-commerce space, particularly from larger retailers like Amazon, which acquired Zappos in 2009 (Hsieh, 2010). Managing the integration with Amazon while maintaining its unique company culture and brand identity has been an ongoing challenge for Zappos. Furthermore, the rapidly changing retail landscape, driven by technological advancements and shifting consumer preferences, has required Zappos to continuously innovate and adapt its business model to stay competitive.

LESSONS LEARNED

Zappos's journey offers several important lessons for businesses looking to implement Entrepreneurial Marketing strategies. One key lesson is the importance of maintaining a customer-centric approach, as Zappos has done by making customer service a core part of its business strategy. Additionally, fostering strong two-way communication with customers is critical for building trust, gathering valuable feedback, and creating a loyal customer base. The value of strategic alliances is also evident in Zappos's success, as its partnerships with suppliers and technology companies have been crucial in expanding its product offerings and enhancing its e-commerce platform. Leveraging Informal Marketing Research allows companies to stay agile and responsive to customer needs, ensuring that their products and services remain relevant in a competitive market. Finally, deep Market Immersion is essential for understanding industry trends and anticipating changes in the market, which can help businesses stay ahead of the competition (Hsieh, 2010; Frei & Morriss, 2012). These lessons highlight the importance of being adaptable, innovative, and customer-focused in today's fast-paced business environment.

LITE DIAGNOSTIC TOOL

CASE STUDY: BRIGHT HARVEST OR MISSED SEASON?

Executive Summary: Bright Harvest is a $45 million regional distributor of organic produce grounded in sustainability and authenticity. Founded by a former organic farmer with a bold vision and a deep commitment to ethical sourcing, the company achieved rapid growth through values-based branding and an entrepreneurial drive. Yet in 2025, Bright Harvest faces a pivotal moment. Customer churn is rising, partnerships are eroding, and internal misalignment is stalling its ability to adapt. At the heart of the tension is a founder-led culture rooted in instinct and identity, now clashing with the need for customer insight, operational rigor, and scalable systems. As Bright Harvest approaches its strategic-planning retreat, the leadership team must confront whether its growth model is sustainable—and what kind of company it wants to become.

1. **Company Background:** Bright Harvest Organics (BHO) was founded in 2017 by Taylor Ramos, a second-generation organic farmer passionate about creating a transparent, values-driven food-supply chain. Taylor envisioned a company that connected small farms to conscious consumers—emphasizing fairness, traceability, and storytelling. Beginning with just five farm partners and a refrigerated van, BHO delivered seasonal produce to independent grocers across Northern California.

The company's early success came from its authenticity, vibrant brand identity, and emotional resonance with millennial and Gen Z customers.

It used "Meet the Farmer" content, sustainable packaging, and social media takeovers to humanize its product. From 2019 to 2022, Bright Harvest scaled rapidly—expanding into Oregon and Southern California, launching a direct-to-consumer (DTC) subscription box, and becoming a darling in regional sustainability circles. By 2023, the company had over sixty farm partners, four hundred retail accounts, and a team of fifty-five employees.

2. The Founder's Vision: Taylor, now thirty-nine, remains the company's central figure. Equal parts mission-driven and action-oriented, Taylor is widely admired for vision, charisma, and decisiveness. Employees describe them as "intensely loyal," "deeply intuitive," and "always in motion." Taylor's oft-repeated motto—"If we wait for the data, we're already behind"—underscores their approach.

Taylor distrusts bureaucracy. Departmental meetings are ad hoc. Strategic plans are sketched on whiteboards, evolving midcycle. KPIs are optional. Customer feedback is considered important, but not in any formalized or structured way. Taylor continues to review all product and branding decisions personally and retains final say over partnerships, packaging, and messaging.

Despite advice to the contrary, Taylor declined offers from large grocers and investors that seemed misaligned with the brand's ethos. "We're not here to scale industrially," Taylor once said in a staff meeting. "We're here to grow with integrity."

3. Momentum—and Cracks: Bright Harvest's rise was marked by instinctual wins: a viral video campaign featuring farm families, a partnership with a wellness influencer, and exclusive sourcing deals that helped BHO thrive during a supply-chain crunch. Its DTC subscription box launched with no dedicated e-commerce team but succeeded on the strength of brand trust and community loyalty. Investors took notice. A seed round in 2021 from a mission-aligned food fund pushed the company's valuation over $100 million.

But in 2023, signs of strain emerged. Subscription churn climbed to

22 percent. A key grocery chain in San Diego dropped BHO due to inconsistent delivery schedules and lack of promo tracking. Customer-service tickets regarding late boxes, missing items, and unclear communication rose steadily. Internally, operations and marketing were growing increasingly disconnected.

4. A New Perspective: In early 2024, BHO hired Maya Patel as director of growth. Maya brought a strong track record from a DTC food-tech company and immediately proposed initiatives to strengthen retention and improve operational discipline. These included CRM systems, a net-promoter score (NPS) program, segmentation strategies, and structured customer-feedback loops.

However, Maya's initiatives faced resistance. Taylor expressed skepticism about the need for "corporate tools," and several staff members echoed the sentiment that data shouldn't replace relationships. Projects were delayed or deprioritized. Maya's email performance tests were shelved. A pilot feedback survey was never launched.

Maya pushed for a partnership with a fast-growing plant-based meal-kit company. She saw it as a strategic alignment in values and audience. Taylor rejected it outright, saying, "Their brand is diluted. Ours is pure."

5. Cultural Friction: As 2025 approached, internal tensions became more visible:

- **Maya:** "Churn is telling us something, but we're not listening. If we don't act on customer data, we're just guessing."
- **Taylor:** "Data didn't get us here. Intuition did. You want us to trade our voice for a spreadsheet?"
- **Farm Partnerships Director:** "Farms are loyal, but I'm getting more calls about payment timing and delivery confusion."
- **Ops VP:** "Expansion into Oregon stretched us thin. We need to fix fulfillment before we grow again."

Bright Harvest had hired four experienced staff from outside firms in the past year. None had stayed longer than eight months. Interviews revealed a pattern: unclear priorities, reactive planning, and a culture that prized improvisation over systems.

6. The Customer View: Interviews with three longtime subscribers revealed issues with box-content consistency, vague delivery communication, and lackluster customer-service interactions. While they loved the company's values, all said they'd recently considered canceling. "I want to stay with Bright Harvest," one said, "but I feel like they've stopped listening."

A regional grocery buyer voiced similar concerns:

"We love the mission. But they don't meet us halfway. No sell-through data. No co-marketing planning. We're not sure they're serious about retail."

7. Strategic Crossroads: Bright Harvest now faces four critical tensions:

- **Instinct vs. Insight**—Can the company retain its identity while building structured-feedback systems?
- **Founder Control vs. Organizational Scalability**—Will Taylor allow decentralization of decision-making?
- **Growth vs. Discipline**—Should Bright Harvest pause expansion to address retention and operational issues?
- **Values vs. Flexibility**—Can the brand evolve without compromising its mission?

The upcoming 2025 strategy retreat will determine whether the company leans into its legacy model—or transforms into something more adaptable.

8. Observed Strategic Behaviors: Student analysis is required to classify the company's behavior using the Strategic Orientation Index™. Consider:

Are decisions shaped more by proactiveness and risk-taking, or by market feedback?

How does the company engage with customer data and competitor insights?

What role does internal coordination and marketing discipline play?

9. Decision Prompt: You have been invited to join Bright Harvest's 2025 planning retreat as a strategic advisor. Based on the company's behavior and posture:

How would you assess their current strategic orientation?

What are their strengths—and what's holding them back?

Which strategic posture are they most aligned with today?

What are the potential consequences of continuing on their current path?

10. Strategic Options: Taylor is preparing a proposal for the board. Four paths are on the table:

A. Expand into Colorado and Arizona using the current model.

B. Pause expansion, implement CRM and VOC tools, and improve retention.

C. Seek acquisition by a values-aligned parent while momentum remains.

D. Pilot Maya's insight-driven model in one region while maintaining founder control elsewhere.

What would you recommend—and why?

CASE STUDY: NIMBLETECH SOLUTIONS— CHASING GROWTH WITHOUT ALIGNMENT

1. OPENING VIGNETTE

The executive team at NimbleTech Solutions had gathered for what was supposed to be a routine quarterly strategy sync. The VP of sales, energized by a recent swing through prospective enterprise accounts, pushed for a bold new pivot. "We've got five big logos on the hook," she said. "All we need to do is adapt our roadmap slightly to support a few custom requests."

The CTO's jaw tightened. "We can't just hack in features on a whim," she countered. "Our last three roadmap deviations have added six months of tech debt."

The CEO—a founder known for rallying the troops with start-up grit—looked conflicted. His dream was growth, but not at the cost of losing the team. The head of product, normally quiet, finally spoke: "We're not aligned. This isn't a strategy session—it's a food fight."

Silence followed. The room didn't lack intelligence. It lacked shared behavior. And the rift was widening.

2. COMPANY BACKGROUND

NimbleTech Solutions was founded in 2017 with a mission: Simplify the management of distributed IoT devices in manufacturing environments. Its flagship product, ControlLink, allowed enterprise teams to remotely monitor, update, and secure industrial equipment via a centralized dashboard. The product hit product-market fit quickly, and by 2022, the company had scaled to $42 million in ARR and closed a $75 million Series C funding round.

Leadership included:

- CEO & Co-founder Alan Hsu: a visionary product leader with deep roots in the IoT space
- CTO Leena Kumar: known for her precision, discipline, and aversion to technical shortcuts
- CRO Michelle Reyes: recently hired from a hypergrowth fintech with a reputation for dealmaking at all costs
- VP of Product Jordan Wu: a loyalist and early team member, now stuck between competing functions

As NimbleTech matured, it added layers of structure—new departments, objectives and key results, and a professionalized middle-management tier. But alignment eroded. The original founder-led cohesion that once substituted for process was no longer enough. Teams began pulling in different directions.

3. BEHAVIORAL SIGNALS EMERGE

Engineering prided itself on disciplined codebases, long-term stability, and backward compatibility. Leena made it clear: Reliability and uptime were non-negotiable. Yet Sales, buoyed by Michelle's fintech bravado, operated in a culture of promises. Her team often pitched roadmap features as if they already existed.

Marketing conducted regular Voice of Customer surveys, hosted user panels, and generated detailed personas. However, product decisions seemed detached from their insights. Product roadmaps were internally debated more than externally validated.

The CEO, Alan, frequently preached vision in all-hands meetings. He cited Elon Musk, quoted Simon Sinek, and challenged teams to "think 10x." But in decision-making forums, he became risk-averse—opting for incremental moves over bold plays. This behavioral contradiction was demoralizing to his team.

As tensions rose, meetings grew more political. Teams defended turf. Strategy sessions lacked coherence. Alignment had decayed not in principle, but in practice. Behavior was fragmented.

4. INFLECTION POINT

By the first quarter of 2023, revenue growth had slowed from 22 percent year over year to 11 percent. Two major enterprise deals collapsed post-sale due to failed custom implementations. Churn increased in mid-market accounts, and a long-anticipated product launch missed its date by three months.

Internally, turnover among Customer-Success Managers spiked. The Net-Promoter Score dropped from +32 to +17 within one year. In Slack channels and one-on-ones, employees began whispering about dysfunction at the top.

In response, the board pressured Alan to "align the team." He agreed to bring in an external consultant. His mandate: Figure out where the behavioral gaps were—and fix them.

5. THE SOI™ DIAGNOSTIC IS INTRODUCED

The consultant introduced the Strategic Orientation Index™ (SOI™)—a behavioral assessment built around three dimensions:

Entrepreneurial Orientation (EO): how a firm thinks

Market Orientation (MO): how a firm listens

Entrepreneurial Marketing (EM): how a firm acts

Each executive team completed a behavioral survey, rating Nimble-Tech across nine subconstructs:

EO: Innovativeness, Proactiveness, Risk-Taking

MO: Customer Orientation, Competitor Orientation, Interfunctional Coordination

EM: Growth Orientation, Opportunity Orientation, Two-Way Contact with Customers, Value Creation Through Alliances, Informal Research and Market Immersion

Patterns emerged. Engineering rated EO extremely low. They viewed product stability as strategic. Sales gave themselves high marks for EM but were weak on coordination. Marketing scored highest on MO, especially Customer Orientation. Product was middling across the board.

The behavioral picture was clear: NimbleTech listened well, but acted sporadically and thought conservatively. Behaviorally, they were a Reluctant Responder.

6. MAPPING THE QUADRANT

When the SOI™ results were plotted on the quadrant, NimbleTech landed in the bottom-right:

- **High MO**
- **Low EO**
- **Inconsistent EM**

This placed them in the **Reluctant Responder** persona: organizations that hear the market clearly but fail to act decisively or think entrepreneurially.

The CEO was stunned. "But we were founded to take risks," he said. "We disrupted the space."

The consultant responded, "Your founding story is entrepreneurial. But your current behavior isn't."

This moment changed the tone. Leaders began seeing the dissonance between self-perception and execution.

7. PERSONA FRICTION

Each functional leader operated from a different behavioral model. Michelle (CRO) acted like a Fearless Inventor—aggressive, opportunistic, short-cycle focused. Leena (CTO) embodied elements of a Reluctant Responder—cautious, risk-averse, methodical. Marketing wanted to be an Insightful Optimizer but lacked authority. Product hovered between personas.

The result: constant misfires. Sales sold features Engineering wouldn't build. Marketing warned about trends that Product ignored. Product launched on spec instead of insight.

Meetings turned toxic. Alignment was impossible because no one shared the same behavioral lens. This wasn't a strategy problem. It was a quadrant collision.

8. INTERVENTION AND STRATEGIC ACTION PLAN

The consultant facilitated a quadrant-based behavioral debrief. Each department presented how they scored and where they believed they *should* be. This forced a painful, but productive reckoning.

Three changes followed:

1. **Quarterly Innovation Sprints (EO Rebalancing):**

    Every quarter, each department would pilot one initiative outside its comfort zone.

    Engineering experimented with rapid prototyping weeks.

    Sales piloted verticalized offerings, instead of custom requests.

2. **Customer-Immersion Framework (EM Formalization):**

Marketing, Sales, and CX co-created a "Customer Learning Loop."

Every sixty days, teams reviewed anonymized call transcripts, churn data, and win/loss insights.

3. **Behavioral Playbook Launch (Leadership Modeling):**

The CEO published five "Behavioral Commitments."

Example: "We will tolerate small, intelligent risks over safe stagnation."

Each department was required to operationalize these commitments.

9. SIX MONTHS LATER

Six months after the intervention, NimbleTech rescored their SOI™. The new results showed:

EO scores up 28 percent, especially in Engineering and Product

EM behaviors adopted more formally, with shared KPIs, quarterly retrospectives

MO held steady but was now tied to actual decisions

The Net-Promoter Score climbed back to +29. Churn decreased 18 percent. The new product line launched on time, and customer usage exceeded forecast.

But more importantly, leaders had a shared language. They didn't argue about strategy in the abstract. They debated behavior. They understood their quadrant—and were moving together.

10. TEACHING NOTE PROMPTS

What quadrant was NimbleTech in before the diagnostic? What quadrant were they moving toward?

Which subconstructs of EO, MO, or EM caused the most internal tension?

How did leadership behaviors enable or hinder quadrant alignment?

If you were the consultant, what next step would you recommend to reinforce the quadrant shift?

What risks remain if one department backslides into a previous persona?

Strategic Implication: Strategic alignment isn't just structural—it's behavioral. Firms must assess the gaps between how they think, listen, and act, and decide whether those patterns are producing competitive advantage.

CHAPTER 11

ENHANCING FIRM PROFITABILITY THROUGH STRATEGIC ORIENTATIONS AND ENTREPRENEURIAL MARKETING

Measuring firm profitability is fundamental for understanding a business's financial health and making informed strategic decisions. Profitability metrics allow businesses to evaluate their efficiency in generating profit relative to their revenue, assets, and equity, which are crucial indicators of overall performance (Brigham & Ehrhardt, 2022). This chapter explores the importance of these metrics, strategies for improving profitability, and tools for accurate measurement, with a particular focus on how Market Orientation (MO), Entrepreneurial Orientation (EO), and Entrepreneurial Marketing (EM) can drive profitability through innovative, customer-centric, and proactive approaches.

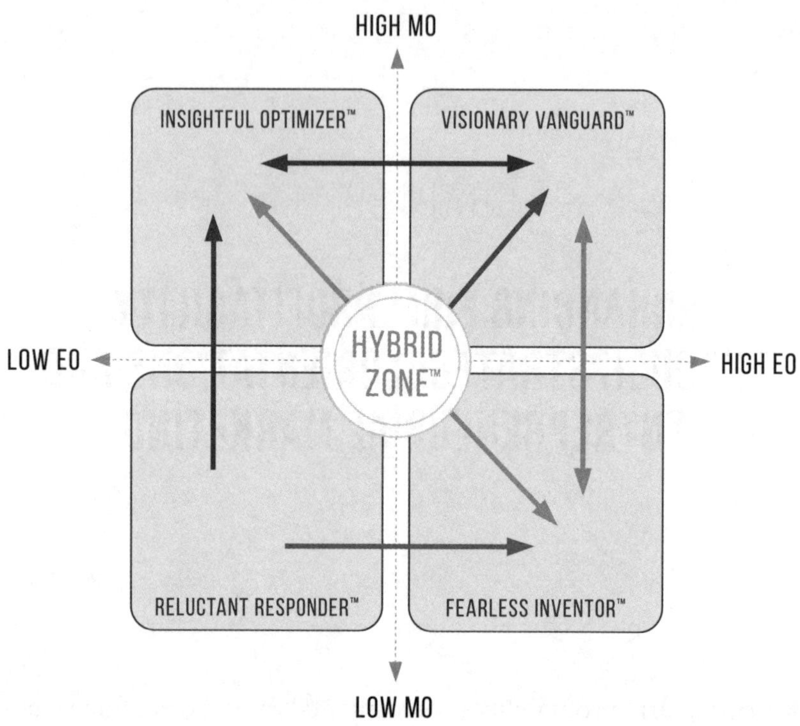

DYNAMIC QUADRANT MIGRATION

Firms evolve in nonlinear ways. This map highlights typical and atypical movement patterns across strategic personas—capturing how EO, MO, and EM behaviors shift in response to internal and external pressures.

UNDERSTANDING FIRM PROFITABILITY

DEFINITION AND KEY CONCEPTS

Profitability metrics are essential indicators that provide insights into a firm's financial performance, particularly its ability to generate profit (Ross, Westerfield, & Jordan, 2019). The key concepts include:

Gross Profit Margin: This metric indicates the percentage of revenue that exceeds the cost of goods sold, measuring how efficiently a company uses its resources to produce goods (Higgins, 2020). A higher gross profit margin suggests that a company can cover its operating expenses and still achieve profitability. To improve gross profit margin, companies can focus on reducing production costs, negotiating better terms with suppliers, or increasing the selling price of their products while maintaining or improving quality.

Operating Profit Margin: This reflects the percentage of revenue remaining after deducting operating expenses, offering insights into a company's operational efficiency (Brealey, Myers, & Allen, 2021). Operating profit margin can be enhanced by optimizing operational processes, such as automating manual tasks, outsourcing non-core activities, or implementing lean manufacturing techniques. Reducing unnecessary expenditures and improving cost control measures are also critical to increasing this margin.

Net Profit Margin: This shows the percentage of revenue that remains as profit after all expenses, including taxes and interest, providing a comprehensive view of overall profitability (Parrino, Kidwell, & Bates, 2020). To improve net profit margin, businesses should focus on increasing sales, reducing costs, and improving efficiency across all operations. Strategies could include launching new revenue streams, renegotiating terms with creditors to lower interest payments, and optimizing tax strategies through deductions and credits.

Return on Assets (ROA): ROA measures how effectively a company uses its assets to generate profit (Damodaran, 2021). A higher ROA indicates that the company is efficiently using its assets to create earnings. Businesses can improve their ROA by either increasing net income or reducing total assets through asset-optimization strategies, such as selling underperforming assets, improving asset turnover, or investing in more productive assets.

Return on Equity (ROE): ROE indicates how well a company generates profit from shareholders' equity, reflecting the efficiency of using investors' funds (Megginson & Smart, 2021). To enhance ROE, companies can focus on increasing net income through profit-maximizing strategies, such as expanding high-margin product lines, reducing debt to lower interest expenses, or utilizing financial leverage to increase shareholder returns without diluting equity.

Earnings Before Interest, Taxes, Depreciation, and Amortization (EBITDA): EBITDA evaluates a company's operating performance without the impact of financing and accounting decisions (Kaplan & Atkinson, 2020). By focusing on EBITDA, businesses can assess their core operational performance and identify areas for improvement. Enhancing EBITDA can be achieved through cost-cutting measures, increasing operational efficiency, or expanding the company's revenue base through strategic business development. Historically, profitability metrics have been pivotal in assessing financial performance and guiding strategic business decisions. Companies have long relied on these metrics to understand their ability to generate income, manage costs, and achieve sustainable growth (Higgins, 2020). In the modern business environment, where competition is fierce and market conditions fluctuate rapidly, continuously monitoring these metrics is more critical than ever (Brigham & Ehrhardt, 2022). Historically, firms that excel in profitability metrics have demonstrated greater resilience in economic downturns and have been better positioned to capitalize on growth opportunities during economic upswings.

THE ROLE OF MARKET ORIENTATION (MO) IN ENHANCING PROFITABILITY

Market Orientation (MO) refers to the organizational culture and practices that prioritize understanding and meeting the needs and desires of customers. It involves a strong focus on gathering market intelligence, disseminating this information throughout the organization, and responding effectively to market demands (Kohli & Jaworski, 1990). Properly implemented, MO can significantly enhance a firm's profitability by ensuring that the company remains aligned with customer expectations and market trends.

MO EMPIRICALLY SUPPORTED PERFORMANCE STATISTICS

Companies that exercise Market Orientation (MO) generally experience significantly higher profitability compared to those that do not. Studies have consistently shown that firms with a strong Market Orientation tend to achieve better financial performance, higher customer satisfaction, and greater competitive advantage.

Market Orientation represents a firm's capability to generate, disseminate, and respond to market intelligence—placing the customer at the center of strategic decisions.

In their foundational study, Narver and Slater (1990) concluded: "A market-oriented firm recognizes that there are numerous ways by which additional benefits can be created for the buyer. This quest for and ultimate fulfillment of customer needs translates into superior performance" (p. 22). A business that increases its Market Orientation will improve its profitability.

Jaworski and Kohli (1993) found that Market Orientation is positively related to business performance and employee commitment. Firms that emphasize market intelligence and responsiveness are better able to adapt to market needs, which in turn enhances financial performance. "The results indicate that a Market Orientation is positively related to overall business performance" (p. 63).

A meta-analysis by Kirca, Jayachandran, and Bearden (2005) confirmed significant positive correlations between MO and key performance metrics:

- Profitability (**r** = **0.25**)
- Sales growth (**r** = **0.27**)
- Market share (**r** = **0.26**)

Market Orientation is a driver of superior business performance across industries and contexts. "Our meta-analysis reveals a positive association between market orientation and performance (r = .32, p < .05)" (p. 31).

Kumar, Jones, Venkatesan, and Leone (2011) also confirmed this link in longitudinal models, stating: "Market orientation should have a more pronounced effect on a firm's profit than sales because a market orientation focuses efforts on customer retention rather than on acquisition" (p. 26).

CUSTOMER-CENTRICITY AND PROFITABILITY

A market-oriented firm places a high value on customer satisfaction and loyalty, which are critical drivers of profitability (Narver & Slater, 1990). By consistently gathering and analyzing customer feedback, companies can tailor their products and services to better meet customer needs, leading to higher satisfaction rates. Satisfied customers are more likely to become repeat buyers, refer others, and remain loyal to the brand, all of which contribute to increased revenue and profitability (Kotler, 2003). Furthermore, market-oriented companies are better equipped to identify and capitalize on emerging customer trends, allowing them to stay ahead of competitors. This proactive approach enables businesses to innovate continuously, offering products and services that resonate with customers and meet their evolving needs, thereby driving sustained profitability (Deshpandé, Farley, & Webster, 1993).

MARKET INTELLIGENCE AND PROFITABILITY

Effective Market Orientation relies heavily on the collection and utilization of market intelligence. This involves not only understanding customer preferences but also monitoring competitor activities, market conditions, and broader economic trends (Kohli & Jaworski, 1990). By leveraging this intelligence, firms can make informed decisions about product development, pricing strategies, and marketing campaigns, all of which can enhance profitability. For instance, understanding competitors' strengths and weaknesses allows a firm to position itself more effectively in the market, offering superior value propositions that attract and retain customers. Additionally, by anticipating changes in the market environment, companies can adjust their strategies proactively, minimizing risks and maximizing opportunities for profit growth (Narver & Slater, 1990).

INTERFUNCTIONAL COORDINATION AND PROFITABILITY

A key aspect of Market Orientation is interfunctional coordination, which involves the collaborative efforts of various departments to create value for customers (Narver & Slater, 1990). When departments such as marketing, sales, R&D, and customer service work together, they can deliver a more cohesive and satisfying customer experience. This collaboration ensures that all parts of the organization are aligned with the company's market-oriented goals, leading to more effective execution of strategies that enhance profitability. For example, when R&D teams are informed by customer feedback collected by the marketing department, they can develop products that better meet market demands. Similarly, when sales teams are aware of marketing strategies and customer insights, they can tailor their sales pitches more effectively, leading to higher conversion rates and increased sales (Kohli & Jaworski, 1990).

THE ROLE OF ENTREPRENEURIAL ORIENTATION (EO) IN ENHANCING PROFITABILITY

Entrepreneurial Orientation (EO) refers to a firm's strategic posture that emphasizes innovation, proactiveness, and risk-taking (Lumpkin & Dess, 1996). Companies with a strong EO are often more agile, able to adapt to changing market conditions, and better positioned to capitalize on new opportunities. These attributes are essential for driving profitability in today's dynamic and competitive business environment.

EO EMPIRICALLY SUPPORTED PERFORMANCE STATISTICS

Entrepreneurial Orientation (EO) also has a strong correlation with improved profitability and overall business performance. Companies that exhibit a high level of Entrepreneurial Orientation typically outperform those that do not in several key financial and strategic areas. Entrepreneurial Orientation reflects a firm's propensity to innovate, take risks, and act proactively. Numerous empirical studies support EO's positive relationship with firm performance.

A meta-analysis by Rauch, Wiklund, Lumpkin, and Frese (2009) found a robust overall EO–performance relationship: "The meta-analytic correlation between EO and performance is r = .242, which is significant and moderately strong" (p. 770). This finding holds across industries, firm sizes, and countries.

Wiklund and Shepherd (2005) demonstrated that EO positively impacts firm growth, especially when combined with organizational learning and resource availability. "The results of our study show that EO is positively related to performance" (p. 83). Firms with a strong Entrepreneurial Orientation are likely to achieve higher growth due to their willingness to take risks, innovate, and act proactively.

In a study comparing new ventures and established firms, Su, Xie, and Li (2011) observed: *"We find that the relationship between EO and performance is inverse U-shaped in new ventures but positive in established firms"* (p. 558).

Overall, companies with a high level of Entrepreneurial Orientation are more likely to achieve superior financial performance, market leadership, and long-term growth compared to those that are less entrepreneurial.

INNOVATION AND PROFITABILITY

Innovation is a core component of EO and plays a crucial role in enhancing profitability (Covin & Slevin, 1991). Firms that prioritize innovation are constantly seeking new ways to create value, whether through the development of new products, services, or business models. This focus on innovation enables companies to differentiate themselves from competitors, offering unique solutions that attract customers and command premium prices.

Innovative firms are also more likely to tap into unmet market needs, creating entirely new revenue streams that contribute to profitability. Additionally, innovation can lead to cost savings through the introduction of more efficient processes or technologies, further boosting profit margins (Lumpkin & Dess, 1996).

PROACTIVENESS AND PROFITABILITY

Proactiveness, another key element of EO, involves anticipating and acting on future market opportunities before competitors do (Lumpkin & Dess, 1996). Proactive firms are often the first to market with new products or services, allowing them to capture market share quickly and establish a strong competitive position. This early mover advantage often translates into higher profitability as these firms can set the market standards and enjoy brand recognition and customer loyalty.

Moreover, proactive firms are better equipped to navigate market changes and disruptions. By continuously scanning the environment for emerging trends and potential threats, these companies can pivot quickly, adjusting their strategies to maintain profitability even in volatile markets (Covin & Slevin, 1991).

THE IMPACT OF PROPERLY IMPLEMENTED ENTREPRENEURIAL MARKETING (EM) ON FIRM PROFITABILITY

Entrepreneurial Marketing (EM) is a strategic approach that combines innovative marketing practices with the entrepreneurial mindset, focusing on maximizing the potential of limited resources, exploiting market opportunities, and building strong customer relationships (Morris, Schindehutte, & LaForge, 2002). When properly implemented, EM can significantly enhance a firm's profitability by fostering growth, enhancing customer loyalty, and driving innovation.

EM EMPIRICALLY SUPPORTED PERFORMANCE STATISTICS

Entrepreneurial Marketing (EM), which combines innovative, risk-taking, and proactive marketing strategies with a deep customer focus, has been shown to significantly enhance profitability and overall business performance. Companies that effectively implement EM often see marked improvements in various financial metrics compared to those that do not. Entrepreneurial Marketing blends entrepreneurial behavior with marketing discipline—emphasizing innovation, risk-taking, proactivity, and customer intensity in strategic execution.

Morris, Schindehutte, and LaForge (2002) argued that EM behaviors facilitate opportunity recognition and enhance the firm's ability to adapt to rapidly changing markets, ultimately improving financial performance (p. 5). While conceptual, their framework is widely cited in empirical follow-ups.

Becherer, Haynes, and Fletcher (2006) studied small businesses and found that: Firms with stronger Entrepreneurial Marketing practices report higher levels of both profitability and revenue growth.

Kraus, Harms, and Fink (2010) provided empirical support by showing that EM positively impacts both competitive advantage and firm performance: Results indicate that Entrepreneurial Marketing strongly influences the market and financial performance of young ventures. The authors note that firms exhibiting higher levels of EM practices tend to experience improved performance metrics, including profitability and revenue growth.

Miles and Darroch (2006) examined EM in larger firms and concluded: "Firms adopting Entrepreneurial Marketing processes (EMPs) will engage in marketing processes that emphasize opportunity creation and/or discovery, evaluation, and exploitation" (p. 485).

Large firms can, and must, effectively leverage Entrepreneurial Marketing processes for competitive advantage.

Hanaysha and Al-Shaikh (2022) found that specific EM dimensions like customer intensity and value creation positively impact firm performance: "The findings revealed that six out of seven identified constructs of Entrepreneurial Marketing hold a significant impact over performance of entrepreneurial Firms" (p. 2).

Integration of EM has significant positive effects on firm performance, highlighting their strategic relevance.

GROWTH ORIENTATION AND PROFITABILITY

A key component of EM is Growth Orientation, which emphasizes the importance of seeking new opportunities and scaling operations to achieve long-term success (Miles & Darroch, 2006). Firms that adopt a growth-oriented mindset are more likely to explore and capitalize on new market opportunities, diversify their product offerings, and expand their customer base. This approach leads to increased revenue streams and, ultimately, higher profitability. Growth Orientation encourages businesses to be proactive in identifying market trends and consumer needs, allowing them to develop products or services that meet emerging demands. This proactive stance not only drives sales but also positions the firm as a leader in innovation, creating a competitive advantage that translates into sustained profitability (Ireland, Hitt, & Sirmon, 2003).

OPPORTUNITY ORIENTATION AND PROFITABILITY

Opportunity orientation, another critical element of EM, involves the continuous search for and exploitation of market opportunities that align with the firm's capabilities and strategic goals (Hills & Hultman, 2011). Firms that are adept at recognizing and seizing opportunities are better positioned to introduce new products, enter untapped markets, and leverage strategic partnerships, all of which contribute to increased profitability. For example, by identifying gaps in the market or underserved customer segments, firms can introduce tailored solutions that address specific needs, thereby capturing a larger market share. Additionally, opportunity orientation often leads to the development of innovative marketing campaigns that resonate with target audiences, driving brand loyalty and repeat business, which are crucial for long-term profitability (Morris et al., 2002).

TWO-WAY CUSTOMER CONTACT AND PROFITABILITY

Total customer focus, particularly through Two-Way Customer Contact, is central to EM and has a direct impact on profitability (Hills, Hultman, & Miles, 2008). Engaging in meaningful dialogues with customers allows firms to gather valuable insights into customer preferences, behaviors, and pain points. This information can be used to refine products, improve customer service, and tailor marketing strategies, all of which enhance customer satisfaction and loyalty. When customers feel heard and valued, they are more likely to remain loyal to the brand, leading to increased customer-retention rates and lower acquisition costs (Kotler, 2003). Loyal customers tend to spend more over time, provide positive word-of-mouth referrals, and are less sensitive to price increases, all of which contribute to improved profit margins (Reichheld, 2003).

VALUE CREATION THROUGH ALLIANCES AND PROFITABILITY

EM emphasizes the importance of creating value through strategic alliances and partnerships. By collaborating with other firms, suppliers, or even customers, businesses can access new resources, technologies, and markets that would otherwise be difficult or costly to reach independently (Ireland et al., 2003). These alliances can lead to cost savings through shared resources, co-marketing opportunities, and enhanced innovation, all of which positively impact profitability. For instance, strategic partnerships can enable firms to leverage complementary strengths, such as combining innovative technology with established distribution channels, to deliver superior value to customers. This collaborative approach not only enhances the firm's market position but also reduces operational costs, thereby boosting profitability (Morris et al., 2002).

INFORMAL MARKETING RESEARCH AND PROFITABILITY

Informal Marketing Research, or the practice of leveraging non-traditional research methods to gather market intelligence, is a hallmark of EM (Hills & Hultman, 2011). This approach allows firms to remain agile and responsive to market changes without the need for extensive and costly formal research processes. By using informal methods such as direct customer feedback, social media listening, and observational techniques, businesses can quickly adapt their strategies to align with market dynamics. The agility provided by Informal Marketing Research enables firms to make informed decisions swiftly, reducing the risk of missed opportunities and costly mistakes. Moreover, this approach often leads to a deeper understanding of the target market, allowing firms to develop products and services that better meet customer needs, thus enhancing customer satisfaction and driving profitability (Stokes, 2000).

MARKET IMMERSION AND PROFITABILITY

Market Immersion, or the deep involvement in and understanding of the market and customer environment, is another critical aspect of EM (Hills et al., 2008). Firms that are deeply immersed in their markets are better equipped to anticipate changes, identify emerging trends, and understand the competitive landscape. This knowledge enables them to act quickly and decisively, capitalizing on opportunities before competitors do. Market Immersion fosters innovation by encouraging firms to think creatively about how to meet customer needs and solve problems. This innovative approach often results in the development of unique products and services that differentiate the firm from its competitors, leading to increased market share and profitability (Morris et al., 2002). Additionally, by staying closely connected to the market, firms can build stronger relationships with customers, further enhancing loyalty and profitability.

OVERALL IMPACT OF EM ON FIRM PROFITABILITY

When EM is properly implemented, it drives profitability through multiple avenues: enhanced growth potential, improved customer retention, increased innovation, and effective resource utilization. By focusing on key elements such as Growth Orientation, opportunity orientation, customer engagement, Value Creation Through Alliances, Informal Marketing Research, and Market Immersion, firms can build a robust and adaptable business model that thrives in dynamic environments (Morris et al., 2002).

STRATEGIES FOR IMPROVING PROFITABILITY THROUGH ENTREPRENEURIAL MARKETING

REVENUE GROWTH

To drive profitability, businesses must focus on strategies that directly enhance revenue. Practical steps include:

Market Expansion: Entering new markets can significantly increase the customer base and, consequently, revenue. Conducting thorough market research can help identify opportunities in untapped regions or demographics (Porter, 1985). This can involve expanding geographically, targeting new customer segments, or exploring emerging markets. For successful market expansion, businesses should tailor their products or services to the preferences and cultural nuances of the new market, establish a local presence, and build relationships with local partners and distributors.

Product Diversification: Introducing new products or services tailored to different customer needs can boost sales and attract a broader audience (Ansoff, 1965). Product diversification can take the form of creating new product lines, modifying existing products to appeal to different customer segments, or offering complementary products that enhance the overall value proposition. Diversification also reduces the risk associated with relying on a single product or market, making the business more resilient to market fluctuations.

Pricing Strategies: Implementing pricing strategies such as premium pricing, discount pricing, and value-based pricing can optimize revenue. Understanding customer perceived value and competitive pricing is crucial for setting prices that maximize profit margins (Nagle, Hogan, & Zale, 2016). Premium pricing can be effective for products with a strong brand or unique value proposition, while discount pricing may be used to increase sales volume or penetrate a competitive market. Value-based pricing involves setting prices based on the perceived value to the customer rather than the cost of production, which can lead to higher profitability if executed correctly.

COST MANAGEMENT

Efficient cost management is essential for improving profitability. Businesses can implement the following strategies:

Cost Reduction: Identify and eliminate unnecessary expenses without compromising quality. This could involve renegotiating supplier contracts to secure better prices or terms, optimizing inventory levels to reduce carrying costs, or implementing energy-saving measures to lower utility bills (Horngren, Datar, & Rajan, 2021). Another approach could be to evaluate and streamline processes to eliminate redundant tasks or activities that do not add value to the customer or the business.

Efficient Resource Utilization: Optimize the use of resources such as labor, materials, and technology. Techniques like lean manufacturing and just-in-time inventory can help reduce waste and improve efficiency (Womack & Jones, 1996). Companies should also consider investing in technology that automates repetitive tasks, allowing employees to focus on higher-value activities. Regular audits of resource allocation can identify areas where resources are underutilized or misallocated, leading to more effective use of company assets.

Supply-Chain Optimization: Improving supply-chain efficiency can reduce costs and enhance profitability. Strategies include consolidating suppliers to achieve economies of scale, streamlining logistics to reduce transportation costs, and adopting technology to track and manage supply-chain processes (Christopher, 2016). Businesses should also consider implementing supply-chain-management software that provides real-time data, allowing for quicker adjustments and reducing the risk of supply-chain disruptions.

OPERATIONAL EFFICIENCY

Operational efficiency plays a crucial role in profitability. The following steps can enhance efficiency:

Process Improvement: Streamline business processes to reduce waste and increase productivity. Employ methodologies such as Six Sigma or Lean to identify inefficiencies and implement corrective actions (George, 2002). Process improvement can involve re-engineering workflows, automating manual tasks, and removing bottlenecks that slow down production or service delivery. Regular process audits can help maintain efficiency gains and identify new areas for improvement.

Technology Integration: Adopt advanced technologies to automate processes and improve productivity. Technologies like enterprise-resource-planning systems, automation, and AI can significantly reduce operational costs and improve accuracy (Brynjolfsson & McAfee, 2014). By integrating technology across various functions such as finance, HR, and supply chain, businesses can enhance data accuracy, reduce manual errors, and make more informed decisions. Additionally, investing in predictive analytics can help forecast demand, optimize inventory, and plan production schedules more effectively.

Employee Training: Invest in employee training and development to enhance skills and efficiency. Well-trained employees are more productive and can contribute to cost-saving initiatives (Noe, Hollenbeck, Gerhart, & Wright, 2019). Providing continuous learning opportunities helps employees stay up-to-date with the latest industry trends and technologies, enabling them to perform their tasks more effectively.

Encouraging a culture of continuous improvement where employees are empowered to suggest process enhancements can also lead to significant efficiency gains.

FINANCIAL MANAGEMENT

Strong financial-management practices are critical to sustaining and improving profitability. Key strategies include:

Effective Budgeting: Develop and adhere to a budget to control expenses and allocate resources efficiently. Regularly review budgets against actual performance and make adjustments as necessary (Kaplan & Atkinson, 2020). Businesses should create detailed budgets that account for all potential expenses, including variable costs, and forecast revenue realistically. Monthly or quarterly budget reviews can help track financial performance, identify areas of overspending, and adjust spending accordingly to stay within budget.

Debt Management: Manage debt effectively to minimize interest expenses and maintain financial stability. This may involve refinancing high-interest debt to lower interest rates, paying down debt aggressively when cash flow is strong, or restructuring debt to improve cash-flow management (Brigham & Ehrhardt, 2022). Keeping a healthy balance between debt and equity financing is crucial for maintaining financial flexibility and avoiding overleverage, which can lead to financial distress.

Investment in High-Return Projects: Allocate capital to projects with a high return on investment to maximize profitability. Use tools like Net Present Value (NPV) and Internal Rate of Return (IRR) to evaluate potential projects (Damodaran, 2021). Prioritizing investments that offer the highest potential returns while aligning with the company's strategic goals can drive long-term growth and profitability. Additionally, conducting thorough risk assessments before investing in new projects can help mitigate potential losses.

IMPORTANCE OF PROFITABILITY METRICS

Profitability metrics are vital for several reasons:

Performance Assessment: These metrics provide a clear picture of a company's financial health and operational efficiency (Brigham & Ehrhardt, 2022). By regularly tracking profitability metrics, businesses can assess whether they are meeting their financial goals and identify areas where performance is lacking. This assessment allows for timely interventions to correct course and improve overall financial health.

Decision-Making: Profitability metrics aid in making informed decisions regarding investments, cost management, and strategic planning (Kaplan & Atkinson, 2020). By understanding which aspects of the business are most profitable, companies can allocate resources more effectively and prioritize initiatives that offer the greatest return on investment. Decision-makers can also use these metrics to identify underperforming areas and develop strategies to address them.

Investor Confidence: High profitability metrics can attract investors and boost their confidence in the company's potential, leading to better funding opportunities (Damodaran, 2021). Investors are more likely to invest in companies that demonstrate strong profitability metrics, as these indicate a lower risk of financial distress and a higher potential for returns. Consistently strong profitability metrics can also lead to higher stock prices and improved market valuations.

Benchmarking: These metrics enable comparisons with industry peers, helping identify areas for improvement and best practices (Higgins, 2020). By benchmarking profitability metrics against industry standards, companies can gauge their competitive position and identify areas where they may be lagging. This information can be used to implement best practices and improve performance relative to competitors.

TOOLS FOR MEASURING PROFITABILITY

FINANCIAL STATEMENTS

Financial statements offer a comprehensive view of a company's financial performance and profitability:

Income Statement: The income statement, also known as the profit and loss statement, summarizes revenue, expenses, and net profit over a specific period, providing a clear view of profitability (Ross, Westerfield, & Jordan, 2019). Regular analysis of the income statement allows businesses to track their profitability trends, identify areas of improvement, and make data-driven decisions about cost management and revenue generation.

Balance Sheet: The balance sheet offers a snapshot of a company's assets, liabilities, and shareholders' equity, helping assess financial stability (Parrino, Kidwell, & Bates, 2020). Analyzing the balance sheet can help businesses understand their liquidity position, capital structure, and ability to fund future growth. It also provides insights into how well the company is managing its resources and liabilities.

Cash-Flow Statement: The cash-flow statement tracks cash inflows and outflows, offering insights into liquidity and cash management (Higgins, 2020). By regularly reviewing cash-flow statements, businesses can ensure they maintain sufficient cash reserves to meet operational needs, invest in growth opportunities, and service debt. Positive cash flow is a key indicator of financial health and sustainability.

FINANCIAL RATIOS

Financial ratios provide insights into various aspects of profitability and financial performance:

Profitability Ratios: Ratios like gross profit margin, operating profit margin, and net profit margin offer insights into a company's ability to generate profit from its operations (Brigham & Ehrhardt, 2022). These ratios can be used to assess the effectiveness of pricing strategies, cost management, and operational efficiency. Businesses should regularly calculate and compare these ratios to identify trends and make necessary adjustments to improve profitability.

Efficiency Ratios: Ratios such as return on assets and return on equity measure the efficiency of a company's use of its resources to generate profit (Megginson & Smart, 2021). These ratios are critical for evaluating how well a company is utilizing its assets and equity to generate earnings. Improving these ratios often involves optimizing resource allocation, improving asset utilization, and enhancing operational efficiency.

Liquidity Ratios: Liquidity ratios, including the current ratio and quick ratio, measure a company's ability to meet its short-term obligations and manage cash flow (Ross, Westerfield, & Jordan, 2019). Maintaining healthy liquidity ratios is essential for ensuring that the business can cover its immediate financial commitments without resorting to expensive short-term borrowing. Businesses should monitor these ratios regularly to avoid liquidity crises.

PERFORMANCE DASHBOARDS

Performance dashboards provide real-time insights into key profitability metrics and performance indicators:

Key Performance Indicators (KPIs): Tracking KPIs helps monitor and assess profitability. Dashboards can visualize and analyze KPIs in real time, aiding in quick decision-making (Brynjolfsson & McAfee, 2014). KPIs may include metrics like revenue growth, customer-acquisition cost, and customer-lifetime value. By displaying these metrics on a dashboard, businesses can quickly identify trends and make data-driven decisions to enhance profitability.

Benchmarking: Performance dashboards allow companies to compare their profitability metrics with industry benchmarks, helping identify areas for improvement (Higgins, 2020). Benchmarking against industry standards helps businesses understand where they stand relative to competitors and identify best practices that can be adopted to improve performance. Dashboards can facilitate this process by providing visual comparisons and highlighting gaps that need to be addressed.

Data Visualization: Data-visualization tools make it easier to understand financial data by presenting trends, patterns, and insights in a visual format (Few, 2012). Effective data visualization can help businesses quickly grasp complex financial information, identify key drivers of profitability, and communicate insights to stakeholders. By using graphs, charts, and other visual aids, businesses can enhance the clarity and impact of their financial analysis.

CONCLUSION

Measuring firm profitability is essential for assessing a company's financial health and making informed business decisions. By understanding key profitability metrics, employing effective measurement techniques, and implementing strategies for improving profitability through Market Orientation (MO), Entrepreneurial Orientation (EO), and Entrepreneurial Marketing (EM), businesses can optimize their operations and achieve sustainable growth. The concepts and techniques outlined in this chapter provide a comprehensive framework for evaluating and enhancing firm profitability, setting the stage for continued success in a competitive business environment.

Strategic Implication: Profitability is not just a financial outcome—it reflects behavioral alignment. Misalignment between EO, MO, and EM often shows up first in missed growth, then in eroded margins.

CHAPTER 12

ENTREPRENEURIAL MARKETING BEYOND SMALL BUSINESSES

Entrepreneurial Marketing (EM) is traditionally associated with small businesses and start-ups, primarily due to its focus on agility, creativity, and resourcefulness. These characteristics are often essential for smaller enterprises that lack the vast resources of larger corporations. However, the principles of EM are not only applicable to small businesses; they can also be a powerful strategy for larger corporations. Large organizations, with their substantial resources and established market presence, can leverage the principles of EM to foster innovation, respond swiftly to market changes, and maintain a competitive edge in their respective industries. This chapter explores why Entrepreneurial Marketing is advantageous for businesses of all sizes, including detailed case studies and scholarly references to underscore its broader applicability (Kraus et al., 2012).

THE CORE PRINCIPLES OF ENTREPRENEURIAL MARKETING

EM is characterized by its proactive, innovative, and risk-taking approach. These core principles of EM can be applied across various business sizes and industries, driving growth and sustaining competitive advantages. For larger businesses, understanding and implementing these principles can lead to more dynamic and resilient strategies that ensure long-term success.

Customer-Centricity: Prioritizing customer needs and feedback is at the heart of Entrepreneurial Marketing. This principle involves not only understanding current customer preferences but also anticipating future needs through continuous engagement and interaction. In large corporations, customer-centricity can manifest in various ways, such as through personalized marketing campaigns, customer-service initiatives, and the development of products and services that align with customer expectations. For instance, companies like Amazon and Apple have built their reputations on their ability to listen to and meet customer needs. Amazon's focus on customer satisfaction is evident in its Amazon Prime membership program, which was developed in response to customer desires for faster shipping and better value (Stone, 2013). Apple's customer-centric approach is demonstrated through its seamless ecosystem of products and services, which are designed to provide a cohesive and user-friendly experience (Morris et al., 2002). By continuously gathering customer feedback and using it to inform business decisions, these companies maintain high levels of customer loyalty and satisfaction.

Innovation and Creativity: Innovation and creativity are fundamental to EM, encouraging businesses to continuously seek new ways to engage customers and differentiate themselves from competitors. For larger organizations, fostering a culture of innovation and creativity can lead to the development of groundbreaking products and services that set the company apart in the marketplace. For example, Google's "20% time" policy, where employees are allowed to work on side projects, has led to the creation of some of its most successful products, such as Gmail and Google Maps (Iyer & Davenport, 2008). This policy not only encourages creativity but also empowers employees to take ownership of innovative ideas, leading to a more engaged and motivated workforce. In a larger business context, innovation can also involve investing in research and development (R&D) to explore new technologies and market opportunities as in the case of Tesla, which heavily invests in R&D and has revolutionized the automotive industry with its innovative electric vehicles and autonomous-driving technology. By fostering a culture of innovation and creativity, large organizations can stay ahead of the competition and continuously deliver value to their customers.

Agility and Flexibility: The ability to adapt quickly to market changes is crucial for maintaining relevance in today's fast-paced business environment. Larger corporations, although typically less nimble than start-ups, can implement agile methodologies in their operations to become more responsive to market demands. Agility in large organizations can be achieved by adopting a decentralized decision-making process, which allows for quicker responses to market trends and customer needs. This can involve cross-functional teams working iteratively to develop and refine products based on customer feedback (Rigby, Sutherland, & Takeuchi, 2016). For example, Procter & Gamble has adopted agile methodologies in its product-development process, allowing the company to bring new products to market faster and more efficiently (Lafley & Martin, 2013). By fostering agility and flexibility, large organizations can better navigate market uncertainties and capitalize on emerging opportunities.

Resourcefulness: Making the most of available resources is a hallmark of Entrepreneurial Marketing. While large organizations often have vast resources at their disposal, the challenge lies in utilizing them effectively to achieve business objectives. Resourcefulness in a large business context can involve leveraging existing assets, such as brand reputation, customer data, and technological infrastructure, to drive growth and innovation. Strategic partnerships and alliances, particularly with start-ups and smaller firms, can also provide fresh ideas and innovative solutions, helping larger companies stay ahead of the curve (Morris, Schindehutte, & LaForge, 2002). For instance, the partnership between Google and Nest, a start-up that developed smart-home products, allowed Google to enter the smart-home market and expand its product offerings . By being resourceful and leveraging strategic partnerships, large organizations can extend their reach and explore new market opportunities without significant capital investment.

LEVERAGING ENTREPRENEURIAL MARKETING TO GROW FROM AN SME TO A LARGER BUSINESS

Entrepreneurial Marketing is not just a strategy for established corporations or start-ups; it plays a crucial role in helping small and medium-sized enterprises (SMEs) transition into larger, more established businesses. As SMEs grow, they face unique challenges, including scaling operations, entering new markets, and managing increased complexity. EM, with its focus on innovation, customer-centricity, agility, and resourcefulness, provides a roadmap for SMEs to navigate these challenges and achieve sustainable growth.

1. BUILDING A SCALABLE CUSTOMER-CENTRIC STRATEGY

One of the foundational principles of EM is customer-centricity, which involves placing the customer at the center of all business activities. For SMEs, building a scalable customer-centric strategy is essential for growth. As businesses expand, maintaining a deep understanding of customer needs and preferences becomes increasingly complex, but it is also critical for sustaining competitive advantage.

To achieve this, SMEs must invest in tools and technologies that enable them to gather and analyze customer data at scale. Customer-relationship-management systems, for example, allow businesses to track customer interactions, preferences, and feedback, providing valuable insights that can inform marketing strategies, product development, and customer-service initiatives (Chaffey & Ellis-Chadwick, 2019). SMEs can also use social media platforms to engage with customers directly, gather real-time feedback, and build strong relationships. These tools help SMEs stay connected with their customer base even as they grow, ensuring that their offerings remain relevant and appealing.

Moreover, SMEs should focus on creating personalized experiences for their customers, even as they scale. Personalization can be achieved through data-driven marketing strategies that tailor messages, offers, and products to individual customer segments. This approach not only enhances customer satisfaction but also fosters loyalty, which is crucial for long-term growth (Peppers & Rogers, 2016). By maintaining a customer-centric focus, SMEs can differentiate themselves from larger competitors and build a loyal customer base that supports their growth.

2. INNOVATING TO STAY COMPETITIVE

Innovation is a key driver of growth for SMEs looking to transition into larger businesses. In the context of EM, innovation goes beyond developing new products; it encompasses finding new ways to deliver value to customers, exploring untapped markets, and rethinking business models.

For SMEs, fostering a culture of innovation is critical. This involves encouraging employees to experiment with new ideas, take calculated risks, and learn from failures. SMEs can adopt practices such as regular brainstorming sessions, innovation workshops, and cross-functional teams to generate fresh ideas and drive innovation across the organization (Tidd & Bessant, 2020). Additionally, SMEs should consider investing in research and development to explore new technologies and market opportunities. While R&D can be resource-intensive, it can also lead to breakthrough innovations that give SMEs a competitive edge.

SMEs can also leverage strategic partnerships to accelerate innovation. By collaborating with other companies, research institutions, or technology providers, SMEs can gain access to new knowledge, resources, and markets. For example, a technology SME might partner with a university to develop cutting-edge solutions, or a retail SME might collaborate with a logistics company to improve its supply-chain efficiency. These partnerships can help SMEs bring innovative products and services to market more quickly, driving growth and expansion (Kraus et al., 2012).

Furthermore, SMEs should be open to adopting new business models that align with changing market conditions and customer needs. For instance, the shift toward subscription-based services, which provide customers with ongoing value and generate recurring revenue, has been successfully adopted by companies of all sizes. By experimenting with new business models, SMEs can uncover new revenue streams and expand their market reach, paving the way for growth.

3. ENHANCING AGILITY AND FLEXIBILITY

Agility and flexibility are critical for SMEs as they navigate the challenges of growth. Unlike larger organizations, SMEs often have fewer bureaucratic layers, which allows them to respond more quickly to market changes and customer demands. However, as SMEs grow, maintaining this agility becomes more challenging. EM provides a framework for SMEs to retain their agility and flexibility as they scale.

One way SMEs can enhance their agility is by adopting agile methodologies in their operations. Agile methodologies, which emphasize iterative development, cross-functional collaboration, and continuous improvement, allow businesses to respond quickly to market changes and customer feedback (Rigby et al., 2016). For example, an SME that develops software might use agile practices to release new features frequently, gather user feedback, and make rapid adjustments based on that feedback. This approach not only improves the quality of the product but also ensures that it meets the evolving needs of customers.

In addition to adopting agile methodologies, SMEs should focus on building a flexible organizational structure that can adapt to changing circumstances. This might involve creating small, autonomous teams that are empowered to make decisions quickly, or implementing a flat organizational hierarchy that encourages open communication and collaboration. By fostering a flexible and adaptive culture, SMEs can navigate the complexities of growth while remaining responsive to market opportunities.

SMEs can also enhance their flexibility by diversifying their product or service offerings. Diversification reduces reliance on a single product line or market, making the business more resilient to market fluctuations. For example, a manufacturing SME that initially focused on producing a single type of product might expand its offerings to include complementary products or services, thereby reducing its exposure to market risks. This diversification strategy allows SMEs to tap into new revenue streams and support their growth objectives.

4. LEVERAGING RESOURCEFULNESS FOR SUSTAINABLE GROWTH

Resourcefulness is a core tenet of EM, particularly for SMEs that often operate with limited resources. As SMEs grow, they must continue to maximize their resources effectively to ensure sustainable growth. This involves making strategic decisions about where to allocate resources, identifying opportunities to optimize operations, and leveraging partnerships to extend their capabilities.

One way SMEs can leverage resourcefulness is by adopting a lean approach to business operations. Lean practices focus on minimizing waste, improving efficiency, and delivering value to customers with the least amount of resources. For example, an SME in the manufacturing sector might implement lean manufacturing techniques to reduce production costs, improve product quality, and shorten lead times (Womack & Jones, 2010). By streamlining operations, SMEs can free up resources that can be reinvested in growth initiatives, such as expanding into new markets or developing new products.

In addition to adopting lean practices, SMEs should explore opportunities to form strategic alliances and partnerships that enable them to access new resources and capabilities. For example, an SME might partner with a larger company to gain access to advanced technologies, or collaborate with other SMEs to share resources and reduce costs. These partnerships can provide SMEs with the scale and expertise needed to compete with larger players, while also opening up new growth opportunities (Morris et al., 2002).

Moreover, SMEs should focus on building a strong brand that resonates with their target audience. A well-established brand not only attracts customers but also enhances the company's ability to secure financing, attract talent, and form strategic partnerships. SMEs can leverage their brand to differentiate themselves in the market, build customer loyalty, and drive growth. This might involve investing in marketing and public relations efforts that raise brand awareness, or developing a brand narrative that highlights the company's unique value proposition.

5. STRATEGIC MARKET EXPANSION

For SMEs looking to grow into larger businesses, expanding into new markets is a key strategy. Market expansion allows SMEs to reach a broader audience, increase revenue, and diversify their customer base. However, successful market expansion requires careful planning and execution, guided by the principles of EM. Before entering a new market, SMEs should conduct thorough market research to understand the competitive landscape, customer needs, and potential challenges. This research should inform the development of a market-entry strategy that aligns with the company's strengths and resources. For example, an SME that specializes in sustainable products might target markets with a high demand for eco-friendly solutions, or an SME with a strong online presence might focus on expanding into digital markets (Kraus et al., 2012).

SMEs should also consider the most effective market-entry mode, whether it be exporting, franchising, joint ventures, or direct investment. Each mode has its own advantages and risks, and the choice will depend on factors such as the level of control desired, resource availability, and market conditions. For example, an SME might choose to enter a new market through a joint venture with a local partner, allowing it to leverage the partner's knowledge of the market while sharing the risks and rewards.

Once the market-entry strategy is in place, SMEs should focus on building strong relationships with local customers, partners, and stakeholders. This involves adapting products and marketing strategies to meet local preferences and cultural norms, as well as investing in customer service to ensure a positive customer experience. By building strong local relationships, SMEs can establish a foothold in new markets and drive long-term growth.

EM IN LARGE CORPORATIONS: CASE STUDIES AND STRATEGIES

Several large corporations have successfully integrated EM principles into their operations, demonstrating that these strategies are not confined to small businesses. The following case studies of Amazon and Google illustrate how large organizations can benefit from Entrepreneurial Marketing practices.

CASE STUDY: AMAZON

Amazon exemplifies how a large corporation can benefit from EM. The company's relentless focus on customer satisfaction, innovation, and agility has made it a leader in the e-commerce space. Amazon's approach to Entrepreneurial Marketing includes customer-centric innovation, where initiatives like Amazon Prime and Amazon Web Services (AWS) were developed by closely listening to customer needs and market trends (Stone, 2013). The success of Amazon Prime, for example, can be attributed to the company's ability to anticipate customer demands for faster shipping and enhanced services. By offering a subscription-based model, Amazon has not only increased customer loyalty but also created a steady stream of revenue. AWS, on the other hand, was developed in response to the growing demand for cloud-computing services, and it has since become a major revenue driver for Amazon (Brynjolfsson, Hu, & Rahman, 2013). Additionally, Amazon's ability to pivot quickly and enter new markets has been crucial to its success. The introduction of Amazon Fresh and its venture into physical stores with Amazon Go demonstrate its agile response to market opportunities. Amazon Fresh was developed to capitalize on the growing trend of online grocery shopping, while Amazon Go introduced a new shopping experience by eliminating the need for checkout lines through the use of advanced technology (Stone, 2013). These initiatives showcase Amazon's ability to innovate and adapt to changing market conditions, solidifying its position as a market leader.

CASE STUDY: GOOGLE

Google's marketing strategies also reflect EM principles, particularly in fostering an innovative culture. Google encourages employees to spend 20 percent of their time on projects outside their usual responsibilities, leading to the creation of innovative products like Gmail and Google Maps (Iyer & Davenport, 2008). This policy not only fosters creativity but also promotes a sense of ownership and empowerment among employees, which in turn drives innovation. The company's user-centric approach ensures that the development of products and services is heavily influenced by user feedback and data-driven insights, maintaining Google's position at the forefront of technology and user experience. For example, the development of Google Maps was driven by the company's desire to provide users with accurate and easy-to-use navigation tools, and it has since become one of the most widely used mapping services in the world . Google's focus on innovation is also evident in its acquisition strategy. By acquiring companies like YouTube and Android, Google has expanded its product portfolio and strengthened its market position in the video-sharing and mobile-operating-system markets, respectively . These acquisitions have not only added value to Google's business but also allowed the company to tap into new revenue streams and maintain its competitive edge.

THE ADVANTAGES OF EM FOR LARGER BUSINESSES

Adopting EM principles can offer several advantages for larger businesses, including enhanced customer loyalty, increased innovation, market agility, and a competitive edge. These benefits are crucial for large organizations seeking to thrive in today's dynamic business environment.

Enhanced Customer Loyalty: By adopting a customer-centric approach, larger businesses can build stronger relationships and loyalty among their customer base. This involves not only listening to customers but also engaging them in meaningful ways, such as through personalized marketing campaigns and customer-service initiatives (Rust & Lemon, 2001). For example, Starbucks has successfully built a loyal customer base by offering personalized rewards through its mobile app, which tracks customer preferences and offers tailored promotions (Schultz & Gordon, 2011). This level of personalization makes customers feel valued and appreciated, leading to increased brand loyalty and repeat business. Additionally, larger organizations can use customer data to create more targeted marketing campaigns that resonate with specific segments of their audience. By leveraging advanced analytics and machine learning, companies can predict customer behavior and tailor their offerings accordingly, further enhancing customer satisfaction and loyalty (Chaffey & Smith, 2017).

Increased Innovation: Larger businesses often have more resources to invest in research and development, allowing them to explore new technologies and market opportunities. By fostering an entrepreneurial mindset within their teams, these companies can drive significant innovation, leading to the development of new products and services that meet evolving market demands (Chesbrough, 2003). For instance, IBM's focus on innovation has led to the development of its Watson AI platform, which has revolutionized industries such as health care, finance, and customer service (Kelly III & Hamm, 2013). By encouraging employees to think creatively and take risks, large organizations can unlock new sources of growth and remain competitive in their respective markets.

Market Agility: While larger companies might not be as inherently nimble as start-ups, adopting EM principles can help them become more responsive to market changes. Market agility allows larger organizations to quickly capitalize on emerging trends and mitigate risks more effectively (Rigby et al., 2016). For example, Netflix's transition from a DVD rental service to a streaming platform is a testament to its market agility. By recognizing the shift in consumer preferences toward online streaming, Netflix was able to pivot its business model and become a dominant player in the entertainment industry (Hastings & Meyer, 2020). This ability to adapt to changing market conditions has been critical to Netflix's success and ongoing growth.

Competitive Edge: EM enables larger businesses to differentiate themselves in the marketplace through unique value propositions and innovative marketing strategies. This differentiation can be a key factor in maintaining a competitive edge in crowded industries (Kuratko, 2009). For example, Apple's emphasis on design and user experience has set it apart from other technology companies, making its products highly desirable among consumers (Isaacson, 2011). By continuously innovating and offering products that meet customer needs, Apple has maintained its position as a market leader in the technology industry. Additionally, companies like Nike have used EM principles to create strong brand identities and emotional connections with consumers, further solidifying their competitive positions (Knight, 2016).

IMPLEMENTING EM IN LARGER ORGANIZATIONS

For larger organizations looking to integrate EM principles, several strategies can be effective. These strategies involve fostering an entrepreneurial culture, implementing agile methodologies, establishing customer-feedback loops, and forming strategic partnerships. Each of these strategies plays a critical role in helping large organizations successfully adopt EM practices.

Foster an Entrepreneurial Culture: Encouraging creativity, risk-taking, and innovation at all levels of the organization is crucial for fostering an entrepreneurial culture. This can be achieved through initiatives like innovation labs, hackathons, and incentivizing employees to propose new ideas. As noted in Chapter 2, 3M's famous "15% rule" allows employees to spend 15 percent of their work time on projects of their own choosing, which has led to the creation of some of the company's most successful products, such as Post-it Notes (Collins & Porras, 1997). By creating an environment where employees feel empowered to experiment and take risks, organizations can tap into a wealth of creative potential and drive innovation across the company. Additionally, leadership plays a key role in fostering an entrepreneurial culture by setting the tone and encouraging a mindset that embraces change and innovation (Morris et al., 2002). Leaders should promote a culture of continuous learning and improvement, where employees are encouraged to challenge the status quo and seek out new opportunities for growth.

Agile Methodologies: Implementing agile methodologies in marketing and product development increases responsiveness to market changes. Agile methodologies involve iterative processes, cross-functional teams, and a focus on continuous improvement. Agile marketing practices allow for rapid experimentation, learning, and scaling successful initiatives (Rigby et al., 2016). For example, Spotify's use of agile practices has allowed the company to continuously innovate its music-streaming service, offering new features and improvements based on user feedback (Kniberg & Ivarsson, 2012). By adopting agile methodologies, larger organizations can enhance their ability to respond to market shifts and customer demands, ultimately leading to better business outcomes.

Customer-Feedback Loops: Establishing robust mechanisms for collecting and acting on customer feedback is essential for maintaining a customer-centric approach. This can include regular surveys, focus groups, and leveraging social media insights to inform business decisions. Continuous feedback loops ensure that the company remains in tune with customer needs and can quickly adapt to changing preferences (Schneider & Bowen, 1999). For example, Dell's "IdeaStorm" platform allows customers to submit and vote on ideas for new products and services, providing the company with valuable insights into customer preferences and expectations. By incorporating customer feedback into the decision-making process, organizations can ensure that their products and services align with customer needs and expectations, leading to higher satisfaction and loyalty.

Strategic Partnerships: Forming alliances with start-ups and smaller firms can bring fresh ideas and innovations into the company. These partnerships can provide access to new technologies, markets, and business models, helping larger organizations stay competitive and innovative (Morris et al., 2002). For example, General Electric (GE) has partnered with numerous start-ups through its GE Ventures program, which invests in early-stage companies working on innovative technologies (Immelt, Govindarajan, & Trimble, 2009). These partnerships have allowed GE to explore new markets and develop cutting-edge products, such as advanced health-care solutions and energy-efficient technologies. By leveraging the expertise and agility of smaller firms, larger organizations can enhance their own innovation capabilities and stay ahead of industry trends.

HOW TO IMPLEMENT THIS IN YOUR BUSINESS: SCALING ENTREPRENEURIAL MARKETING PRACTICES

Scaling Entrepreneurial Marketing practices in a large organization requires a strategic approach that involves assessing current marketing strategies, expanding innovation across departments, leveraging resources for market expansion, and forming strategic alliances and partnerships. Each of these steps is critical for successfully implementing EM at scale.

Assess Current Marketing Strategies: The first step in scaling EM practices is to evaluate how your current marketing strategies align with Entrepreneurial Marketing principles. This involves conducting a thorough analysis of your existing marketing practices, identifying areas where these practices can be scaled or adapted for a larger business environment. This assessment should be ongoing, ensuring that marketing strategies remain aligned with the company's growth objectives and market conditions (Kraus et al., 2012). For example, a company might assess its digital-marketing efforts to determine whether they are effectively reaching the target audience and driving engagement. If gaps are identified, the company can explore new digital channels, such as social media or influencer marketing, to enhance its reach and impact. Additionally, companies should regularly review their marketing metrics to ensure that they are achieving the desired outcomes and making adjustments as needed.

Expand Innovation Across Departments: To successfully implement EM practices, it's important to encourage a culture of innovation beyond the marketing department. This involves implementing cross-departmental initiatives that promote innovative thinking in product development, customer service, and operations. Establishing innovation hubs or task forces within various departments can help explore new ideas and initiatives, fostering a company-wide entrepreneurial spirit (Morris et al., 2002). For example, Ford Motor Company has created an innovation center that brings together engineers, designers, and marketers to collaborate on new vehicle concepts and technologies. By breaking down silos and encouraging collaboration across departments, organizations can drive innovation and create products and services that meet the evolving needs of their customers.

Leverage Resources for Market Expansion: Larger organizations have significant resources at their disposal, and these resources can be leveraged to expand into new markets. This involves investing in advanced market research tools and technologies that provide deeper insights into customer behavior and market trends. By using these insights, companies can identify and explore new market segments or geographic regions for expansion (Chesbrough, 2003). For instance, Coca-Cola has leveraged its extensive distribution network and brand recognition to enter new markets around the world, tailoring its products to meet local tastes and preferences (Isdell & Beasley, 2011). By effectively utilizing their resources, larger organizations can achieve sustainable growth and establish a strong presence in new markets.

Form Strategic Alliances and Partnerships: Forming strategic alliances with other companies, industry experts, or tech firms can provide large organizations with new opportunities for innovation and growth. These partnerships can help companies enter new markets, innovate faster, or offer new products and services to their customers (Kuratko, 2009). For example, Microsoft's partnership with LinkedIn has allowed the company to integrate LinkedIn's professional networking platform with its Office 365 suite, offering enhanced tools for business users (Nadella, 2017). By forming strategic alliances, larger organizations can access new technologies, markets, and expertise, enabling them to stay competitive in a rapidly changing business environment.

CONCLUSION

Entrepreneurial Marketing is not just a strategy for small businesses; its principles of innovation, customer-centricity, agility, and resourcefulness can significantly benefit larger organizations as well. By embracing EM, larger businesses can enhance their competitiveness, foster innovation, and build stronger customer relationships, leading to sustained growth and success in dynamic market environments (Morris et al., 2002). As large organizations continue to navigate an increasingly complex and competitive landscape, the ability to think and act entrepreneurially will be a key determinant of their success. Implementing EM practices requires a strategic approach, but the potential rewards in terms of innovation, customer loyalty, and market agility make it a worthwhile endeavor. By integrating these principles into their operations, large businesses can unlock new opportunities for growth and achieve long-term success.

Strategic Implication: Large firms can practice Entrepreneurial Marketing—but only if leaders protect space for agility. Bureaucracy, not scale, is the real barrier. Revisit whether your systems enable or hinder entrepreneurial action.

CHAPTER 13

COMMON CHALLENGES AND HOW TO OVERCOME THEM

Entrepreneurial Marketing offers a wealth of opportunities for growth and innovation, yet it is accompanied by significant challenges. These challenges often stem from resource constraints, market uncertainty, difficulties in customer acquisition and retention, and the complexity of building brand awareness. This chapter examines these common challenges and provides strategies to overcome them. By understanding and addressing these issues, businesses can optimize their marketing efforts, enhance customer engagement, and achieve sustainable growth (Morris et al., 2002).

COMMON CHALLENGES IN ENTREPRENEURIAL MARKETING

RESOURCE CONSTRAINTS

Resource constraints, particularly in financial, human, and technological areas, are a frequent hurdle for businesses, especially start-ups and small enterprises (Carson et al., 1995). Limited budgets restrict the scope of marketing activities, which may impede a company's ability to compete effectively. Similarly, constraints in human resources, such as a small team or lack of specialized marketing expertise, can hinder the execution of complex strategies. Technological limitations, including outdated systems or lack of access to advanced tools, further compound these challenges. To overcome these constraints, businesses must prioritize strategically and leverage available resources creatively (Hills & Hultman, 2013).

STRATEGIES FOR OVERCOMING RESOURCE CONSTRAINTS

Prioritize Initiatives: Focusing on marketing initiatives that offer the highest potential impact is crucial. By targeting high-impact projects, businesses can ensure their limited resources are used effectively. Projects that align with strategic goals and provide a strong return on investment should be prioritized (Barney, 1991). This targeted approach allows companies to maximize results without overextending resources. Regularly reassessing priorities is also important to stay aligned with evolving business needs (Kotler & Keller, 2016).

Leverage Technology: Affordable digital tools and platforms can significantly enhance marketing efforts. Numerous cost-effective technologies are available to help businesses streamline operations and improve outcomes. For instance, social media platforms provide powerful marketing tools that are either free or low-cost, enabling companies to reach large audiences with minimal expense (Kaplan & Haenlein, 2010). Content-management systems and email-marketing platforms are also valuable for boosting efficiency. Additionally, analytics tools offer insights that support data-driven decision-making, optimizing marketing efforts (Chaffey & Ellis-Chadwick, 2019).

Outsource and Partner: Outsourcing certain marketing functions to specialized agencies or freelancers can provide access to expertise without the costs associated with hiring full-time staff. For example, businesses can outsource tasks such as graphic design, content creation, or SEO optimization to experts who can deliver high-quality work efficiently

(Quinn, 1999). Strategic partnerships with other businesses can also help share resources and capabilities, extending a company's reach and impact. Such collaborations may lead to innovative marketing strategies that would be difficult to achieve independently (Dyer & Singh, 1998).

Bootstrap Marketing: Cost-effective strategies like content marketing, social media marketing, and guerrilla marketing can be highly effective for businesses with limited budgets. Bootstrap marketing emphasizes creativity and resourcefulness, allowing companies to make a significant impact with minimal financial investment. Content marketing, for example, involves creating valuable, relevant content that attracts and engages an audience, building brand awareness and customer loyalty over time. Social media marketing utilizes platforms such as Instagram, Twitter, and LinkedIn to reach broad audiences with little financial outlay. Guerrilla marketing, which relies on unconventional and often low-cost tactics, can also generate substantial buzz and brand recognition (Levinson, 1984).

MARKET UNCERTAINTY

Market uncertainty, including changing customer preferences, economic fluctuations, and competitive dynamics, presents significant challenges for Entrepreneurial Marketing. Businesses must continuously adapt to market shifts to stay competitive (Knight, 2000). Customer preferences can change rapidly due to trends, technological advancements, or economic conditions. Economic fluctuations, such as recessions or sudden market booms, can also impact consumer spending and business operations. Additionally, competitive dynamics, including the entrance of new competitors or changes in existing competitor strategies, add further complexity. Navigating this uncertainty requires a proactive, flexible approach (Porter, 1980).

STRATEGIES FOR NAVIGATING MARKET UNCERTAINTY

Continuous Market Research: Regular market research is essential to stay informed about customer needs, industry trends, and competitive dynamics. This research is critical for understanding the external environment and making informed decisions (Kotler & Armstrong, 2018). By closely monitoring market shifts, businesses can adjust their strategies to meet changing demands and mitigate risks. This includes tracking current customer behavior and anticipating future trends based on industry analysis. Continuous research ensures that companies remain agile and responsive, which is crucial in today's fast-paced markets (McDaniel & Gates, 2013).

Scenario Planning: Developing multiple scenarios based on different market conditions and planning strategic responses for each scenario is a valuable tool for managing uncertainty. Scenario planning helps organizations prepare for various potential futures by envisioning and planning for different outcomes (Schoemaker, 1995). This approach allows businesses to be better prepared for unexpected changes in the market, reducing the impact of uncertainty. Having contingency plans in place enables companies to respond more effectively to both opportunities and threats as they arise. Scenario planning also encourages long-term thinking and helps align organizational goals with potential market conditions (Chermack, 2011).

Agile Approach: An agile approach to marketing, which allows for quick adjustments based on real-time data and feedback, is highly effective in uncertain environments. Agile marketing emphasizes flexibility, collaboration, and customer-centricity (Denning, 2015). It involves iterative planning, rapid prototyping, and continuous improvement, enabling businesses to respond swiftly to changes in the market or customer preferences. Staying agile allows companies to experiment with different tactics, learn from the results, and pivot quickly when necessary. Agile marketing fosters a culture of innovation and adaptability, which is essential for success in today's volatile markets (Beck et al.,

2001). Modern strategy execution increasingly aligns with Agile principles, emphasizing adaptability over static planning to respond to rapidly shifting market conditions. This reflects McGrath's (2013) assertion that sustainable competitive advantage has eroded, giving way to a series of **transient advantages** that require organizations to constantly reconfigure resources and behaviors to stay ahead.

Risk Management: Identifying and evaluating potential risks and developing strategies to mitigate them are crucial components of effective marketing in uncertain times. Risk management involves assessing the likelihood and impact of various risks, such as economic downturns or competitive pressures (Hopkin, 2018). By implementing measures to reduce vulnerability, businesses can better withstand the effects of unexpected events. Regular risk assessments help keep the company aware of potential threats and prepared to address them proactively. Maintaining a risk-aware culture within the organization enhances overall resilience and sustainability (Lam, 2014).

CUSTOMER ACQUISITION AND RETENTION

Acquiring and retaining customers are fundamental challenges for businesses, particularly in competitive markets. For new and emerging businesses, building a customer base from scratch can be daunting. Moreover, retaining customers in the face of stiff competition requires a deep understanding of customer needs and effective engagement strategies. Successfully acquiring and retaining customers involve delivering a compelling value proposition, engaging with customers meaningfully, and fostering loyalty through consistent, high-quality experiences (Reichheld & Sasser, 1990).

STRATEGIES FOR EFFECTIVE CUSTOMER ACQUISITION AND RETENTION

Value Proposition: Clearly communicating the unique value proposition of products and services is vital for attracting and retaining customers. A strong value proposition differentiates a business from its competitors by highlighting the benefits and solutions it offers to address customer needs (Anderson et al., 2006). By effectively articulating what makes their offerings unique, businesses can attract customers who are looking for specific solutions that match their needs. This clear communication also helps set customer expectations, which, when met or exceeded, can lead to higher satisfaction and loyalty.

Customer Engagement: Engaging with customers through personalized communication, social media, and customer-service interactions is essential for building long-term relationships. Personalized engagement helps businesses connect with customers on a deeper level, making them feel valued and understood (Peppers & Rogers, 2016). Social media platforms provide opportunities for real-time interaction, allowing businesses to respond to customer inquiries, share updates, and create a community around their brand. Effective customer service further reinforces these relationships by addressing concerns promptly and professionally, enhancing overall customer satisfaction.

Loyalty Programs: Implementing loyalty programs that reward customers for their repeat business and engagement can significantly improve retention rates. Loyalty programs incentivize customers to continue choosing a brand by offering rewards such as discounts, exclusive access to new products, or personalized perks (Sharp & Sharp, 1997). These programs not only encourage repeat purchases but also foster a sense of belonging and appreciation among customers. Additionally, well-designed loyalty programs can provide valuable insights into customer preferences and behavior, enabling businesses to tailor their offerings more effectively.

Content Marketing: Using content marketing to attract, educate, and engage customers is an effective strategy for both acquisition and retention. By providing valuable, relevant content, businesses can establish themselves as thought leaders in their industry and build trust with their audience (Pulizzi, 2014). Content marketing can take many forms, including blog posts, videos, infographics, and social media content, all designed to address customer needs and interests. Over time, this consistent delivery of quality content helps to nurture relationships, convert leads into customers, and keep existing customers engaged with the brand.

MEASURING MARKETING EFFECTIVENESS

Measuring the effectiveness of marketing efforts and demonstrating return on investment can be challenging, particularly for businesses with limited resources and data. However, it is crucial for understanding the impact of marketing activities and making informed decisions. By tracking key performance indicators, utilizing analytics tools, and conducting regular reviews, businesses can assess the success of their marketing strategies and identify areas for improvement (Pfeifer & Farris, 2004).

STRATEGIES FOR MEASURING MARKETING EFFECTIVENESS

Key Performance Indicators (KPIs): Defining and tracking KPIs are essential for measuring the success of marketing initiatives. KPIs provide a quantifiable measure of performance, helping businesses to evaluate whether they are meeting their marketing goals (Reibstein, 2009). Common KPIs include conversion rates, customer-acquisition cost, customer lifetime value, and return on marketing investment. By regularly monitoring these metrics, businesses can gain insights into the effectiveness of their strategies and make data-driven decisions to optimize performance.

Analytics Tools: Utilizing analytics tools is crucial for tracking and analyzing marketing performance. Tools such as Google Analytics, social media analytics, and customer-relationship-management systems provide valuable data on customer behavior, campaign performance, and overall return on investment (Chaffey & Ellis-Chadwick, 2019). These tools help businesses identify which strategies are working and where adjustments are needed. In addition to providing real-time insights, analytics tools can also forecast trends, allowing businesses to anticipate changes and adapt accordingly.

A/B Testing: Conducting A/B testing allows businesses to evaluate the effectiveness of different marketing strategies and tactics. A/B testing involves comparing two versions of a marketing element—such as an email subject line or a landing page—to determine which performs better (Kohavi et al., 2009). This method provides concrete data on what resonates with customers, enabling businesses to optimize their campaigns based on actual user behavior. Regular A/B testing can lead to incremental improvements that significantly enhance overall marketing effectiveness.

Regular Reviews: Regularly reviewing marketing performance is essential for assessing progress and identifying areas for improvement. Periodic reviews, involving key stakeholders, provide an opportunity to reflect on what has been achieved and to recalibrate strategies as needed (Clark, 2000). These reviews should include a thorough analysis of KPIs, insights from analytics tools, and the results of any A/B testing conducted. By maintaining a cycle of continuous evaluation and adjustment, businesses can ensure that their marketing efforts remain aligned with their goals and responsive to market changes.

BUILDING BRAND AWARENESS

Building brand awareness in a crowded and competitive market is another significant challenge for businesses, especially for new and emerging companies. Strong brand awareness is critical for attracting customers, differentiating from competitors, and establishing a lasting presence in the market. To build brand awareness effectively, businesses must leverage a combination of content marketing, social media engagement, public relations, and influencer partnerships (Aaker, 1996).

STRATEGIES FOR BUILDING BRAND AWARENESS

Content Marketing: Creating and sharing valuable, relevant content are powerful ways to build brand awareness. Content marketing allows businesses to connect with their target audience by addressing their needs and interests (Pulizzi, 2014). This content can take various forms, such as blog posts, videos, infographics, and social media updates, all of which serve to educate, inform, and engage potential customers. Over time, consistent content delivery helps establish the brand as a trusted authority in its field, leading to increased recognition and loyalty.

Social Media Marketing: Leveraging social media platforms is essential for reaching and engaging with a broad audience. Social media allows businesses to interact with customers in real time, share content, and build a community around their brand (Kaplan & Haenlein, 2010). By maintaining an active and consistent presence on platforms like Facebook, Instagram, Twitter, and LinkedIn, businesses can amplify their reach and foster direct connections with their audience. Social media also provides opportunities for viral marketing, where compelling content can quickly spread, significantly boosting brand awareness.

Public Relations: Utilizing public relations strategies to generate media coverage and build credibility is another effective way to increase brand awareness. Public relations efforts can include press releases, media pitches, and thought leadership articles that highlight the company's expertise and achievements (Grunig & Hunt, 1984). Positive media coverage not only enhances visibility but also builds trust among consumers, as third-party endorsements are often seen as more credible than self-promotion. Effective PR strategies can position a brand as a leader in its industry, attracting attention from both customers and partners.

Influencer Marketing: Collaborating with influencers and industry experts can significantly expand a brand's reach and credibility. Influencer marketing involves partnering with individuals who have a strong following in a particular niche and can endorse the brand to their audience (Freberg et al., 2011). By selecting influencers whose values and audience align with the brand, businesses can tap into new markets and build trust through authentic, third-party endorsements. Influencer partnerships can also generate valuable content, such as reviews, testimonials, and social media posts that further reinforce brand awareness.

COMMON CHALLENGES IN ENTREPRENEURIAL MARKETING AND SPECIFIC OBSTACLES OF EM FACTORS

RESOURCE CONSTRAINTS AND GROWTH ORIENTATION

Resource constraints, particularly in financial, human, and technological areas, are a frequent hurdle for businesses, especially start-ups and small enterprises (Carson et al., 1995). These constraints directly impact a company's Growth Orientation, which focuses on expanding market share, product offerings, and revenue. Pursuing growth with limited resources can strain organizational processes, leading to inefficiencies and making it difficult to balance growth with profitability (Gilbert et al., 2006). Additionally, aligning growth objectives with volatile market conditions can be challenging.

Strategies for Overcoming Growth-Related Obstacles: Businesses should prioritize sustainable-growth strategies that align with their resource capabilities. Incremental growth opportunities that build on existing strengths can be more manageable and less risky. Leveraging technology to automate and streamline processes helps mitigate operational challenges associated with growth. Regular market assessments ensure that growth strategies remain relevant, and adopting a phased approach to scaling—where growth targets are aligned with specific milestones—can keep expansion efforts sustainable.

MARKET UNCERTAINTY AND OPPORTUNITY ORIENTATION

Market uncertainty, including changing customer preferences, economic fluctuations, and competitive dynamics, presents significant challenges for Entrepreneurial Marketing, particularly in terms of Opportunity Orientation. Identifying and pursuing new market opportunities involve significant risks, such as financial loss or resource misallocation (Kirzner, 1997). Moreover, opportunity overload—where too many potential opportunities dilute focus—can hinder effective strategy implementation (Shane & Venkataraman, 2000).

Strategies for Navigating Market Uncertainty and Opportunity Orientation: Businesses should adopt a systematic approach to evaluating opportunities, using criteria like market potential, alignment with core competencies, and resource requirements. A portfolio approach—pursuing multiple opportunities with staggered investments—spreads risk and increases the likelihood of success. Flexibility in strategy allows for rapid pivots if an opportunity proves less viable. Regular market research and scenario planning help businesses stay informed and prepared for various market conditions.

CUSTOMER ACQUISITION, RETENTION, AND TWO-WAY CUSTOMER CONTACT

Acquiring and retaining customers are fundamental challenges, particularly in competitive markets. Two-Way Customer Contact, which involves engaging customers in dialogue, is crucial for understanding their needs and building long-term relationships. However, cutting through the noise in crowded markets to capture customer attention is difficult (Prahalad & Ramaswamy, 2004). Additionally, small businesses may lack the resources to maintain consistent, meaningful engagement across multiple platforms.

Strategies for Overcoming Customer-Contact Obstacles: To enhance customer engagement, businesses should focus on creating personalized, relevant content that resonates with their audience. Leveraging data analytics allows for more tailored interactions, while customer-relationship-management systems can streamline communication and ensure all interactions are tracked. Prioritizing the most relevant communication channels and building a strong brand narrative that emotionally connects with customers can further deepen engagement.

VALUE CREATION THROUGH ALLIANCES

Value Creation Through Alliances involves forming strategic partnerships to enhance value propositions and gain a competitive edge. While strategic alliances can offer significant benefits, they also come with challenges. Finding the right partners who share the same values, goals, and commitment to quality can be difficult (Hitt et al., 2000). Furthermore, managing the relationship requires clear communication, mutual trust, and a well-defined governance structure. Differences in corporate culture, operational practices, and strategic priorities can lead to conflicts that undermine the partnership. Additionally, small businesses may face power imbalances in alliances with larger firms, limiting their influence over key decisions.

Strategies for Overcoming Alliance Obstacles: To address these challenges, businesses should conduct thorough due diligence before entering into alliances, ensuring that potential partners are a good strategic and cultural fit. Establishing clear, mutually agreed-upon goals and governance structures at the outset can help prevent misunderstandings and conflicts down the line. Regular communication and joint problem-solving sessions can also strengthen the partnership and ensure that both parties remain aligned. For small businesses, leveraging niche expertise or unique value propositions can help balance power dynamics in partnerships with larger firms. Additionally, businesses should be prepared to exit alliances that no longer serve their strategic interests.

INFORMAL MARKETING RESEARCH

Informal Marketing Research involves using non-traditional, often intuitive methods to gather market insights. While this approach can be flexible and cost-effective, it also presents challenges. The lack of structure in informal research methods can lead to incomplete or biased data, which may result in misguided marketing decisions (Zikmund et al., 2013). Additionally, relying too heavily on intuition or anecdotal evidence can overlook critical market trends or customer needs. Informal research methods may also lack the rigor needed to convince stakeholders of their validity, particularly when competing for resources with more formal, data-driven approaches.

Strategies for Enhancing Informal Research: To mitigate these challenges, businesses should complement informal research with more structured methods where possible. For example, informal customer interviews can be supplemented with surveys or focus groups to validate findings and provide more comprehensive insights. Businesses should also develop a systematic approach to informal research, including documenting findings and cross-referencing them with other data sources to identify patterns and trends. Encouraging a culture of curiosity and continuous learning can help teams refine their informal research skills and improve the quality of insights gathered. When presenting findings to stakeholders, framing informal research as exploratory and highlighting its role in generating new hypotheses can increase its credibility.

MARKET IMMERSION

Market Immersion refers to deeply understanding the market by staying closely attuned to industry trends, customer behaviors, and competitive dynamics. However, achieving true Market Immersion can be challenging, especially in fast-paced industries where trends change rapidly. Keeping up with the latest developments requires significant time and effort, which can be overwhelming for small businesses with limited resources (Day, 1994). Additionally, the sheer volume of information available can make it difficult to discern what is truly relevant and actionable. Businesses may also struggle to translate market insights into concrete strategies that drive competitive advantage.

Strategies for Overcoming Market-Immersion Challenges: To overcome these obstacles, businesses should prioritize continuous learning and stay engaged with industry networks, events, and publications. Developing a focused approach to market research—identifying the key areas of the market that are most critical to success—can help manage the information overload. Using technology to track and analyze market data can also provide a more structured and efficient way to stay immersed in the market. Additionally, businesses should regularly revisit and refine their market strategies based on new insights, ensuring that they remain relevant and competitive. Building a culture of agility and openness to change can further enhance the effectiveness of Market-Immersion efforts.

CONCLUSION

Entrepreneurial Marketing, while full of potential for growth and innovation, presents its own set of challenges that businesses must navigate to succeed. By addressing resource constraints, managing market uncertainty, effectively acquiring and retaining customers, measuring marketing effectiveness, and building brand awareness, businesses can overcome these obstacles and position themselves for sustained success. The strategies and practical tips provided in this chapter offer valuable guidance for businesses looking to enhance their Entrepreneurial Marketing efforts. By implementing these strategies, businesses can not only survive in a competitive landscape but thrive by achieving their growth objectives.

Strategic Implication: Behavioral transformation takes intention. Identify where resistance is most entrenched—in culture, systems, or leadership—and attack those areas of resistance systematically.

CHAPTER 14

PRACTICAL STEPS TO IMPLEMENT ENTREPRENEURIAL MARKETING

Entrepreneurial Marketing is not merely a set of strategies; it represents a holistic approach that integrates innovation, risk-taking, and proactive tactics to foster growth and maintain competitive advantage. Implementing Entrepreneurial Marketing requires a structured yet flexible framework that can adapt to evolving market conditions while driving innovation within the organization. This chapter outlines practical steps for implementing Entrepreneurial Marketing, including setting SMART goals, developing actionable strategies, executing plans efficiently, and measuring performance effectively. By adhering to these steps, businesses can cultivate a robust Entrepreneurial Marketing system that supports sustainable growth and continuous innovation, ultimately leading to long-term success (Morris et al., 2020).

SETTING GOALS

IMPORTANCE OF CLEAR AND ACHIEVABLE GOALS

Establishing clear and achievable goals is fundamental to guiding an organization's direction and focus. Goals act as a strategic roadmap, ensuring that every effort is aligned with the company's overarching vision. Moreover, well-defined goals serve as benchmarks that allow organizations to measure progress and make necessary adjustments to strategies. Without clear goals, businesses may face challenges in coordinating efforts across departments, leading to inefficiencies and missed opportunities (Kotler et al., 2017).

TECHNIQUES FOR SETTING SMART GOALS

Specific: Goals should be unambiguous and detailed, clearly outlining what the organization aims to achieve. This specificity helps minimize misunderstandings and ensures that efforts are aligned across all departments. For example, instead of a vague goal like "increase market share," a specific goal would be "increase market share in the North American region by 10 percent within the next twelve months." The more detailed the goal, the easier it becomes to create actionable strategies to achieve it (Doran, 1981).

Measurable: To evaluate the success of a goal, it must be quantifiable, allowing the organization to track progress and make data-driven decisions. Measurable goals provide clear criteria for success, such as "achieve a 15 percent increase in annual revenue by the end of the fiscal year." This clarity enables organizations to monitor their progress consistently and adjust strategies to stay on course, ultimately ensuring that they meet their targets (Locke & Latham, 2002).

Achievable: Goals must be realistic and attainable, taking into consideration the organization's resources and constraints. Setting goals that are too ambitious can lead to frustration and demotivation, while goals that are too easy may not challenge the organization enough to reach its full potential. An example of an achievable goal could be "launch three new products in the next fiscal year," assuming that the company has the necessary resources and capabilities to do so (Ryan, 2012).

Relevant: Every goal should align with the broader business objectives and contribute to long-term success. Relevant goals ensure that resources are used efficiently and that every action taken is purposeful. For instance, a goal to "expand into the e-commerce market to diversify revenue streams" would be relevant if the company's long-term objective is to increase its market presence online. This alignment keeps the organization focused on what truly matters and drives strategic initiatives that support overall business growth (SMART, 2018).

Time-Bound: Goals should have a clear deadline, which creates a sense of urgency and helps prioritize tasks. Time-bound goals prevent procrastination and ensure that efforts are concentrated on achieving the goal within the set timeframe. For example, "enter the Asian market within the next two years" sets a specific timeframe that motivates the organization to act promptly and systematically monitor progress. Having a deadline encourages accountability and helps track progress over time (Doran, 1981).

DEVELOPING STRATEGIES

IMPORTANCE OF STRATEGIC PLANNING

Strategic planning is crucial for translating goals into actionable steps, providing a clear direction for the organization. It ensures that resources are allocated effectively and that all efforts are aligned with the company's objectives. Without a solid strategic plan, even the most well-defined goals can remain out of reach, as the organization may lack the structured approach necessary to achieve them. A strong strategic plan not only outlines the steps needed to reach the goals but also anticipates potential obstacles and includes contingency plans to address them, ensuring that the organization remains resilient and adaptable (Porter, 1996).

TECHNIQUES FOR DEVELOPING EFFECTIVE STRATEGIES

Market Analysis: Conducting thorough market research and analysis is essential for understanding customer needs, industry trends, and competitive dynamics. This information is critical for crafting strategies that are not only effective but also sustainable in the long term. By identifying gaps in the market and potential areas for growth, businesses can position themselves more strategically and tailor their offerings to meet customer demands. Continuous market analysis helps companies stay ahead of trends, anticipate changes, and make informed decisions that align with market realities, ensuring long-term competitiveness (Kotler & Keller, 2016).

SWOT Analysis: A SWOT analysis helps organizations evaluate their strengths, weaknesses, opportunities, and threats, providing a comprehensive view of their competitive position. This analysis is crucial for identifying internal capabilities and external opportunities that can be leveraged for growth. Similarly, understanding weaknesses and threats allows the organization to mitigate risks and improve where necessary. Regularly conducting a SWOT analysis ensures that the organization remains agile and responsive to changes in the business environment, allowing it to capitalize on opportunities and defend against potential threats (Gürel & Tat, 2017).

Value Proposition: Clearly defining a unique value proposition is essential for differentiating the business in a crowded market. The value proposition should address specific customer needs and explain why the company's product or service is the best choice. A strong value proposition serves as the foundation for all marketing strategies, guiding messaging, branding, and customer engagement efforts. By continuously refining the value proposition, businesses can ensure they remain relevant and competitive, consistently delivering value that resonates with their target audience (Anderson, Narus, & van Rossum, 2006).

Customer Segmentation: Segmenting the target market based on demographics, behaviors, and preferences allows businesses to tailor their strategies to meet the specific needs of different customer groups. This targeted approach increases the effectiveness of marketing campaigns and improves customer satisfaction by addressing the unique characteristics of each segment. By understanding these distinctions, businesses can develop personalized offerings that resonate more deeply with customers, enhancing brand loyalty. Effective customer segmentation also helps optimize marketing budgets by focusing resources on the most profitable segments, leading to better returns on investment (Wedel & Kamakura, 2012).

Marketing Mix: Developing a well-balanced marketing mix—comprising product, price, place, and promotion—ensures that all aspects of the marketing strategy are aligned with the organization's goals and value proposition. The marketing mix must be carefully tailored to the target market, considering factors like customer preferences, competitive positioning, and market conditions. Regularly reviewing and adjusting the marketing mix allows businesses to adapt to changes in the market and maintain their competitive edge. This adaptability is crucial for sustaining long-term success and responding to evolving consumer needs (Borden, 1964).

TACTICS FOR IMPLEMENTING THE SIX FACTORS OF ENTREPRENEURIAL MARKETING

Implementing the six factors of Entrepreneurial Marketing requires a combination of strategic insight and practical application. Below are detailed tactics for each factor:

1. GROWTH ORIENTATION

Growth Orientation emphasizes the pursuit of opportunities that contribute to the overall expansion of the business. Tactics to implement Growth Orientation include:

Continuous Innovation: Encourage a culture of innovation where new ideas are regularly tested and implemented. This can be achieved by setting aside dedicated time for brainstorming sessions, encouraging cross-functional collaboration, and rewarding innovative thinking.

Organizations that prioritize innovation are better positioned to discover new growth opportunities, leading to sustained competitive advantage. Continuous innovation ensures that the company remains relevant in a rapidly changing market and can capitalize on emerging trends (Drucker, 1985).

Scalable Business Models: Develop and refine business models that are scalable, meaning they can grow without a proportionate increase in costs. This might involve investing in technology that automates key processes, expanding product lines that have a low marginal cost, or entering new markets with high growth potential. Scalable models are essential for sustaining long-term growth, as they allow the organization to maximize returns on investment without being constrained by resource limitations. A scalable business model is a critical component of a growth-oriented strategy, enabling the business to expand efficiently and sustainably (Hess, 2010).

Market Expansion: Identify and pursue opportunities to expand into new markets. This can include geographical expansion, targeting new customer segments, or introducing existing products into different industries. Successful market expansion often requires thorough market research, strategic partnerships, and tailored marketing strategies that resonate with the new audience. By expanding into new markets, businesses can diversify their revenue streams, reduce dependence on a single market, and achieve long-term stability and growth. Market expansion also provides opportunities to learn from new customer bases and innovate based on their unique needs (Ansoff, 1957).

Performance Metrics: Implement metrics that specifically measure growth-related outcomes, such as revenue-growth rate, market-share expansion, and customer-acquisition costs. Regularly review these metrics to ensure the organization remains focused on growth objectives and can quickly adapt strategies as needed. By monitoring performance metrics, businesses can identify areas of success and opportunities for improvement, enabling them to make data-driven decisions that drive growth. Effective use of performance metrics also fosters accountability and transparency within the organization, ensuring that everyone is aligned with the company's growth goals (Kaplan & Norton, 1992).

2. OPPORTUNITY ORIENTATION

Opportunity orientation involves recognizing and capitalizing on market opportunities that others may overlook. Tactics for fostering opportunity orientation include:

Environmental Scanning: Regularly conduct environmental scans to identify emerging trends, potential disruptions, and new opportunities. This might involve monitoring industry reports, attending conferences, and engaging with thought leaders. A proactive approach to environmental scanning helps businesses stay ahead of competitors and capitalize on trends before they become mainstream. By staying informed about the external environment, organizations can anticipate changes and position themselves to take advantage of new opportunities as they arise (Daft & Weick, 1984).

Flexible Strategy Development: Develop strategies that are flexible enough to adapt to new opportunities as they arise. This can be achieved by maintaining a dynamic strategic-planning process that allows for adjustments based on real-time market feedback. Flexibility in strategy development ensures that the organization can pivot quickly when new opportunities are identified, maximizing the potential for success. A flexible strategy also enables the company to respond to unforeseen challenges and shifts in the market, maintaining resilience and agility in a competitive landscape (Mintzberg, 1994).

Risk Management: Implement steps robust risk-management practices to evaluate and mitigate the risks associated with pursuing new opportunities. This includes conducting thorough market research, developing contingency plans, and ensuring the organization has the resources to handle potential setbacks. Effective risk management allows businesses to pursue opportunities with confidence, knowing that they are prepared to address any challenges that may arise. By balancing risk and reward, organizations can make informed decisions that drive growth while minimizing potential downsides (Hillson, 2002).

Entrepreneurial Mindset: Foster an entrepreneurial mindset within the organization by encouraging employees to think creatively and take calculated risks. This can be achieved through training programs, leadership that models entrepreneurial behavior, and a reward system that recognizes innovative contributions. An entrepreneurial mindset is crucial for identifying and capitalizing on new opportunities, as it empowers employees to challenge the status quo and seek out new ways to create value. By embedding an entrepreneurial mindset into the company culture, organizations can cultivate a workforce that is proactive, innovative, and driven to pursue growth (Gartner, 1988).

3. TWO-WAY CUSTOMER CONTACT

Two-Way Customer Contact focuses on engaging with customers in a way that fosters dialogue and mutual understanding. Tactics for implementing this factor include:

Customer-Feedback Loops: Establish formal and informal feedback loops that allow customers to share their opinions, experiences, and suggestions. This can be done through surveys, social media interactions, and direct customer outreach. Regularly analyzing this feedback helps businesses stay attuned to customer needs and preferences, ensuring that products and services remain relevant. By acting on customer feedback, organizations can build stronger relationships and increase customer loyalty, which is crucial for long-term success (Griffin & Hauser, 1993).

Personalized Communication: Implement personalized communication strategies that make customers feel valued and understood. This can involve using customer data to tailor marketing messages, sending personalized offers, or following up with customers after a purchase. Personalization helps create a more engaging customer experience, leading to higher satisfaction and repeat business. Moreover, personalized communication fosters trust, as customers feel that the company understands and cares about their unique needs, which can significantly enhance brand loyalty and customer retention (Peppers & Rogers, 1997).

Active Listening: Train customer-service and sales teams to practice active listening during interactions with customers. Active listening involves fully concentrating, understanding, responding, and remembering what the customer says, which enhances the quality of the interaction. This approach not only helps in resolving customer issues more effectively but also provides valuable insights into customer sentiments and desires. Organizations that excel in active listening are better positioned to anticipate and meet customer needs proactively, leading to improved customer satisfaction and loyalty (Brownell, 2012).

Community Building: Foster a sense of community among your customers by creating platforms where they can interact with each other and with the company. This could be through online forums, social media groups, or customer events. Building a community allows customers to share their experiences and learn from one another, which enhances brand loyalty. Additionally, it creates opportunities for the company to gather insights and feedback in a more organic and continuous manner, fostering a deeper connection with the customer base (Muniz & O'Guinn, 2001).

4. VALUE CREATION THROUGH ALLIANCES

Value Creation Through Alliances emphasizes the importance of partnerships and collaborations in enhancing the value offered to customers. Tactics to implement this factor include:

Strategic Partnerships: Identify and establish strategic partnerships with other organizations that complement your business. These partnerships can provide access to new markets, technologies, and customer segments that might otherwise be difficult to reach. By collaborating with partners, businesses can enhance their offerings and create more comprehensive solutions for customers. Additionally, strategic partnerships can lead to cost-sharing and risk mitigation, making them a valuable tool for achieving growth and sustaining competitive advantage in the long term (Dyer, Kale, & Singh, 2001).

Co-Branding Opportunities: Explore co-branding opportunities with companies that have a strong market presence or a complementary product line. Co-branding can enhance brand credibility, increase exposure, and create new value propositions for customers. For example, a technology company might collaborate with a software provider to offer an integrated solution that adds more value to the end-user. Successful co-branding initiatives can lead to increased market share and customer loyalty for both brands involved, as customers perceive greater value from the combined offering (Blackett & Boad, 1999).

Joint Ventures: Consider forming joint ventures with other companies to pursue new business opportunities or enter new markets. Joint ventures allow organizations to pool resources, share risks, and combine expertise to achieve objectives that might be challenging independently. For example, entering a foreign market with a local partner can provide valuable insights and reduce the risks associated with international expansion. Joint ventures can lead to significant value creation by leveraging the strengths of both partners, fostering innovation, and accelerating growth in new and existing markets (Beamish & Lupton, 2009).

Supplier Collaboration: Collaborate closely with suppliers to enhance the quality and efficiency of your products or services. This can involve co-developing new materials, improving supply-chain processes, or implementing just-in-time delivery systems. By working closely with suppliers, businesses can create more value for customers through improved product quality, faster delivery times, and reduced costs. Supplier collaboration also fosters long-term relationships that can lead to continuous innovation and mutual growth, ensuring a sustainable competitive advantage (Cousins & Lawson, 2007).

5. INFORMAL MARKETING RESEARCH

Informal Marketing Research involves gathering market intelligence through non-traditional and often unstructured methods. Tactics for implementing this factor include:

Customer Observation: Observe customers in their natural environments to gain insights into their behaviors, preferences, and pain points. This can be done through in-store observations, tracking online behavior, or analyzing customer interactions with products. Unlike formal surveys, observation allows businesses to understand customers' unarticulated needs and identify opportunities for innovation. Insights gained from customer observation can inform product development and marketing strategies, making them more aligned with actual customer behaviors, leading to more relevant and successful offerings (Belk, 2006).

Employee Insights: Leverage the insights of frontline employees who interact with customers daily. Employees in sales, customer service, and support roles often have valuable observations about customer needs and challenges that might not be captured through formal research. Encouraging employees to share their insights can provide the business with a more nuanced understanding of the customer experience. By incorporating these insights into decision-making processes, companies can make more informed and effective strategic choices, enhancing their responsiveness to customer needs (Prahalad & Hamel, 1990).

Social Media Monitoring: Use social media-monitoring tools to track conversations, trends, and sentiments related to your brand and industry. Social media platforms provide a wealth of real-time data that can reveal customer opinions, emerging trends, and potential issues. By analyzing social media data, businesses can respond quickly to customer concerns, capitalize on trending topics, and refine their marketing messages. Social media monitoring also helps in identifying brand advocates and influencers who can amplify your message to a broader audience, enhancing brand visibility and customer engagement (He, Zha, & Li, 2013).

Informal Networking: Engage in informal networking with industry peers, customers, and thought leaders to gather insights and ideas. This can involve attending industry events, participating in online forums, or simply having casual conversations with stakeholders. Informal networking provides access to a diverse range of perspectives and can uncover new opportunities that formal research might miss. Additionally, it helps build relationships that can be beneficial for future collaborations and partnerships, leading to a stronger industry presence and enhanced business growth (Uzzi, 1997).

6. MARKET IMMERSION

Market Immersion involves deeply embedding the organization within the market to gain an intimate understanding of customer needs and market dynamics. Tactics to implement this factor include:

On-the-Ground Experience: Encourage key decision-makers to spend time in the field, interacting with customers, suppliers, and competitors. This hands-on experience provides a direct understanding of market conditions and customer challenges, which can inform more effective decision-making. By being present in the market, leaders can identify trends, challenges, and opportunities that might not be apparent from a distance. On-the-ground experience also fosters stronger relationships with customers and partners, enhancing the organization's reputation and trustworthiness, which is crucial for long-term success (Narver & Slater, 1990).

Immersive Training Programs: Develop training programs that immerse employees in the customer experience, such as shadowing customers or participating in customer-journey-mapping exercises. These programs help employees understand the customer perspective, which can improve product development, marketing strategies, and customer service. Immersive training also encourages empathy and a customer-centric mindset throughout the organization. By seeing the world through the customer's eyes, employees are better equipped to meet their needs and exceed their expectations, leading to higher customer satisfaction and loyalty (Schneider & Bowen, 1995).

Cross-Functional Teams: Create cross-functional teams that include members from different departments to work together on Market-Immersion projects. These teams can collaborate on initiatives such as market research, product development, and customer engagement. By combining diverse perspectives, cross-functional teams can develop more innovative solutions and ensure that all aspects of the business are aligned with market needs. Cross-functional collaboration also breaks down silos within the organization, leading to more cohesive and effective strategies that resonate with the target market (Griffin & Hauser, 1996).

Continuous Learning: Foster a culture of continuous learning where employees and leaders alike are encouraged to stay informed about market trends, customer behaviors, and industry developments. This can be achieved through regular training sessions, access to industry publications, and participation in professional development opportunities. Continuous learning ensures that the organization remains agile and responsive to changes in the market, which is critical for maintaining a competitive edge. By staying informed, businesses can anticipate customer needs and adapt their strategies proactively, ensuring long-term relevance and success (Senge, 1990).

CONCLUSION

Implementing Entrepreneurial Marketing requires a strategic approach that is both structured and flexible, allowing businesses to innovate and adapt to an ever-changing market landscape. By setting clear, achievable goals and developing well-informed strategies, organizations can align their efforts toward sustained growth and competitive advantage. The key to success lies in the effective execution of these strategies, supported by continuous monitoring and adjustment based on performance metrics.

Moreover, the six factors of Entrepreneurial Marketing—Growth Orientation, Opportunity Orientation, Two-Way Customer Contact, Value Creation Through Alliances, Informal Marketing Research, and Market

Immersion—provide a robust framework for navigating the complexities of today's business environment. Each factor contributes uniquely to the overall success of the organization, whether by driving innovation, fostering customer relationships, or enabling deeper market insights.

By applying the tactics outlined in this chapter, businesses can cultivate a proactive and dynamic marketing approach that not only responds to current market demands but also anticipates future opportunities. This holistic strategy ensures that the organization remains resilient, adaptable, and poised for long-term success.

Strategic Implication: Implementation fails when there's no behavior blueprint. Leaders should treat Entrepreneurial Marketing not as a mindset, but as a repeatable process embedded into daily activity.

CHAPTER 15

THE FUTURE OF ENTREPRENEURIAL MARKETING

The landscape of Entrepreneurial Marketing is rapidly evolving, driven by technological advancements, shifting consumer expectations, and emerging market trends. This chapter delves into these key trends and offers actionable strategies for businesses to adapt, innovate, and maintain a competitive edge in a dynamic environment. By embracing change and fostering a culture of continuous improvement, businesses can secure sustainable growth and profitability in the future. The following sections will explore the most critical trends shaping the future of Entrepreneurial Marketing and provide a roadmap for businesses aiming to future-proof their operations.

1. DIGITAL TRANSFORMATION

Digital transformation is no longer a luxury but a necessity for businesses striving to remain competitive in today's fast-paced market. It involves the integration of digital technologies across all areas of a business, fundamentally altering how it operates and delivers value to customers. This transformation is not just about adopting new technologies but about rethinking how business processes, customer interactions, and employee roles are structured. As businesses embrace digital transformation, they unlock new opportunities for growth, efficiency, and customer engagement (Dean & McMullen, 2007).

KEY ASPECTS OF DIGITAL TRANSFORMATION

Digital Customer Experience: Enhancing the customer experience through digital channels is paramount in the digital age. Businesses must focus on creating seamless and personalized interactions across websites, mobile apps, and social media platforms. This includes utilizing customer data to anticipate needs and deliver tailored experiences, ensuring that every digital touchpoint adds value to the customer journey (Lemon & Verhoef, 2016; Rawson et al. 2013). The goal is to create a cohesive and responsive environment where customers feel understood and valued at every stage of their interaction with the brand . Companies like Amazon have set the standard for digital customer experience, utilizing AI to personalize recommendations and streamline the shopping process, thus setting a benchmark for other businesses to follow.

Data-Driven Decision-Making: The ability to collect, analyze, and act on data is a significant advantage in modern marketing. Data-driven decision-making allows businesses to refine their strategies based on real-time insights, making marketing efforts more targeted and effective (Wedel & Kannan, 2016). By leveraging data analytics, companies can identify trends, predict customer behavior, and optimize their marketing campaigns for better outcomes. This approach not only enhances the accuracy of marketing efforts but also increases the overall efficiency of business operations. For example, Netflix uses sophisticated data analytics to recommend content to its users, driving engagement and reducing churn.

Automation and AI: Automation and artificial intelligence (AI) are transforming how businesses approach marketing. These technologies streamline processes, reduce human error, and free up resources to focus on more strategic tasks. For example, AI-powered chatbots can provide instant customer support, while predictive analytics can offer personalized product recommendations (Hoyer et al., 2010). The integration of AI and automation tools enables businesses to operate at scale while maintaining a high level of personalization, ultimately leading to improved customer satisfaction and increased revenue. Moreover, AI-driven content-creation tools are beginning to assist in generating marketing materials, from personalized emails to social media posts, allowing marketers to focus on higher-level strategic initiatives.

E-Commerce and Online Sales: The shift toward e-commerce has accelerated, with more consumers preferring online shopping over traditional retail experiences. Businesses must adapt by optimizing their e-commerce platforms to provide a seamless shopping experience, from product discovery to checkout (Adner, 2017; Jacobides et al., 2018). This involves implementing user-friendly interfaces, secure-payment gateways, and efficient logistics systems. Additionally, businesses should leverage digital-marketing strategies such as search-engine optimization (SEO), social media advertising, and email marketing to drive traffic and conversions on their e-commerce platforms. The rise of social commerce, where transactions are integrated directly into social media platforms, represents a significant evolution in this space, offering new avenues for engagement and sales.

FUTURE OF GROWTH ORIENTATION

Growth Orientation has always been a defining characteristic of entrepreneurial ventures, reflecting the desire to scale and expand rapidly. In the future, growth will increasingly depend on a business's ability to leverage technology, innovate, and adapt to global market trends.

Technology-Driven Growth: The integration of advanced technologies such as artificial intelligence (AI), machine learning, and blockchain will play a pivotal role in driving growth for entrepreneurial businesses.

These technologies enable businesses to scale operations efficiently, enter new markets, and offer innovative products and services (Bharadwaj et al., 2023). For instance, AI can optimize supply-chain operations, while blockchain can enhance transparency and security in transactions, fostering trust among customers and partners. Companies that successfully harness these technologies will be able to accelerate their growth trajectory by improving operational efficiency and opening new revenue streams.

Sustainable Growth Practices: With the increasing emphasis on sustainability, future growth strategies will need to balance profitability with environmental and social responsibility. Businesses that adopt sustainable practices, such as reducing carbon footprints and using renewable resources, will likely see long-term benefits, including enhanced brand reputation and customer loyalty (Shepherd & Patzelt, 2011). Sustainable growth is not just about expansion but about creating value that endures over time. This shift toward sustainability is driven by growing consumer awareness and demand for ethical products, as well as regulatory pressures that are pushing businesses to adopt greener practices.

Global Market Expansion: The future of Growth Orientation will also involve expanding into global markets, facilitated by digital platforms and e-commerce. Entrepreneurs will need to navigate diverse cultural, regulatory, and economic environments to succeed globally. This requires a deep understanding of local markets and the ability to adapt marketing strategies to fit different cultural contexts (Lemon & Verhoef, 2016; Rawson et al. 2013). The expansion into emerging markets, where digital adoption is on the rise, presents significant opportunities for growth. However, this expansion will require businesses to be agile and culturally sensitive, tailoring their offerings to meet the unique needs of each market.

2. PERSONALIZATION AND OPPORTUNITY ORIENTATION

Personalization is becoming increasingly important as customers expect more tailored experiences from the brands they interact with. Personalization involves understanding and catering to the specific needs and preferences of individual customers, rather than adopting a one-size-fits-all approach. Businesses that excel in personalization can foster stronger customer relationships, increase brand loyalty, and boost sales by delivering relevant and timely content, offers, and interactions (Arona et al., 2008).

KEY ASPECTS OF PERSONALIZATION

Customer Segmentation: Effective personalization begins with customer segmentation, where businesses categorize their audience based on various factors such as demographics, behaviors, and preferences. By understanding these segments, businesses can create targeted marketing campaigns that resonate with specific groups. For instance, younger audiences might respond better to social media engagement, while older segments may prefer email communication. Segmentation allows businesses to allocate resources more efficiently and increase the likelihood of conversion by addressing the unique needs of each group. Advanced segmentation techniques, such as psychographic and behavioral segmentation, are becoming more prevalent, enabling businesses to connect with customers on a deeper level.

Personalized Communication: Personalized communication is about more than just addressing customers by name; it's about crafting messages that align with their interests and needs. By analyzing customer data, businesses can create tailored messages that speak directly to the recipient's current situation or past interactions with the brand. For example, a customer who frequently purchases outdoor gear might receive recommendations for related products or upcoming promotions on similar items. This level of personalization helps in building stronger connections with customers and encourages repeat business (Huang & Rust, 2021). The advent of AI-driven personalization tools, which can dynamically adjust content in real time based on user behavior, is set to revolutionize how businesses communicate with their audiences.

Behavioral Targeting: Behavioral targeting takes personalization a step further by using data on customers' online behaviors to deliver targeted ads and content. This includes tracking browsing history, purchase behavior, and social media activity to create a comprehensive profile of each customer. Businesses can then use this information to serve ads that are relevant to the customer's interests, increasing the likelihood of engagement and conversion. For example, a customer who frequently searches for running shoes might see ads for new athletic apparel or exclusive discounts on footwear. This approach ensures that marketing efforts are aligned with customer intent, making them more effective (Lanbrecht & Tucker, 2013).

Customer-Journey Mapping: Mapping the customer journey involves understanding the various steps a customer takes when interacting with a brand, from initial awareness to post-purchase support. By identifying these touchpoints, businesses can tailor their marketing efforts to meet customer needs at each stage. For instance, during the consideration phase, providing detailed product comparisons or customer testimonials might be more effective than a simple promotional offer. Understanding the customer journey also helps in identifying potential pain points where customers might drop off, allowing businesses to proactively address these issues and improve the overall experience (Richardson, 2010).

FUTURE OF OPPORTUNITY ORIENTATION

Opportunity Orientation is the ability to recognize and seize new opportunities as they arise. As markets become more dynamic and competitive, this dimension will become even more critical for entrepreneurial success.

Agility and Flexibility: The future will favor businesses that can quickly adapt to changes in the market and capitalize on emerging opportunities. This requires a mindset that values agility and flexibility, allowing entrepreneurs to pivot their strategies in response to market shifts. For example, the rapid adoption of remote work during the COVID-19 pandemic created opportunities for businesses offering digital-collaboration tools, which were quickly seized by agile companies. This ability to quickly pivot in response to changing market conditions will be crucial for businesses to thrive in an increasingly volatile and uncertain environment. Companies that can swiftly adjust their strategies, reallocate resources, and innovate in response to new challenges will be better positioned to capitalize on emerging opportunities and mitigate risks (Hoyer et al., 2010). The future will see more businesses adopting agile methodologies, not just in product development but across all areas of operation, enabling them to respond to changes with greater speed and efficiency.

Data-Driven Opportunity Identification: As big data and analytics tools become more sophisticated, businesses will increasingly rely on data to identify opportunities. By analyzing trends, customer behavior, and market conditions, businesses can uncover hidden opportunities and act on them swiftly. Data-driven decision-making reduces the risks associated with new ventures and allows businesses to validate opportunities before committing significant resources. For instance, predictive analytics can help businesses forecast market trends and consumer demand, enabling them to launch products or services at the optimal time. The ability to harness data effectively will be a key competitive advantage in the future, as businesses that can anticipate and act on market changes will be more likely to succeed (McAfee & Brynjolfsson, 2012).

Collaborative Innovation: The future of Opportunity Orientation will also involve collaborative innovation, where businesses partner with other organizations, including competitors, to co-create new products and services. This approach allows businesses to pool resources, share risks, and access new markets more effectively. Collaborative innovation can lead to breakthrough opportunities that might not be achievable by a single organization. For example, partnerships between tech companies and health-care providers have led to the development of innovative digital-health solutions that combine the strengths of both industries. As businesses increasingly recognize the value of collaboration, we can expect to see more cross-industry partnerships that drive innovation and create new opportunities for growth (Chesbrough, 2003).

3. TWO-WAY CUSTOMER CONTACT AND VALUE CREATION THROUGH ALLIANCES

Two-Way Customer Contact emphasizes the importance of engaging in meaningful, interactive communication with customers. As customer expectations evolve, businesses will need to adopt new strategies to maintain and enhance this dimension.

KEY ASPECTS OF TWO-WAY CUSTOMER CONTACT

Personalized Customer Interactions: The future will see a greater emphasis on personalized customer interactions, driven by advancements in AI and machine learning. These technologies allow businesses to analyze customer data and tailor communications to individual preferences and behaviors. Personalized interactions foster deeper connections with customers, making them feel valued and understood, which can lead to increased loyalty and advocacy. For instance, AI-driven chatbots can provide customers with instant, personalized responses based on their previous interactions and preferences, enhancing the overall customer experience (Huang & Rust, 2021).

Customer Co-Creation: Businesses will increasingly involve customers in the creation of products and services, leveraging their insights and feedback to enhance offerings. This approach not only ensures that products meet customer needs but also strengthens the customer relationship by making them feel like valued partners in the process (Hoyer et al., 2010). Customer co-creation can lead to innovative solutions that resonate more strongly with the market. For example, LEGO's Ideas platform allows fans to submit their own designs for new LEGO sets, some of which are turned into actual products. This not only engages customers but also helps the company stay attuned to market trends and preferences.

Real-Time Engagement: As consumers become more accustomed to instant communication, businesses will need to adopt real-time engagement strategies. This includes using chatbots, social media, and live streaming to interact with customers instantly and address their concerns or questions. Real-time engagement enhances the customer experience by providing timely and relevant responses, which can significantly impact customer satisfaction and retention. For example, brands like Nike have successfully used live streaming to launch new products, allowing customers to interact with the brand in real time and providing a more immersive and engaging experience (Grewal, Roggeveen & Norfalt, 2017).

FUTURE OF VALUE CREATION THROUGH ALLIANCES

Value Creation Through Alliances refers to the strategic partnerships and collaborations that businesses form to enhance their offerings and achieve mutual benefits. The future will see a greater reliance on alliances as businesses seek to navigate an increasingly complex and interconnected global market.

Strategic Ecosystems: In the future, businesses will form strategic ecosystems, where multiple organizations collaborate to create value for customers. These ecosystems can include suppliers, distributors, technology providers, and even competitors, all working together to deliver comprehensive solutions (Adner, 2017; Jacobides et al., 2018). Strategic ecosystems allow businesses to leverage each other's strengths, reduce costs, and accelerate innovation, leading to greater value creation. For example, the collaboration between Apple and various app developers has created a robust ecosystem around the iOS platform, benefiting both the company and its partners.

Cross-Industry Collaborations: As industries converge, cross-industry collaborations will become more common. These collaborations allow businesses to explore new markets, diversify their offerings, and create innovative solutions that combine expertise from different sectors (Adner, 2017; Jacobides et al., 2018). For instance, the partnership between automotive companies and tech firms to develop autonomous vehicles is a prime example of how cross-industry collaboration can lead to groundbreaking innovations. Such collaborations not only drive technological advancements but also open up new revenue streams and market opportunities.

Sustainable Partnerships: The future of Value Creation Through Alliances will also emphasize sustainability, with businesses forming partnerships that align with their environmental and social goals. These sustainable partnerships not only enhance brand reputation but also contribute to long-term success by addressing the growing demand for ethical and responsible business practices. For example, Unilever's partnerships with NGOs and local communities to promote sustainable sourcing practices have helped the company reduce its environmental impact while also strengthening its brand image. As consumers increasingly prioritize sustainability, businesses that can demonstrate their commitment to ethical practices through strategic partnerships will have a competitive advantage (Porter & Kramer, 2011).

4. INFORMAL MARKETING RESEARCH AND MARKET IMMERSION

Informal Marketing Research involves gathering market insights through non-traditional methods, such as direct customer interactions, observations, and gut feelings. As data becomes more accessible and technology advances, the future of this dimension will see a blend of traditional and digital research methods.

KEY ASPECTS OF INFORMAL MARKETING RESEARCH

Social Listening and Sentiment Analysis: The future of Informal Marketing Research will be heavily influenced by social-listening tools that allow businesses to monitor online conversations and analyze customer sentiment. These tools provide real-time insights into customer opinions, preferences, and emerging trends, enabling businesses to make informed decisions. Social listening complements traditional research methods by providing a continuous stream of data that reflects the ever-changing market landscape. For instance, a company like Coca-Cola might use social listening to track consumer sentiment about new product launches, allowing them to make adjustments based on real-time feedback (He, Zha & Li, 2013).

Crowdsourced Insights: Businesses will increasingly turn to crowdsourcing to gather insights from a broader audience. Crowdsourced insights can be obtained through online communities, forums, and social media platforms, where customers and stakeholders share their opinions and ideas. This approach allows businesses to tap into a diverse pool of knowledge and perspectives, leading to more comprehensive and accurate market research. For example, platforms like Kickstarter not only help companies raise funds but also provide valuable insights into consumer demand and preferences before a product is even launched (Bayus, 2013).

Intuitive Decision-Making: Despite the rise of data-driven approaches, intuitive decision-making will remain an important aspect of Informal Marketing Research. Entrepreneurs often rely on their instincts and experience to make quick decisions in uncertain situations. The future will see a more balanced approach, where data and intuition work together to guide marketing strategies. This hybrid approach ensures that businesses can respond swiftly to market changes while staying grounded in their vision and values. Companies like Tesla have demonstrated the value of this approach, where visionary leadership and data-driven insights have combined to drive innovation and market success (Kahneman & Klein, 2009).

FUTURE OF MARKET IMMERSION

Market Immersion involves deeply understanding and engaging with the market to identify opportunities and stay ahead of competitors. As markets become more complex and dynamic, businesses will need to adopt more sophisticated strategies to achieve true Market Immersion.

Immersive Technologies: The future of Market Immersion will be shaped by immersive technologies such as virtual reality (VR) and augmented reality (AR). These technologies allow businesses to create realistic simulations of market environments, enabling them to test products, services, and marketing strategies in a controlled setting. For example, a retailer might use VR to simulate a store layout and observe how customers navigate the space, gaining valuable insights into their behavior. This not only enhances the customer experience but also helps businesses optimize their offerings based on real-world interactions (Poncin & Mimouon, 2014).

Customer-Centric Innovation: Businesses will increasingly focus on customer-centric innovation, where Market Immersion involves directly engaging with customers to co-create solutions. This approach ensures that products and services are designed with the customer in mind, leading to higher satisfaction and loyalty (Lemon & Verhoef, 2016; Rawson et al. 2013). Customer-centric innovation requires businesses to be constantly attuned to customer needs and willing to iterate on their offerings based on feedback. Companies like Apple have mastered this approach, continuously refining their products based on user feedback to maintain their market leadership.

Global Market Immersion: As globalization continues to influence markets, businesses will need to immerse themselves in diverse cultural and economic environments to remain competitive. This involves understanding local customs, consumer behavior, and regulatory frameworks, as well as building relationships with local stakeholders. Global Market Immersion allows businesses to tailor their strategies to different regions, enhancing their ability to succeed in international markets. For example,

Starbucks's success in entering new markets has often been attributed to its deep understanding of local cultures and consumer preferences, which has allowed the brand to adapt its offerings and marketing strategies to suit each market (Moon & Quelch, 2006).

CONCLUSION

As we conclude this exploration of Entrepreneurial Marketing, it's clear that the future is both exciting and challenging. The six dimensions of Entrepreneurial Marketing—Growth Orientation, Opportunity Orientation, Two-Way Customer Contact, Value Creation Through Alliances, Informal Marketing Research, and Market Immersion—will continue to be the pillars that support entrepreneurial ventures in an increasingly complex and dynamic business environment.

The trends and strategies discussed in this chapter highlight the importance of adaptability, innovation, and a customer-centric approach. Digital transformation will redefine how businesses operate, pushing them to leverage technology in ways that enhance efficiency and customer engagement. The growing demand for personalized experiences will require businesses to understand their customers at a deeper level, using data to deliver tailored interactions that foster loyalty and trust.

Opportunity Orientation will be essential as markets evolve, with businesses needing to remain agile and responsive to new trends and challenges. The ability to recognize and seize opportunities will be a key differentiator for successful ventures. Similarly, Value Creation Through Alliances will become even more critical, as businesses seek to navigate an interconnected world by forming strategic partnerships that drive innovation and value.

Informal Marketing Research and Market Immersion will continue to provide the insights necessary for businesses to stay ahead of the competition. As data becomes more accessible and technologies like VR and AR offer new ways to engage with markets, businesses will need to combine traditional and digital research methods to gain a comprehensive understanding of their environment.

Looking forward, the future of Entrepreneurial Marketing will be shaped by the ability to embrace change and leverage the six EM dimensions to create sustainable and impactful business strategies. Entrepreneurs who can master these dimensions will not only survive but thrive in the face of uncertainty, leading their ventures to new heights of success.

As you close this book, consider how these principles apply to your own business or entrepreneurial journey. The landscape may shift, but the core values of Entrepreneurial Marketing—adaptability, innovation, and customer focus—will always be relevant. By staying informed, being proactive, and maintaining a growth mindset, you can ensure that your venture is well equipped to navigate the future of marketing and achieve lasting success.

The future is uncertain, but for those who are prepared, it is filled with opportunities. Embrace the changes, innovate relentlessly, and always keep the customer at the heart of your strategies. In doing so, you will not only secure the future of your business but also contribute to shaping the future of the entrepreneurial landscape.

START WHERE YOU ARE: PUTTING THE SOI™ INTO ACTION

Every business wants to grow. But growth isn't just a function of market conditions—it's a direct result of how well your firm is aligned around three invisible forces: entrepreneurial energy, market intelligence, and marketing behavior. That's what the Strategic Orientation Index™ (SOI™) was designed to uncover. Throughout this book, you've explored how Entrepreneurial Orientation (EO), Market Orientation (MO), and Entrepreneurial Marketing (EM) interact—and how misalignment among them silently erodes performance. You've seen that strategy isn't just about vision—it's about behavior. And now, you know how to diagnose it.

But insight without action is a trap. If you've identified your firm as a

Fearless Inventor, Insightful Optimizer, Reluctant Responder, Hybrid, or Visionary Vanguard, the next step is to convert that insight into aligned decisions. Maybe that means shifting investment, hiring differently, or rethinking how you engage customers. Maybe it means reorganizing teams or revisiting product-market fit. No matter where you begin, the most important thing is to begin. Because alignment isn't a light switch—it's a lever you pull intentionally, over time.

The SOI™ gives you more than a label—it gives you language. It gives you a way to talk about strategic misalignment without blame. It gives your executive team a shared vocabulary for why things feel off, even when performance isn't bad yet. And it gives consultants, educators, and team leaders a framework for shaping growth that's grounded in both theory and behavior. This isn't a new business fad. It's a practical system rooted in academic rigor and built for modern complexity.

Strategic Implication: The future favors firms that move fast, listen deeply, and act with courage. Codify your own version of Entrepreneurial Marketing—and ensure it lives not in your decks, but in your decisions.

So what should you do next?

- Invite your leadership team to participate in a guided SOI™ workshop.
- If you're an educator or consultant, explore licensing opportunities to use SOI™ in your courses or client engagements.
- You don't have to guess where to start anymore. You have a framework. You have a persona. And now, you have a path.

LICENSING THE SOI™ FRAMEWORK

The SOI™ model and assessment tools are available for licensed use across three core application areas:

University Programs: Graduate business schools and executive education programs can license the SOI™ for use in capstone projects, strategic planning modules, and market-strategy simulations. A university license includes teaching guides, classroom diagnostics, and case studies.

Consulting Firms: Strategy advisors, marketing agencies, and growth consultants can integrate the SOI™ into discovery workshops, leadership retreats, and strategic-planning engagements. Licensed firms receive facilitator kits, customizable persona grids, and client-ready templates to accelerate alignment and drive results.

Corporate Teams: Firms seeking to institutionalize the SOI™ across departments can engage in facilitated implementation and team-level training. This includes executive workshops, persona mapping across business units, and quarterly alignment diagnostics.

All licensed partners gain access to updated SOI™ tools, new use cases, and the latest version of the assessment system via our private partner portal.

GET STARTED

To inquire about licensing options or facilitated discovery sessions, visit kylejharkema.com. Whether you're an educator, consultant, or executive leader, we're here to help you apply the SOI™ framework in a way that drives real strategic clarity—and sustainable performance.

REFERENCES

Aaker, D.A. 1991. *Managing Brand Equity: Capitalizing on the Value of a Brand Name.* The Free Press.

Aaker, D.A. 1996. *Building Strong Brands.* Free Press.

Aaker, D.A. 1998. *Strategic Market Management (5th ed.).* John Wiley & Sons.

Accenture. 2019. "The Omni-Experience Imperative: Redefining Customer Experience in the Digital Age." Retrieved from https://www.accenture.com/us-en/insights/digital/omni-experience.

Adams, R., J. Bessant, and R. Phelps. 2006. "Innovation Management Measurement: A Review." *International Journal of Management Reviews* 8(1), 21-47.

Adner, R. (2017). "Ecosystem as structure: An actionable construct for strategy." *Journal of Management* 43(1): 39–58.

Aguilar, F.J. 1967. *Scanning the Business Environment.* Macmillan.

Allen, F. 1994. *Secret Formula: How Brilliant Marketing and Relentless Salesmanship Made Coca-Cola the Best-Known Product in the World.* HarperCollins.

Amabile, T.M. 1988. "A Model of Creativity and Innovation in Organizations." *Research in Organizational Behavior* 10(1), 123-167.

Amabile, T.M. 1996. *Creativity in Context: Update to the Social Psychology of Creativity.* Westview Press.

58(3), 53-66.

Anderson, J.C., J.A. Narus, and W. van Rossum. 2006. "Customer Value Propositions in Business Markets." *Harvard Business Review* 84(3), 90-99.

Ansoff, H.I. 1957. "Strategies for Diversification." *Harvard Business Review* 35(5), 113-124.

Ansoff, H.I. 1965. *Corporate Strategy: An Analytic Approach to Business Policy for Growth and Expansion*. McGraw-Hill.

Argyris, C., and D.A. Schön. 1974. *Theory in Practice: Increasing Professional Effectiveness*. Jossey-Bass.

Arora, N., X. Dreze, A. Ghose, et al. 2008. "Putting One-to-One Marketing to Work: Personalization, Customization, and Choice." *Marketing Letters* 19(3), 305-321.

Atuahene-Gima, K., & Ko, A. 2001. An empirical investigation of the effect of market orientation and entrepreneurship orientation alignment on product innovation. *Organization Science*, 12(1), 54–74.

Baker, W.E., and J.M. Sinkula, 2009. "The Complementary Effects of Market Orientation and Entrepreneurial Orientation on Profitability in Small Businesses." *Journal of Small Business Management* 47(4), 443-464.

Barney, J. 1991. "Firm Resources and Sustained Competitive Advantage." *Journal of Management* 17(1), 99-120.

Bayus, B. L. 2013. Crowdsourcing new product ideas over time: An analysis of the Dell IdeaStorm community. *Management Science*, 59(1), 226–24

Beamish, P.W., N.C. Lupton. 2009. "Managing Joint Ventures." *The Academy of Management Perspectives* 23(2), 75-94.

Becherer, R. C., Haynes, P. J., & Fletcher, L. P. 2006. Paths to profitability: A comparison of rural and urban entrepreneurs. *Journal of Small Business Strategy*, 17(1), 27–39.

Becherer, R.C., P.J. Haynes, and L.P. Fletcher. 2006. "Paths to Profitability in Owner-Operated Firms: The Role of Entrepreneurial Marketing." *Journal of Business and Entrepreneurship* 18(1), 17–31.

Beck, K., M. Beedle, A. van Bennekum, et al. 2001. *Manifesto for Agile Software*

Development. Agile Alliance. Retrieved from https://agilemanifesto.org/.

Belfiore, M. 2007. *Rocketeers: How a Visionary Band of Business Leaders, Engineers, and Pilots Is Boldly Privatizing Space*. HarperCollins.

Belk, R.W. 2006. *Handbook of Qualitative Research Methods in Marketing*. Edward Elgar Publishing.

Benioff, M., and C. Adler. 2009. *Behind the Cloud: The Untold Story of How Salesforce.com Went from Idea to Billion-Dollar Company—and Revolutionized an Industry*. Jossey-Bass.

Bharadwaj, A., O. A. El Sawy, P. A. Pavlou, and N. V. Venkatraman. 2013. "Digital Business Strategy: Toward a Next Generation of Insights." *MIS Quarterly* 37(2): 471–482.

Bharadwaj, A., El Sawy, O. A., Pavlou, P. A., & Venkatraman, N. 2023. Digital business strategy and value creation: Framing the next frontier. *MIS Quarterly*, 47(1), 1–26.

Bharadwaj, A., O.A. El Sawy, P.A. Pavlou, and N.V. Venkatraman. 2013. "Digital Business Strategy: Toward a Next Generation of Insights." *MIS Quarterly* 37(2): 471–482.

Bhasin, H. 2020, July 27. "Dollar Shave Club marketing strategy." *Marketing* 91.

Bhuian, S. N., Menguc, B., & Bell, S. J. 2005. Just entrepreneurial enough: The moderating effect of entrepreneurship on the relationship between market orientation and performance. *Journal of Business Research*, 58(1), 9–17

Birkinshaw, J., Bouquet, C., & Barsoux, J.-L. 2011. The 5 myths of innovation. MIT Sloan Management Review, 52(2), 43–50.

Bjerke, B., and C. M. Hultman. 2002. *Entrepreneurial Marketing: The Growth of Small Firms in the New Economic Era*. Edward Elgar Publishing.

Blackett, T., and B. Boad, eds. 1999. *Co-Branding: The Science of Alliance*. Springer.

Blank, S. 2013. *The Four Steps to the Epiphany: Successful Strategies for Products That Win*. K&S Ranch.

Borden, N. H. 1964. "The Concept of the Marketing Mix." *Journal of Advertising Research* 4(2): 2–7.

Boudette, N. E. 2017. "Tesla to Offer New Autopilot Features This Year, Musk Says." *The New York Times*.

Bourne, M., and P. Bourne. 2011. *Handbook of Corporate Performance Management.* Wiley.

Bower, J. L. 1970. *Managing the Resource Allocation Process.* Harvard Business School Press.

Brealey, R. A., S. C. Myers, and F. Allen. 2021. *Principles of Corporate Finance.* 13th ed. McGraw-Hill Education.

Brenner, M. 2019. "Starbucks Customer Engagement: How to Do It Right." *Marketing Insider Group.*

Brigham, E. F., and M. C. Ehrhardt. 2022. *Financial Management: Theory & Practice.* 16th ed. Cengage Learning.

Brown, J. S., and P. Duguid. 2000. *The Social Life of Information.* Harvard Business School Press.

Brown, T. 2008. "Design Thinking." *Harvard Business Review* 86(6): 84–92.

Brownell, J. 2012. *Listening: Attitudes, Principles, and Skills.* 5th ed. Pearson Education.

Brush, C. G., P. G. Greene, and M. M. Hart. 2001. "From Initial Idea to Unique Advantage: The Entrepreneurial Challenge of Constructing a Resource Base." *Academy of Management Executive* 15(1): 64–78.

Brynjolfsson, E., and A. McAfee. 2014. *The Second Machine Age: Work, Progress, and Prosperity in a Time of Brilliant Technologies.* W. W. Norton & Company.

Brynjolfsson, E., Y. J. Hu, and M. S. Rahman. 2013. "Competing in the Age of Omnichannel Retailing." *MIT Sloan Management Review* 54(4): 23–29.

Bulik, B. S. 2006. "Dove's 'Real Beauty' Draws Real Dollars." *Advertising Age.*

Burkus, D. 2013. *The Myths of Creativity: The Truth About How Innovative Companies and People Generate Great Ideas.* Jossey-Bass.

Buttle, F. 2009. *Customer Relationship Management: Concepts and Technologies.* Routledge.

Buttle, F., and S. Maklan. 2019. *Customer Relationship Management: Concepts and Technologies.* Routledge.

Butterfield, S. 2020. "The CEO of Slack on adapting in response to a global crisis." *Harvard Business Review* (July–August).

Cameron, K. S., and R. E. Quinn. 2006. *Diagnosing and Changing Organizational*

Culture: Based on the Competing Values Framework. Revised ed. Jossey-Bass.

Camp, R. C. 1989. *Benchmarking: The Search for Industry Best Practices That Lead to Superior Performance.* ASQC Quality Press.

Capell, K. 2008. "Zara Thrives by Breaking All the Rules." *Bloomberg Businessweek.*

Carson, D., S. Cromie, P. McGowan, and J. Hill. 1995. *Marketing and Entrepreneurship in SMEs: An Innovative Approach.* Prentice Hall.

Carson, D., A. Gilmore, C. Perry, and K. Gronhaug. 1995. *Marketing and Entrepreneurship in SMEs: An Innovative Approach.* Pearson Education.

Catmull, E., and A. Wallace. 2014. *Creativity, Inc.: Overcoming the Unseen Forces That Stand in the Way of True Inspiration.* Random House.

Chaffey, D., and F. Ellis-Chadwick. 2019. *Digital Marketing: Strategy, Implementation and Practice.* Pearson Education.

Chaffey, D., & Smith, P. R. 2017. Digital marketing excellence: Planning, optimizing and integrating online marketing (6th ed.). *Routledge*

Chen, I. J., and K. Popovich. 2003. "Understanding Customer Relationship Management (CRM): People, Process, and Technology." *Business Process Management Journal* 9(5): 672–688.

Chermack, T. J. 2011. *Scenario Planning in Organizations: How to Create, Use, and Assess Scenarios.* Berrett-Koehler Publishers.

Chesbrough, H. 2003. *Open Innovation: The New Imperative for Creating and Profiting from Technology.* Harvard Business Review Press.

Chouinard, Y. 2006. *Let My People Go Surfing: The Education of a Reluctant Businessman.* Penguin Books.

Chouinard, Y., and V. Stanley. 2016. *Let My People Go Surfing: The Education of a Reluctant Businessman.* Penguin.

Christensen, C. M. 1997. *The Innovator's Dilemma: When New Technologies Cause Great Firms to Fail.* Harvard Business Review Press.

Christensen, C. M., M. E. Raynor, and R. McDonald. 2015. "What Is Disruptive Innovation?" *Harvard Business Review* 93(12): 44–53.

Christopher, M. 2016. *Logistics & Supply Chain Management.* 5th ed. Pearson Education Limited.

Clark, B. H. 2000. "Managerial Perceptions of Marketing Performance: Efficiency,

Adaptability, Effectiveness, and Satisfaction." *Journal of Strategic Marketing* 8(1): 3–25.

Collins, J. C., and J. I. Porras. 1996. "Building Your Company's Vision." *Harvard Business Review* 74(5): 65–77.

Collins, J. C., and J. I. Porras. 1997. *Built to Last: Successful Habits of Visionary Companies*. Harper Business.

Collinson, E., and E. Shaw. 2001. "Entrepreneurial Marketing—A Historical Perspective on Development and Practice." *Management Decision* 39(9): 761–766.

Collis, D. J., and C. A. Montgomery. 1995. *Corporate Strategy: A Resource-Based Approach*. McGraw-Hill/Irwin.

Colson, E. 2019. "What AI-driven decision making looks like." *Harvard Business Review* (digital article).

Contractor, F. J., and P. Lorange. 2002. *Cooperative Strategies and Alliances*. Emerald Group Publishing.

Cooper, A. 1999. *The Inmates Are Running the Asylum*. SAMS.

Cousins, P. D., and B. Lawson. 2007. "The Effect of Socialization Mechanisms and Performance Measurement on Supplier Integration in New Product Development." *British Journal of Management* 18(3): 311–326.

Corbett, A. C. 2007. Learning asymmetries and the discovery of entrepreneurial opportunities. *Journal of Business Venturing*, 22(1), 97–118

Covin, J. G., and D. Miller. 2014. "International Entrepreneurial Orientation: Conceptual Considerations, Research Themes, Measurement Issues, and Future Research Directions." *Entrepreneurship Theory and Practice* 38(1): 11–44.

Covin, J. G., & Slevin, D. P. 1989. Strategic management of small firms in hostile and benign environments. *Strategic Management Journal*, 10(1), 75–87. https://doi.org/10.1002/smj.4250100107

Covin, J. G., and D. P. Slevin. 1991. "A Conceptual Model of Entrepreneurship as Firm Behavior." *Entrepreneurship Theory and Practice* 16(1): 7–25.

Crawford, C. M., and A. Di Benedetto. 2011. *New Products Management*. 10th ed. McGraw-Hill/Irwin.

Croll, A., and B. Yoskovitz. 2013. *Lean Analytics: Use Data to Build a Better Startup*

Faster. O'Reilly Media.

Cross, R., and A. Parker. 2004. *The Hidden Power of Social Networks: Understanding How Work Really Gets Done in Organizations*. Harvard Business Review Press.

Cusumano, M. A. 2010. *Staying Power: Six Enduring Principles for Managing Strategy and Innovation in an Uncertain World*. Oxford University Press.

Dabholkar, P. A. 1996. "Consumer Evaluations of New Technology-Based Self-Service Options: An Investigation of Alternative Models of Service Quality." *International Journal of Research in Marketing* 13(1): 29–51.

Daft, R. L., and K. E. Weick. 1984. "Toward a Model of Organizations as Interpretation Systems." *Academy of Management Review* 9(2): 284–295.

Damanpour, F. 1991. "Organizational Innovation: A Meta-Analysis of Effects of Determinants and Moderators." *Academy of Management Journal* 34(3): 555–590.

Damodaran, A. 2021. *Corporate Finance: Theory and Practice*. 4th ed. Wiley.

Dane, E., & Pratt, M. G. 2007. Exploring intuition and its role in managerial decision making. *Academy of Management Review*, 32(1), 33–54.

Danziger, P. N. 2018. "How Sephora Built an Empire on Understanding Its Customer." *Forbes*.

Das, T. K., and B. S. Teng. 1998. "Between Trust and Control: Developing Confidence in Partner Cooperation in Alliances." *Academy of Management Review* 23(3): 491–512.

Das, T. K., and B. S. Teng. 2000. "A Resource-Based Theory of Strategic Alliances." *Journal of Management* 26(1): 31–61.

Davenport, T. H., and J. G. Harris. 2007. *Competing on Analytics: The New Science of Winning*. Harvard Business Review Press.

Davenport, T. H., and L. Prusak. 1998. *Working Knowledge: How Organizations Manage What They Know*. Harvard Business Review Press.

Davenport, T., A. Guha, D. Grewal, and T. Bressgott. 2020. "How AI Will Change the Future of Marketing." *Journal of the Academy of Marketing Science* 48(1): 24–42.

Day, G. S. 1994. "The Capabilities of Market-Driven Organizations." *Journal of Marketing* 58(4): 37–52.

Dean, T.J., and J.S. McMullen. 2007. "Toward a theory of sustainable entrepreneurship: Reducing environmental degradation through entrepreneurial action." *Journal of Business Venturing* 22(1): 50–76.

Deming, W. E. 1986. *Out of the Crisis*. MIT Press.

Denison, D. R., and A. K. Mishra. 1995. "Toward a Theory of Organizational Culture and Effectiveness." *Organization Science* 6(2): 204–223.

Denning, S. 2015. *The Age of Agile: How Smart Companies Are Transforming the Way Work Gets Done*. AMACOM.

Dess, G. G., & Picken, J. C. 2000. Changing roles: Leadership in the 21st century. *Organizational Dynamics*, 28(3), 18–34.

Deshpandé, R., J. U. Farley, and F. E. Webster. 1993. "Corporate Culture, Customer Orientation, and Innovativeness in Japanese Firms: A Quadrad Analysis." *Journal of Marketing* 57(1): 23–37.

Doran, G. T. 1981. "There's a S.M.A.R.T. Way to Write Management's Goals and Objectives." *Management Review* 70(11): 35–36.

Doz, Y. L., and G. Hamel. 1998. *Alliance Advantage: The Art of Creating Value Through Partnering*. Harvard Business School Press.

Doz, Y. L., and M. Kosonen. 2010. "Embedding Strategic Agility: A Leadership Agenda for Accelerating Business Model Renewal." *Long Range Planning* 43(2–3): 370–382.

Drucker, P. F. 1954. *The Practice of Management*. Harper & Row.

Drucker, P. F. 1985. *Innovation and Entrepreneurship: Practice and Principles*. Harper & Row.

Dumas, C. 2007. *Leadership in Non-Profit Organizations*. Palgrave Macmillan.

Dyer, J. H., and K. Nobeoka. 2000. "Creating and Managing a High-Performance Knowledge-Sharing Network: The Toyota Case." *Strategic Management Journal* 21(3): 345–367.

Dyer, J. H., and H. Singh. 1998. "The Relational View: Cooperative Strategy and Sources of Interorganizational Competitive Advantage." *Academy of Management Review* 23(4): 660–679.

Dyer, J. H., P. Kale, and H. Singh. 2001. "How to Make Strategic Alliances Work." *MIT Sloan Management Review* 42(4): 37–43.

Edmondson, A. 1999. "Psychological Safety and Learning Behavior in Work Teams." *Administrative Science Quarterly* 44(2): 350–383.

Edmondson, A. C., and J. F. Harvey. 2017. "Cross-Boundary Teaming for Innovation: Integrating Research on Teams and Knowledge in Organizations." *Human Resource Management Review* 27(4): 347–360.

Evans, J. R., and W. M. Lindsay. 2017. *Managing for Quality and Performance Excellence*. Cengage Learning.

Few, S. 2012. *Show Me the Numbers: Designing Tables and Graphs to Enlighten*. 2nd ed. Analytics Press.

Fiet, J. O. 2002. *The Systematic Search for Entrepreneurial Discoveries*. Quorum Books.

Fillis, I. 2010. "The Art of the Entrepreneurial Marketer." *Journal of Research in Marketing and Entrepreneurship* 12(2): 87–107.

Finn, A., and U. Kayande. 1999. "Unmasking a Phantom: A Psychometric Assessment of Mystery Shopping." *Journal of Retailing* 75(2): 195–217.

Freberg, K., K. Graham, K. McGaughey, and L. A. Freberg. 2011. "Who Are the Social Media Influencers? A Study of Public Perceptions of Personality." *Public Relations Review* 37(1): 90–92.

Frei, F., and A. Morriss. 2012. Uncommon Service: How to Win by Putting Customers at the Core of Your Business. *Harvard Business Review Press*.

Fried, J., and D. H. Hansson. 2010. *Rework*. Crown Business.

Gagné, M., & Deci, E. L. 2005. Self-determination theory and work motivation. *Journal of Organizational Behavior*, 26(4), 331–362.

Gallagher, L. 2017. *The Airbnb Story: How Three Ordinary Guys Disrupted an Industry, Made Billions of Dollars, and Created Plenty of Controversy*. Houghton Mifflin Harcourt.

Gansky, L. 2010. *The Mesh: Why the Future of Business Is Sharing*. Penguin Books.

Gartner, W. B. 1988. "Who Is an Entrepreneur? Is the Wrong Question." *American Journal of Small Business* 12(4): 11–32.

Gawer, A., and M. A. Cusumano. 2002. *Platform Leadership: How Intel, Microsoft, and Cisco Drive Industry Innovation*. Harvard Business Review Press.

Gawer, A., and M. A. Cusumano. 2014. "Industry Platforms and Ecosystem

Innovation." *Journal of Product Innovation Management* 31(3): 417–433.

George, M. L. 2002. *Lean Six Sigma: Combining Six Sigma Quality with Lean Production Speed*. McGraw-Hill.

Gerstner, L. V. 2002. *Who Says Elephants Can't Dance?*. HarperBusiness.

Gilbert, B. A., P. P. McDougall, and D. B. Audretsch. 2006. "New Venture Growth: A Review and Extension." *Journal of Management* 32(6): 926–950.

Gilliland, N. 2016, November 16. How Glossier has used Instagram to create a cult following. *Econsultancy*. HYPERLINK "https://econsultancy.com/how-glossier-has-used-instagram-to-create-a-cult-following/?utm_source=chatgpt.com" https://econsultancy.com/how-glossier-has-used-instagram-to-create-a-cult-following/.

Gilmore, A., D. Carson, and K. Grant. 2001. "SME Marketing in Practice." *Marketing Intelligence & Planning* 19(1): 6–11.

Gittell, J. H. 2005. *The Southwest Airlines Way: Using the Power of Relationships to Achieve High Performance*. McGraw-Hill.

Gladwell, M. 2000. *The Tipping Point: How Little Things Can Make a Big Difference*. Little, Brown.

Glover, S., H. Friedman, and G. Jones. 2002. "The Relationship Between Ethical Climate and Organizational Commitment in Manufacturing Organizations." *Journal of Business Ethics* 41(3): 241–249.

Goodman, J. 2014. *Customer Experience 3.0: High-Profit Strategies in the Age of Tech-Savvy Customers*. AMACOM.

Govindarajan, V., and C. Trimble. 2010. *The Other Side of Innovation: Solving the Execution Challenge*. Harvard Business Review Press.

Granovetter, M. 1973. "The Strength of Weak Ties." *American Journal of Sociology* 78(6): 1360–1380.

Griffin, A., and J. R. Hauser. 1993. "The Voice of the Customer." *Marketing Science* 12(1): 1–27.

Griffin, A., and J. R. Hauser. 1996. "Integrating R&D and Marketing: A Review and Analysis of the Literature." *Journal of Product Innovation Management* 13(3): 191–215.

Grunig, J. E., and T. Hunt. 1984. *Managing Public Relations*. Holt, Rinehart &

Winston.

Grewal, D., Roggeveen, A. L., & Nordfält, J. 2017.The future of retailing. *Journal of Retailing*, 93(2), 95–101.

Gulati, R. 1998. "Alliances and Networks." *Strategic Management Journal* 19(4): 293–317.

Gulati, R., N. Nohria, and A. Zaheer. 2000. "Strategic Networks." *Strategic Management Journal* 21(3): 203–215.

Gurran, N., and P. Phibbs. 2017. "When Tourists Move In: How Should Urban Planners Respond to Airbnb?" *Journal of the American Planning Association* 83(1): 80–92.

Guttentag, D. 2015. "Airbnb: Disruptive Innovation and the Rise of an Informal Tourism Accommodation Sector." *Current Issues in Tourism* 18(12): 1192–1217.

Gürel, E., and M. Tat. 2017. "SWOT Analysis: A Theoretical Review." *Journal of International Social Research* 10(51): 994–1006.

Hagedoorn, J. 1993. "Understanding the Rationale of Strategic Technology Partnering: Interorganizational Modes of Cooperation and Sectoral Differences." *Strategic Management Journal* 14 (5): 371–385.

Halligan, B., and Shah, D. 2009. *Inbound Marketing: Get Found Using Google, Social Media, and Blogs*. Wiley.

Hamel, G. 2006. "The Why, What, and How of Management Innovation." *Harvard Business Review* 84 (2): 72–84.

Hamel, G., and Prahalad, C. K. 1989. "Strategic Intent." *Harvard Business Review* 67 (3): 63–76.

Hamel, G., and Prahalad, C. K. 1994. *Competing for the Future*. Harvard Business Review Press.

Hamel, G., and Valikangas, L. 2003. "The Quest for Resilience." *Harvard Business Review* 81 (9): 52–63.

Hanaysha, J. R., and AlShaikh, M. E. 2022. "Entrepreneurial Marketing and Firm Performance: The Role of Customer Intensity and Value Creation." *Sustainability* 14 (18): 11444.

Hansen, M. T., and Birkinshaw, J. 2007. "The Innovation Value Chain." *Harvard Business Review* 85 (6): 121–130.

Hart, S. L., and Dowell, G. 2011. "Invited Editorial: A Natural Resource Based View of the Firm: Fifteen Years After." *Journal of Management* 37 (5): 1464–1479.

Hastings, R., and Meyer, E. 2020. *No Rules Rules: Netflix and the Culture of Reinvention.* Penguin Press.

Hatch, M. J., and Schultz, M. 2008. *Taking Brand Initiative: How Companies Can Align Strategy, Culture, and Identity Through Corporate Branding.* John Wiley & Sons.

Hayashi, A. M. 2001. "When to Trust Your Gut." *Harvard Business Review* 79 (2): 59–65.

He, W., Zha, S., and Li, L. 2013. "Social Media Competitive Analysis and Text Mining: A Case Study in the Pizza Industry." *International Journal of Information Management* 33 (3): 464–472.

Helms, M. M., and Nixon, J. 2010. "Exploring SWOT Analysis—Where Are We Now?" *Journal of Strategy and Management* 3 (3): 215–251.

HennigThurau, T., Gwinner, K. P., and Gremler, D. D. 2010. "Electronic WordofMouth Via ConsumerOpinion Platforms: What Motivates Consumers to Articulate Themselves on the Internet?" *Journal of Interactive Marketing* 18 (1): 38–52.

Heskett, J. L., Jones, T. O., Loveman, G. W., Sasser, W. E., Jr., & Schlesinger, L. A. 1994. "Putting the service-profit chain to work." *Harvard Business Review,* 72(2), 164–174.

Hess, E. D. 2010. *Grow to Greatness: Smart Growth for Entrepreneurial Businesses.* Stanford University Press.

Higgins, R. C. 2020. *Analysis for Financial Management.* 12th ed. McGrawHill Education.

Highsmith, J. 2004. *Agile Project Management: Creating Innovative Products.* AddisonWesley.

Hills, G. E., & Hultman, C. M. 2008. "Entrepreneurial marketing: Conceptual and empirical research opportunities." *Marketing Theory,* 8(3), 305–312.

Hills, G. E., Hultman, C. M., & Miles, M. P. 2008. "The evolution and development of entrepreneurial marketing. " *Journal of Small Business Management,* 46(1), 99–112.

Hills, G. E., and Hultman, C. M. 2011. "Entrepreneurial Marketing: Conceptual and Empirical Research Opportunities." *Entrepreneurship Theory and Practice* 33 (1): 129–145.

Hills, G. E., and Hultman, C. M. 2013. "Entrepreneurial Marketing: Conceptual and Empirical Developments." *International Journal of Entrepreneurship and Innovation Management* 14 (1): 3–14.

Hillson, D. 2002. "Extending the Risk Process to Manage Opportunities." *International Journal of Project Management* 20 (3): 235–240.

Hitchner, J. R. 2011. *Financial Valuation: Applications and Models*. John Wiley & Sons.

Hitt, M. A., Ireland, R. D., Sirmon, D. G., and Trahms, C. A. 2011. "Strategic Entrepreneurship: Creating Value for Individuals, Organizations, and Society." *Academy of Management Perspectives* 25 (2): 57–75.

Holt, D., & Cameron, D. 2010. Cultural strategy: Using innovative ideologies to build breakthrough brands. *Oxford University Press*.

Homburg, C., Workman, J. P., and Jensen, O. 2000. "Fundamental Changes in Marketing Organization: The Movement Toward a Customer-Focused Organizational Structure." *Journal of the Academy of Marketing Science* 28 (4): 459–478.

Hopkin, P. 2018. *Fundamentals of Risk Management: Understanding, Evaluating, and Implementing Effective Risk Management*. Kogan Page Publishers.

Horngren, C. T., Datar, S. M., and Rajan, M. V. 2021. *Cost Accounting: A Managerial Emphasis*. 17th ed. Pearson Education.

Hoyer, W.D., R. Chandy, M. Dorotic, M. Krafft, and S.S. Singh. 2010. "Consumer co-creation in new product development." *Journal of Service Research* 13(3): 283–296.

Hsieh, T. 2010. *Delivering Happiness: A Path to Profits, Passion, and Purpose*. Grand Central Publishing.

Huang, M. H., and Rust, R. T. 2021. "Engaged to a Robot? The Role of AI in Service." *Journal of Service Research* 24 (1): 30–41.

Huang, M.-H., & Rust, R. T. 2021. "A strategic framework for artificial intelligence in marketing." *Journal of the Academy of Marketing Science*, 49, 30–50

Hughes, M., and Morgan, R. E. 2007. "Deconstructing the Relationship Between Entrepreneurial Orientation and Business Performance at the Embryonic Stage of Firm Growth." *Industrial Marketing Management* 36 (5): 651–661.

Hult, G. T. M., Ketchen, D. J., Jr., & Nichols, E. L., Jr. (2003). "Organizational learning as a strategic resource in supply management." *Journal of Operations Management*, 21(5), 541–556.

Ibarra, H., and Hunter, M. 2007. "How Leaders Create and Use Networks." *Harvard Business Review* 85 (1): 40–47.

Immelt, J. R. 2016. "How I Remade GE." *Harvard Business Review* 94 (11): 41–49.

Immelt, J. R., Govindarajan, V., and Trimble, C. 2009. "How GE Is Disrupting Itself." *Harvard Business Review* 87 (10): 56–65.

Ireland, R. D., Hitt, M. A., and Sirmon, D. G. 2003. "A Model of Strategic Entrepreneurship: The Construct and Its Dimensions." *Journal of Management* 29 (6): 963–989.

Ireland, R. D., Hitt, M. A., and Vaidyanath, D. 2002. "Alliance Management as a Source of Competitive Advantage." *Journal of Management* 28 (3): 413–446.

Isaacson, W. 2011. *Steve Jobs*. Simon & Schuster.

Isdell, N. W., and Beasley, D. 2011. *Inside CocaCola: A CEO's Life Story of Building the World's Most Popular Brand*. St. Martin's Press.

Ishibashi, K., and Watanabe, C. 2004. "Technology Substitution and the Survival of Incumbents: Coevolution of Innovation Strategies and Technology Trajectories." *Technovation* 24 (9): 775–788.

Iyer, B., and Davenport, T. H. 2008. "Reverse Engineering Google's Innovation Machine." *Harvard Business Review* 86 (4): 58–68.

Jacobides, M.G., C. Cennamo, and A. Gawer. 2018. "Towards a theory of ecosystems." *Strategic Management Journal* 39(8): 2255–2276.

Jaworski, B. J., and Kohli, A. K. 1993. "Market Orientation: Antecedents and Consequences." *Journal of Marketing* 57 (3): 53–70.

Jehn, K. A. 1995. "A Multimethod Examination of the Benefits and Detriments of Intragroup Conflict." *Administrative Science Quarterly* 40 (2): 256–282.

Jenkins, S. 2016. *The Best Digital Marketing Campaigns in the World: Mastering the Art of Customer Engagement*. Kogan Page Publishers.

Johanson, J., and J.E. Vahlne. 2009. "The Uppsala Internationalization Process Model Revisited: From Liability of Foreignness to Liability of Outsidership." *Journal of International Business Studies* 40 (9): 1411–1431.

Kahneman, D. 2011. *Thinking, Fast and Slow*. Farrar, Straus and Giroux.

Kahneman, D., & Klein, G. (2009). Conditions for intuitive expertise: A failure to disagree. *American Psychologist*, 64(6), 515–526.

Kahneman, D., and A. Tversky. 1979. "Prospect Theory: An Analysis of Decision Under Risk." *Econometrica* 47 (2): 263–292.

Kanter, R. M. (1983). The change masters: Innovation and entrepreneurship in the American corporation. *Simon & Schuster*.

Kaplan, A. M., and M. Haenlein. 2010. "Users of the World, Unite! The Challenges and Opportunities of Social Media." *Business Horizons* 53 (1): 59–68.

Kaplan, R. S., and A. A. Atkinson. 2020. *Advanced Management Accounting*. 4th ed. Pearson.

Kaplan, R. S., and D. P. Norton. 1992. "The Balanced Scorecard—Measures That Drive Performance." *Harvard Business Review* 70 (1): 71–79.

Kaplan, R. S., & Norton, D. P. (2004). Strategy maps: Converting intangible assets into tangible outcomes. *Harvard Business School Press*.

Keating, G. 2012. "Netflix, Inc.: The 'Comeback' King." *Journal of Business Case Studies (JBCS)* 8 (3): 231–240.

Kelley, T., and J. Littman. 2001. *The Art of Innovation: Lessons in Creativity from IDEO, America's Leading Design Firm*. Currency/Doubleday.

Kelly III, J. E., and S. Hamm. 2013. *Smart Machines: IBM's Watson and the Era of Cognitive Computing*. Columbia University Press.

Khatri, N., & Ng, H. A. (2000). The role of intuition in strategic decision making. *Human Relations*, 53(1), 57–86.

Kilenthong, P. 2011. *An Empirical Investigation of Entrepreneurial Marketing and the Role of Entrepreneurial Orientation*. Doctoral dissertation, University of Illinois at Chicago. https://indigo.uic.edu.

Kim, W. C., & Mauborgne, R. 2005. Blue ocean strategy: How to create uncontested market space and make the competition irrelevant. *Harvard Business School Press*.

Kirca, A. H., S. Jayachandran, and W. O. Bearden. 2005. "Market Orientation: A Meta-Analytic Review and Assessment of Its Antecedents and Impact on Performance." *Journal of Marketing* 69 (2): 24–41.

Kirzner, I. M. 1997. "Entrepreneurial Discovery and the Competitive Market Process: An Austrian Approach." *Journal of Economic Literature* 35 (1): 60–85.

Kniberg, H., and A. Ivarsson. 2012. *Scaling Agile @ Spotify with Tribes, Squads, Chapters & Guilds*. Spotify Labs.

Knight, F. H. 1921. *Risk, Uncertainty, and Profit*. Houghton Mifflin.

Knight, G. A. (2000). Entrepreneurship and marketing strategy: The SME under globalization. *Journal of International Marketing*, 8(2), 12–32.

Knight, P. (2016). Shoe Dog: A Memoir by the Creator of Nike. *Scribner*.

Kohavi, R., R. Longbotham, D. Sommerfield, and R. M. Henne. 2009. "Controlled Experiments on the Web: Survey and Practical Guide." *Data Mining and Knowledge Discovery* 18 (1): 140–181.

Kohli, A. K., and B. J. Jaworski. 1990. "Market Orientation: The Construct, Research Propositions, and Managerial Implications." *Journal of Marketing* 54 (2): 1–18.

Kotler, P. 2003. *Marketing Management*. 11th ed. Pearson Prentice Hall.

Kotler, P., and G. Armstrong. 2018. *Principles of Marketing*. 17th ed. Pearson.

Kotler, P., and K. L. Keller. 2016. *Marketing Management*. 15th ed. Pearson Education.

Kotler, P., H. Kartajaya, and I. Setiawan. 2017. *Marketing 4.0: Moving from Traditional to Digital*. Wiley.

Kotter, J. P. 1996. *Leading Change*. Harvard Business Review Press.

Kraus, S., R. Harms, and M. Fink. 2010. "Entrepreneurial Marketing: Moving Beyond Marketing in New Ventures." *International Journal of Entrepreneurship and Innovation Management* 11 (1): 19–34.

Kraus, S., J. C. Rigtering, M. Hughes, and V. Hosman. 2012. "Entrepreneurial Orientation and the Business Performance of SMEs: A Quantitative Study from the Netherlands." *Review of Managerial Science* 6 (2): 161–182.

Kumar, V., and A. Pansari. 2016. "Competitive Advantage Through Engagement." *Journal of Marketing Research* 53 (4): 497–514.

Kumar, V., and D. Shah. 2009. "Customer Lifetime Value: Research and Practice." *Journal of Marketing* 73 (6): 121–123.

Kumar, V., E. Jones, R. Venkatesan, and R. P. Leone. 2011. "Is Market Orientation a Source of Sustainable Competitive Advantage or Simply the Cost of Competing?" *Journal of Marketing* 75 (1): 16–30.

Kuratko, D. F. 2009. *Entrepreneurship: Theory, Process, and Practice.* Cengage Learning.

Kuratko, D. F., J. S. Hornsby, and J. G. Covin. 2014. "Diagnosing a Firm's Internal Environment for Corporate Entrepreneurship." *Business Horizons* 57 (1): 37–47.

Kvale, S. 1996. *InterViews: An Introduction to Qualitative Research Interviewing.* SAGE Publications.

Lafley, A. G., and Martin, R. L. 2013. *Playing to Win: How Strategy Really Works.* Harvard Business Review Press.

Lambrecht, A., & Tucker, C. (2013). When does retargeting work? Information specificity in online advertising. *Journal of Marketing Research,* 50(5), 561–576.

Lane, P. J., and Lubatkin, M. 1998. "Relative Absorptive Capacity and Interorganizational Learning." *Strategic Management Journal* 19 (5): 461–477.

Lashinsky, A. 2012. *Inside Apple: How America's Most Admired—and Secretive—Company Really Works.* Business Plus.

Lavie, D. 2006. "The Competitive Advantage of Interconnected Firms: An Extension of the Resource-Based View." *Academy of Management Review* 31 (3): 638–658.

Lemon, K. N., and Verhoef, P. C. 2016. "Understanding Customer Experience Throughout the Customer Journey." *Journal of Marketing* 80 (6): 69–96.

Leonard, D., and Rayport, J. F. 1997. "Spark Innovation Through Empathic Design." *Harvard Business Review* 75 (6): 102–113.

Levinson, J. C. 1984. *Guerrilla Marketing: Secrets for Making Big Profits from Your Small Business.* Houghton Mifflin.

Lieberman, M. B., and Montgomery, D. B. 1988. "First-Mover Advantages." *Strategic Management Journal* 9 (S1): 41–58.

Liker, J. K. 2004. *The Toyota Way: 14 Management Principles from the World's*

Greatest Manufacturer. McGraw-Hill.

Liker, J. K., and Hoseus, M. 2008. *Toyota Culture: The Heart and Soul of the Toyota Way.* McGraw-Hill.

Locke, E. A., and Latham, G. P. 2002. "Building a Practically Useful Theory of Goal Setting and Task Motivation: A 35-Year Odyssey." *American Psychologist* 57 (9): 705–717.

Lotz, A. D. 2017. *Portals: A Treatise on Internet-Distributed Television.* University of Michigan Press.

Lumpkin, G. T., and G.G. Dess. 1996. "Clarifying the Entrepreneurial Orientation Construct and Linking It to Performance." *Academy of Management Review* 21 (1): 135–172.

Lumpkin, G. T., and G.G. Dess. 2001. "Linking Two Dimensions of Entrepreneurial Orientation to Firm Performance: The Moderating Role of Environment and Industry Life Cycle." *Journal of Business Venturing* 16 (5): 429–451.

Mangram, M. E. 2012. "The Globalization of Tesla Motors: A Strategic Marketing Plan Analysis." *Journal of Strategic Marketing* 20(2): 1–20.

Markowitz, H. 1952. "Portfolio Selection." *The Journal of Finance* 7(1): 77–91.

Marquis, C., and L. Velez-Villa. (2013). Warby Parker: Vision of a "Good" Fashion Brand (Harvard Business School Case). Boston, *MA: Harvard Business School.*

McAfee, A., and E. Brynjolfsson. 2008. "Investing in the IT That Makes a Competitive Difference." *Harvard Business Review* 86(7/8): 98–107.

McAfee, A., and E. Brynjolfsson. 2012. "Big Data: The Management Revolution." *Harvard Business Review* 90(10): 60–68.

McDaniel, C., and R. Gates. 2013. *Marketing Research Essentials.* 8th ed. Wiley.

McDonald, K., and D. Smith-Rowsey. 2016. *The Netflix Effect: Technology and Entertainment in the 21st Century.* Bloomsbury Academic.

McGrath, R. G. 2013. *The End of Competitive Advantage: How to Keep Your Strategy Moving as Fast as Your Business.* Harvard Business Review Press.

McKeown, M. 2012. *The Strategy Book.* Financial Times Prentice Hall.

Megginson, W. L., and S. B. Smart. 2021. *Introduction to Corporate Finance.* 5th ed. Cengage Learning.

Miles, M. P., and J. Darroch. 2006. "Large Firms, Entrepreneurial Marketing

Processes, and the Cycle of Competitive Advantage." *European Journal of Marketing* 40(5/6): 485–501.

Miles, M. P., and J. Darroch. 2006. "Large Firms, Entrepreneurial Marketing Processes, and the Cycle of Competitive Advantage." *European Journal of Marketing* 40(5/6): 485–501.

Miller, D. 1983. "The Correlates of Entrepreneurship in Three Types of Firms." *Management Science* 29(7): 770–791.

Miller, D., and P. H. Friesen. 1982. "Innovation in Conservative and Entrepreneurial Firms: Two Models of Strategic Momentum." *Strategic Management Journal* 3(1): 1–25.

Mintzberg, H. 1979. *The Structuring of Organizations: A Synthesis of the Research*. Prentice Hall.

Mintzberg, H. 1994. "The Fall and Rise of Strategic Planning." *Harvard Business Review* 72(1): 107–114.

Moon, Y., & Quelch, J. A. (2006). Starbucks: Delivering customer service. *Harvard Business School Publishing*.

Morgan, N. A., E. W. Anderson, and V. Mittal. 2005. "Understanding Firms' Customer Satisfaction Information Usage." *Journal of Marketing* 69(3): 131–151.

Morris, M. H., & Sexton, D. L. (1996). The concept of entrepreneurial intensity: Implications for company performance. *Journal of Business Research*, 36(1), 5–13.

Muniz, A. M., and T.C. O'Guinn. 2001. "Brand Community." *Journal of Consumer Research* 27(4): 412–432.

Musk, E. 2013. "The Mission of Tesla." Retrieved from https://www.tesla.com/blog/mission-tesla.

Nadella, S. 2017. *Hit Refresh: The Quest to Rediscover Microsoft's Soul and Imagine a Better Future for Everyone*. Harper Business.

Nagle, J. 2018. "Sephora's Omni-Experience: Analyzing the Beauty Brand's Digital Transformation." *Retail TouchPoints*.

Nagle, T.T., J. Hogan, and J. Zale. 2016. *The Strategy and Tactics of Pricing: A Guide to Growing More Profitably*. 6th ed. Pearson.

Narver, J. C., and S.F. Slater. 1990. "The Effect of a Market Orientation on

Business Profitability." *Journal of Marketing* 54 (4): 20–35.

Nisen, M. 2013. "Nike's Genius Move to Stay Ahead of Competitors." *Business Insider*.

Noble, C. H., Sinha, R. K., & Kumar, A. (2002). Market orientation and alternative strategic orientations: A longitudinal assessment of performance implications. *Journal of Marketing*, 66(4), 25–39.

Noe, R.A., J.R. Hollenbeck, B. Gerhart, B. et al. 2019. *Human Resource Management: Gaining a Competitive Advantage*. 11th ed. McGraw-Hill Education.

Norman, D. A. 2002. *The Design of Everyday Things*. Basic Books.

O'Grady, J. (2009). Apple Inc. Greenwood Press.

Oliver, R. L. 2014. *Satisfaction: A Behavioral Perspective on the Consumer*. Routledge.

O'Reilly, C.A., and M.L. Tushman. 2016. *Lead and Disrupt: How to Solve the Innovator's Dilemma*. Stanford Business Books.

Osterwalder, A., & Pigneur, Y. (2010). *Business model generation: A handbook for visionaries, game changers, and challengers*. Wiley.

Pang, B., and L. Lee. 2008. *Opinion Mining and Sentiment Analysis. Foundations and Trends in Information Retrieval* 2 (1–2): 1–135.

Parkhe, A. 1993. "Strategic Alliance Structuring: A Game Theoretic and Transaction Cost Examination of Interfirm Cooperation." *Academy of Management Journal* 36 (4): 794–829.

Parrino, R., D. S. Kidwell, and T. W. Bates. 2020. *Fundamentals of Corporate Finance*. 4th ed. Wiley.

Pendergrast, M. 2000. *For God, Country, and Coca-Cola: The Definitive History of the Great American Soft Drink and the Company That Makes It*. 2nd ed. Basic Books.

Penrose, E. T. 1959. *The Theory of the Growth of the Firm*. Oxford University Press.

Peppers, D., and M. Rogers. 1999. *The One to One Manager: Real-World Lessons in Customer Relationship Management*. Currency Doubleday.

Petersen, J. A., T. Kushwaha, and V. Kumar. 2018. "Marketing Communication Strategies and Consumer Financial Decision Making: The Role of National Culture." *Journal of Marketing* 82 (3): 35–52.

Pfeffer, J., and R. I. Sutton. 2000. *The Knowing-Doing Gap: How Smart Companies*

Turn Knowledge into Action. Harvard Business School Press.

Pfeifer, P. E., and P. W. Farris. 2004. "The Elasticity of Customer Value to Retention: The Duration of a Customer Relationship." *Journal of Interactive Marketing* 18 (2): 20–31.

Piller, F. T., A. Vossen, and C. Ihl. 2012. "From Social Media to Social Product Development: The Impact of Social Media on Co-Creation of Innovation." *Die Unternehmung* 66 (1): 7–27.

Pinchot, G. 1985. *Intrapreneuring: Why You Don't Have to Leave the Corporation to Become an Entrepreneur.* Harper & Row.

Pine, B. J., and J. H. Gilmore. 1999. *The Experience Economy: Work Is Theater & Every Business a Stage.* Harvard Business School Press.

Polman, P. (2014). Letter from the CEO: Unilever Sustainable Living Plan. Unilever. https://www.unilever.com/sustainable-living/

Polanyi, M. (1966). The tacit dimension. Routledge & Kegan Paul.

Poncin, I., & Mimoun, M. S. B. (2014).

The impact of "e-atmospherics" on physical stores: A conceptual framework.

Journal of Retailing and Consumer Services, 21(5), 851–859.

Porter, M. E. 1979. "How Competitive Forces Shape Strategy." *Harvard Business Review* 57 (2): 137–45.

Porter, M. E. 1980. *Competitive Strategy: Techniques for Analyzing Industries and Competitors.* Free Press.

Porter, M. E. 1985. *Competitive Advantage: Creating and Sustaining Superior Performance.* Free Press.

Porter, M. E. 1996. "What Is Strategy?" *Harvard Business Review* 74 (6): 61–78.

Porter, M. E., and M. R. Kramer. 2006. "Strategy and Society: The Link Between Competitive Advantage and Corporate Social Responsibility." *Harvard Business Review* 84 (12): 78–92.

Porter, M. E., & Kramer, M. R. (2011). Creating shared value: How to reinvent capitalism—and unleash a wave of innovation and growth. *Harvard Business Review,* 89(1–2), 62–77.

Prahalad, C. K., and G. Hamel. 1990. "The Core Competence of the Corporation." *Harvard Business Review* 68 (3): 79–91.

Prahalad, C. K., and V. Ramaswamy. 2004a. *The Future of Competition: Co-Creating Unique Value with Customers*. Harvard Business Review Press.

Prey, R. 2016. "Musica Analytica: The Datafication of Listening." *Popular Music* 35 (2): 269–92.

Pulizzi, J. 2014. *Epic Content Marketing: How to Tell a Different Story, Break Through the Clutter, and Win More Customers by Marketing Less*. McGraw-Hill.

Quinn, J. B. 1999. "Strategic Outsourcing: Leveraging Knowledge Capabilities." *Sloan Management Review* 40 (4): 9–21.

Rauch, A., J. Wiklund, G.T. Lumpkin, et al. 2009. "Entrepreneurial Orientation and Business Performance: An Assessment of Past Research and Suggestions for the Future." *Entrepreneurship Theory and Practice* 33 (3): 761–787.

Rawson, A., E. Duncan, and C. Jones. 2013. "The Truth About Customer Experience." *Harvard Business Review* 91 (9): 90–98.

Reibstein, D. J. (2009). Linking marketing to financial consequences. *Marketing Science Institute Working Paper*, 09-102.

Reichheld, F.F. 2003. "The One Number You Need to Grow." *Harvard Business Review* 81 (12): 46–54.

Reichheld, F.F. 2006. *The Ultimate Question: Driving Good Profits and True Growth*. Harvard Business Review Press.

Reichheld, F.F., and W.E. Sasser. 1990. "Zero Defections: Quality Comes to Services." *Harvard Business Review* 68 (5): 105–111.

Renault Group. 2019. "The Renault-Nissan-Mitsubishi Alliance: A Success Story." Retrieved from Renault Group.

Richardson, A. (2010, November). Using customer journey maps to improve customer experience. *Harvard Business Review*.

Ries, E. 2011. *The Lean Startup: How Today's Entrepreneurs Use Continuous Innovation to Create Radically Successful Businesses*. Crown Business.

Rigby, D.K., J. Sutherland, and H. Takeuchi. 2016. "Embracing Agile." *Harvard Business Review* 94 (5): 40–50.

Ring, P. S., and A.H. Van de Ven. 1994. "Developmental Processes of Cooperative Interorganizational Relationships." *Academy of Management Review* 19 (1): 90–118.

Robertson, D., and B. Breen. 2013. *Brick by Brick: How LEGO Rewrote the Rules of Innovation and Conquered the Global Toy Industry*. Crown Business.

Rogers, B. 2015. "The Social Costs of Uber." *University of Chicago Law Review Online* 82 (1): 85–102.

Rogers, E.M. 2003. *Diffusion of Innovations*. 5th ed. Free Press.

Ross, S.A., R. Westerfield, and B.D. Jordan. 2019. *Fundamentals of Corporate Finance*. 12th ed. McGraw-Hill Education.

Rothaermel, F.T. 2013. *Strategic Management: Concepts and Cases*. McGraw-Hill/Irwin.

Rust, R. T., and K.N. Lemon. 2001. "E-Service and the Consumer." *International Journal of Electronic Commerce* 5 (3): 85–101.

Ryan, R.M. 2012. *The Oxford Handbook of Human Motivation*. Oxford University Press.

Sadler-Smith, E. (2016). The role of intuition in entrepreneurship and business venturing decisions. *European Journal of Work and Organizational Psychology*, 25(2), 212–225.

Sawhney, M., R.C. Wolcott, and I. Arroniz. 2006. "The 12 Different Ways for Companies to Innovate." *MIT Sloan Management Review* 47 (3): 75–81.

Saxenian, A. 1994. *Regional Advantage: Culture and Competition in Silicon Valley and Route 128*. Harvard University Press.

Schein, E.H. 2010. *Organizational Culture and Leadership*. 4th ed. Jossey-Bass.

Schilling, M.A. 2013. *Strategic Management of Technological Innovation*. McGraw-Hill/Irwin.

Schmidt, E., and J. Rosenberg. 2014. *How Google Works*. Grand Central Publishing.

Schneider, B., and D.E. Bowen. 1995. *Winning the Service Game*. Harvard Business School Press.

Schoemaker, P.J.H. 1995. "Scenario Planning: A Tool for Strategic Thinking." *Sloan Management Review* 36 (2): 25–40.

Schouten, J.W., and J.H. McAlexander. 1995. "Subcultures of Consumption: An Ethnography of the New Bikers." *Journal of Consumer Research* 22 (1): 43–61.

Schultz, H. 2019. *From the Ground Up: A Journey to Reimagine the Promise of America*. Random House.

Schultz, H., and J.Y. Gordon. 2011. *Onward: How Starbucks Fought for Its Life Without Losing Its Soul.* Rodale Books.

Schumpeter, J.A. 1934. *The Theory of Economic Development: An Inquiry into Profits, Capital, Credit, Interest, and the Business Cycle.* Harvard University Press.

———. 1942. *Capitalism, Socialism, and Democracy.* Harper & Brothers.

Shoham, A., Rose, G. M., & Kropp, F. 2005. "Market orientation and performance: A meta-analysis." *Marketing Intelligence & Planning,* 23(5), 435–454.

Senge, P. M. 1990. *The Fifth Discipline: The Art & Practice of the Learning Organization.* Doubleday/Currency.

Shane, S., and S. Venkataraman. 2000. "The Promise of Entrepreneurship as a Field of Research." *Academy of Management Review* 25 (1): 217–226.

Shane, S. (2000). Prior knowledge and the discovery of entrepreneurial opportunities. *Organization Science,* 11(4), 448–469.

Sharp, B., and A. Sharp. 1997. "Loyalty Programs and Their Impact on Repeat-Purchase Loyalty Patterns." *International Journal of Research in Marketing* 14 (5): 473–486.

Shepherd, D. A., & H. Patzelt. (2011). "The new field of sustainable entrepreneurship: Studying entrepreneurial action linking 'what is to be sustained' with 'what is to be developed.'" *Entrepreneurship Theory and Practice* 35(1): 137–163.

Siegel, E. 2013. *Predictive Analytics: The Power to Predict Who Will Click, Buy, Lie, or Die.* John Wiley & Sons.

Sirmon, D.G., and M.A. Hitt. 2009. "Contingencies Within Dynamic Managerial Capabilities: Interdependent Effects of Resource Investment and Deployment on Firm Performance." *Strategic Management Journal* 30 (13): 1375–1394.

Slater, S.F., and J.C. Narver. 1998. "Customer-Led and Market-Oriented: Let's Not Confuse the Two." *Strategic Management Journal* 19 (10): 1001–1006.

Slater, S.F., E.M. Olson, and G.T.M. Hult. 2006. "The Moderating Influence of Strategic Orientation on the Strategy Formation Capability-Performance Relationship." *Strategic Management Journal* 27 (12): 1221–1231.

Slovic, P. 1987. "Perception of Risk." *Science* 236 (4799): 280–285.

Smith, W.R. 1956. "Product Differentiation and Market Segmentation as

Alternative Marketing Strategies." *Journal of Marketing* 21 (1): 3–8.

Spekman, R.E., T.M. Forbes, L.A. Isabella, and T.C. MacAvoy. 1998. "Alliance Management: A View from the Past and a Look to the Future." *Journal of Management Studies* 35 (6): 747–772.

Spiggle, S. 1994. "Analysis and Interpretation of Qualitative Data in Consumer Research." *Journal of Consumer Research* 21 (3): 491–503.

Starbucks Corporation. 1996. "Starbucks and PepsiCo Ready-to-Drink Coffee Products." Retrieved from Starbucks Stories & News.

Stokes, D. 2000. "Putting Entrepreneurship into Marketing: The Processes of Entrepreneurial Marketing." *Journal of Research in Marketing and Entrepreneurship* 2 (1): 1–16.

Stone, B. 2013. *The Everything Store: Jeff Bezos and the Age of Amazon.* Little, Brown and Company.

Stringham, E.P., J.K. Miller, and J.R. Clark. 2015. "Overcoming Barriers to Entry in an Established Industry: Tesla Motors." *California Management Review* 57 (4): 85–103.

Su, Z., Xie, E., & Li, Y. (2011). Entrepreneurial orientation and firm performance in new ventures and established firms: An empirical examination. *International Journal of Entrepreneurial Behavior & Research*, 17(6), 558–586.

Sundararajan, A. 2016. *The Sharing Economy: The End of Employment and the Rise of Crowd-Based Capitalism.* MIT Press.

Teece, D.J. 2010. "Business Models, Business Strategy and Innovation." *Long Range Planning* 43(2–3): 172–194.

Teece, D.J. 2014. "The Foundations of Enterprise Performance: Dynamic and Ordinary Capabilities in an (Economic) Theory of Firms." *The Academy of Management Perspectives* 28(4): 328–352.

Teece, D.J., G. Pisano, and A. Shuen. 1997. "Dynamic Capabilities and Strategic Management." *Strategic Management Journal* 18(7): 509–533.

Thomke, S. 2003. *Experimentation Matters: Unlocking the Potential of New Technologies for Innovation.* Harvard Business School Press.

Thomke, S. 2020. *Experimentation Works: The Surprising Power of Business Experiments.* Harvard Business Review Press.

Tidd, J., and J. Bessant. 2020. *Managing Innovation: Integrating Technological, Market, and Organizational Change*. John Wiley & Sons.

Tushman, M.L., and C.A. O'Reilly. 1996. "Ambidextrous Organizations: Managing Evolutionary and Revolutionary Change." *California Management Review* 38(4): 8–30.

Ulwick, A.W. 2005. *What Customers Want: Using Outcome-Driven Innovation to Create Breakthrough Products and Services*. McGraw Hill.

Uzzi, B. 1997. "Social Structure and Competition in Interfirm Networks: The Paradox of Embeddedness." *Administrative Science Quarterly* 42(1): 35–67.

Vance, A. 2015. *Elon Musk: Tesla, SpaceX, and the Quest for a Fantastic Future*. Ecco.

Varian, H.R. 2009. *Intermediate Microeconomics: A Modern Approach*. 8th ed. W.W. Norton & Company.

Verhoef, P. C., P.K. Kannan, and J.J. Inman. 2015. "From Multi-Channel Retailing to Omni-Channel Retailing: Introduction to the Special Issue on Multi-Channel Retailing." *Journal of Retailing* 91(2): 174–181.

Vise, D.A., and M. Malseed. 2005. *The Google Story: Inside the Hottest Business, Media, and Technology Success of Our Time*. Delta.

Vlasic, B., and B. Stertz. 2000. *Taken for a Ride: How Daimler-Benz Drove off with Chrysler*. HarperCollins.

Vogus, T.J., and K.M. Sutcliffe. 2007. "Organizational Resilience: Towards a Theory and Research Agenda." *IEEE International Conference on Systems, Man and Cybernetics*, 3418–3422.

Wack, P. 1985. "Scenarios: Shooting the Rapids." *Harvard Business Review* 63(6): 139–150.

Wack, P. 1985. "Scenarios: Uncharted Waters Ahead." *Harvard Business Review* 63(5): 72–89.

Wagner, K. 2017. "Spotify and Uber Will Let You Play Your Own Music During Rides." *Recode*. Retrieved from Recode.

Wasson, C.R. 2000. "Ethnography in the Field of Design." *Human Organization* 59(4): 377–388.

Wedel, M., and W.A. Kamakura. 2012. *Market Segmentation: Conceptual and Methodological Foundations*. 2nd ed. Springer Science & Business Media.

Wedel, M., & Kannan, P. K. (2016). Marketing analytics for data-rich environments. *Journal of Marketing*, 80(6), 97–121.

Wessel, M., & Christensen, C. M. (2016). Surviving disruption. *Harvard Business Review*, 94(12), 46–53.

Wiklund, J., and D. Shepherd. 2003. "Knowledge-Based Resources, Entrepreneurial Orientation, and the Performance of Small and Medium-Sized Businesses." *Strategic Management Journal* 24(13): 1307–1314.

Wiklund, J., and D. Shepherd. 2005. "Entrepreneurial Orientation and Small Business Performance: A Configurational Approach." *Journal of Business Venturing* 20(1): 71–91. https://doi.org/10.1016/j.jbusvent.2004.01.001.

Womack, J.P., and D.T. Jones. 1996. *Lean Thinking: Banish Waste and Create Wealth in Your Corporation*. Simon & Schuster.

Yip, G.S. 2003. *Total Global Strategy II*. Prentice Hall.

Zahra, S.A. 1993. "A Conceptual Model of Entrepreneurship as Firm Behavior: A Critique and Extension." *Entrepreneurship Theory and Practice* 17(4): 5–21.

Zahra, S. A., & Covin, J. G. (1995). Contextual influences on the corporate entrepreneurship–performance relationship: A longitudinal analysis. *Journal of Business Venturing*, 10(1), 43–58.

Zahra, S.A., and D.M. Garvis. 2000. "International Corporate Entrepreneurship and Firm Performance: The Moderating Effect of International Environmental Hostility." *Journal of Business Venturing* 15(5–6): 469–492.

Zahra, S.A., and J.A. Pearce. 1989. "Boards of Directors and Corporate Financial Performance: A Review and Integrative Model." *Journal of Management* 15(2): 291–334.

Zappos. 2012. *Delivering Happiness: A Path to Profits, Passion, and Purpose*. Business Plus.

Zervas, G., Proserpio, D., & Byers, J. W. (2017). The rise of the sharing economy: Estimating the impact of Airbnb on the hotel industry. *Journal of Marketing Research*, 54(5), 687–705.

Zhou, K. Z., Yim, C. K., & Tse, D. K. (2005). The effects of strategic orientations on technology- and market-based breakthrough innovations. *Journal of Marketing*, 69(2), 42–60.

Zikmund, W.G., B.J. Babin, J.C. Carr, et al. 2013. *Business Research Methods*. 9th ed. Cengage Learning.

Zollo, M., and S.G. Winter. 2002. "Deliberate Learning and the Evolution of Dynamic Capabilities." *Organization Science* 13(3): 339–351.

Zook, C., and J. Allen. 2003. "Growth Outside the Core." *Harvard Business Review* 81(12): 66–73.

ABOUT THE AUTHOR

 Dr. Kyle Harkema, DBA, MBA, is a distinguished scholar-practitioner with a wealth of experience at the intersection of academia and industry. With an academic foundation built on rigorous study and research, combined with extensive practical experience in the business world, Dr. Harkema epitomizes the modern scholar-practitioner—a professional who not only understands theoretical frameworks but also knows how to apply them in real-world contexts.

KEY HIGHLIGHTS OF PROFESSIONAL AND ACADEMIC EXPERIENCE

Marketing Leadership and Innovation: Dr. Harkema has a robust background in marketing, having led strategic-marketing initiatives across various industries. His experience includes developing and executing marketing strategies that drive brand growth, enhance customer engagement, and increase market share. Dr. Harkema has a deep understanding of consumer behavior, market trends, and competitive analysis, which he leverages to create impactful marketing campaigns. His work has involved everything from digital marketing and social media strategies to traditional advertising and public relations, demonstrating his versatility and expertise in the field.

Academic Excellence: Dr. Harkema's academic credentials are equally impressive. He holds a Doctor of Business Administration (DBA) and a Master of Business Administration (MBA), which provide him with a strong foundation in both research and applied business practices. His academic pursuits have focused on areas such as strategic management, entrepreneurship, and marketing, with a particular emphasis on how these disciplines intersect with real-world challenges.

Published Research and Thought Leadership: As a scholar, Dr. Harkema has contributed to the academic community through research that addresses critical business issues. He explores topics such as entrepreneurial marketing, strategic decision-making, and the role of leadership in organizational success. His ability to translate complex theoretical concepts into practical insights is highly regarded.

Educator and Mentor: Dr. Harkema is also a dedicated educator, teaching at the university level, where he brings his professional experience into the classroom. His teaching philosophy emphasizes the importance of blending theory with practice, preparing students to navigate the complexities of the modern business world. As a mentor, he has guided numerous students and professionals, helping them develop the skills and knowledge needed to excel in their careers.

Consultant and Advisor: Beyond academia, Dr. Harkema has served as a consultant and advisor to businesses, where he applies his scholarly insights to solve practical problems. His expertise in strategic planning, market analysis, and organizational development has helped companies achieve significant improvements in performance and competitiveness.

THE IMPORTANCE OF SCHOLAR-PRACTITIONERS

The importance of scholar-practitioners like Dr. Harkema cannot be overstated. In a world where business landscapes are continuously evolving, the ability to bridge the gap between theory and practice is crucial. Scholar-practitioners serve as vital conduits, ensuring that academic insights are not only relevant but also actionable. They bring a unique perspective, blending scholarly rigor with practical insights, which is essential for fostering innovation, improving business practices, and guiding future leaders.

Dr. Harkema's work exemplifies this role. His research and teaching are deeply informed by his hands-on experience in the business world, allowing him to offer students and colleagues a nuanced understanding of both the theoretical and practical aspects of business management. This dual expertise enables him to develop strategies and solutions that are both theoretically sound and practically viable, making a significant impact on the organizations and individuals he engages with.

As a scholar-practitioner, Dr. Harkema is committed to advancing knowledge while simultaneously ensuring that this knowledge has a tangible, positive impact on the business community. His approach not only enriches academic discourse but also empowers businesses to adapt, grow, and succeed in an increasingly complex environment.